The
Suicide Archive

The Suicide Archive

READING RESISTANCE IN THE
WAKE OF FRENCH EMPIRE

DOYLE D. CALHOUN

Duke University Press   *Durham and London*   2024

© 2024 Duke University Press
All rights reserved
Printed and bound by CPI Group (UK) Ltd, Croydon, CR0 4YY
Project Editor: Ihsan Taylor
Designed by Courtney Leigh Richardson
Typeset in Garamond Premier Pro and QuadraatSansPro by
Westchester Publishing Services

Library of Congress Cataloging-in-Publication Data
Names: Calhoun, Doyle D., [date] author.
Title: The suicide archive : reading resistance in the wake of French empire / Doyle D. Calhoun.
Description: Durham : Duke University Press, 2024. |
Includes bibliographical references and index.
Identifiers: LCCN 2023057405 (print)
LCCN 2023057406 (ebook)
ISBN 9781478030744 (paperback)
ISBN 9781478026501 (hardcover)
ISBN 9781478059738 (ebook)
Subjects: LCSH: Enslaved persons—Suicidal behavior. | Suicide in literature. | Suicide in art. | Slavery—Psychological aspects. | Postcolonialism. | France—Colonies—Administration. | Africa—Colonization—Psychological aspects. | BISAC: SOCIAL SCIENCE / Ethnic Studies / American / African American & Black Studies | POLITICAL SCIENCE / Colonialism & Post-Colonialism
Classification: LCC HT1176 .C35 2024 (print) | LCC HT1176 (ebook) |
DDC 306.3/6209171244—dc23/eng/20240416
LC record available at https://lccn.loc.gov/2023057405
LC ebook record available at https://lccn.loc.gov/2023057406

Cover photo: Still from Ousmane Sembène's *Black Girl* (Criterion Collection, 2017), courtesy of Janus Films with permission from Alain Sembène. Restored by Cineteca di Bologna / L'Immagine Ritrovata laboratory, in association with the Sembène Estate, Institut National de l'Audiovisuel (INA), Eclair Laboratories, and the Centre National de Cinématographie. Restoration funded by The Film Foundation's World Cinema Project.

For my parents

Suicide sometimes changes the course of history.

MOHAMED MBOUGAR SARR

Death is private, a path down which none
can follow, but also public, because each death is
simultaneously the end of the world.

HERMANN BURGER

CONTENTS

Preface · ix

INTRODUCTION. *In Articulo Mortis* · 1

1 · CHORAL HISTORIES: Suicide and
Slavery in the French Atlantic · 39

2 · ORAL ARCHIVES: The "Talaatay Nder"
Narrative in Wolof and French · 77

3 · SCREEN MEMORIES: Ousmane Sembène's
Black Girl between Image, Icon, and Archive · 113

4 · MULTIPLE EXPOSURES: Geologies
of Suicidal Resistance · 161

5 · STRANGE BEDFELLOWS: On Suicide
Bombing and Literature · 201

CONCLUSION. The Suicide Archive:
A Social Document · 235

Acknowledgments · 241   Notes · 243
Bibliography · 283   Index · 315

PREFACE

There is no good way to write about suicide. I return to versions of this thesis throughout this book, but the difficulty of writing about something that should not be written about and the tragic valences of which cannot be overstated should be legible at the outset. Studies of suicide, including this one, are marked by belatedness, trespass, and failure.

The Suicide Archive is about death and dying, physical and psychological pain, and almost unfathomable loss. It takes up harrowing, sometimes violent representations of personal and collective suffering. It is traversed and troubled by the real risks involved in writing about "other people's deaths [...] as something [some]one 'reads.'"[1] With respect to visual culture, Sampada Aranke has framed these stakes in powerful terms, writing that looking at images of Black pain and anti-Black violence, "coupled with the question of whether or not to write about them, exhausts an already fatigued image-cast that centers anti-Black violence as an everyday visual practice."[2] How to look upon and write about death, disappearance, and dispossession; how to write about the looking, too: these ethical and methodological quandaries permeate *The Suicide Archive*.

To suggest that there is no good way to write about suicide does not mean nothing can be gained from writing about it. Rather, I want to inscribe my own positioning, misgivings, and trespasses as integral to this undertaking. Despite its subject matter, this is a hopeful book insofar as it is also a story about resourcefulness and survival, about new ways of looking at the past, and about how, in the present, we might become more compassionate and skillful readers of histories of loss—how we might create something lasting "on this broken ground."[3]

Faced with and motivated by the complexity of its object, *The Suicide Archive* creates an analytical field for holding the multiple, competing resonances of suicide in tension. The historical, sociopolitical, and literary contexts of French slavery and colonization in Africa and the Caribbean—especially their archives and afterlives—bring the stakes of reading suicide and/as resistance in the wake of empire into focus. They serve as case studies here. Beyond my own disciplinary formation as a scholar of literature in French, the "Frenchness" of this project pushes back against the specific ways (political) suicide has been historicized, theorized, and canonized, especially in literary studies, *as something distinctly French*—as a product of the French Revolution, Romantic ideal, expression of nineteenth-century malaise, sign of existential ennui, or philosophical limit.[4] I locate the genesis of suicide as a political language and practice of freedom in extremis not in Romantic impulses or Republican values but in the experiences of empire and state violence.

This book argues that *the history of resistance to French empire is also a history of suicide* while recognizing that this dimension of the historical record has been overlooked.[5] *The Suicide Archive* addresses this critical imbalance by showing that literature and, more broadly, aesthetic works (novels, poetry, performance, film, visual artworks) have long registered what otherwise recedes from view. In the absence of archival sources or in the presence of overdetermined (post)colonial scripts, aesthetic works keep alive occulted histories of suicidal resistance. With respect to suicide, aesthetic works do what colonial-imperial accounts and traditional historiographies have failed to do: they stay with suicide, attempting to dwell in its potentially incommensurable significations. They provide, to borrow Édouard Glissant's phrasing, a means of "saying without saying while saying all the while" (*dire sans dire tout en disant*).[6] In some cases, they make recessed or "secret" histories of suicidal resistance available in writing and accessible to the collective historical consciousness for the first time.

The history of suicide under slavery is an ineluctable departure point for a study of suicidal resistance in the world(s) of French colonialism and the cultural productions that emerged in its wake. But it is, for reasons I hope will become clear, neither the end point nor the political horizon of this book, which dedicates an introduction and two chapters (1–2) to suicide in the Atlantic world (the Caribbean and the African littoral) before moving farther afield—to post-Independence Senegal (chapter 3), Algeria (chapter 4), and Morocco (chapter 5). Across this expansive chronology and far-ranging geography, chattel slavery in the Atlantic world remains a central historical and conceptual framework for two main reasons: first, for the powerful ways it lays bare many of the challenges involved in interpreting or "reading" forms of death and dispossession in contexts of unfreedom as resistance; second, for the ways fields such as Black Atlantic studies, slavery and freedom studies, and Black studies have sharply and sensitively engaged questions of archives and archiving in relation to the production of historical knowledge. It is largely for these reasons that I have found it necessary and useful to begin this book with an overview of suicide under French slavery in my introduction before turning to some of the book's larger claims, presenting its key terms (*suicide archive, suicidal resistance, the rhetorical force of suicide*), and focusing on its aesthetic archive, which remains haunted by but moves beyond the Black Atlantic.

In *The Suicide Archive*, I am interested in charting a capacious genealogy and telling a complicated, though far from complete, story about individuals who in the face of extreme violence violently disappeared themselves. This story does not adhere to neat chronologies or national borders. It tracks suicidal resistance across a diverse corpus and different historical, cultural, and linguistic contexts. This is not without risks or disadvantages as a scholarly undertaking. Readers will not find here an exhaustive historical accounting or watertight philosophical argument about voluntary death in the French-speaking world. What I offer is something less ambitious but hopefully more generative and elastic: a new way of thinking and writing about suicide, coloniality, and their archives in relation to literary history.

By considering suicidal resistance in the *longue durée* and extending the historical limits of French colonization into the present, I connect suicide as a response to enslavement and empire to other forms of liberatory political violence and examples of what Achille Mbembe calls "transformation through destruction."[7] The far edge of this task becomes clearest in my final chapter, where I consider the case of the suicide bomber and "sacrificial violence."[8] The individual whose suicide kills other people continues to figure a limit to thinking on contemporary violence even though such acts are less frequent and claim fewer victims than colonizing war, drone strikes, and military occupations. This book engages with such complexities and decalages.[9]

The Suicide Archive considers how antislavery and anticolonial suicide belongs more to our present moment than might be thought. The experiences of empire, Atlantic slavery, and colonization continue to haunt the world(s) that emerged in the wake of official abolition and decolonization in profound ways. Current forms of structural inequality, systemic violence, and racial injustice against Black and Arab minorities in the Francosphere are outgrowths of colonial, postcolonial, and neocolonial asymmetries. They have their origins in a past that refuses to remain past, to inflect Henry Rousso's famous characterization of Vichy France.[10]

Debates around colonial history, historical memory, and the afterlives of French slavery and colonization have only gathered urgency in recent years with global #BlackLivesMatter and #mustfall initiatives, as well as calls to "decolonize" curricula and defund the police. These movements are powerful precisely for their transnational scope and transhistorical consciousness. By drawing connections across temporal, spatial, and linguistic boundaries, they condemn and combat anti-Black and anti-Arab violence as far-reaching, deeply historical systems—from the legacies of Atlantic slavery to present-day policing and the flagrant disregard of governments for African life in the context of irregular migration. The parallels between the murder of George Floyd by police in 2020 in the United States and, in France, #JusticePourAdama, referring to the death of Adama Traoré, a twenty-four-year-old Black Frenchman who died in police custody in 2016, are a case in point. In June 2022, twenty-three Black African men were beaten to death by officers at the Morocco-Melilla border. Even more recently, in June 2023, as I finished writing this book, outrage over the policing of and excessive use of force against Black and Arab minorities in France erupted after the shooting of the seventeen-year-old Nahel M. during a police stop. Such violence is not new. It is contiguous with the deathscape of French colonialism, which continues to produce Black/African life as precarious and disposable *in the present*.

The Suicide Archive offers ways forward for thinking through long-standing legacies of "legitimate" state violence by examining the archives of transatlantic slavery and colonization alongside contemporary literary and extraliterary discourses. If past forms of colonial and postcolonial state violence persist in the present, then older forms of resistance, including suicide, can be seen to shadow contemporary modes of refusal and protest. They inspire new practices of freedom and fugitivity. The aesthetic works examined in this book make such genealogies explicit.

The Suicide Archive is primarily a work of literary-historical criticism, although it is perhaps better described as a work of transdisciplinary criticism by someone who happens to be (primarily) a literary-historical scholar. As a complex and largely untold story, suicidal resistance invites new modes of critical and ethical engagement. The ciphered and secret nature of suicide, especially under colonization, calls for working at the interstices and fringes of established discourses, sounding out silences in scriptural accounts, and attending to unconscious or repressed content. *The Suicide Archive* lays out a transgressive interpretive practice that reads and writes across languages, media, archives, and intellectual traditions. By allying close reading and "politicized looking" across languages and media with forensic archival research, oral history, and an investigative mode, this book endeavors to connect aesthetic forms with real lives lost.[11] In this sense, it is inscribed in an ongoing project of accounting, however imperfectly, for the human toll of centuries of colonial violence in a time of unfinished decolonization.

Above all, this book is an invitation to a mode of literary-historical inquiry based on following traces, compiling evidence, and attempting to render unheard whispers audible. This is a hermeneutic practice that I hope will have "enough capaciousness to travel."[12]

INTRODUCTION

IN ARTICULO MORTIS

I had to be on-site, see the corpses, to learn these facts, for the death of an enslaved man [*un nègre*] is considered of so little importance by authorities and *the masters take so much care to keep the death a secret*. We can conclude these are not the only suicides that have occurred here over the past nine months.

ABBÉ DUGOUJON, *Lettres sur l'esclavage dans les colonies françaises* (1845)

Memory on Trial

The year is 1804. In Basse-Terre, the capital of the French colony of Guadeloupe, a cadaver awaits judgment: a dead man and his "memory" (*mémoire*) are standing trial.[1] In the austere prose of a handwritten procès-verbal, the details of the suicide and postmortem trial of an enslaved man named Azor emerge.[2] On the evening of 27 April, Azor asked his enslaver, Cabre, a printer and bookseller on the island, for money to buy some sweetbread to accompany the dinner of fried fish he was preparing. Cabre gave him the money, and Azor returned home about ten minutes later. Shortly after that, around 8 p.m.,

Azor took an empty pistol from Cabre's bedroom, loaded it with ammunition, placed the barrel against his temple, and "blew his brains out" (*s'est brûlé la cervelle*). The following day, Azor's act of self-destruction was tried as a criminal offense. The details of the trial are summarized in the *minutes du greffe*, court records collating statements and documents from Azor's enslaver and members of the judicial police who arrived on scene the following day to inspect Azor's body.[3]

In French jurisprudence, self-killing was criminalized throughout the Ancien Régime in metropolitan France and in France's colonies into the first decades of the nineteenth century.[4] It was among a handful of crimes (treason, duels, armed rebellions) singled out in Jean-Baptiste Colbert's Criminal Ordonnance of 1670 as the basis for a postmortem trial of "the cadaver or *the memory* of the deceased" (*faire le procès au cadavre ou à la mémoire du défunt*) (Titre XXII, Article 1).[5] In practice, this meant that judges designated someone—ideally a relative of the suicide, so long as they could read and write—as a *curateur* who would speak and be interrogated on behalf of "the cadaver [...] if it still existed [...] or the deceased's memory" (Titre XXII, Article 2). A *curateur* also was named in cases where the defendant was "mute or deaf or [...] refused to respond" (Titre XVIII). The recourse to a *curateur* and to a suicide's "memory" were legal means of making death and disappearance speak.

In 1670, suicide was not yet named as such. The act appears in Colbert's Ordonnance as *homicide de soi-même* (murder of the self). Not until 1734, via the Abbé Prévost, did the English word *suicide*, coined in 1643 from Latin *sui* (self) and *caedes/cide* (killing), enter French, joining existing periphrases (*homicide de soi-même, meurtre de soi-même, attentat contre soi-même*) and giving rise to new expressions (*mort suicide, suicide prémédité, suicide commis en sa personne, suicide involuntaire*).[6] As historian Dominique Godineau writes, over the course of the next century "suicide" was renamed and recategorized; a host of new verbal expressions entered usage in French, including the reflexive *se suicider*.[7] These neologisms (*s'homicider soi-même, se défaire soi-même, se noyer le cœur, se détruire soi-même, attenter à ses jours, attenter contre soi-même, s'assassiner, se donner soi-même la mort, s'abréger les jours*) gave names to an act that was hardly "new" and that had been condemned by the Church and European governments since the Middle Ages.[8] But the criminalization, prosecution, and codification of suicide *as suicide* throughout the eighteenth century was novel and increasingly a topic of public debate.[9]

In the archives of French slavery and colonization, the notion of putting "memory" on trial takes on powerful, far-ranging resonances. Indeed, the legal expression *faire le procès à la mémoire* emerges as a prescient metaphor for the stakes of France's ever-deferred reckoning with its colonial past. From the legacies of chattel slavery in the Atlantic world to the violence of the Algerian War of Independence, to the more recent history of France's irradiation of numerous sites in the Sahara and Pacific Ocean and systemic violence against Black and Arab minorities, France remains embroiled in "memory wars" related to crimes for which it has yet to stand trial and bodies it refuses to claim.

In Azor's case, the trial of "memory" raises questions that are far from metaphorical. The criminalization of suicide under French law supposed *mens rea* (that is, "intent or knowledge of wrongdoing"). Although many considered the postmortem trials and punishments of suicides unusually cruel, this fact was not especially remarkable for your average French *citoyen*, free men and women, who ended their days.[10] But for enslaved people who died by suicide, the supposition of *mens rea* meant they were tried posthumously as criminals whose insurrectional acts threatened public order and not as "property" (*biens meubles*), as they were inscribed in the Code Noir (1685), the legal decree defining the conditions of chattel slavery in France's colonies.[11] In a perverse paradox of French colonial law, suicide was one of the only instances where enslaved Africans appeared legally as "persons," momentarily gaining the juridical "force" of autonomous subjects.[12]

That a detailed record of Azor's death exists is extraordinary. As Christopher M. Church points out, natural disasters and civil unrest throughout the French Caribbean "destroyed numerous governmental records and administrative minutes" and "incinerated countless written accounts."[13] Moreover, as my epigraph from the Catholic priest and abolitionist writer Abbé Casimir Dugoujon makes clear, the deaths of enslaved men, women, and children were ascribed little importance beyond numerical (and monetary) value. Registers of deaths of the enslaved captured the sparsest details: name, approximate age, gender, and racial category (*nègre, négresse, mulâtresse, nègre nouveau-né*); time and place of death; and the identity of the enslaver. From the same year as Azor's trial, death records of the enslaved in Guadeloupe are so chillingly succinct that Azor's procès-verbal reads like a biographical document by comparison.[14]

In addition to being an individual, private, and deeply personal response to psychological pain and emotional distress, suicide was an insurrectional act that directly disordered and undermined the slave economy. It was kept "secret" in France's colonies for multiple reasons—not least of which was financial gain.[15] Under colonial insurance policies, enslavers were not reimbursed for the loss of enslaved men and women who died by suicide. This stipulation contrasted with indemnification policies applied to other causes of death, which could be the legitimate basis for insurance claims.[16] In his *Traité des assurances et des contrats à la grosse* (1783), considered the authoritative text on commercial maritime law during the eighteenth and nineteenth centuries, Balthazard-Marie Émérigon spells out this grim calculus:

> If animals or the enslaved [*des Nègres*] have died a natural death, or even when the enslaved [*des Nègres*], in desperation, have taken their own lives, the Insurer is not bound by it; because these are losses arrived at by nature, or the defect of the thing [*le vice de la chose*], or sometimes by negligence of the Master, which cannot be imputed to the Insurer, if he is not expressly responsible for it; another thing would be if they were drowned in a storm or killed in a fight.[17]

By dying by their own hands, enslaved Africans deprived enslavers of forced human labor as well as any monetary compensation.

For these same reasons—withdrawal of labor, refusal of colonial power—suicide could be a form of personal revenge. As Church explains, fire was the slave's preferred tool of insurrection throughout the French Atlantic, leading the governor of Guadeloupe to declare in 1899 that, at one point in Caribbean history, "the torch was the only instrument of vengeance left to the slave."[18] But suicide and death by fire(arm)—or rope, or drowning, or any number of other means—arguably were the slave's true "last resort." As Jean Raynaud writes in his unpublished study on suicide under colonization, *Essai sur le suicide en Afrique noire* (1934–35), suicide, not arson, was the slave's "only vengeance, his only means of protest, to show that even in taking everything from him they [could] not take away his final right": that is, the right to die.[19]

When the suicides of enslaved men, women, and children were recorded in official documents, as in the case of Azor, colonial administrators were at pains to demonstrate the infrequency of such acts and to show that they were not linked directly to the routinized violence of enslavement. If the body of the suicide could not be covered up or disappeared, then it was important to demonstrate that the death was the result of mental pathology. An example of this tendency from one of the highest levels of colonial oversight is the report published by the Minister of the Navy and Colonies—Ange René Armand, the baron de Mackau—who in 1845 instituted a series of policies known as the Lois Mackaus intended to ameliorate the status of the enslaved before outright abolition.[20] In his report, Mackau presents scant data on slave suicide to demonstrate the efficacy of his new legislation, aiming to show that under the new Mackau Laws slaves were less desperate and, ultimately, less suicidal. Of the nineteen suicides reported by Mackau, only one—after a failed attempt at *marronage*—is connected indirectly to the actual conditions of enslavement.

The rest are explained in purely psychological terms (*chagrin, ivresse, aliénation mentale, désespoir*). This psychological "turn" in explaining slave suicide by no means reflects sensitivity to the psychological traumas of enslavement or awareness of the unconscious effects of colonialism—psychoanalytic phenomena that have received lucid, indeed clinical, analysis in works by thinkers such as Albert Memmi (*The Colonizer and the Colonized*, 1957), Frantz Fanon (*The Wretched of the Earth*, 1961), and Achille Mbembe (*Critique of Black Reason*, 2013).[21] Nor should it be read as a precursor to the ideation-to-action theories of suicide guiding modern studies of the progression from suicidal ideation to suicide attempts.[22] Rather, such explanations come directly from the repertoire of eighteenth-century "causes" for suicide in metropolitan France—which included *chagrin, ennui, faiblesse d'esprit, mélancolie, ivresse, démence*, and *maladie de folie*.[23] Their application in colonial contexts pathologized and naturalized suicidal ideation among the colonized. Suicide and its attendant explanations (melancholia, chagrin, nostalgia, ennui) were theorized in colonial pseudoscience as "maladies des nègres"—afflictions to which the enslaved supposedly were predisposed.[24]

The minutes of the trial of Azor reflect this self-absolving tendency, locating the suicidal impulse in the psyche of the enslaved man and not the murderous system entrapping him. It is noted simply that his enslaver "could not imagine the motive that led Azor to destroy himself [*se détruire*], having always treated him well." The act seemed premeditated, the report speculates, because Azor would have had to buy ammunition beforehand. Perhaps some of the money requested for sweetbread went toward this purchase.

In his statement, a member of the judicial police suggests that Azor's suicide invited the revival of a particular form of public postmortem punishment: "In the past, those who put an end to their existence by violent means were stretched and quartered [*traînait sur la claie*], it would perhaps be appropriate for this example to be reinstated." Known as the *supplice de la claie* or the *claie d'infamie*, this form of torture involved desecrating the body of a suicide by stretching the corpse across a wooden frame that was hitched to a horse and dragged through streets and public squares.[25] Popularized in Ancien Régime France, the *claie d'infamie* was employed throughout metropolitan France and France's colonies as a suicide deterrent, along with other grisly spectacles of "biopower"—the term Michel Foucault uses to describe techniques of administering and regulating human life to produce subjugated bodies.[26] Many of these punishments were specific to voluntary death, such as hanging suicides by their feet after postmortem trials: an inversion of traditional hangings, intended to dehumanize the cadaver, stringing it up like an animal or, according to Christian symbolism, the head pointed downward signifying eternal damnation.[27] Such practices were outlawed in the metropole following the French Revolution when suicide was decriminalized; they persisted in France's colonies—sites that remained governed not by the revolutionary ideals of *liberté, égalité, fraternité*, but by regimes of Black death or what Achille Mbembe calls "necropolitics."[28]

Under French slavery, the *claie d'infamie* and other forms of desecration (decapitation and dismemberment) were popular forms of punishment for slave suicide because it was thought that defiling the cadavers of the enslaved prevented the transmigration of souls and thus would discourage enslaved men and women from seeking out such a fate.[29] Forms of postmortem desecration joined a grim repertoire of torture techniques that terrorized the bodies of the enslaved, whether dead or alive. Some of these torture spectacles also applied to free French subjects who bucked colonial authorities, such as Millet de la Girardière and Pierre Barse.[30] Widely deployed and perfected under slavery, techniques of torture, mutilation, desecration, and humiliation continued to haunt the postslavery moment long after they disappeared from use in France's colonies. This is especially true in the Caribbean and Indian Ocean, in the contexts of indentured labor, and in Africa, where colonial strategies of oppression, violence, forced labor, and policing directly informed postcolonial regimes.[31] The morbid "display" of colonized bodies and the literal conditions of forced displacement and captivity extended well into the twentieth century in the form of France's *zoos humains* (human zoos), colonial expositions where many "participants" died under horrific conditions, from untreated injuries and illnesses, or from suicide.[32]

Despite the suggestion of the judicial police, it is unclear whether Azor's body was desecrated or displayed. This, along with other details, is absent from the minutes of the trial in 1804. Other key facts, equally absent from the court records, allow us to grasp the significance of Azor's act of self-destruction more fully and to understand the political backdrop against which his suicide and trial unfolded. Azor only recently had been re-enslaved. He lived as a free man for almost a decade, from the time of the first French abolition of slavery in 1794 until Napoleon Bonaparte's troops, led by General Antoine Richepanse, landed in Guadeloupe in 1802 to reestablish slavery. Azor witnessed and likely participated in the fierce, anti-French resistance mounted against Napoleon's army by the formerly enslaved: a resistance movement that culminated in the suicides of its leaders Joseph Ignace, who shot himself at Baimbridge—and whose head was displayed on a pike in Pointe-à-Pitre—and Louis Delgrès, who detonated a massive suicide bomb, exploding himself along with three hundred of his followers and many French troops at Matouba in a last stand against Richepanse's men. Azor's trial in the last week of April 1804 occurred less than a month after Napoleon's Code Civil des Français was adopted (21 March 1804), though it would not reach Guadeloupe until late 1805. When it did, it applied only to French citizens, not to the (re)enslaved, whose lives—and deaths—remained governed by the Code Noir.[33] Though meager in detail, the minutes of Azor's trial are enough to excavate a singular human tragedy and a recessed genealogy of suicidal resistance to French slavery and colonization.

Suicide under Slavery

Azor's trial distills a pervasive and harrowing historical reality: Amerindians and sub-Saharan Africans frequently resisted capture, enslavement, and re-enslavement at the hands of Europeans—and, in the case of the trans-Saharan trade in human beings, North African slavers—through suicide.[34] Throughout Africa and the Caribbean, captive Africans and besieged Caribs leaped from great heights; tore open their throats; consumed dirt, sand, and ash.[35] They refused to eat; deliberately exposed themselves to the elements or to illness; dashed their heads against rocks or the sides of slave ships; self-asphyxiated by "swallowing" their tongues; choked, hanged, poisoned,[36] burned, shot, and drowned themselves to avoid capture or to put an end to their enslavement.[37] Suicidal resistance to slavery was so widespread from the very beginning of the slave trade that one of the earliest "how-to" books on maritime commerce, Jacques Savary's *Le parfait négociant* (1675), encouraged captains to set sail as quickly as possible because captives were at risk for suicide the moment they were taken onboard.[38]

Suicide under slavery was a devastating, deeply complicated gesture carried out by enslaved men, women, and occasionally children, individually and collectively. Its timeline cannot easily be arrested with the second abolition of French slavery in 1848, when old forms of enslavement and forced labor adapted, persisted, and transformed—not least through the many permutations of indentured servitude or *engagisme*, based in Napoleon III's policy of *rachat préalable*, instituted in 1856, which effectively replaced chattel slavery in France's Caribbean, African, and Indian Ocean colonies.[39] In other French-occupied territories, especially the Sahara-Sahel region—in places like Morocco, Algeria, Mauritania, and Mali—local forms of slavery continued well into the first half of the twentieth century and, in some cases, until Independence. Antislavery suicide casts a long shadow on the world the French empire made, from the Atlantic to the Indian Ocean to North Africa.

The vehemency and violence with which enslaved and colonized persons were prepared to die on their own terms and by their own hands contradicted long-held European assumptions that suicide was a "Western" phenomenon and that Africans, in general, did not take their own lives.[40] The belief that Africans did not kill themselves contrasted with an eighteenth- and nineteenth-century French Orientalist fascination with "exotic" cultures of suicide, such as the Indian sati or the seppuku of Japanese samurai. Within the racist imperial imaginary, Africans were thought not sufficiently "civilized" to exhibit a behavior that, by the nineteenth century, Europeans considered a marker of modern malaise. In a short medical treatise titled "Le suicide parmi les noirs" (1894), Georges Liengme, a French medical missionary working in South Africa, thus expresses genuine surprise at discovering suicide among "pre-contact" African societies:

> A Black man tired of life! That's not part of the African idyll. And yet, no offense to those who still believe in the reality of this idyll, there are suicides even among Africans who have not yet come into contact with the Whites of civilized life. Let us declare it straight away, cases of suicide are rarer than in civilized countries; this is easily understood. They increase when Indigenous populations live near Whites.[41]

Suicide was thought to be virtually unknown south of the Sahara. However, as French colonial presence in Africa increased throughout the eighteenth, nineteenth, and early twentieth centuries, authors began to revisit the idea that African societies were somehow "immune" to suicide. They faced overwhelming evidence to the contrary.

Throughout the slave trade and the emergent slave societies in the Caribbean basin and along the African littoral during the seventeenth, eighteenth, and nineteenth centuries, the suicides of enslaved persons were widespread enough that Europeans dissertated at length about ways to keep Africans from destroying themselves.[42] In Cuba, during the 1840s, the rates of slave suicide on certain plantations became so high that an emergency colonial committee was convened to identify ways of discouraging suicide among the enslaved population.[43] After slavery was finally abolished in France's colonies in 1848, suicide among indentured laborers continued at rates high enough to provoke ongoing concern among plantation owners.[44]

For white abolitionists such as Victor Schœlcher, suicide most clearly exposed the horrors of the slave trade and plantation system. As a "direct, immediate consequence" and "striking condemnation" of slavery, it made a compelling ethical and rhetorical argument for abolition.[45] For slavers, planters, and ship captains, slave suicide was anything but a moral quandary. It indexed a failure of European control and incurred a material loss through the destruction of the salable "goods" of human cargo. Throughout the Atlantic slave trade, Europeans conducted (pseudo)medical and sociological studies on slave suicide as part of a cottage industry of colonial science—a body of interested "nosopolitical" medical knowledge related to slavery.[46]

The statistics on slave suicide, though sketchy and hard to come by, are staggering: abolitionist Benjamin Frossard cites one voyage of a certain Captain Phillips, who refused to take measures to dissuade suicide among the enslaved, leading to a loss of almost half (320 out of 700) of the captives on board.[47] These were "suicide epidemics" (*épidémies de morts volontaires*), in which suicidality spread like a "contagion."[48] More than a revolt—during which enslavers could "justify" the murder of the enslaved and make a legitimate insurance claim—collective suicide was to be avoided at all costs.[49] Along these lines, enslavers introduced specific disciplinary sanctions and uniquely cruel punishments for suicidal captives, including holding burning coals to the lips of captives who refused to eat, pouring molten lead into the mouths of suicidal slaves, or cutting off their legs or arms in order to "terrify" captives away from attempting suicide.[50] Enslavers strategically manipulated Indigenous slave religiosity to shape views of voluntary death by convincing the enslaved that transmigration was possible only if the body remained intact after death. They developed new instruments to prevent self-destruction, such as the *speculum oris*, a vise used to force-feed suicidal slaves, and cross-shaped wooden bits to prevent captives from self-asphyxiating by swallowing their tongues (figure I.1).[51] They installed nets around the gunwales of slave ships to discourage captive Africans from leaping overboard.[52] It is one of the great ironies of imperial history that Europeans first extensively innovated with methods of suicide prevention and experimented with technologies of "keeping alive" in the context of chattel slavery in the Atlantic world: a necropolitical institution maintained through Black death.[53]

For captive and enslaved Africans, suicide had other significations and participated in other ecologies of meaning. Within many African cosmologies, the transition between life and death is not viewed as an absolute rupture. As Ghanaian philosopher Kwasi Wiredu writes, "The African world of the dead [...] is in no sense another world, but rather a part of this world, albeit a conceptually problematic part."[54] Voluntary death could be viewed as a means of agency, reunion, return, and transmigration or metempsychosis.[55] It was a form of fugitivity and "Afro-Atlantic flight."[56] This belief gave rise to the figure of the "flying African" who resisted enslavement, disappeared, and soared home to Africa through death.[57] Originally rooted in the collective suicide of seventy Nigerian captives at a site in Georgia now known as Igbo or Ebos Landing, flying Africans were part of what Sophie Nahli Allison has characterized as

FIGURE I.1. A *speculum oris*, a vise used to force-feed suicidal slaves. Source: Schomburg Center for Research in Black Culture, New York Public Library. "A vise used on slave ships to force open the mouths of slaves for feeding purposes," New York Public Library Digital Collections, accessed 3 June 2022, https://digitalcollections.nypl.org/items/510d47df-9d3d-a3d9-e040-e00a18064a99.

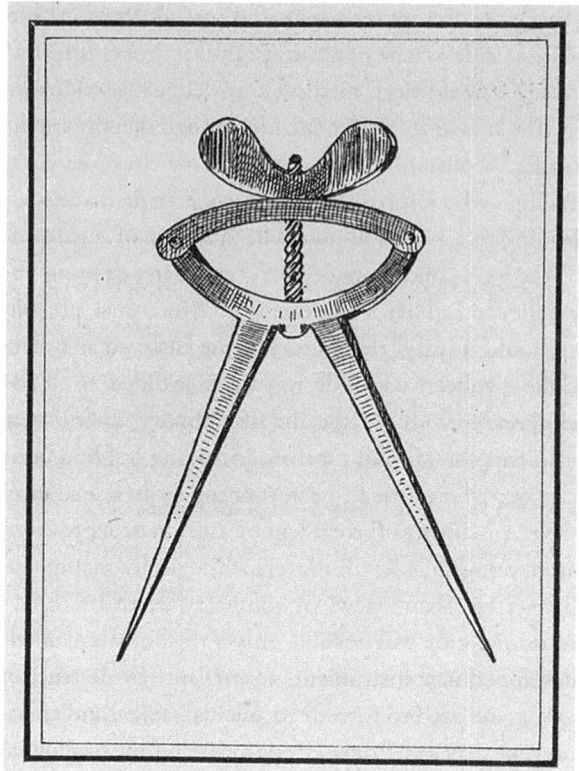

"an oral archive of resistance" connecting voluntary death to an emancipatory flight from slavery and movement toward Black liberation.[58] This defiance of tyranny through death resonates with Huey Newton's concept of "revolutionary suicide" and the Black pan-African liberation movements of the late twentieth century.[59]

Less attention has been given to the cultural contexts and systems of meaning of suicide in Africa, especially in sites along the West African slave route, where self-destruction not only long served as a form of resistance to conquest, capture, and enslavement but also was viewed as a self-affirming and self-preserving dignifying act. For his part, Léopold Sédar Senghor reads suicide as a manifestation of Black African *dyom* (*jom*) or "dignity" in Wolof and thus as a pan-African value and Indigenous African philosophical concept older than both Islam and Christianity.[60]

As the suicide of Azor in 1804 suggests, suicide sometimes was premeditated and carefully planned, but often the suicides and parasuicides of enslaved persons were spontaneous and improvisatory.[61] They took advantage of the temporary disorder generated by an insurrection,[62] or capitalized on sudden access to something that could be transformed into a means of self-destruction: a bit of twine, a blade, a shard of glass, a poisonous substance, a body of water.[63] Suicide also occurred as a direct response to severe corporal punishments or threats thereof.[64] Many enslaved men and women died by suicide in prison while awaiting public torture and execution.[65]

Some enslaved individuals dressed entirely in white before taking their own lives, suggesting that voluntary death had certain ritualistic vestimentary markers associated with it. This appears to be true not only in the French Caribbean but across the Atlantic world.[66] In Jessey Torrey's *A Portraiture of Domestic Slavery* (1817), for instance, we find a haunting image of an enslaved woman's "flight" from slavery: an engraving of a Black woman, barefoot in a luminous white shift, leaping from the open window of a garret into an otherwise empty cobblestone street (figure I.2).[67] The illustration captured a real incident: the attempted suicide of an enslaved woman named Anna, who in 1815 leaped from the top floor of George Miller's "slave tavern" on F Street in Washington, DC. Miraculously, she survived, despite breaking both legs and badly injuring her back.

Such visual representations of suicide under slavery are rare and noticeably absent from studies of the imaging of suicide in the Western world.[68] But images of slave suicide circulated widely throughout the French and British Atlantic worlds during the eighteenth and nineteenth centuries. The different editions of Thomas Day and John Bicknell's antislavery epistle in verse *The Dying Negro*, first published in 1773 and dedicated to Jean-Jacques Rousseau, featured frontispieces depicting an enslaved man in chains and clothed in a bright white loincloth, wielding a dagger as he prepares to kill himself (figures I.3 and I.4). Like the account of Anna's leap, Day's and Bicknell's poem was based on a real event: the suicide of an enslaved man reported in the *Morning Chronicle and London Advertiser* of 28 May 1773.

In the French press of the nineteenth century, we find more graphic depictions of slave suicide. In the Sunday, 22 August 1886, issue of the *Journal des Voyages*, the entire front page was taken up by a dramatic scene by Georges Lemoine, an engraver who illustrated Émile Zola's and Guy de Maupassant's novels. Reminiscent of the spectacular, often gruesome images in the *Illustrated Police News*, a British crime tabloid whose explicit illustrations brought suicide into public view, Lemoine's engraving portrays an enslaved African man in a white jumpsuit, his hands tied behind his back, crushing his head between two railway cars (figure I.5).

"— but I did not want to go, and I jump'd out of the window.—"

To you this unpolluted blood, I pour,
To you that Spirit which ye gave restore.

FIGURES I.2–I.5. Visual representations of suicide under slavery, eighteenth–nineteenth centuries. Figure I.2: Anna's leap. Source: Jesse Torrey, *A portraiture of domestic slavery, in the United States: with reflections on the practicability of restoring the moral rights of the slave, without impairing the legal privileges of the possessor; and a project of a colonial asylum for free persons of colour: including memoirs of facts on the interior traffic in slaves, and on kidnapping: Illustrated with engravings* (Philadelphia, 1817), 46. Figure I.3: Frontispiece to *The dying negro*, 2nd ed. Source: Thomas Day and John Bicknell, *The dying negro, a poem* (London: Flexney, 1775), n.p. Figure I.4: Frontispiece to *The dying negro*, 3rd ed. Source: Thomas Day and John Bicknell, *The dying negro, a poem: By the late Thomas Day and John Bicknell, Esquires. To which is added, a fragment of a letter on the slavery of the negroes. By Thomas Day, Esq. Embellished with a frontispiece* (London: John Stockdale, 1793), 26, digitized by the British Library (11644.d.57). Figure I.5: Frontpage image of 22 August 1886 edition of *Journal des voyages*. Source: "Les esclaves au Brésil—Il se fit écraser la tête entre deux tampons," *Journal des voyages*, no. 476 (22 August 1886): [1] (n.p.).

In some cases, suicide under French slavery was a spectacular and highly visible "performance" in which self-fashioning and self-finishing radically coincided.[69] Schœlcher describes one striking "scene" of suicide in Martinique in 1844 when an enslaved man hanged himself from a tree below the windows of the governor's residence, providing a powerful indictment of slavery and the colonial administration shortly before abolition.[70] Writing about the period leading up to the Revolution of Saint-Domingue, Antoine Métral describes witnessing "up to thirty slaves take their own lives [*se donner la mort*], on the same day, at the same hour, ending their misery together, and in the throes of death, letting the joy of breaking the chains of slavery burst forth together."[71] In other cases, suicides sought death through slower, less visible means, such as willful exposure to the elements or to disease and starvation, and other "suicide-like" behaviors.[72] Sometimes death by suicide came after a psychotic break resulting from the traumas and violence of slavery, at which point the enslaved person was said to have "lost their mind";[73] at other times one was simply "overcome with grief" (*prise de chagrin*) or "desperation" (*désespoir*).

Schœlcher documents the suicide of an enslaved woman named Justine in these terms, describing how she began to consume dirt before cutting her throat:

> On September 8, 1846, an enslaved woman [*une négresse*] Justine, belonging to the Boulogne estate (Guadeloupe), added one more name to the great and solemn protest of those individuals made desperate by servitude. [...] She was overcome with grief [*prise de chagrin*], as the Creoles say, and, we are assured, began to eat dirt. To prevent her from doing so, she had been tied to the bar for a few days when, on September 8, she cut her throat with a knife.[74]

Consuming dirt or other soil-like substances—a practice known as *geophagia* or diagnosed as the medical condition *pica*—is a nearly universal phenomenon.[75] In the case of slavery, however, ingesting dirt, ash, chalk, and other non-food items was a well-known suicidal or parasuicidal resistance practice, diagnosed in the racialized colonial medical discourse as the disease "cachexia Africana."[76] In abolitionist and proslavery texts alike, it was connected to other illnesses, such as "drapetomania," a "morbid desire to flee servitude" believed to be "a kind of madness congenital to black slaves."[77] The Père Labat diagnoses it as a symptom of *la mélancolie noire* (black melancholy), which, he writes, leads the enslaved "to eat earth, ash, lime and other things of that nature."[78] Labat's *mélancolie noire*, although it sounds something like a "postcolonial melancholia" (Paul Gilroy) or Afropessimism (Frank Wilderson) *avant la lettre*, recalls the vocabulary of psychological explanations for suicide during the eighteenth century.[79] Labat's "diagnosis" further reflects the rapidly growing body of pseudomedical and ethnographic literature on enslaved and colonized populations, groups that were thought to be predisposed to extreme chagrin, nostalgia, desperation, depression, suicidal ideation, and languorous voluntary deaths.[80] We find avatars of this belief in European depictions of enslaved and/or displaced Black subjects from Oroonoko to Ourika.

In his *Guide médical aux Antilles* (1834), Michel-Gabriel Levacher similarly identifies geophagia as a method of *lent suicide* (slow suicide) common among the enslaved, writing that "the afflictions of the soul give rise, among slaves [*chez le nègre*], to the resolution to poisoning and decided them to these slow suicides [...]. Despondency [*chagrin*] seizes their soul; they become indolent and pusillanimous; they eat dirt in order to put an end to their existence."[81] He further notes that enslaved men and women regularly self-poisoned by ingesting dirt and other substances so that they would be too sick to work, encouraging their children to do the same.[82] The practice was so common that enslavers placed "mouth-locks" on slaves to prevent them from earth-eating.[83] In his *Voyage pittoresque et historique au Brésil* (1834–39), the French artist Jean Debret depicts a young enslaved woman in a mouth-lock (figure I.6), describing the "distressing spectacle of the tinplate mask in which the face of this victim is enveloped—a sinister indicator of the resolution she had made to die [*se faire mourir*] by eating earth."[84] Debret adds, in a footnote, that "this force of character, called a vice by slaveowners, is most commonly found among certain African peoples [*nations nègres*] impassioned by liberty."[85]

In each case, the suicides and parasuicidal practices of enslaved persons inspired fear, uncertainty, anger, distress, and grief—but also, occasionally, resolve and approbation—in the immediate enslaved and free communities, for the slave trade and plantation system, and among global abolitionist networks.[86] As a state of exception that Orlando Patterson termed "social death" and Mbembe theorizes as "necropolitics," chattel slavery upended—indeed inverted—basic positivist assumptions about the sanctity of life, and thus about the meaning or value of taking one's life.[87] In this context, suicide could hardly be considered a straightforward act of resistance—a defiant triumph, a principled martyrdom—nor a simple capitulation to colonial power.[88] It is better understood as a harrowing event: a personally, politically, and historically charged act of life-affirming necroresistance. The political, historical, and cultural significance of slave suicide resounded far beyond the circumstances and context of a singular act of individual or collective self-killing.

FIGURE I.6. Detail of illustration from *Voyage pittoresque et historique au Brésil*, vol. 2 (1835) showing an enslaved woman wearing a mouth-lock to prevent her from eating dirt. Source: "Une visite à la campagne" (planche 10) in Jean Baptiste Debret, *Voyage pittoresque et historique au Brésil, ou, Séjour d'un artiste français au Brésil, depuis 1816 jusqu'en 1831 inclusivement [. . .]* (Paris: Didot Frères, 1834–39), vol. 2 (1835), [169] (n.p.).

Azor's Silence

While it remains possible to trace and historicize European attitudes toward slave suicide across various sources (legal archives, insurance policies, scientific treatises, coroners' reports, newspaper articles, abolitionist tracts, literary texts), discerning the meanings of voluntary death for members of the enslaved and colonized community is a more difficult endeavor. In the case of French slavery, this difficulty is part of a profound "silence" conditioning access to the voices of the enslaved and formerly enslaved.[89] This is the spectral silence of Azor, whose own "voice" appears under erasure, ventriloquized in a procès-verbal forgotten in French archives.

The silence of Azor is paradigmatic insofar as erasure and absence haunt and hinder any study of suicide under slavery.[90] This is not only because many records related to French slavery and colonization have been damaged or destroyed.[91] Nor is it simply because, as Christopher L. Miller writes in *The French Atlantic Triangle* (2007), there "*are no real slave narratives in French*," or, as Louis Sala-Molins asserts, because "we have at our disposal [in French] not a single written testimony on the reality of slavery coming from a slave."[92] Compared to a rich Anglo-American scriptural tradition of firsthand accounts of slavery by the formerly enslaved—texts such as Phillis Wheatley's poetry, Ottobah Cugoano's *Thoughts and Sentiments on the Wicked Traffic of the Slav-*

ery and Commerce of the Human Species (1787), and Olaudah Equiano's *Interesting Narrative* (1789)—lack of more direct access to stories about slavery appears stark and daunting.[93] At the very least, it requires other ways of doing history. It demands, as Church writes, reading "against the grain of documents produced at the top in order to arrive at an image from below."[94]

It is important not to overstate such challenges. Blanket claims about silences, absences, and aporia structuring the archive of slavery and colonization risk fetishizing disappearance and impasse. It is true, as historian Terri Snyder writes in her pathbreaking study of suicide and slavery in British North America, *The Power to Die* (2015), that the enslaved did not leave suicide notes.[95] But it is equally true that suicide, as the case of Azor shows, was one of the few means by which the enslaved appeared themselves onto the historical and legal record. There is a further risk, in insisting on archival lacunae, of suggesting that "silencing" is something that belongs to the colonial past—something other people did and contemporary scholarship and modern record-keeping stand to undo. The reality is that suicide perhaps suffers most from critical silences here and now: namely, a continued reticence on the part of scholars toward integrating acts of self-destruction into mainstream accounts of French slavery and colonization. Following Michel-Rolph Trouillot, we might characterize this as the "silence of resistance thrown against a superior silence."[96] In contrast to the extensive literature on suicide in metropolitan France from the eighteenth century onward, there is a near total silence with respect to the suicides of enslaved or colonized peoples.

This is not to say that metropolitan literature failed to register the phenomenon of suicide as a response to colonizing violence. While representations of suicide in French literature frequently fed racist tropes of "principled" Africans who honorably (and freely) "chose" death over enslavement, suicide served a range of rhetorical and political ends within humanitarian and abolitionist discourses. Some of the most important, widely circulated works of abolitionist fiction in French depict the suicides of enslaved persons centrally or at key moments.[97] Gabriel Mailhol's *Le philosophe nègre* (1764), for instance, opens with the exiled African prince Tintillo preparing to slit his own throat. He evokes the horrors of the Middle Passage in precise terms, mordantly noting that "in the course of the voyage, we *only* found that 189 had stabbed, suffocated, or hanged themselves."[98] In *Paul et Virginie* (1788)—a text idyllically remembered by French literature's most famous suicide, Emma Bovary ("She had read *Paul et Virginie*...")—the fugitive enslaved woman covered in scars who throws herself at Virginie's feet in desperation is headed to drown herself. Finally, in Victor Séjour's "Le Mulâtre" ("The Mulatto," 1837), a short story about miscegenation whose plot revolves around the cruelties of the Code Noir, the titular "mulatto," Georges, carries out patricide and suicide.[99] The phenomenon of slave suicide would seem to occupy a more important place in abolitionist literature and in philosophical reflections on Atlantic slavery than has been acknowledged previously.

The forms of contemporary silencing regarding the interrelation of suicide, slavery, and colonization are pervasive. As philosopher Ian Hacking writes, while suicide may seem like a "timeless option"—discussed by essayists as varied as Cicero, Hume, and Sartre—its theorization can be historicized: "It might better be described as a French obsession."[100] By the end of the long nineteenth century—a period coinciding with France's most intense imperial expansion into North and West Africa—the nascent medical and sociological literature included "so much information about French suicides that [Émile] Durkheim could use suicide to measure social pathology."[101]

It is revealing that the father of suicidology makes only two references to France's colonies in *Le suicide* (1897), both in footnotes. First, in his discussion of "fatalistic suicide" (*le suicide fataliste*), Durkheim struggles to find contemporary examples, noting that this type of suicide is "of so little importance today" and "it is so difficult to find examples of it that it seems useless for us to linger here."[102] He turns instead to historical examples, evoking the history of French slavery as a distant past and abstract problem, musing, Is it not "to this type [of suicide] that the suicides of slaves are connected, which are said to be frequent under certain conditions?"[103] Durkheim returns to France's far-flung colonies in a footnote on military suicides, where he observes that increases in military suicide "occurred exactly at the moment when the period of colonial expansion was beginning."[104] Writing during France's bloody occupation of Algeria, Durkheim's concern is for *French* soldiers who cannot bear the traumas of colonizing war, not the thousands of Africans destroying themselves and their cities in deadly acts of resistance against French conquest. The oversight and bracketing of histories of suicidal resistance to French colonizing violence continue to organize critical reflections on suicide today. At the time of this writing, more scholarly attention continues to be accorded to the "suicide epidemic" that took place in metropolitan France during the 2000s—and especially to the thirty-five deaths by suicide of French employees in 2019—than to the countless suicides during the long, ongoing histories of French slavery and colonial and neocolonial expansion.[105]

We might speculate as to *why* histories of suicidal resistance in former sites of French empire have not received the critical attention they deserve. Part of this oversight stems from the kinds of memorial impasses and pervasive "silences" (archival, historical, critical, and otherwise) related to French slavery and colonization discussed earlier. Moreover, it seems worth pointing out that only very recently have forms of resistance to French slavery received sustained scholarly attention.[106] Nor is suicide-as-abnegation easily integrated into triumphant narratives of abolition, independence, and nation-building or positivist historical accounts. Though occasionally recuperated as revolutionary acts (the suicide of Delgrès, for instance), there exist innumerable other, less spectacular, and in many ways far lonelier, suicides that fall through the cracks of grand historical accounts.

So-called borderline or "limit" cases, such as suicide bombing and self-burning protests, put additional pressure on a term—*suicide*—that covers a range of behaviors and outcomes and that today, as Drew Daniel writes in his study of suicide in early modern English literature, *Joy of the Worm* (2022), is "saddled with overfamiliar connotations of pathology and mood disorder."[107] For this reason, Daniel prefers the term *self-killing* to *suicide* throughout his study, especially given that during the early modern period, the former term was supplanted by the latter, and the semantic and cultural shifts engendered by the transition were significant. I, on the other hand, use these terms—as well as others, such as *voluntary death*, *self-destruction*, and *death by suicide*—somewhat interchangeably, not because such fine-grained distinctions are not useful or illuminating but because (1) by the late eighteenth century, when this study begins, the word *suicide* had entered French, in everyday parlance and legal documents; and (2) the primary aesthetic works analyzed here vary greatly in how they refer to instances of self-killing. To put it another way, in my own analytical language I tend to prefer contemporary conventions ("to die by suicide" versus "to commit suicide") but defer to the works under analysis when it comes to tracking how suicide is named.

I suspect, too, that the fact that suicide remains a cultural taboo in much of the French-speaking (and, for that matter, English-speaking) world remains a sticking point and might otherwise discourage work on a topic that engages so many disciplines (psychology, history, sociology, anthropology, literature, philosophy). There is, relatedly, the bald fact that suicide is extremely difficult to write and read about. This is true not only on a methodological level but also on a personal, emotional, and psychosomatic level. As I write in my preface, there simply is no "good" way to write about suicide. There is even the risk, or fear, that reading and writing about suicide, or consuming various kinds of media related to suicide, encourages suicidal ideation—though many studies suggest that the opposite is true, that such activities serve as "protective factors."[108] None of this fully explains the frequency and interest with which various kinds of scholarship are carried out on suicide in metropolitan France, from the Middle Ages to the present, in contrast to the near total lack of scholarly attention to suicide in countries formerly colonized by France and/or part of the so-called Global South. This disparity speaks more readily, I think, to a long and ongoing history of violent indifference to Black and African life.

Archiving Suicide, Reading Resistance

For these reasons, the phenomenon of suicidal resistance under and after French empire is not easily accommodated within existing interpretive frameworks or consistently legible within traditional archives. Alongside other forms of bodily resistance such as marronage, self-mutilation, hunger strikes, parasuicide, and infanticide, suicide under slavery and colonization revealed a troubling threshold between forms of self-destruction and forms of self-actualization. It served as a bodily contestation of unlivable violence and a revolutionary appeal for an altogether different order: a world-breaking and world-making act at the irreducible intersection between technologies of the self and assemblages of the state, private and public spheres.

Suicide refused capture and containment, rejecting the regime of terror to which the enslaved and colonized were subject. As Gayatri Spivak writes, suicide marks an attempt to "go outside of the space-time enclosure when that enclosure means oppression, colonial or gendered or both, undoing history and geography by inscribing the body with death."[109] In the case of slavery, suicide rejected "enclosure" by identifying the world itself *as* enclosure: a structure of containment that, as Tyrone Palmer suggests, "extends to the literal captivity of Blackness in the first instance as that which articulates the World scale."[110] Through suicide, enslaved Africans reclaimed their stolen bodies, refused enclosure—refused the world—and dramatically rejected the status of commodity ascribed to them under the Code Noir but at an immeasurable cost.

One of the through lines of this book, then, is the idea that suicide under slavery and colonization articulates a radical demand for Black freedom at the very moment of death or *in articulo mortis*—that it is a practice of freedom and fugitivity in extremis.[111] At the same time, I share Stephen Best's uneasiness with respect to what he identifies in *None like Us* (2018) as "a certain habit of mind that is triggered when we deal with issues of slavery and death": namely, "a tendency to toggle between positions of martyrdom and nihilism, agency and dispossession."[112] Instead, Best turns to different and, I think, more interesting and complicated questions, asking "whether self-immolation presents a problem for history *writing*; whether [suicide] can even be made available to historical consciousness"; and, elsewhere, "whether the story of slavery"—and here I would add *the story of suicide under slavery*—"can ever be narrated 'from below.'"[113] Are acts of self-suppression, self-immolation, or self-extinguishment, as Best suggests, "unaccountable events [...] being conscripted to ends for which they cannot give account"?[114] Do they, as Constantin Fasolt proposes, constitute a "limit" of history?[115] Such questions require going beyond slavery and Blackness into the murky territory of "consider[ing] the sorts of problems [suicide] poses *for* interpretation," for history, and for meaning more generally.[116]

Departing from the premise that suicide *does* pose problems for interpretation and for the writing of history—indeed, for writing and narration in general—I ask *how*, in suicide's wake, aesthetic forms open up dialogic and polyphonic ways of writing history by attending to points of suicidal resistance. How do such works model alternative modes of archiving suicide? How do they respect and reserve—and here I am interested in the etymologies of these words (*respect*, from *re* + *specere*, "to look (back) at"; *reserve*, from *re* + *servare*, "to keep, to hold back")—what is inaccessible, unsayable, unshareable, and unknowable about suicide?[117]

Organizing Principles, Conceptual Threads

Near the end of her study of philosophy in the African novel, *The African Novel of Ideas* (2021), Jeanne-Marie Jackson traces a literary genealogy of what she calls "philosophical suicide."[118] In a chapter titled "Bodies Impolitic: African Deaths of Philosophical Suicide," Jackson writes against a long tradition of scholarship on suicide in Anglophone African literature—exemplified by the deaths of Okonkwo in Chinua Achebe's *Things Fall Apart* (1958) and Elesin in Wole Soyinka's *Death and the King's Horseman* (1975)—clearing space for a different kind of dying. Focusing on "alienated, contemplative characters whose intellectual dispositions lead them [...] to court death," she unearths an underexamined lineage in African letters in which "self-reflection" and "self-killing" are entangled, doomed pursuits.[119] But then, in something of an aside, Jackson remarks, "There are, of course, other suicides in modern African literature."[120] It is these "other suicides" and the possibility of reading suicide "otherwise" that this book brings into focus.

The Suicide Archive explores how aesthetic works give shape to the untransmissible and unsayable: the resistance of the subaltern who speaks through dying. It tracks how literary, cinematic, and visual art forms figure and extend subversive genealogies of African and Afro-Caribbean suicidal resistance in former sites of French empire. The aesthetic works examined here all recognize suicide as a moment of subalternity coming to crisis. They frequently return to "the scene of the crime," to suicides evoked in passing in colonial-era documents, or occasionally taken up by post-Independence narratives of liberation and nation-building, unloosing them from overdetermined meanings and placing them at the center of their creative responses to the colonial past. Across different media, genres, languages, and vocabularies, suicide emerges as a volatile and resistant political language in extremis, a source of insurrectional potential, and a way of voicing a message when no other means will get through.

Entextualizing Suicide

The passage from acts of self-killing to their appearance in/as text warrants some theorization. In her study of the printing of death in colonial West Africa, Stephanie Newell draws on the sociolinguistic notion of "entextualization" or, as she explains, "the transformation of a process into a cultural object that can be interpreted in the manner of text."[121] I find this notion useful both for describing what aesthetic works "do" to suicide and for characterizing my own critical practice. As Michael Silverstein writes, entextualization is the "process of coming to textual formedness."[122] It involves moving a "text" or fragment of discourse from one context to another in the process of creating a new, circulable text. In writing about death and dying, entextualization, Newell suggests, helps "one to appreciate the cultural processes through which a material corpse passes en route to becoming part of a printed corpus of materials about death."[123] The aesthetic works examined throughout this book all *entextualize* suicides, real and imagined, through citational and intertextual moves that extract suicide from an original context (an archival document, an oral history, a historical record, a newspaper article, a literary work) and reinscribe it in another. Of course, colonial-imperial accounts and official documents entextualize suicide, too; it is often in these discursive environments that suicide first is framed or produced *as* resistance. A key difference, however, and what serves as a criterion of selection for the constellation of aesthetic works discussed in *The Suicide Archive*, is that the entextualizations of suicide that interest me here foreground and amplify what I call the "rhetorical force" of suicide, a notion fleshed out later in this introduction. Each of the primary works discussed in *The Suicide Archive* entextualizes traces of "real" suicides, but not to arrive at a straightforward historical account. Rather, such works write into and against historical accounts or existing archives in complex and generative ways, rethinking and rerouting previous entextualizations of suicide to new ends.

The works explored here achieve this rethinking and rerouting not only by entextualizing suicide but also by narrativizing and, in many cases, novelizing it. Although I draw on a range of materials and media, novels and narratives occupy an important place in this book. The status of the novel, especially the historical novel, in African, Caribbean, and "postcolonial" literary studies has been subject to extensive scrutiny. I want neither to dwell on those debates here nor to fully bracket them. At this juncture in literary studies—in the wake of work by scholars such as Edward Said, Homi Bhabha, and, more recently, Eileen Julien—it seems relatively uncontroversial to point out, as Firdous Azim does, that "the novel is tied to the historical task of colonial, commercial and cultural expansion" (we might add "nationalism" and "globalization") and that its study historically has privileged supposedly "Western" notions such as textuality, modernity, capital accumulation, and liberalism.[124]

The novel as *one possible form* among many for the suicide archive is what most interests me. This boils down to what Jackson calls "the form's inbuilt principles and capacities": namely, in Bakhtin's formulation, the fact that the novel is "multiform in style and variform in speech and voice," that it can "swallow" other genres and registers.[125] This tracks with Greg Forter's suggestion that the postcolonial resuscitation of the novel "develops critiques of colonialism that are totalizing in their ambitions—that oblige us to think beyond both the nation and recent, mono-oceanic paradigms for superseding it" while "enabl[ing] the genre to uncover traces of previous life worlds that resist the totalizing designs of capital."[126] In this sense, the novel form facilitates my gradual expansion of aspects of the Black Atlantic paradigm to other contexts and other bodies of water, namely the Mediterranean and the Seine, as well as my attempts to uncover traces of worlds that have ended on the way to imagining worlds that might yet be.

The origins of the French *roman* in "romance" introduces another fold into this discussion. It prompts us to ask, Is the "subject" of suicide romantic or tragic? Should the story of suicidal resistance be told as romance or tragedy? Such concerns are at the center of David Scott's thesis in *Conscripts of Modernity* (2004) about the narrative frames used to conceptualize colonial history.[127] The works examined throughout *The Suicide Archive* all emerge in tension with narrative and generic frames, even the ones most readily ascribed to them. They resist or refuse the categories of "tragedy" and "romance," as well as "epic." The idiom of suicidal resistance sheds a different kind of light on such distinctions. I call these aesthetic works "suicide archives" in their own right.

On "Suicidal Resistance"

The Suicide Archive studies suicide with its political twin, resistance, positing suicide as a form of necroresistance and a resistant form of subaltern speech.[128] Aesthetic works, I argue, train our capacity to recognize and read this fatal and fragile idiom. These two terms—*suicide* and *resistance*—are the organizing poles and conceptual pillars of this inquiry. That does not mean, however, that they are stable categories. Nor are they synonyms (*suicide* ≠ *resistance*). Rather, *The Suicide Archive* examines the affinities, tensions, and interplay between "suicide" and "resistance," exploring the risks and rewards of reading them alongside one another.

The term *suicidal resistance* deployed throughout this book describes a double gesture and double bind. It names a real mode of political resistance in which people resist myriad forms of oppression through self-destruction. For Michel Foucault, suicide is one of the many "points of resistance" dispersed throughout any power network.[129] Foucault writes:

> In order to exercise a relation of power, there must be on both sides at least a certain form of liberty [...] a power can only be exercised over another to the extent that the latter still has the possibility of committing suicide, of jumping out of the window or of killing the other. That means that in relations of power, there is necessarily the possibility of resistance, for if there were no possibility of resistance—of violent resistance, of escape, of ruse, of strategies that reverse the situation—there would be no relations of power.[130]

The possibility of suicide as resistance shadows all regimes of power—especially, this book shows, gendered and colonial regimes of power.

"Resistance" also gets at a more general feature of suicide: the extent to which the act simultaneously calls out for and resists interpretation. All suicides confront us with an opaque, dysgraphic, "impossible" text whose author disappears the moment their message comes into being. Suicide resists, even forecloses, attempts at understanding insofar as we want to know *why*, but never can with absolute certainty, not even in the case of a suicide note.[131] The aesthetic works I analyze here do not pretend to achieve any such access, which can only ever be illusory. Their subversive potential resides in how they show that this latter dimension of "resistance"—the resistance of a message whose meaning is never assured—gains urgency and power in contexts where suicide also functions as a practice of bodily resistance and political dissidence, when suicide becomes what James C. Scott calls a "weapon of the weak."[132]

I call this dimension the *rhetorical force* of suicide: its capacity to serve as political speech act, as both counter-conduct and counter-discourse. The rhetorical force of self-killings derives from suicide's tendency to signify in ways that cannot be considered purely referential and that evade or unsettle official discursive channels. This is the source of suicide's power and precarity as a political idiom. Aesthetic works unfold the double gesture and double bind of suicidal resistance, attuning us to the act's subversive political potential and activating its rhetorical force. They do so, moreover, without domesticating the recalcitrant power of suicide to resist decipherment, foreclose meaning, and keep its silence. The rhetorical force of suicide is my way of drawing out a distinction between the kinds of readings of suicide made available to us through literary versus purely historical lenses.

Understanding suicide as a speech act and, for all intents and purposes, a mode of writing in and out of the archive demands further explanation. Throughout my attempts at close reading and "politicized looking" in this book, I enlist a series of figures, tropes, and metaphors related to language, languaging, textual or sonic production, and forms of marking to get at the *rhetorical force of suicide*. These include impossible inscription/text/speech; trace, ash (Derrida); ghost-writing (Spivak); dysgraphia (Sharpe); glossolalia (Best); idiom; signal, signifier, sign; cipher; and scream. Many of these figures emerge directly from the aesthetic or theoretical works under analysis. They reveal something fundamental and unassimilable about suicide, something I have tried to describe in my thinking of suicidal resistance and the rhetorical force of suicide here: namely, the ways suicide compels and vexes interpretative activity; the inkling that suicide has a semiotics related to but distinct from natural language; and the difficulty of ever fully recuperating suicide to a theory of speech or writing. These all contribute to the strangeness of suicide as a political idiom.

The rhetorical force of suicide flickers in and out of focus. Once again, I find Best's insights useful here, specifically his theorization of the precarious and resistant archival writing he names *rumor*. Best describes rumor's ontology in the archive as "an appearance made possible only in its disappearance; an aspiration registered at the moment of its suppression; a power that reaffirms itself by liquidating its sources."[133] He continues, "Rumor's paraphrase, translation, and transcription *amplifies, rather than dampens, its semantic instability*."[134] One could readily substitute *suicide* for *rumor* in the archive and in Best's definition. Of course, in French, *rumeur* is not simply gossip or everyday prattle but also a murmur—of voices, the sea, the wind. It names a phonic and haptic middle ground between articulate language and unintelligible noise, often analogized to but distinct from speech.

I am most interested and invested in pursuing a version of Best's claim: that suicide-as-rumor resists the interpretive, literary, and hermeneutic activity brought to bear on it by amplifying semantic instability. In and out of the archive, we receive suicide in a mediated and mendacious form—as "paraphrase, translation, and transcription"—not in its original idioms, death and disappearance, which cannot be translated, which are untranslatable. This is part of a more diffuse claim—an instinct, really—in *The Suicide Archive*: that we should resist recuperating suicide to meaning too quickly or completely, that we should learn to dwell in what is irrecuperable, what can never be redressed, recovered, or saved, and that the tools of literary criticism can help us do this. Such an endeavor takes inspiration from what Brent Hayes Edwards calls a "queer practice of the archive": "an approach to the material preservation of the past that deliberately aims to retain what is elusive, what is hard to pin down, what can't quite be explained or filed away according to the usual categories."[135]

It is noteworthy that in the language of psychoanalysis, "resistance" takes on different, even inverse, meanings from its use in political vocabularies—meanings that are closer to what is at issue in my understanding of suicide's rhetorical force. "Resistance" is the name Sigmund Freud gives to precisely what blocks the psyche's passage to freedom: refractory behaviors—including suicide itself—that Freud initially observed in his female patients in response to his insistence that they "remember the past."[136] Resistance is something that requires "working-through."[137] In this sense, as Jacqueline Rose writes in *The Last Resistance* (2007), resistance is not "the action of the freedom fighter, the struggle against tyranny, the first stirring of the oppressed" but "the mind at war with itself, blocking the path to its own freedom and, with it, its ability to make the world a better, less tyrannical place."[138] In psychoanalysis, resistance becomes "resistance of the conscious to the unconscious" and thus resistance to treatment and analysis in general.[139] Rose's title, "the last resistance," comes directly from Freud's inventory of forms of resistance and anticathexis (repression, transference, gain from illness, etc.) in his addenda to "Inhibitions, Symptoms and Anxiety" (1926).[140] The "last [resistance] to be discovered," Freud writes, is "also the most obscure though not always the least powerful one."[141] The resistance of suicide draws its power from obscurity.

Throughout *The Suicide Archive*, I attempt to hold these different understandings of resistance—as political opposition, as repression of the unconscious, as obstacle to analysis and recovery, as refusal of cure—in tension. They are ultimately all "political," however, insofar as each deals with the relation of suicide to structures of power or to the language of power.

On "Suicide Archives"

If "suicide" and "resistance" form the conceptual pillars organizing this study, then "archive" names its method and fundamental challenge. As the trial of Azor demonstrates, the relation of suicide to the scriptural-imperial archive is complex. The legibility of suicide as resistance is never certain. In the archive of slavery and colonization, suicide appears under erasure or in highly overdetermined frames.

The evidential and existential uncertainty of suicide's status within traditional archives compounds the challenges of writing about death and dispossession under slavery and colonization more generally. Scholars in fields such as Black Atlantic studies and slavery and freedom studies have engaged directly with how the archival turn in twentieth-century Americanist historicism often translates to "a desire [...] to recover black subjects from archives structured by violence and dispossession" and the attendant challenges, pitfalls, and problems "recovery" poses.[142] They have pointed to the ways in which the task of recovery, though "fundamental to historical writing and research," is impossible when it comes to archives built on exclusion and occlusion.[143]

We find versions of this thesis—about the impossibility/necessity of recovery, about the violence of the archive—in works across various subdisciplines, but its formulation in recent feminist scholarship is most powerful and especially salient here. For Saidiya Hartman in "Venus in Two Acts" (2008), a text I return to throughout this book, the archive is "a death sentence, a tomb, a display of the violated body, an inventory of property."[144] For Marisa Fuentes in *Dispossessed Lives* (2016), "violence is transferred from the enslaved bodies to the documents that count, condemn, assess, and evoke them."[145] For Jennifer Morgan in *Reckoning with Slavery* (2021), "archives make it impossible to receive African women as other than historically obscure, damaged, and violated."[146] In *Ordinary Notes* (2023), as part of her preliminary dictionary of untranslatable Blackness, Christina Sharpe dedicates "Note 176," an entry by Dionne Brand, to the term *archive*, defined as "a compendium, usually fissured, listings of events, *seams from which Black life must be extracted, extrapolated*."[147]

Despite the violence of the archive and the impossibility of redress, recovery appeals to our sensibilities as scholars and humans. Best parses this critical impulse—really a longing and projection—as follows:

> No one wants to be erased from history.... Obliterated. Snuffed out. And most scholars of slavery are drawn into the vortex of lives lost in the very moment in which they are found, quite in earnest, out of a longing to bear witness to violent extermination and in the hope that such witness may occasion compassionate resuscitation.[148]

Best's assertion—"No one wants to be erased from history"—would seem justification enough for such "earnest" efforts to recover lives lost, indeed for a whole model of doing history: I would not want to be erased, forgotten, obliterated, *so let me find you*.

Where does that leave us in cases of self-erasure, self-disappearance, self-obliteration, self-liquidation? What about the resistance of invisibility and anonymity? What does it mean to find someone who did not want to be found, who wanted to remain lost? There is a real—unresolved—ambivalence throughout *The Suicide Archive* regarding how to write about the lives and deaths of people who, for reasons unknowable, desired to no longer exist: how to handle the traces of people who perhaps only wanted to disappear and can no longer answer for themselves.

WHILE MY READING-WRITING praxis is in sustained dialogue with Spivak, especially her analysis of female subaltern suicide in "Can the Subaltern Speak?" (1988)—as well as in later essays[149]—the title of this book takes direct inspiration from and seeks to expand Suman Gupta's notion of a "suicide archive." In *Usurping Suicide* (2017), Gupta defines the "suicide archive" as an aggregate of official or unofficial "suicide texts" pertaining to a specific case of suicide. In Gupta's formulation, the suicide archive is a "fluid," open-ended formation encompassing "explicit statements by the person committing suicide (such as a suicide note), the manner and setting of its performance (in public or private, as spectacle or ritual, etc.), the testimonials of witnesses," as well as "records for public purposes, such as reports and media accounts, and findings and assessments by various investigators (for the legal record, for news reportage, etc.)."[150] A suicide archive incorporates "possible linkages and framings that may already be publicly anticipated" between a suicide and its context—what Gupta calls "pressing social concerns"—and between one suicide and another.[151]

The literary is missing from this list and from Gupta's initial definition of "suicide archive," thereby omitting recourse, in suicide's wake, to the aesthetic—as well as the possibility of reading the act itself, and not merely the texts it gives rise to, *literarily*. For all its insights, *Usurping Suicide* reaffirms the critical borders of suicide studies, focusing on highly public, widely reported suicides, predominantly from Europe and the Global North. The only "African" example in the wider study is the much-discussed suicide of Mohamed Bouazizi, the twenty-six-year-old street vendor who set himself on fire in front of the governor's office in Sidi Bouzid, Tunisia, on 17 December 2010, and whose self-immolation is regarded as the "spark" that set off the Jasmine Revolution in Tunisia as well as a series of uprisings across North Africa and the Middle East, often called the "Arab Spring."[152]

The Suicide Archive charts a different course and proposes an alternative history of resistance to French empire by (1) taking seriously the fundamentally literary and dysgraphic dimensions of suicide archives as fungible, surreptitious textual formations; and (2) foregrounding the capacity of aesthetic works to function as "anarchives" (Lia Brozgal) or "other-archives" (Brahim El Guabli) of suicidal resistance in their own right, that is, as *suicide archives*.[153] My book turns to the singular affordance of the aesthetic, which I argue provides ways forward for thinking about suicide—and about the kinds of problems it poses for history, interpretation, and memory—that trouble easy binarisms of resistance and oppression, martyrdom and nihilism. Aesthetic forms lay bare the terrible tensions and tragic paradoxes that characterize suicidal resistance.

Structure and Itinerary

The Suicide Archive begins in the eighteenth century in the French Atlantic world and ends in the present day in North and West Africa. Each chapter bears witness to how people have actively, vehemently, and violently resisted their enslavement, colonization, and settler occupation from the dawn of French colonial expansion to the present. I pay particular attention to histories of female suicidal resistance, which historically have been less available to collective historical consciousness and even more coercively framed in the colonial archive. Many of the aesthetic works discussed in *The Suicide Archive* centrally represent female suicide, and it seems important to point out this fact as a feature not only of this book but of aesthetic representations of suicide more generally. There is a long literary genealogy of female suicides—most often authored by men—from Dido, Antigone, and Cleopatra to Ophelia to Anna Karenina and Emma Bovary. In the nineteenth century, as Margaret Higonnet writes, "women's suicide becomes a cultural obsession."[154] This extends to more recent theoretical reflections on suicide and/as resistance: Spivak's inaugural reading-writing of suicide in "Can the Subaltern Speak" is a post-factum reading of *female* suicide. The "impossible message" that her essay makes legible is inscribed in the death of the young Indian woman Bhubaneswari Bhaduri, who hanged herself in her father's apartment in North Calcutta to avoid having to participate in a political assassination. She had waited until she was menstruating to preempt the charge that she knew would inevitably be ascribed to her hanged, female-gendered body: an illicit pregnancy. The obsession with women's suicide carries over to contemporary debates around the figure of the female suicide bomber and the role of women as agents of political violence, topics I return to in my final chapter.

All this is to say that I attempt to constellate concerns of race, gender, and social status in my readings of individual works and in my discussions of the interrelation between suicidal resistance and systemic violence. Put another way, suicide, in my reading, is always "political," even in its most private and personal iterations. On some level, it is always a refusal of the world as it is currently structured. Reading suicide, attending to the act's rhetorical force, requires an acknowledgment of the ways in which suicides also become records of rampant social inequality and injustice, especially with respect to race- and gender-based violence in colonial and ostensibly postcolonial contexts.

The five chapters of *The Suicide Archive* cover broad terrain, effectively retracing the historical and geographic contours of the French Atlantic Triangle in reverse and revisiting the sites of some of the most intense episodes of French colonizing violence. They also cover key moments in the history of French empire and thus different imperial and neo-imperial formations. Chapters 1 and 2 deal with the period of French slavery and its abolitions (roughly the late seventeenth century to the mid-nineteenth century), examining collective antislavery suicides on the Caribbean and African sides of the Atlantic Triangle. Chapter 3 occurs at a flex point, focusing on the decade leading up to and immediately following Senegalese Independence (1960). This chapter opens up *The Suicide Archive* to a more diasporic framework, to transhistorical links, global networks, and South–North migratory routes, all while remaining profoundly haunted by the Middle Passage and antislavery suicide. It marks a further transition toward a focus, in the back half of this book, on individual suicide, political protest, and suicide in Independence and post-Independence struggles on the continent. In chapter 4, the backdrop is Algeria during the outright anticolonial war of the 1950s and 1960s, then the civil war and state violence of the 1990s. In chapter 5, the setting is Morocco during the post-9/11 era and the war on terror.

Across these chapters, the "shadows" of slave suicide and of anti-Black violence loom large. The transatlantic and trans-Saharan slave trades continue to haunt West and North Africa not only as metaphor but also as historical effect and affect.[155] Colonial techniques of corporal punishment, forced labor, and imprisonment introduced under slavery directly informed France's colonial policies throughout Africa, the Indian Ocean, and Asia after abolition and later were adopted and transformed by postcolonial regimes. This genealogy of violence is perhaps most evident in the origins of the Code de l'Indigénat (the Native Code)—implemented first in Algeria in 1881 before being extended to all of France's colonies and aspects of which remained in place until after Independence—in the text of the Code Noir.

The five chapters of *The Suicide Archive* also span important shifts in French legal history: suicide was decriminalized in the Code Pénal of 1791, the Napoleonic Code Civil of 1804, and the Code Pénal of 1810 but remained a punishable offense under slavery. This fact reflects the different and inferior legal status ascribed to the enslaved under the various iterations of the Code Noir (1685) in place until the abolition of 1848, and later to colonized subjects under the Code de l'Indigénat (introduced in 1881 and abolished between 1944 and 1947).

Despite its loosely chronological structure, precolonial, colonial, and postcolonial texts are juxtaposed throughout *The Suicide Archive*. Part of the argument of this book is that suicide scrambles conventions of chronology and historiography in formative ways. Each of the individual timelines, historical moments, and locales explored in this book is entangled with others: the past surges up in the present, colony bleeds into postcolony, "Africa" makes itself known and felt in France, the Atlantic and Mediterranean haunt and shadow one another.[156] In this focus on entanglement and intersection—connections, crossings, and hauntings—*The Suicide Archive* draws on recent contextual approaches to imperial history and memory such as *histoire croisée* or "crossed history" (Michael Werner and Bénédicte Zimmerman); "multidirectional" and "knotted" memory (Michael Rothberg); "entangled history" (Gregor Feindt); "history hesitant" (Lisa Lowe); and "potential history" (Ariella Aïsha Azoulay).[157] Lowe's mobilization of "hesitation" as archival method and Azoulay's notion of "potential history" are especially resonant with the project of *The Suicide Archive*. The former marks an attempt, as Lowe writes, to "provide a space, a different temporality [. . .] [to] reckon with the connections that could have been but were lost and are thus not yet—before we conceive the freedoms yet to come."[158] The latter cautions us against the progressive impulse to consign violence to a colonial past in the name of a decolonized future, urging us instead toward "a form of being with others, both living and dead, across time, against the separation of the past from the present," toward an undisciplined history focused on activating and amplifying dormant possibilities.[159] The suicide archive provides this different temporality, this space of reckoning.

Taken together, the five chapters of this study articulate a far-ranging genealogy of suicidal resistance that unsettles imperial cartographies by connecting Atlantic, sub-Saharan, Maghrebi, and French geographies and temporalities. Each chapter may stand on its own and might be read independently of others, but chapters benefit most from being read within this broader architecture, which begins and ends with suicide bombs, positioning suicide under slavery and suicide terrorism as two poles, challenging us to think about resistance in different, often unsettling, ways. The chapters of *The Suicide Archive* effectively alternate between two dominant modes or settings of suicide and their attendant images: fire (ashes, explosions, burning) and water (oceans, rivers, drowning). This allows for connections to be drawn across texts but also between lexicons—from Azor's death by firearm (*il s'est brûlé la cervelle*, literally "he burned his head") to the trajectories of the *harragas* who "burn" the sea. It reflects the ways suicide archives travel in unpredictable and unsettling ways. Across the book, "suicide" itself is revealed to be a highly unstable category. It emerges, variously, as a response to different kinds of unfreedom; to enslavement, colonial oppression, and occupation; to experiences of migration, alienation, and displacement; to racism, psychological abuse, and trauma; to incredible structural and state violence; to rampant inequality; and as the expression of a desire to be closer to God, to reach "paradise." It is carried out individually and collectively, in ways both private and public.

CHAPTER 1, "CHORAL HISTORIES," explores the interplay between memory and resistance in literary texts that creatively mine and transform a silenced history of slave suicide in the French Atlantic world. Building on my analysis of the paradoxes of suicide under French slavery made legible by the trial of Azor, I read Fabienne Kanor's fugue-like text *Humus* (2006) and Daniel Maximin's quasi-epistolary novel *L'isolé soleil* (1981) together, showing how both works find creative forms for histories of suicide that fall out of frame in historiographical accounts of French slavery or are obscured in national narratives of resistance and emancipation. Kanor and Maximin decenter and regender masculinist narratives by magnifying the real and imagined archival traces of enslaved women in their literary rewritings of collective suicide.

Whereas Kanor takes up a virtually unknown episode of collective female suicide under French slavery, Maximin's novel topples the famous "epic" of the collective suicide of Louis Delgrès and his followers in order to bear witness to less visible, more "secret" histories of suicidal resistance. Their literary texts crack open monumentalized accounts of slavery, clearing space for more complicated forms of resistance to surface and other voices to be heard. In my conclusion to this chapter, I turn to contemporary debates around historical memory, showing how Kanor's and Maximin's novels participate in important, ongoing conversations about commemorating the history of slavery and abolition.

Chapter 2, "Oral Archives," maintains focus on suicide as a response to capture and enslavement but turns to the African "side" of the French Atlantic Triangle, examining the oral history and translingual literary responses surrounding a national tragedy in Senegalese history that is almost unknown outside Senegal. The Talaatay Nder, or "Tuesday of Nder," refers to a collective suicide at the beginning of the nineteenth century, when an entire village of women and children self-immolated to escape enslavement. The Talaatay Nder reveals some of the complexities of French colonization in West Africa and the challenges of studying slave systems in isolation: the raid and razing of Nder by North African raiders were indirectly provoked by French encroachments in the region. Moreover, they occurred in the immediate wake of the official abolition of the transatlantic (but not trans-Saharan) slave trade (1818) in France, when a clandestine Atlantic trade remained active and while France continued to support and maintain local forms of slavery throughout the Sahara-Sahel region.

Reading across languages and archives, I reconstruct the history of the women of Nder's suicidal resistance and trace its multiple entextualizations. I examine how Senegalese writers have represented and repurposed the Talaatay Nder narrative in literature through readings of Alioune Badara Bèye's French-language historical tragedy *Nder en flammes* (1988) and Boubacar Boris Diop's first Wolof-language novel, *Doomi Golo: Nettali* (2003), a complex example of African "world literature." In these texts, the antislavery suicides of the women of Nder become hymnals of female resistance and expressions of feminist nationalisms. I conclude this chapter by considering another "afterlife" of the Talaatay Nder in Mohamed Mbougar Sarr's novel *La plus secrète mémoire des hommes* (2021), which connects the women's self-immolation to fire protests that spread throughout Senegal in the wake of Bouazizi's self-burning in Tunisia.

Chapter 3, "Screen Memories," uses the oral archive of the Talaatay Nder unearthed in the preceding chapter and the metaphorics of slave suicide explored in chapter 1 to reread perhaps the most iconic suicide in Francophone African cinema and literature: that of Diouana, the protagonist of Ousmane Sembène's short story "La Noire de..." (1962) and its eponymous film adaptation, *La Noire de...* (1966) / *Black Girl* (2017). Considered in the wake of the resistance of Nder, Diouana's suicide more clearly rehearses and reactivates local histories of suicidal resistance to oppression and exile. It resonates with a transatlantic genealogy of antislavery suicide as well as with many suicidal migration narratives—from Ousmane Socé Diop's *Mirages de Paris* (1937) to Fatou Diome's *Le ventre de l'Atlantique* (2003) to Khalid Lyamlahy's *Évocation d'un mémorial à Venise* (2023).

This chapter examines the myriad forms of "screening" that have characterized Diouana's story from the 1950s to the present. Drawing on Freud's notion of a "screen memory," a visual memory that covers or conceals another, I revisit the meanings of "resistance" as repression and opposition to recovery or analysis—themes explored further in the following chapter. As the cartographic and chronological boundaries of *The Suicide Archive* gradually expand and multiply, more supple interpretative frames become necessary. To this end, chapters 3 and 4 collectively elaborate a critical lexicon grounded in visual grammars, forms of exposure and spectacle, and the camera image as heuristics for activating layered histories of suicidal resistance.

Chapter 4, "Multiple Exposures," extends the theoretical frames for representing female suicide developed in earlier chapters and for considering the relationship between memory and resistance. Focusing on the work of the Constantine-born writer Nourredine Saadi (1944–2017), I lay out a history of Algerian suicide in the *longue durée*. I build on earlier discussions, in chapters 1 and 3, of the Atlantic as a watery burial ground or "seametary" (Hakim Abderrezak) in the works of writers like Kanor, Diome, and Sembène to establish a genealogy of suicidal resistance centered on Constantine's defining geological feature, the Rhummel River Gorge, which I show to be a fluvial geography of tragedy and terror, peopled by the ghosts of drowned women.

Taking cues from how images, especially photographs, circulate in Saadi's work, I develop a literary hermeneutic informed by photographic techniques of exposure as a means of accessing sedimented histories of loss. Through the notion of *multiple exposure*, I argue for an associative poetics of superimposition that supplies more supple "frames" for thinking French colonial history and suicide together. I focus on twin novels by Nourredine Saadi, *La nuit des origines* (2005) and *Boulevard de l'abîme* (2017). Both are set between Constantine and Paris, but their timelines and geographies constantly fold back on themselves, moving between the civil war of the 1990s, the Algerian War for Independence decades earlier, and the colonial and precolonial periods. Like Sembène's Diouana and Diome's Salie, the female protagonist of these novels, Abla, finds herself in exile in France—simultaneously longing and unable or unwilling to return home. Her suicide, like Diouana's, is heavily mediated—recounted as a long flashback through the narrative frame of a police investigation or *enquête*. In the wake of Diouana's suicide, we are better positioned to read Abla's suicide as a moment of colonial memory coming to crisis.

Chapter 5, "Strange Bedfellows," forms an unsettling coda to my reflections on the relationship between suicide, archive, resistance, violence, history, and aesthetics. Focusing on suicide terrorism, this chapter shows how literature and literary criticism supply other discursive forms for theorizing contemporary violence. Aesthetic works articulate different modes of understanding and open up conceptual possibilities where official discourses meet the limit of suicide bombing, laying out hermeneutical and ethical alternatives by way of fiction.

My reading focuses on Mahi Binebine's novel about the 2003 Casablanca suicide bombings, *Les étoiles de Sidi Moumen* (2010). Binebine's novel creates a bridge from previous chapters since he explicitly connects the situation of the suicide bomber to the history of terrorism in Algeria during the Black Decade and to the trajectories of sub-Saharan and North African migrants or *harraga*, who risk everything to reach foreign shores. This discussion of the relationship between irregular migration, on the one hand, and suicide bombing, on the other, is enriched by turning to one of Binebine's earlier novels, *Cannibales* (1999), which shares formal and thematic concerns with *Les étoiles de Sidi Moumen*. Binebine's exploration of suicide bombing is noteworthy both for its innovative narrative frame—the novel is narrated by a dead terrorist—and for its queering of the terrorist fiction genre. Through its ghostly narration and "queer form," Binebine's novel contests the idea that there is no mode, no adequate language, for understanding the suicide bomber. It unsettles the masculinist posturing most often associated with acts of suicide terrorism, making available a queer subtext that keeps focus on the oppressive postcolonial state.

My conclusion, "The Suicide Archive: A Social Document," returns to the questions of memory, meaning, and reckoning raised here in the introduction. I reflect on the role of archives and archiving in writing histories of loss and on the yield of reading aesthetic works as archives, especially amid ongoing debates about memorial approaches to colonial history and the status of African archives.

I

Arm'd with thy sad last gift—the pow'r to die,
Thy shafts, stern fortune, now I can defy;
Thy dreadful mercy points at length the shore,
Where all is peace, and men are slaves no more;
This weapon, ev'n in chains, the brave can wield,
And vanquish'd, quit triumphantly the field.

THOMAS DAY AND JOHN BICKNELL,
The Dying Negro (1773)

· I ·

CHORAL HISTORIES

Suicide and Slavery in the French Atlantic

Imagine, if you can, the swirling red of mounting to the deck, the ramp they climbed, the black sun on the horizon, vertigo, the dizzying sky plastered to the waves.

ÉDOUARD GLISSANT, *Poetics of Relation* (1990)

The Ramp They Climbed

Thirty years before Azor's trial in Basse-Terre and the same year Thomas Day's poetic epistle about slave suicide, *The Dying Negro*, began circulating in print, a slave ship called *Le Soleil* (*The Sun*) left the French port city of Nantes for the West Coast of Africa.[1] On New Year's Eve, 1773, the ship reached Badagry in present-day Nigeria. Over the next three months, 382 Africans were captured, traded, and taken onboard.[2] The captain of *Le Soleil* was a middle-aged Frenchman named Louis Mosnier; he (or his secretary) kept a careful record of the voyage.[3] *Le Soleil* was heading for Saint-Marc (Sen Mak), Haiti, where she arrived on 16 June 1774 after nearly three months at sea. Before the ship left the Nigerian coast, there were problems.

On 15 January 1774, seven women were "burned alive" in the dugout pits or *zomaï* where captive Africans were sequestered while awaiting departure for the Americas (ironically, the Fon/Fɔ̀ngbè term *zomaï* translates to "a place fire cannot go"). It is unclear whether the fire was a tragic accident—a blaze that spread quickly in hermetically sealed close quarters—or a deliberate act of rebellion. Mosnier simply notes the event as a loss of cargo.

On 23 March 1774, the thirty-eight-man crew of *Le Soleil* was preparing to set sail (Mosnier lists their official departure date as the following day). The Bight of Bénin—the part of the Gulf of Guinea where *Le Soleil* dropped anchor—was storm-tossed. The sea, Mosnier writes, was "extremely rough and the wind was howling."

It is not entirely clear what happened next, how the women broke free of their chains. Perhaps they were brought up from the hold to be "danced"—a practice by which the enslaved were forced above deck for exercise to keep them physically fit for the market. The inclement weather and the fact that the ship was soon getting underway make this scenario unlikely. What is clear is that fourteen women suddenly appeared standing together on the *dunette*, the most elevated section of the aft poop deck at the rear of the ship. To have gotten there, they must have climbed the ladder or ramp quickly, before the crew caught on. If the sea was rough, this could not have been easy, and the ramp they climbed would have been narrow and steep. The women's eyes would not have had time to adjust from the darkness of the hold to the bright light of day. Even if it had been cloudy, the contrast would have been stark, disorienting, vertiginous. Fourteen women, standing together. Then they jumped.

Mosnier writes that it happened in total synchrony: "14 Black women [*Noires*] all together, at the same time, in a single movement." The description of the women's striking unison is the only point in the captain's report where his otherwise unflinching language falters and we glean a flicker of something else—awe, perhaps fear. Then he returns to business as usual and to the terse language of inventory. Only seven of the women could be recovered. One of them died on deck. She was in bad shape already. Six returned to the hold. The rest drowned or were eaten by sharks.[4] The 382 became 374.

THIS CHAPTER FOCUSES ON literary works that take suicide in the French Atlantic as a crucible for thinking through the colonial past as well as the profound silences that continue to condition historical memory related to French slavery in the present. The works discussed actively unsettle the relationship of slave suicide to the colonial-imperial script by writing into the gaps in dominant discourses and constructing alternative suicide archives. They crack open monumentalized accounts of slavery to clear space for more complicated forms of resistance and unarchived voices by finding creative, choral forms for histories of suicide that fall out of the frame in historiographical accounts of French slavery or are obscured in national narratives of resistance and emancipation.

I focus on two novels that were published over two decades apart but share thematic and formal concerns in their entextualizations of collective antislavery suicides. First, French Martinican writer Fabienne Kanor's fugue-like text *Humus* (2006; English translation, 2020), engages directly with how enslaved women are disappeared from historical records and radically silenced within the imperial archive.[5] In *Humus*, Kanor excavates the little-known episode of collective female suicidal resistance described above, an event for which almost no written trace remains: when fourteen enslaved African women threw themselves overboard from the French frigate *Le Soleil* as it left the coast of West Africa in 1774. Departing from the ship captain's succinct, dispassionate report of the women's leap and the recovery attempts that ensued, *Humus* interrogates and expands a written trace discovered in the archive in Nantes into a polyvocal text: an imaginative attempt to hear the voices of the drowned. Next, I move on to Guadeloupean writer Daniel Maximin's intricate quasi-epistolary novel *L'isolé soleil* (1981; *Lone Sun*, 1989), which proposes a fractured history of suicidal resistance to French slavery by exploding the "epic" text of the collective suicide of Louis Delgrès (1766–1802) and three hundred of his followers at Matouba in 1802 into a series of fragmented texts-in-progress. Centering loosely on the attempts of the aspiring writer Marie-Gabriel to develop a polyphonic account of Antillean history, and specifically of the "épopée Delgrès," *L'isolé soleil* contests and subverts masculinist narratives of suicidal resistance heroes, rehabilitating the role of female insurgents such as Solitude, who fought alongside Delgrès, or those who resisted in less visible ways and who have been ignored in dominant colonial and postcolonial scripts.[6] Like Kanor's *Humus*, Maximin's *L'isolé soleil* makes room for what masculinist accounts of slave suicide obscure, toppling Guadeloupe's national epic of resistance and a "statuefied" version of the Antillean past.

In the conclusion to this chapter, I expand on the question of "statuefication" with respect to suicide in/and the Antillean past since Kanor's and Maximin's novels make explicit arguments *against* monumentalizing approaches to colonial history. This puts the novels into tension with the contexts of their publication, reception, and circulation (the 1980s for Maximin, the early

2000s for Kanor), which bore witness to new memorial initiatives in France, Martinique, and Guadeloupe to commemorate the Slave Trade. More recently, the desecration and toppling of statues related to imperial history throughout the French Caribbean—including those of abolitionist Victor Schœlcher, Empress Joséphine Bonaparte, and French colonizer Pierre Belain d'Esnambuc—have sparked debates about the historical memory at stake in Kanor's and Maximin's novels and in this chapter.[7] Examining such debates in connection with literary texts prepares the ground for considering more ephemeral though no less powerful approaches to histories of suicide. This theme is taken up in the following chapter, which focuses on the oral history and literary responses surrounding a second episode of collective female suicidal resistance to slavery, one for which no physical monument exists.

Requiem, Rumor

The story of the women of *Le Soleil* reaches us as "rumor" in the archive: as little more than a murmur—a few spare lines that "radiate with a sense of historical impossibility" and raise more questions than they answer.[8] What were the women's names? Did they conspire? If so, how? Did they speak the same language? What became of the women returned to the hold?

Mosnier's original report and whatever personal *journal de bord* or ship's log he kept are now lost. What remains is the record of a record: the transcription from the same year of a navigation report (*rapport de navigation* or *rapport de mer*) filed by Mosnier with the Admiralty of Nantes, the administrative unit responsible for the French navy and local maritime law, now conserved in the Departmental Archives in Nantes:

> [Mosnier] a déposé pareillement en ce greffe que le 23 mars dernier; il se seroit jetté de dessus la dunette à la mer et dans les lieux 14 femmes noires toutes ensemble et dans le même tems par un seul mouvement; ayant alors le canot sur le pont et la chalouppe étant employée a chercher l'ancre de tangon; qu'ayant a la mer pour embarcation une pirogue de 33 pieds fillée de barriere; que pendant le temps que tout l'équipage fut occupé à baller de lavant la d. pirogue; quelque diligence qu'on put faire la mer etant extrêmement grosse et agitée ventant avec tourmente; les requins en avoient déjà mangé plusieurs avant qu'il y eut même du monde embarqué, qu'on parvint cependant à pouvoir en sauver 7 dont une mourut à 7 heures du soir, étant fort mal lorsqu'elle fut sauvée; qu'il s'en est trouvé 8 de perdues dans cet évènement de quoi il a aussi déposé procès-verbal.[9]

([Mosnier] also filed in this registry that on 23 March last, fourteen black women apparently had thrown themselves into the sea and onto the decks from the poop deck, all together and at the same time in a single movement; the dinghy at this point being on the bridge and the rowboat being used to pull up the boom anchor; that having at sea with them a 33-foot skiff lined with a barrier; that during this time the whole crew was busy scrubbing down this skiff; whatever haste they made, the sea being extremely rough and choppy, blowing a gale; the sharks had already eaten several of them before the crew had even set out, that seven were saved nonetheless, one of whom died at seven o'clock, being in very bad shape when she was rescued; that eight therefore were lost in this incident, of which he also filed a procès-verbal.)

Over two hundred years later, Fabienne Kanor transcribed part of the same text and appended it to her novel *Humus* (2006) as an epigraph. Kanor first discovered the citation from Mosnier and the history of the unnamed women of *Le Soleil* by dint of what she later would call "a necessary chance."[10] While traveling in Senegal, she visited Gorée Island, one of the best-known and most significant *lieux de mémoire* in West Africa related to the French slave trade. In an exhibition on slave revolts in the upper-level gallery of the Maison des esclaves, she found a brief reference to the women's leap in 1774: a story "the size of a footnote, an example among others of the captives' insubordination."[11] The sense that there was something more to this "anecdote" of suicidal resistance prompted Kanor to dig deeper, unearthing and inventing a suicide archive of her own.

Kanor effectively retraced Mosnier's transatlantic voyage from two centuries earlier. Her itinerary followed the bare archival trace and spectral signposts left in the wake of *Le Soleil*. Traveling first to Nantes, she visited the archives, where she consulted and transcribed the report. She then went to Badagry, where *Le Soleil* traded in human beings between December 1773 and March 1774. Moving on to Bénin, she visited the palaces of Abomey and, in Ouidah, several sites along the West African slave route that all feature in the novel.[12] Finally, Kanor returned to the Antilles—first to Guadeloupe and then to Martinique—where she finished drafting her novel.

In *Humus*, Kanor appropriates this meager archival trace encountered in the slave port of Gorée and preserved in the archives in Nantes in her own polyphonic narrative. Mosnier's report becomes the point of imaginative departure for sounding out the stories of the unnamed women of *Le Soleil* and reading the phantom text of their suicide. As if pressing her ear to the dog-eared page of Mosnier's report, Kanor excavates an alternate text in *Humus*: a choral narrative declined in the feminine plural—a requiem for the drowned. Splitting open a third-person account of suicidal resistance made by one Frenchman, Kanor produces a fugue for the Middle Passage: a contrapuntal, musical text declaimed by the captive African women of *Le Soleil*, who narrate their fatal leap and "flight" from slavery in the first person. Here the etymology and meaning in French are instructive: *fugue* comes from the Latin *fuga*, meaning "flight," related to *fugere*, "to flee," and can designate a psychological state of rupture. As fugue, *Humus* connects the suicidal leap of the women of *Le Soleil* to the fugitive movement of the maroon, the flight of the flying African, and the fugue state as a response to severe trauma.

Through its direct engagement with the text of Mosnier's report, Kanor's *Humus* provides a powerful literary response to Marisa J. Fuentes's historiographical query: How can we narrate "the fleeting glimpses of enslaved subjects," especially enslaved women, within traditional archives?[13] This is a question that preoccupies many of the authors explored in this book: not how to recover the irrecoverable, per se, but how to tell new stories from fragments, traces, whispers. Kanor's novel, which takes off from the account of a real (failed) recovery attempt in the archive of transatlantic slavery, offers a possible model in its choral architecture. A "vessel" in the fullest sense, *Humus* is a liquid text resounding with the voices of the drowned.

IN ITS SUBJECT AND praxis, *Humus* resembles other fictionalized representations of French slavery, including Maximin's *L'isolé soleil*, discussed in the second half of this chapter. *Humus* shares in and inflects the memorial projects of texts like Édouard Glissant's *Le quatrième siècle* (1964), Patrick Chamoiseau's *L'esclave vieil homme et le molosse* (1997), Maryse Condé's *Moi, Tituba, sorcière... Noire de Salem* (1986), and Évelyne Trouillot's *Rosalie l'infâme* (2003).[14] *Humus* also enters into conversation with more recent work, such as Léonora Miano's *La saison de l'ombre* (2013) and David Diop's *La porte du voyage sans retour* (2021), which reconstitute the "sides" of the French Atlantic Triangle perhaps least available to historical memory and rarely represented in literature: the European trade in slaves along the coasts of Africa.[15] Such works, as Christopher Miller puts it, attempt "to fill in the missing French-language, first-person testimony of slaves born in Africa."[16]

Despite its designation as a *roman* (novel) and its origins in an actual, documented episode of suicidal resistance during the Middle Passage, *Humus* is, emphatically, *not* a historical novel. As will be the case with *L'isolé soleil* and Marie-Gabriel—who writes against dominant tropes of Antillean history—

the narrator of *Humus* breaks with the generic frames most often used to re-present the colonial past, especially histories of suicide within slavery. Following the excerpt from Mosnier's report, *Humus* opens with a direct, second-person address disabusing readers of any expectations that what follows is a straightforward account of French slavery: "Leave here all hopes, you who think perhaps that a story about slavery is necessarily an adventure novel. An epic tale, a tragic epic [. . .]. Abandon all hope, you who surely hope that I am going to tell you such a story [*histoire*]."¹⁷ The narrator's "avertissement" echoes the bleak warning on the gates of Hell in Dante's *Divine Comedy* (*lasciate ogne speranza, voi ch'intrate,* "leave here all hope, you who enter"). It makes *Humus* a textual portal opening onto the hellscape of the *cale*, the hold of the slave ship—a *porte du voyage sans retour.*¹⁸

The suggestion is that we, the readers, will be "taken" and "chained"—held captive—by this haunting text: "You will be captured [*pris*]. Chained [*enchaînés*] in spite of yourself to the words" (14). We are enjoined to listen to the women of *Le Soleil*, to the ghostly "chorus" (*chœur*) of their beating hearts (*cœur*): "Like these ghosts [*ombres*] chained up long ago, the reader is from here on condemned to remain still. Just to listen, with no other distraction, to this chorus of women. To hear again [*entendre encore*], at the risk of being intoxicated [*s'étourdir*], these beating hearts" (14). Kanor's novel "condemns" the reader to an exercise of ethical listening, attempting to hear a spectral chorus of enslaved women as they recite the text of their collective suicide.

Adopting an apophatic mode of address reminiscent of Toni Morrison's *Beloved* ("This is not a story to pass on . . ."), *Humus* progressively undoes its own genericity. This *histoire* is not a *histoire*, the narrator insists, but something else entirely: "This story [*histoire*] is not a story. But a poem. This story is not a story, but an attempt to slip into a space where there are no longer witnesses to speak, where man, plunged into the darkness of the sea, in this endless blue-black, faces the worst trial there is: the death of speech, aporia" (14). In *Humus*, Kanor attempts to access a deep, dark aquatic space of memory and oblivion: something akin to what Derek Walcott memorably calls the "grey vault" of the sea.

Humus frames itself as impossible speech, beginning where language ends, where speech (*la parole*) goes to die. The text takes the silence of the women of *Le Soleil* as its condition of possibility, attempting to "hear" the *rumeur* of their suicidal leap. In Kanor's words, "It is because these women leaped that the captain took up the pen, and the novel could begin. *They leaped not because they had nothing left to say but because they needed to tell of everything that had happened.*"¹⁹ In *Humus*, Kanor marks out a space of textual and sexual difference

CHORAL HISTORIES · 45

in which the story of the women's suicide can surface more fully. As the narrator of the first section of the novel insists, "It all started there. From a desire to trade [*troc*]. Exchange the jargon for speech. The cant [*la langue de bois*] of sailors for the cry of the captives. It all started from a questioning. How to tell, how to retell, this story of men? Without fuss or artifice. Otherwise. And against the reader's expectations" (13). Through a textual "exchange" (*troc*) and telling "otherwise," Kanor substitutes feminine for masculine, "orality" for writing. Counterposing the "wooden" words of sailors with the phonics of the captives' cry, she exchanges the voices above deck with those below: the chorus of interlocking voices of female captives who are "heard" for the very first time.

Chorus

Humus ultimately delivers a "chorus" in fourteen voices in which the leap or "flight" witnessed by Mosnier and his crew in 1774 is recounted through the intersecting perspectives of the women of *Le Soleil*. Yet Kanor does not attempt to recover, resurrect, or restore each of the fourteen women's voices in turn. The novel resists a perfect unity or total harmony, emerging in tension with the women's striking synchrony. Despite its *tour de rôle* structure, the choral architecture of *Humus* is uneven, enacting a general wariness of plenitude and thematizing the inability of any text or archive to achieve total, unmediated access to the voices it contains.

The novel consists of twelve labeled narrative sections, each voiced in the first person by a female speaker designated primarily by the identity ascribed to her before or during captivity, or her role aboard *Le Soleil*: "La muette" (the mute girl), "La vieille" (the old woman), "L'esclave" (the slave), "L'amazone" (the Amazon), "La blanche" (the white girl), "Les jumelles" (the twins, really two narrators, twin captives from Waalo in northern Senegal, the setting of the following chapter), "L'employée" (the conscript), "La petite" (the little one), "La reine" (the queen), "La volante" (the one-who-flies), "La mère" (the mother), and "L'héritière" (the heiress).[20] These names further resemble the practice of naming slave ships with a definite, usually grammatically feminine, noun phrase. In fact, a scan of maritime registers reveals that *La Reine*, *L'Amazone*, and *La Petite Fille* are all slave ships that passed through Nantes during the eighteenth century.[21]

The exceptions to this narrative scheme are the antepenultimate and final sections, "La volante" and "L'héritière." Neither is voiced by a captive woman of *Le Soleil*. "La volante" is the most mobile, least embodied of *Humus*'s narrators. She witnesses but does not physically experience the horrors of slavery.[22]

A nocturnal, visionary presence, she is "the initiate, the mambo, the one-who-flies, the *soukougnante*" (213): an iteration of the *soucougnan* (also called *souklian, volan, volant, gen gagé*), a vampiric sorceress who sheds her human form at night to take the shape of a bird or fireball.[23] Her celestial gaze shuttles the reader between the Old World and the New, depicting the slaving port of Nantes and the plantation society and maroon communities in Saint-Domingue/Haiti/Ayiti on the cusp of insurrection. Her mystic "flight" parallels that of the women of *Le Soleil* who, in their suicidal leap, each become "flying Africans" in turn. "L'héritière" is an inscription of the author, Kanor, and adopts a similarly "aerial" narrative perspective as the narrator travels by airplane from Badagry to Paris to Gosier (244). This final section forms a coda to the first, untitled section of *Humus*, returning us to the novel's scene of writing and depicting the narrator-author facing "the book to come," grappling with the strange "inheritance" of the other women's stories (247).

The remaining narrative sections, each spoken by a captive African woman aboard *Le Soleil*, unfold according to their own idiosyncratic, nonlinear logics. Across this structure, the leap emerges as a haunting refrain. It is elaborated as a series of musical variations on the same theme by which each woman narrates the same event from different positions at different points in time.[24] It is the moment or "movement" through which the various narrative strands of *Humus*—a text that otherwise resists perfect unity and cohesion—harmonize.

In *Humus*, Kanor exchanges a choral "nous" for the "elles" of Mosnier's original report, but she also fractures and transforms Mosnier's account in more substantial ways by using it as the basis for a plurifocalized text that does not purport to tell the whole story. As the narrator of the first section remarks, "I wasn't there, that's the only thing I'm sure about" (13). Kanor shows the narrative structure of her text, like the work of memory related to French slavery, to be open-ended, incomplete, and full of holes. The female narrators of *Humus* all thematize their unknowing, fallibility, and far-from-neutral spaces of enunciation, such that their narratives contrast with the impersonal, technical register of Mosnier's report. The captive women of *Le Soleil* subvert and defy our expectations as narrators and witnesses. They do not recount their own stories with any claim to absolute knowledge or objectivity. They have killed, betrayed, coerced, abandoned, taken captives of their own, and sold others into slavery. They have forgotten names, places, dates. They fail to remember, choose not to remember, or remember imperfectly. They try to forget. They fabricate, invent, and lie.

The paradoxical figure of "La muette," who narrates the first titled section of *Humus*, is emblematic in this respect. A young girl who has been raped by a

French sailor—"One night, they ate my belly"—she narrates without memory or an adequate language, fashioning narrative out of absence (19). She has witnessed everything, but lacks the words to speak of it:

> In the beginning was absence. Say nothing, be nothing. Nothing but a thing that they use. That they use until its insides break.
>
> I saw it all. Don't ask me what. Words lost are lost forever. I'd have to make it up to do it well, to say everything that comes to mind. Words for laughing, for forgetting words, words for acting as if. Who still cares about the details? (17)

Later, recalling the moments after her leap from the *dunette*—the thrashing blur of water and blood, the swarm of sharks, the taste of salt—"La muette" notes: "A story [*une histoire*], what I saw, there, beneath the sea" (21). But she does not reveal what, exactly, she has seen. She wants to speak but has "lost [her] words" (23). The first captive whose "voice" we hear in *Humus* is that of the mute child, an embodiment of what the narrator earlier had called "the death of speech, aporia" (14).

In the absence of articulate language, "La muette" turns to a primitive form of "writing." To make sense of the Middle Passage, she traces signs in the wood of the ship as the African coast vanishes: "When land disappeared behind the great line, I started counting. With my thumbnail, I started scratching [*tracer*]. One day = one line. That's how I went about it. Every day, in the wood, for fear of forgetting one; cutting up time . . . I had never done that before. So I count: twenty-seven scars" (22). This silent code adopted by "La muette" performs quite literally the textual "exchange" (*un désir de troc*) envisioned by Kanor at the beginning of the novel, replacing the *langue de bois* of sailors with signs, or "scars," etched into the wood of the ship.

Like "La muette," "La mère" (the mother), the final captive to recount her leap, is unable, or unwilling, to re-create her death in microscopic detail. Her narration appropriates the original text of Mosnier's report almost verbatim in the first person:

> It was March 23rd, 1774.
>
> I kept my promise. Early that morning, I did as it was written. I threw myself off the poop deck. Whatever haste they made, the sea being extremely rough and choppy, blowing a gale, the shark had already eaten me before the crew had even set off. (224)

"La mère," whose name is homophonous with *la mer* (the sea), narrates from beyond death, from inside the shark who devoured her. Her impossible testimony reaches us from the depths of the Middle Passage, from the "endless blue-black" evoked earlier in the novel as "a space where there are no longer witnesses to speak" (14). But she is speaking—not only from the "belly of the beast" but from "the belly of the Atlantic," to invoke the title of Fatou Diome's novel *Le ventre de l'Atlantique* (2003).[25]

Indeed, despite their different historical settings (Diome's novel takes place in France and Senegal in the present)—and the fact that Diome's novel deals primarily with what her narrator calls the "geographic suicide" of exile, not suicide under slavery—Kanor's *Humus* and Diome's *Le ventre*, published only three years apart, share much, not least their evocation of fateful ocean crossings and the ways they interrogate the imbricated histories of the "Triangle" and the "Hexagon" in relation to Afro-diasporic identity.[26] These themes are taken up powerfully by Maboula Soumahoro's more recent *Le Triangle et l'Hexagone* (2020)—part autobiography, part theoretical treatise, part literary itinerary—in which the author declares herself "daughter" of both France and the Atlantic world: "My ancestry, my origins, my trajectories, and my own history inscribe me in this cultural, political, and intellectual immensity that is the Black Atlantic, a geographic space profoundly shaped by History. I evoke this space, called triangular, which brought together in unprecedented and lasting fashion three continents: Europe, Africa, and the Americas."[27] This is the intercultural space of Kanor's own upbringing—born in France to Martinican parents—and of the final narrator of *Humus*, "L'héritière" (the heiress), who travels around the Triangle and "inherits" a somatic Atlantic history in the *longue durée*.

For Kanor, Diome, and the women of *Le Soleil*—all "daughters of the Atlantic"—*ventre* names the dark center of the Atlantic world. It is the *gouffre-matrice*, the "womb-abyss" of the Middle Passage, what Glissant in *Poétique de la relation* calls the "purple belly" of the sea: "The experience of the abyss [*gouffre*] lies inside and outside the abyss. The torment of those who never escaped it: who went straight from the belly [*ventre*] of the slave ship into the purple belly [*ventre violet*] of the depths of the sea."[28] Purple (*violet*) is the color Glissant gives to the ocean's depths when he bemoans the fates of those enslaved men and women who, like the women of the *Soleil*, never made it to the Americas but sank to the bottom of the Atlantic.

In Kanor's novel, purple is the color of posthumous testimony: the color of blood in deep water. Recalling the moments after her leap as she was devoured alive, "La mère" can only give us an impression, a color—purple: "It happened so fast. Don't expect me to paint you a picture. All that I remember well is the color of the water. Blue + red = purple. Blue + red = purple" (224).

Kanor seems to be picking up threads, or rather hues, not only from Glissant but also from Diome, whose *Le ventre* is etched in shades of "purple ink" (*encre mauve*). In the final pages of *Le ventre de l'Atlantique*, purple becomes a means for the narrator Salie, born in Senegal but living in France, to express and affirm a *transatlantic* identity. Kanor's "equations" build directly on Diome's identarian "admixture," by which Salie advances an "additive" theory of identity, irreducible to its constituent elements:

> Green, yellow, red? Blue, white, red? Barbed wire? Of course! I prefer mauve, that temperate color, a mix of African red heat and cold European blue. What makes purple [*mauve*] beautiful? The blue or the red? [...] I seek my country where they appreciate additive identities [*l'être-additionné*], without separating its various layers. [...] I seek my country where the arms of the Atlantic meet to form the purple [*mauve*] ink that tells of incandescence and sweetness, the burning for existence and the joy of living.[29]

For Diome, purple or *mauve* is the result not of mixing "water" and "blood" but of what Kanor frames in her novel as "the voice of the North meeting the South"—the encounter between Africa and Europe.[30] It is the color of what Dominic Thomas calls "the bilateralism of French-African relations"—the color of migration and hybridity.[31]

Beyond their transatlantic color theory, Kanor, Diome, and Glissant share their identification of the Atlantic as an organizing presence/absence whose historical contours are shaped by the history of slavery. Even in texts ostensibly dealing with a postslavery, postcolonial moment, such as Diome's novel, the links to Atlantic slavery are omnipresent and often explicit.[32] The Atlantic is a haunting and haunted space, as Kanor's ghost chorus in *Humus* shows—an immense maritime burial ground, or what Hakim Abderrezak, writing about the Mediterranean, calls a "seametary."[33] Mati Diop's cinematic "ghost love story" about boat migrations from Senegal, fittingly titled *Atlantics* (2019), takes on this haunted history in more literal terms. From the eighteenth century (Kanor) to present-day migratory routes (Diome, Diop), these depths continue to accumulate histories of loss—bodies and blood in deep water—in the present.

At the same time, Kanor and Diome identify the *ventre* or belly of the Atlantic not only as a fearsome maw, an unfathomable abyss, but also as a womb (from Latin *ventrum*), a generative space of (re)birth. In Kanor, the *ventrum* at issue is clearly the womb of the enslaved. In dying by suicide during the Middle Passage, the women of *Le Soleil* avoid having their reproductive lives legally bound to the institution of French slavery in the Americas through the law of *partus sequitur ventrum* (what leaves follows the womb), which ensured that the status of enslavement passed from enslaved women to their children.

The question of progeny and rebirth becomes clearer later in the mother's narration, as we realize that the "you" (*tu*) she is addressing is not—or not just—the reader but her infant son who, we learn, was swept away by the waves and drowned when she slipped and plunged into the water while boarding *Le Soleil*. This is another parallel, as we will see, to Maximin's novel, which incorporates a lengthy address from a mother to her dead son and not-yet-born daughter (228). The mother's intimate second-person address in *Humus* also encompasses a broader progeny. It addresses everyone living in what Christina Sharpe calls "the wake" and what Saidiya Hartman terms the "afterlife" of slavery, as means of registering how the traces and traumas of Atlantic slavery haunt, interrupt, and shape our present.[34] The mother's *tu*, which rises from the depths, is a reminder that the past of slavery is not past and that the conditions of Black social and physical death it created remain present and future, not "historical," phenomena.

Kanor's mother figure suggests a way forward for remembering and retelling the history of slavery "otherwise." Her final words announce the emergence of something new. Something born out of the dark, damp spaces of the shark, the ship, the sea. Something born of song: "You will be born, safe and sound in the belly of the beast, I mother, I will sing. Red + blue =, red + blue = " (225). The chapter ends with this missing rhyme in French (*je chanterai. Rouge + bleu = [violet]*) that the reader must supply. The mother's sea song heralds a new lyric: the fugue *Humus* channels.

Secondary Rhythms

Across the fugue-like structure of *Humus*, other voices crowd in. Occasionally, the women's self-narration is interrupted by an italicized, third-person omniscient narration in parenthesis that functions as a kind of cinematic *voix-off* or metacommentary: "You can make out the sea in the distance. Nothing extraordinary really. The girl furrows her brow because of the sun, squats down on her heels, and tells a bit" (17). The narratives often incorporate words and strains of poetry, prayer, and song in French, Kréyol, Wolof, and Arabic. A series of female-to-female pairings also emerges such that the separate histories and voices of each of the narrators intersect and cross one another at points: "L'esclave" was the captive of "La reine" before they found themselves in the same *cale*; "La blanche" and "La petite" form an unexpected alliance that spoils; "L'employée," a conscripted worker employed to surveil the female captives, is fascinated by the androgynous Sosi, "L'amazone," and decides to emulate her by leaping with the other women; "L'héritière" is visited in her dreams by "La volante" while composing her final manuscript. *Humus* is the harmonic body in which these contrapuntal musical strains converge, taking on a meaning and "coloration" irreducible to the sum of its parts.

While the twelve labeled narrative sections deliver the polyphonic testimonies of thirteen female narrators (since the narration of "Les jumelles" harbors two voices), the fourteenth "voice" of *Humus*'s fugue is masculine. It is supplied by thirteen short musical texts that precede and succeed each of the twelve narrative sections and appear on the novel's unmarked pages. These are *chants marins* (sea shanties), improvisational lyric bawdies of the type that would have been sung by the male crew of *Le Soleil*.[35] Many concern the figure of Jehan de Nantes, a topman aboard *Le Soleil*, who emerges as a leitmotif across the songs.[36] These masculine lyric refrains—often ludic, sometimes nostalgic—emerge in counterpoint to the rich, harrowing fugue of female voices.

The sea shanties that Kanor splices into her novel are "vulgar" in form and content. Written in dialect, they are characterized by coarse, doggerel rhymes and evoke food, drink, sexual conquest, as well as the tribulations of maritime life. Consider, for instance, the novel's concluding shanty, which follows the narrative of "L'héritière" and marks both the close of *Humus* and the end of Jehan de Nantes's transatlantic wanderings, returning us to Nantes and to the Quai de la Fosse, where *Le Soleil* embarked in 1773:

Oyez bonnes gens et blanches filles
Oyez la fin de ma chanson
L'est pas très gaie, l'est pas très triste
C'est peut-être bien une chanson d'Normands
Depuis qu'il est rentré d'Guinée
Jehan qui s'marrait y rigole plus
Elle a beau dire beau faire Francette
Son homme se noie dans la piquette
Si vous passez un soué par Nantes
Allez-y voir au quai d'la Fosse
Sûrement que vous y croiserez son ombre
Face la rivière en train de gueler
Et un et deux. C'est l'gros Jehan de Nantes
Et trois et quatre. Gabier sur Le Soleil.
Tralala lala. Tralala Lalère.[37]

(Hear ye good people and white lasses
Hear the end of my song

'Tis not very gay, 'tis not very sad
Perhaps it's a Normand's song
Since he sailed back from Guinea
Jehan the joker laughs no more
Francette, tries as she might, says what she will,
But her man drowns himself in cheap drink
If you pass through Nantes one eve
Take a stroll along the Quai de la Fosse
Surely there you will encounter his ghost
Facing the river, freezing
And a-one and a-two. It's Big Ol' Jehan de Nantes
And a-three and a-four. Topman aboard *Le Soleil*
Tralala lala. Tralala lalay.)

This final song, which sees Jehan and *Le Soleil* returning home to Nantes, draws a sharp contrast to the feminine fugue that precedes it. It delimits an audience that de facto excludes the women of *Le Soleil*. It makes a metaphor of their suicide, describing a washed-up topman who now "drowns himself" (*se noie*) in drink.

The textual "labor" performed by these masculine work songs goes beyond a topical gesture at maritime musicality and is more central to Kanor's project in *Humus* than might be apparent for at least three reasons. First, sailors of African descent played an important role in innovating and improvising with the form of the *chant marin* and *chanson de bord*.[38] These sea shanties allow us to detect, in palimpsest, another meter of African work songs and spirituals: musical forms that developed in tandem and in reference to one another. Second, a harrowing detail of the Atlantic slave trade was the fact that music was thought to be a suicide deterrent, capable of lifting the spirits of captives, and deployed during the Middle Passage as a technique of suicide prevention.[39] Finally, the inclusion of sea shanties participates in the general logic of "exchange" structuring Kanor's project, confronting the virile, violating voices of male sailors with the silence of female captives. The result, as Kanor puts it, is "a requiem": "I dare say that the final female voice is hidden in the sailor's voice. More than a simple sea song, you must think of this chant as a requiem—it is the voice of the North meeting the South, the brutal noise of men setting out to sea."[40] *Humus* alternates between two unequal, gendered, "homosocial" spaces of enunciation:[41] one masculine, the other feminine—the first from the (Global) North, the second from the (Global) South. Comprising masculine work songs meant to coordinate the physical movements of sailors as they performed repetitive maritime tasks—to synchronize bodies and voices (*Et un et deux. Et trois et quatre*)—this other, masculine "chorus" throws into relief the deadly synchrony of the women of *Le Soleil* who in their leap also moved as one, at the same time, and to the same tempo (*dans le même temps*).

Inheritance

Humus concludes with "L'héritière" and the question of grappling with histories of slavery and suicide in the present. This final narrative section follows the narrator-author as she struggles to write the other women's stories. Her trajectory reverses the Atlantic Triangle traced by Mosnier and mirrors Kanor's own travels during the genesis of the novel: beginning in Badagry, then Paris, and finally Le Gosier, in Guadeloupe, where the novel takes shape. Her narrative expresses distaste for traditional mechanisms for safeguarding memory, and distrust of the kinds of institutions (archives, museums, exhibitions) that brought the story of *Le Soleil* to Kanor in the first place. Overlooking the bay of Badagry while her novel-to-be lies stagnant, "L'héritière" rejects the museum, the archive, and the written word, preferring instead the haunted act of listening that we can now recognize as being constitutive of Kanor's project in *Humus*: "I never liked museums, or archives, or the written word [*la trace écrite*], so I listen to the sea instead, try to convince myself that the dead are not dead" (238).

Humus ends as it began: as an attempt to listen to a ghostly chorus of the voices of the dead. As she struggles to arrange the discrete narratives of her novel-to-be, "L'héritière" takes her texts on sheet paper (what in French would be called *feuilles volantes*), spreads them out in a ring around her, and lets the women of *Le Soleil* speak:

> In silence, trembling, I sat down in the middle of the room. Arranged my texts in a circle.
>
> Were these the leaves [*feuilles*] of the tree around which we all had to turn? *La volante. La muette. La petite. La vieille* . . . I let the women speak while Pierre hammered his skins. (247)

This final scene takes place in the studio of the narrator's artist friend, whose name mutates over the course of the final passage (Pietr, Pedro, Pierre, Peter) but whom Kanor later identifies in an interview as the Guadeloupean painter Pierre Chadru.[42] Surrounded by the voices of the dead while her friend drums out another rhythm as he prepares his canvases, "L'héritière" finds herself at the center of a summoning circle that recalls the "tree of oblivion," which effaced the memories of the enslaved. The studio—owned by an artist whose names mean "stone" (*pierre, petra*)—becomes an allegory for the writer's work-to-be (*humus*, "earth, ground"). The space is characterized by a proliferation of writing. The studio walls are "tapissé de feuilles blanches"—that is, covered with white canvases on which the artist is painting, as if with ink on paper, "his brush in a great pail of black paint" (247).

The ground is littered with textual detritus, the narrator-author's black-and-white texts fanned out before her. This is the "organic matter," as opposed to monumental stone, that will take shape as *Humus*, whose earthy title recalls Glissant's suggestion in *Poétique de la relation* that "the unknown memory of the abyss" (the Middle Passage) furnishes the "limon" necessary for metamorphosis.[43] As Kanor explains in a later text, *Humus* is "earth that disintegrates but does not disappear. [...] Decomposition of the original soil and its transformation into new organic matter."[44]

Ultimately, writing is given over to silence—then voice:

> When all had been said, and the walls of the room were covered, there was a deep silence in us both. Vertigo. Then words. At last, this cry, too long contained, muffled by the song of the seas and the discourse of men.
>
> "We are the *papas-feuilles*," Peter whispered to me.
>
> I stood up. Before the book to come. Before these walls where the ghosts [*fantômes*] were huddled and would soon fade away. (247)

In its final moments, *Humus* shows the narrator's "feuilles volantes"—the scattered pages of her novel-in-progress, doubled and displaced onto the walls of the studio as Pierre's own visual "texts"—to be the reparative, quasi-mystical tools of traditional Caribbean healers (*papas-feuilles*). The final page (*la dernière feuille*) of the novel is the site where a smothered scream finally surfaces. This is the spectral cry announced at the outset of *Humus*, for which the narrator-author desired to exchange the deadened and deadening "wooden" words of men: "the wooden tongue of the sailors for the cry of the captives" (13). Whereas, at the beginning of the novel, this cry clearly belonged to the captive women of *Le Soleil*, at the novel's close its locus remains ambiguous. It is the *cri* of fourteen African women as they leaped in unison, flashing in the sun before plunging into the sea, but also the exhalative release of the author, who senses her novel now is drawing to a close and who lets out a cry, or a call, of her own—adding her voice to the ghostly chorus before her.

LIKE KANOR'S *HUMUS*, Maximin's *L'isolé soleil* sounds out a silenced history of suicide in the present. Whereas Kanor excavates an episode of suicidal resistance that had all but disappeared from the historical record—a suicide, like Azor's, buried in the colonial archive—Maximin takes on the best-known example of collective suicide in the French Atlantic world. Both literary projects, however, intervene precisely at the vanishing points in dominant scripts where the voices of enslaved women are silenced, obscured, or drowned out. Both reinscribe the suicides of enslaved women within open-ended, ongoing projects of engaging the spectral afterlives of French slavery in the present.

Forgetting Delgrès

Louis Delgrès (1766–1802) was a Martinican-born *homme de couleur libre*—legally, "a free man of color"—and military officer who led the fierce resistance movement against Napoleon's army when French troops, commanded by Antoine Richepanse, landed in Guadeloupe in 1802 to reimpose slavery.[45] Delgrès and some three hundred resistance fighters—men, women, and children, mostly ex-slaves—assembled on the grounds of Habitation Danglemont at Matouba, in the shadow of the volcanic mountain La Soufrière. They lined their plantation stronghold with gunpowder as Richepanse's soldiers climbed the winding road. After waiting for Richepanse's men to be within striking distance, and letting out a resounding battle cry, "Live free or die!"—the *devise* of the French Revolution—Delgrès and his followers exploded themselves rather than be reenslaved, inflicting heavy casualties on the advance guard of French troops.

Today Delgrès is a relatively well-known resistance hero in the Francosphere.[46] But in the decades immediately following his and his followers' suicide on 28 May 1802—the day of his thirtieth birthday—the story of what happened at Matouba immediately receded from view in historical accounts, characterized by what Nick Nesbitt calls "a near total silence" in French archives.[47] The entry on Delgrès in the 1870 edition of Larousse's *Grand dictionnaire universel*, which sets out to "save" Delgrès from obscurity, makes this broadscale forgetting clear:

> DELGRES (Louis), the last defender of Black freedom [*la liberté des noirs*] in Guadeloupe, born in Saint-Pierre (Martinique) in 1772, killed at the capture of Matouba (Guadeloupe) on 28 May 1802. History has preserved the memory of the Black leaders of Saint-Domingue; the name of the mulatto [*mulâtre*] Delgrès, who resisted to the death the soldiers sent to Guadeloupe by the first consul Bonaparte, in 1802, to reestablish slavery there, also deserves to be saved from oblivion [*l'oubli*].[48]

As the *Larousse* suggests, by 1870, history had relegated the name "Delgrès" to oblivion (*l'oubli*), muffling the explosion at Matouba even as it conserved the memory of the leaders of the Haitian Revolution: Toussaint Louverture, Jean-Jacques Dessalines, and Henri Christophe.[49] But the *Larousse* contributes in its own way to the persistent forgetting and silencing around Delgrès, muting the text of his suicide.[50] Delgrès was "killed" resisting "to the death" when, in reality, he and his followers detonated a massive suicide bomb, transforming their bodies into deadly weapons.

The collective forgetting of the suicidal resistance of Delgrès and his followers extended into the twentieth century and, to a large extent, continues in the present. As Laurent Dubois points out, the role played by Delgrès in the events leading up to and immediately following Napoleon's efforts to reimpose slavery in Guadeloupe has been downplayed or absent from the mainstream historiography on French slavery and its abolition, even though these events have received "sustained attention" from Antillean writers.[51] Until his symbolic entrance into the Panthéon in 1998, to which I return in the conclusion to this chapter, there was no public commemoration of Delgrès in metropolitan France. In the "Histoire, histoires" section of *Le discours antillais* (1981)—published the same year as Maximin's novel—Glissant diagnoses the difficulty Delgrès's suicide has posed for historical memory:

> When colonel Delgrès blew himself up with his three hundred men on the powder magazine of Fort Matouba in Guadeloupe (1802), so as not to surrender to the six thousand French soldiers that were surrounding it, the sound of this explosion did not resound [*ne retenti pas*] immediately in the consciousness of the Martinicans and Guadeloupeans. For Delgrès was vanquished a second time by the muffled ruse of the dominant ideology, which succeeded for a time in distorting [*dénaturer*] the meaning of his heroic act and in erasing it from popular memory.[52]

For Glissant, Delgrès was killed twice over: first by the explosion and then in the decades—indeed, centuries—that followed when the "meaning" of his suicide was distorted, dampened, and erased. Delgrès died by suicide resisting French soldiers, but his memory was murdered by an act of collective forgetting, a failure to hear the *rumeur* of his suicide.

For his part, Glissant counters this forgetting and the ambivalence of the *Larousse* definition by redefining Delgrès in the "Glossaire" of *Le discours antillais*:

> Taking with him in death some of the 6,000 French soldiers surrounding him, [Delgrès] exploded himself [*se fit sauter*] along with 300 men on the powder magazine of Fort Matouba in Guadeloupe. They debate as to whether he was a hero who (in 1802) refused the reestablishment of

slavery, or already drunk on "republican" values, not daring to call for total insurrection and thus preferring death to the destruction of his ideal.[53]

Before and after Glissant, Antillean writers, historians, and public intellectuals have commemorated Delgrès, reinscribing his suicide in and *as* history. Gustave Aimard's adventure novel *Le chasseur de rats* (1876), the earliest novelistic treatment of the Delgrès epic, dates from the end of the nineteenth century.[54] However, the real literary rehabilitation of Delgrès's memory in the Caribbean came almost a century later, during the 1950s in the wake of departmentalization (1946) and against the backdrop of the separatist movements that burgeoned throughout the 1960s, '70s, and '80s.[55] Antillean writers such as Aimé Césaire, Daniel Radford, Guy Tirolien, Sonny Rupaire, Daniel Maximin, and Maryse Condé revisited Delgrès's legacy, in French and Kréyol, in verse and prose, while historians such as Germain Saint-Ruf reinterpreted the "épopée Delgrès" as a national epic of resistance.[56] The Pantheonization of Delgrès and Toussaint Louverture in 1998 brought Delgrès more fully into mainstream accounts of French history, while the "memorial turn" of the early 2000s—the period corresponding to the publication of Kanor's and Diome's novels, in the wake of the Taubira Laws (2001), and the bicentenaries of the Haitian Revolution and the first abolition of slavery—renewed public interest in the history of Atlantic slavery. In Guadeloupe, the most visible *lieux de mémoire* commemorating the suicide of Delgrès and his followers, Roger Arékian's sculpture *Mémorial du sacrifice de Louis Delgrès* (2002) at Fort Delgrès, appeared during this period, marking the two hundredth anniversary of Delgrès's death. Since, writers and artists have continued to represent Delgrès and the events of 1802 across various media and genres.[57]

The work of the Guadeloupean poet and novelist Daniel Maximin is unparalleled in the effort to preserve Delgrès's memory. No single author has done more to simultaneously enshrine and interrogate Delgrès's status as literary figure and historical fact. Maximin is largely the reason Delgrès is in the Panthéon in the first place: in 1998, he oversaw the commemorations of the second abolition of slavery of 1848 (Célébration nationale du 150ième anniversaire de l'abolition de l'esclavage) which culminated in the symbolic entry of Delgrès and Toussaint Louverture into the Panthéon crypt in cooperation with the Comité National du Souvenir.[58] In his role as director of cultural affairs in Basse-Terre, he spearheaded the effort to rename Fort Richepanse as Fort Delgrès.[59] While Maximin's civic, public-facing work in Guadeloupe and metropolitan France did much to rehabilitate the figure of Delgrès, monumentalizing him as a French hero, his literary treatment of Delgrès is frequently at odds with, and carefully deconstructs, this memorial stance.

In his first novel, *L'isolé soleil*, Maximin offers a desacralized vision of Delgrès and the epic text of his suicide. Far from erecting a textual "monument" to Delgrès, *L'isolé soleil* interrogates his overdetermined legacy and cracks open the mythologized account of his suicide to bring other forms of resistance, and other suicides, into view and into earshot. In its desacralization of the Delgrès epic, *L'isolé soleil* surfaces the stories of women who, throughout Guadeloupe's history, fought, resisted, survived, and died but have remained invisible. Their archival silence and collective forgetting are even more profound than the one that initially shrouded Delgrès's legacy. While Delgrès's memory now is commemorated in the most hallowed halls of French national identity, the female freedom fighter Solitude has yet to be accepted into the Panthéon.[60] *L'isolé soleil* confronts these discrepancies in historical memory head-on, clearing space for what has remained in the shadow of Delgrès's legacy to bring to light a secret archive of suicide and resistance in the Atlantic world.

AS VARIOUS CRITICS HAVE pointed out, Maximin's "Caribbean trilogy," especially his first novel, *L'isolé soleil*, constitutes the author's inventive rewriting of Antillean, Black Atlantic, and New World (literary) history.[61] Alongside histories and archives of slavery, colonization, resistance, occupation, and departmentalization in the Caribbean, Maximin's work represents literary-historical and artistic developments such as the emergence of the Negritude writers and the dissident journals *Légitime défense* and *Tropiques*; thematizes exchanges between Caribbean writers and the Harlem Renaissance; and explores the history of jazz in France and the Americas. His novels all take seriously the presence of a local literary tradition in Guadeloupean Kréyol, developing an alternative literary-historical archive by incorporating proverbs, tales, and songs in Kréyol, usually untranslated, as well as extended exchanges about the value of Kréyol as a decolonial literary language.[62] The imbrication of literature and history, and the constant relay between literary history and history "proper," are features of a broader strategy of textual "creolization" at work in *L'isolé soleil* (1981)—and in Maximin's subsequent novels *Soufrières* (1987) and *L'île et une nuit* (1995)—through which the Caribbean past itself is shown to be a kind of fiction—what Chris Bongie calls "an invention generated out of desire, a rhetorical *inventio*."[63] Baroque, highly intertextual works, Maximin's novels theorize and perform creolization as a textual practice for writing Caribbean history in and as fiction.[64] Leanna Thomas summarizes this approach usefully as constructing "an imagined past by wrenching archival sources out of their domain and context, and selectively situating them in a narrative replete with cultural and oral traditions."[65] Maximin's texts are concerned as much with writing the Caribbean past anew as they are with revealing the constructedness and fungibility of all histories, especially those related to suicide within French slavery.

In this vein, *L'isolé soleil* takes the *mise-en-fiction* and reordering of Caribbean history as premise and praxis.[66] The novel centers on the efforts of Marie-Gabriel as she endeavors to write a polyvocal, novelistic account of the history of her native Guadeloupe, a text that would "remake the history of my country."[67] Like Kanor's "L'héritière," Marie-Gabriel inherits a story of loss but struggles to put it into writing using existing generic frames. Her *roman historique* initially is intended to reproduce or replace a "paternal" text: the Caribbean history and *journal de voyage* written by her father, Louis-Gabriel. That manuscript disappeared when the Boeing carrying Louis-Gabriel and members of the Guadeloupean independence movement exploded above La Soufrière in 1962, leading to the death of everyone on board. However, Marie-Gabriel's project ultimately is motivated by a fascination and frustration with another paternal narrative: the national epic of Delgrès's suicide.

The two men are connected symbolically in Marie-Gabriel's textual imaginary as Icarus figures—suicidal martyrs who flew too close to the sun and whose fiery deaths almost exactly 160 years apart were witnessed by the same volcano:

> The Boeing 707 *Château de Chantilly*, flying too high to drown, exploded above the volcano at dawn on 22 June 1962, waking a whole people who thought they saw the Soufrière blow up all at once, one hundred and sixty years after the suicide-eruption of Louis Delgrès's rebels. [...] Your musician-father died by accident. But you think that your poet-father committed suicide because he was carrying with him in his saxophone case the only three notebooks of his life's diary. How can one entrust one's whole dreamed life to the plane that is already carrying one's real life? (14–17)

In her text-in-progress, Marie-Gabriel renames her father—whose real name we never learn—to reinforce the symbolic equivalence with Delgrès: "You will name him Louis-Gabriel, Louis like Delgrès, incinerated in our memories, and Gabriel like your grandfather" (17).

In *L'isolé soleil*, the national and family histories incarnated in the twinned figures of Louis Delgrès and Louis-Gabriel provide Marie-Gabriel with the overdetermined historical script that she progressively will unpick and unravel as she finds ways to write Caribbean history, and suicide, otherwise. The words of Kanor's unnamed narrator in the first section of *Humus* might very well apply to Marie-Gabriel's project: "How to tell, how to retell, this story of men? Without fuss or artifice. Otherwise. And against the reader's expectations."[68]

The other characters of the novel similarly express a profound ambivalence toward Delgrès and his legacy—in this sense doubling, refracting, and extending the work of the narrator-author, Marie-Gabriel, as well as Maximin's project of renegotiating and rewriting Guadeloupean history. For instance, in his correspondence with Marie-Gabriel, the Paris-based writer Adrien asks whether "suicide is the only heroism of our islands," pointing out that during the colonial period "whole villages of Caribs threw themselves off the cliffs" and "entire families of slaves poisoned themselves, suffocating the newborns" (86). Marie-Gabriel's mother, Siméa, wonders if suicide is "the only act of heroism that our history can glorify itself with" (186). Even Louis-Gabriel, erected as a hero in his daughter's imaginary, dislikes the heroism of historic figures like Delgrès: "I don't particularly have a taste for heroism. I even think, more often than not, that it is the tree that hides the resistance of the forests" (186). *L'isolé soleil* tracks and enacts Marie-Gabriel's efforts to move beyond Delgrès's heroism and bring the "resistance of the forests" into focus.

Explosive Memory

Maximin's novel unfolds as a complex—and difficult to summarize—constellation of texts-in-progress and archival traces stretching back five generations in Marie-Gabriel's family and covering nearly two centuries of Guadeloupe's history, from the late eighteenth century to the end of the twentieth. In its presentation of this two-hundred-year history, the novel alternates between discursive forms and narrative modes. There are sequences of chronological narration (presumably strands of Marie-Gabriel's historical novel in progress) that reconstruct the different historical periods of *L'isolé soleil*, including the time of slavery and colonization; the lives of Marie-Gabriel's parents, Siméa and Louis-Gabriel, in Paris and Guadeloupe; and Marie-Gabriel's own childhood. There are letters between Marie-Gabriel and her friends Adrien (in Paris) and Antoine (in Guadeloupe) in which they exchange historical, literary, and familial anecdotes and discuss Marie-Gabriel's novel-to-be. There are also excerpts from notebooks that have been transmitted to Marie-Gabriel: *Le cahier de Jonathan*, which dates from the time of colonization and details the role of Marie-Gabriel's ancestors in the anti-French resistance of 1802; *Le journal de Siméa* (Paris, 1939), in which Siméa narrates her time in

Paris before World War II; and *L'air de la mère*, which details Siméa's life and death in Guadeloupe during Vichy occupation under Marshal Philippe Pétain. Poems, songs, tales, proverbs, riddles, formulas, excerpts, and inscriptions are interspersed with citations in French, Kréyol, and occasionally Spanish and English—including the complete text of Delgrès's famous declaration addressed "À l'univers entier" (To the entire universe) on the eve of reoccupation (48–49).

The novel is also traversed by an almost hallucinatory anagrammatic, homophonic, and metathetic play; the title is an example of this (LISOLE <> SOLEIL).[69] The text ends with a short, italicized poetic text signed by Maximin himself (*Daniel*), which furnishes the first line of the author's subsequent novel, *Soufrières*. It is followed by an appendix: a section titled "Repères" (Reference points), reminiscent of the "Repères" and "Glossaire" sections of Glissant's *Le discours antillais* (281–84). These final pages lay out the historical sweep of the novel in a succinct timeline punctuated by important dates and proper names: beginning with Delgrès (an excerpt of the passage from the 1870 *Larousse*) and ending in 1969, with an evocation of Angela Davis's transit through Guadeloupe and her role during the trial of the Soledad Brothers in California.[70] Through this fragmented narrative structure and "exploded chronology,"[71] *L'isolé soleil* finds creative form for registering what has faded out from historical accounts without reifying these silenced histories in turn. In Maximin's novel, the lacunae and *rumeurs* in the colonial archive and the gaps in dominant scripts are not holes to be filled but, rather, spaces of difference and latent potential ripe for a creative project of rearranging and recoding the past.

Across the variegated structure of *L'isolé soleil*, and in each of the novel's separate narrative strands and texts-in-progress, Delgrès's suicide emerges as a particular source of vexation as well as a critical opening; it is the novel's "refrain," to return to the language of *Humus*. Like Marie-Gabriel's father, Delgrès is a glaring presence in whose shadow her own project seems to falter and dim. While Marie-Gabriel dreams initially of crafting a historical novel that would "resurrect the vanished fathers of our history, from Delgrès's eruption to that of the Boeing," she becomes increasingly skeptical of taking the deaths of Delgrès and her father as her points of departure (15). Unsettled by how solitary, and singular, these men appear against the backdrop of the resistance movements they organized and led, she questions the exceptionalism accorded to Delgrès and other suicidal national heroes, such as Joseph Ignace: "But you've noticed to what extent, in all of these tributes, Ignace and [Delgrès] appear alone, isolated [*isolés*] from the people, like two restless spirits [*mal-finis*] soaring above a tufted forest at night" (107). Such mythic figures are "lone suns" (*soleils isolés*) whose suicides eclipse a silent, popular "chorus": "What epic can we compose with such heroes before whom the chorus of the people appears to be nothing but silence and stillness?" (107–8).

In line with Kanor's project of decentering and regendering masculinist accounts of suicidal resistance in *Humus* to amplify a chorus of female voices, Marie-Gabriel desires to write a different kind of history: one that would subvert the received, paternalist narrative of the suicidal hero so omnipresent in Caribbean history—what Reij M. Rosello has analyzed as part of a morbid "cult" of suicidal heroism.[72] At one point, Marie-Gabriel imagines writing "a story [*histoire*] in which only women would appear" (108). Over two decades later, *Humus* can be seen as taking on that task.

Marie-Gabriel does not eschew male figures altogether; instead, she commits herself to the polyvocal and polygeneric textual form that we see reflected in the fragmented, choral architecture of the novel itself:

> You will sink your roots into the ground until you find the source of the bonfires [*feux de joie*]: a tale, a poem, a dance, a song. You will open your eyes, your ears, your mouth, and your hands to the history of your fathers, and you will not fail to make the mothers speak, for they have roots because they bear fruit. (17)

Framed as an apostrophe of the self, Marie-Gabriel's self-reflexive characterization of her writerly praxis equally reads as a critical imperative, enjoining us to open our eyes, ears, mouths, and hands to history. Like the fugitive fugue form of *Humus*, the choral architecture of *L'isolé soleil* serves as a compelling aesthetic argument for more supple reframings of Black Atlantic history through plurifocalized, collective narration.

Marie-Gabriel accomplishes her alternative rewriting of Caribbean history by questioning the received narrative of the Delgrès epic and bringing the events of 28 May 1802 down to human scale: "Sometimes, I have the desire to abandon this eruption of heroism . . . to replace it with a single question, at the head of a chapter left blank: what happened on 28 May 1802? (Then, at the end of the book, I'll give the answer: on that day, Delgrès had just turned thirty.)" (108). She goes on to question and contest the masculine "grammar" of epic accounts of suicidal resistance, which invariably elevate men to the status of solitary saviors and messianic heroes, "all of these Me-I's [*ces Moi-je*] always alone before a silent people" (109). She asks instead whether women also died at Matouba, suspecting that the "masculine plural" has obscured parallel histories of female resistance: "(Did women also die at Matouba? Or was it just a masculine-plural duel, between white and black soldiers, like a game of chess?)" (109).

In *L'isolé soleil*, Marie-Gabriel provides the answers to her own questions by reconstructing the role of her female ancestors in the various resistance movements and crises in Guadeloupean history, tracing a recessed genealogy of female resistance from the time of slavery to the present through the characters Miss Béa and Ti-Carole (who participated in the 1802 anti-French resistance and later fought for abolition), Manman-Louise (who survived the 1897 earthquake and preserved *Le cahier de Jonathan*), and her mother, Siméa (who participated in the anti-Pétainiste resistance under Vichy occupation). The narrative structure of the novel responds to Marie-Gabriel's earlier injunctive "to make the mothers speak." The remaining sections of *L'isolé soleil* (*Le journal de Siméa* and *L'air de la mère*) are given over almost entirely to an *écriture féminine*, in contrast to earlier narrative sequences—*Désirades* (the title of her father's lost manuscript) and *Le cahier de Jonathan* (the notebook kept by the ex-slave Jonathan, which concerns the "Delgrès epic")—in which male figures dominated.

While the "feminine" sequences of *L'isolé soleil* allow the voices and experiences of women to surface more fully in the manner of Kanor's ghostly chorus in *Humus*, they also resist the narcissistic "Moi-je" that Marie-Gabriel identifies as being characteristic of the monumental, masculine grammar of suicidal heroism. In *Le journal de Siméa*, although Marie-Gabriel's mother, Siméa, narrates parts of her own life in prewar Paris in the first person, her *journal intime* is really a letter, addressed to a capacious *tu*. It is an interpellation of her *aérée-morte* (148), the infant son she lost during a forced abortion, and of her daughter not yet conceived: "My son, I keep you, and I declare you my daughter ... You will not hear my high voice, nor will you understand my looks. But you will be the only one to read—and also, sometimes, to write—what I will write from this night on" (121). Her words resonate with the drowned testimony of "La mère," who addresses her dead son and all those living "in the wake."

L'air de la mère echoes and inverts the structure of *Le journal de Siméa*, consisting of an extended second-person narration in which Marie-Gabriel addresses her dead mother, reconstructing Siméa's life in Guadeloupe under Vichy occupation and detailing her work as a nurse and caregiver at a hospital-cum-asylum. Its title, *Air*, recalls the spectral "airiness" of the *aérée-morte*, the dead and the unborn, and the skies in which Delgrès and Louis Gabriel perished in a single blast. As a musical term (*aria*), it resonates with the musicality of Marie-Gabriel's project—and of her bearing, the daughter of a musician-poet—throughout the novel. In the final section of *L'isolé soleil*, *L'exil s'en va aussi*, the narrative voices and scenes of address multiply and expand even further, encompassing the far-ranging correspondence between Marie-Gabriel and her friends Adrien, Antoine, and Ève, and the final signatory, Daniel.

Across the "maternal" sequences of *L'isolé soleil*, the signifier "suicide" gradually accumulates more complex meanings and resonances that point beyond the masculinist epic, heroic, and sacrificial frames associated with Delgrès. Such discursive frames—suicide as sacrifice/martyrdom—are powerful; they continue to condition and conscript readings of suicide, especially suicide bombing, in the present. Like Mahi Binebine's "queering" of the text of suicide bombing in his novel *Les étoiles de Sidi Moumen* (2010)—the focus of chapter 5—Maximin, through Marie-Gabriel, counters the masculinist martyr narrative by setting the "lone sun" of Delgrès's suicide into a more complex constellation. Marie-Gabriel's searching question—*Did women also die at Matouba?*—splits open the sealed text of epic sacrifice, allowing "secret" suicides to surface.

S Is for Suicide

Suicide emerges in *L'isolé soleil* not as a uniquely Antillean form of heroism, limited to the time of colonization, but as a diasporic, essentially African response to conditions of alienation, displacement, and racism. In *Le journal de Siméa* and *L'air de la mère*, Siméa becomes the vector by which the interpretive frames for registering and representing suicide subtly but surely shift. She constructs an alternative archive of suicidal resistance: cataloging secret, silenced acts of self-destruction that are counterpoised to the monumentalized account of Delgrès's heroic sacrifice.

When we first encounter Siméa in the late 1930s, she is a young poet-translator living in Paris during the prewar years, rendering the texts of the Negritude writers Aimé Césaire and Léon-Gontran Damas in French, Creole, and English. At the beginning of her *Journal*, she has fallen in love and conceived a child with a white French architect. Her mother, back in Guadeloupe, refuses to accept the union and organizes a clandestine abortion against Siméa's will by paying a doctor and other women to drug her and forcefully abort the child (113–21). Siméa's life in Paris, in this sense, rehearses and activates a specifically Atlantic intertext, recalling the history of infanticide within slavery described at the opening of the first "notebook" of the novel, *Le cahier de Jonathan*, which evokes "those slave mothers who gently suffocated their daughters at birth in a wet cloth so that they would regain the route to Ethiopia without ever touching down on earth" (29). In *Le journal de Siméa*, infanticide resurfaces not as an act of resistance or a mercy killing but as a murderous weapon against miscegenation.

Siméa's personal and intellectual trajectory in Paris is haunted by the specter of suicide. As a colonized poet-translator in France, she understands her own experience to be shadowed by a metropole-bound journey that never was:

the real suicide of the Malagasy poet Jean-Joseph Rabéarivelo (1903–37) a few years earlier. After being refused passage to Paris to participate in a conference organized as part of the Exposition universelle of 1937, Rabéarivelo died by suicide after swallowing quinine capsules and cyanide. Siméa remembers his history in connection with her own: "Rabéarivelo, our great Malagasy poet who committed suicide in Madagascar, tired of living a life without an emergency exit, that emergency exit for him being the Parisian literary scene, yet another death as a result of promised assimilation, he was refused passage to Paris on the occasion of the Colonial Cultural Congress" (124). In her *Journal*, Siméa recalls having attended the very Congrès from which the poet had been excluded—a humiliation that supposedly precipitated his death (146).

The year 1937, when Rabéarivelo died and the Exposition universelle took place, was also the year that Ousmane Socé published his novel, *Mirages de Paris*, which concerns a suicide related to an earlier colonial exposition (1931). As a tragedy of displacement and *métissage*—a literary corollary to Rabéarivelo's death by "failed assimilation" (*assimiliation manquée*)—*Mirages de Paris* resembles Siméa's experiences in Paris. Her Parisian peregrination, which fulfills Rabéarivelo's French fantasy, regenders and reorients the plot of Socé's novel, in which the Senegalese protagonist, Fara, travels to France and marries a white French woman who dies in childbirth, leading Fara to throw himself into the Seine.[73] In *L'isolé soleil*, Siméa makes this link to Socé's *Mirages* explicit. In a striking moment of intertextuality, she evokes the suicide of Socé's Fara in powerful and surprising terms:

> And it was at that point that Ousmane Socé was concluding his first novel with the suicide of his protagonist, Fara, in the Seine—distraught that Paris had not whitened [*blanchi*] him quickly and completely enough. My child, know this well-guarded secret: there are many suicides among the colonized of Paris. A few bits of ebony wood [*bois d'ébène*] floating down the Seine, having once dreamed of becoming an angel or a crocodile. (126)

For Siméa, the suicide of Socé's Fara is not a romanticized novelistic death through which she recasts her own disenchantment with the metropole but, rather, a means of exposing a pressing historical reality: the human toll of France's racist policy of assimilation. A literary cipher for a secret archive of "real" suicides, including Rabéarivelo's, Fara's death discloses the most "well-guarded secret" of the history of Africans in Paris: the Seine is a fluvial burial ground for the suicides of France's colonial subjects. If Kanor, Diome, Glissant, and others all recognize the Atlantic as an immense "seametary" (Abderrezak),

Siméa does something similar for the Seine. She shows the river to be a grave site with a suicidal history of its own—one that began as early as the 1930s during France's first "experiments" with bringing colonial subjects to Paris, whether to display them in the colonial exhibitions, in human zoos, or for the purposes of education and France's *mission civilisatrice*. Her observation is a prescient one, given that in 1961 the Seine became a crime scene and the site of state violence against colonized Algerians, who were either drowned or had their bodies disposed of in the river—a history explored in some detail in chapter 4. In Siméa's alternative literary history, Fara stands in for countless "colonisés" floating down the Seine like *bois d'ébène* (ebony planks)—a common euphemism used during the *traite clandestine* (illegal slave trade) to refer to human cargo.[74]

The "secret" but apparently pervasive metropole-obsessed suicides recorded by Siméa and transmitted to her dead son and unborn daughter complicate the dominant historical and memorial frames for understanding suicide as a heroic martyrdom, simple capitulation to power, or pure act of resistance. Such frames render suicides like those of Rabéarivelo or Fara—or, as we will see in chapter 3, Diouana—largely invisible. Siméa's excavation and transmission of little-known examples of suicide demonstrate the capacity of literature to construct other suicide archives that register these cryptic deaths even as they disappear from the historical script. The final, ambiguous death of a mute seven-year-old child named Angela depicted in *L'isolé soleil* is an especially striking example of this. Near the end of the novel, it figures a spectral genealogy of suicide that stitches together the various chronotopes of *L'isolé soleil*, from the time of slavery (1780s) to the narrative present (1943).

In *L'air de la mère*, we rejoin Siméa's narrative through Marie-Gabriel's reconstruction of her mother's life in Guadeloupe under Vichy occupation. At this point, Siméa has returned to Guadeloupe to take up work in a hospital; she joins the anti-Pétainiste resistance and meets Louis-Gabriel, whom she later marries. Once more, Maximin excavates a silenced history of resistance that initially only literature seemed to register:[75] Antillean and Guyanese dissidents were excluded from the Conseil national de la Résistance (1943–45), and their role in the Resistance remained absent from historical accounts, not formally recognized until 2011.[76] Under the scrutiny of Pétain's forces, Siméa arranges for some of her patients at the hospital to participate in the Carnaval parade of 1943: a day when French police opened fire on the crowd, killing three civilians, an episode described in Maximin's novel and taken up by Luc Saint-Eloy's play *Blessures secrètes: Port-Louis, 1943* (2017).[77] The night before Carnaval, one of Siméa's patients, the mute child Angela, bestows on her a mysterious gift and transmits an ambiguous message, giving Siméa a white frock to wear at the parade: a nurse's blouse with the letters *sss* embroidered into the fabric using hair collected from the other children at the hospital (178). Associations multiply—Siméa, Soleil, Solitude, Soufrière—prompting Siméa and Louis-Gabriel to devise a game to decode Angela's message: an associative *jeu de mots* in which Louis-Gabriel proposes a theme or category and Siméa produces a word starting with the letter *S*.

As they attempt to unravel Angela's riddle, the associative chains of reference prompted by Louis-Gabriel and provided by Siméa suddenly organize themselves around the novel's key signifier, "suicide":

—Death?
—Death?... Suicide.
—If I say: Verb?
—I have to find a verb that starts with *s*? To sow [*semer*].
—Adjective?
—Spontaneous.
[...]
—If I say to you: Past?
—Suicide. No! Already said it. Souvenir! Too bad, we can't get rid of a word? (179–80)

Connecting her own initial, *S*, to suicide through linguistic play, Siméa improvises a spontaneous text that repeats and resignifies the three terms (*suicide, semence, souvenir*) used earlier in the novel to characterize Delgrès's suicide as a fantasy of a *suicide-semence* that would force the *souvenir des siècles*.[78]

The angelic white dress and its ciphered message "spell" suicide. Eerily evocative of the white garments enslaved men and women traditionally donned before committing suicide, Siméa's white blouse is the same shift Angela puts on before her ambiguous death. Stealing into Siméa's room, the mute Angela—reminiscent of Kanor's "La muette"—slips the white blouse on before slipping out of the hospital, descending to the water's edge, and wading into the sea (215). Siméa learns of Angela's "flight" shortly after from the director of the hospital and grasps the coded message of her disappearance: "Angela was gone. She was seen wearing a white blouse on the way down from Basse-Terre just as the parade was going up. I'm sure she's headed to the sea. I'm not sure if it is to drown" (238). They immediately alert the police that "there's a chance she might kill herself" before setting off to search for her. In addition to evoking the numerous enslaved men, women, and children who "fled" slavery through suicide, Angela's nocturnal flight and watery death directly rehearse the events that led to her muteness and internment in the hospital in the first place:

years prior, she had watched from shore as her father, a fisherman from Marie-Galante, struck out in a dinghy under the cover of darkness to smuggle two men into Dominica; the boat was capsized and engulfed by the swells when a German submarine suddenly surfaced from below it (162–63).

Angela's name, an anagram for *la nage* (swimming), seals her fate: suggestive of the sea swell in which her father disappeared and in which she later drowns. But the name "Angela" harbors additional associations that connect her suicide to other deaths in the novel. The name itself evokes "angel" and thus flight—toward freedom, toward Africa. "Angela" is the name of the enslaved girl found raped and mutilated at the beginning of *L'isolé soleil*, in *Le cahier de Jonathan*; in 1785, her father was "a slave from Louisiana who escaped overboard [*à la nage*] from a slave ship off the coast of La Désirade" (33). The two Angelas are additionally linked by the name of their sisters, Élisa and Elisa. The fathers of both sets of sisters perished in vessels off the coast of Guadeloupe, almost 160 years apart—the same interim between the death of Louis-Gabriel and Louis Delgrès. The first drowned after leaping overboard from a slave ship, the second trying to ferry men to freedom under Vichy occupation in nearby Dominica. In this last respect, Angela's letters recall the insignia traditionally branded onto the skin of individuals who helped enslaved men and women escape to freedom: S.S. for "slave stealer."[79] From the Greek *ángelos*, meaning "messenger," Angela's name also evokes the Angelus, the prayer commemorating the annunciation made to Mary by the archangel Gabriel, thus cleverly encoding Marie-Gabriel's own proper name and suggesting that Angela, like Gabriel, transmits an impossible message.[80] The name has one final incarnation in the novel—this time associated with a member of the living—as Angela Davis, whose clandestine passage through Guadeloupe is described in the final pages of the novel (275–84). In the signifier "Angela," multiple generations of resistance and dissidence, and each of the novel's various narrative strands, converge.

Angela's secretly signifying watery death emerges in counterpoint to the spectacular *éruption-suicide* of Delgrès: a fiery explosion that allowed him to "incinerate" his proper name onto the text of history (*Delgrès, incinéré dans nos mémoires . . .*). By contrast, Angela's suicide by drowning (though it never is definitively termed a "suicide" in the novel) is the only voluntary death in *L'isolé soleil* carried out by a female character—in this case, just a child: a seven-year-old girl who has lost the ability to speak. It happens more or less "offstage." Whereas Delgrès proclaimed a discourse addressed to "the entire universe," in which he fulminated against racial inequality and the horrors of slavery shortly before detonating his collective suicide bomb, the mute Angela disappears silently and solitarily into the night and into the sea.

Angela does not vanish without a trace, however. The title of the final section of *L'air de la mère*, "Renaissance," suggests that Angela will soon be "reborn," at least nominally, in the figure of Angela Davis and is evocative of the role of suicide within slavery as a means for the transmigration of souls. Angela lives on, and traces of her ambiguous end continue to proliferate. At the close of the novel, Siméa reinscribes Angela's cryptic message. In an image recalling both the *bois d'ébène* evoked earlier in the novel to characterize Africans who drowned themselves in the Seine and the way Kanor's "La muette" scratches signs into the wood of the ship in *Humus*, Siméa etches Angela's trinity of letters into the ebony wood of her father's clarinet using a housekey. She then gives the clarinet—now a coded record of Angela's death—to Louis-Gabriel to replace his original instrument, also made of ebony, that Angela, in an uncontrollable fit, had seized and snapped in half during Carnaval shortly before her suicide (185). Finally, Siméa embosses the same letters onto the cover of her notebook, *Le journal de Siméa*, which she transmits to Marie-Gabriel along with "the small engraved ring that Angela had set down on the tambour-conga the night of her escape" (245).

Through these spectral signs sewn in suicide's wake, Angela's death by drowning becomes a dispersed, enigmatic text but also a ciphered model for reading the suicide archive. In her death, she achieves a "suicide-semence" of her own: one that resists the passage of time and continues to signify beyond her own death—though in a more encoded, secretive way than that envisioned by Delgrès. It is only by drawing on the secretive, splintered poetics and anagrammatic play in evidence throughout the novel, that we can render her cryptic suicide legible. In this way, *L'isolé soleil* trains us to see and sound out what is hiding in plain sight.

Conclusion: Where Are Your Monuments?

> Where are your monuments, your battles, martyrs?
> Where is your tribal memory? Sirs,
> in that grey vault. The sea. The sea
> has locked them up. The sea is History.
> DEREK WALCOTT, "The Sea Is History" (1979)

In *L'isolé soleil* and *Humus*, Maximin and Kanor develop plurifocalized, fragmented narrative architectures capable of harboring a multitude of voices: models for an Antillean history yet to be written. In their choral, ciphered forms, both novels make clear aesthetic arguments against monumentalizing approaches to colonial history. But this ambivalence around monuments and martyrs becomes explicit at various points in both novels, too. In *Humus*,

Kanor builds a case against traditional forms of memorialization through the narrative of "La mère": "You say: they've built museums. Plays for reading, thinking, praying. Monuments [*lieux de mémoire*] to which Reds and others flock, adding to the list of those who were not there. You talk. Tell stories of law, damages and interest, of forgiveness, atonement, of reconciliation. But what is the pain worth? Who can say? What is the hell afterwards worth?"[81] In *L'isolé soleil*, Marie-Gabriel's father, Louis-Gabriel, himself named after Delgrès, criticizes memorial (and literary) tendencies to "statuefy" the Antillean past: "Eternity! Delgrès chose to bear witness for eternity. West Indians are always afraid of running out of space, so they seek to defy time. The only solution: turn men into statues. That's the whole goal of our history and, I think, our poetry, too: statuefy slavery, its suffering, and its revolts" (183). This distrust about the statuefication of the Antillean past has only increased since the publication of Kanor's and Maximin's novels. In 2020 and 2021, in the wake of the #mustfall and #BLM movements, the role of monuments in commemorating figures from France's colonial history became a topic of major public debate. Activists performed the work of "toppling" reified versions of the colonial past—explored as *aesthetic* potential and possibility in *Humus* and *L'isolé soleil*—in literal terms by destroying and desecrating multiple statues related to imperial history throughout the French Caribbean. In Martinique and Guadeloupe, these included statues of obvious figureheads of French empire and slavery—Empress Joséphine Bonaparte (whose statue had already been beheaded in the 1990s) and the French colonizer Pierre Belain d'Esnambuc—but also of the abolitionist Victor Schœlcher, whose name is commemorated throughout the Caribbean, arguing that statues should honor Black emancipation leaders instead.[82] The message, evidently, was received in France: every major candidate in the 2022 French presidential elections made a statement on colonial history and memory—a far cry from the 2017 elections, which saw then-candidate Marine Le Pen assert that colonialism was a positive good and François Fillon suggest that colonization was simply a sharing of cultures.[83]

The desacralizing projects of Kanor and Maximin resonate readily with contemporary debates. But at the time of the publication of their novels, Maximin and Kanor were each writing *à contre-courant*: in the case of Maximin, against a long-standing reticence to acknowledge and commemorate colonial history in France; for Kanor, during a sea change with respect to historical memory and amid a flurry of memorial initiatives. In the case of *Humus*, these would be the various "devoir de mémoire" projects that characterized the "memorial turn" of the early 2000s in France, Britain, and the Caribbean: national acts of remembrance such as the Loi Taubira (2001), which legally recognized slavery and the slave trade as crimes against humanity, and the bicentenaries of Haitian Independence, the first abolition of slavery, and Toussaint Louverture's death (2004/3); the activities and publications of the Comité national pour la mémoire et l'histoire de l'esclavage (National Committee for the Memory and History of Slavery, CNMHE); and the unveiling of symbolically empty sites in the Panthéon to commemorate Louverture and Delgrès.[84] In the case of *L'isolé soleil*, published in 1981, Caribbean writers like Maximin, Glissant, and Condé were working against collective amnesia—a persistent and pervasive refusal to formally recognize France's colonial history. It would take almost another two decades, until the 150th anniversary of the second abolition of slavery, for Louverture and Delgrès to officially enter the Panthéon, the same year Laurent Valère's sobering memorial *Cap 110* in Anse Caffard, Martinique, was erected to commemorate the history of the slave trade.

Since the publication of Kanor's and Maximin's novels, both the story of the women of *Le Soleil* and the suicide of Delgrès and his followers have found their way into *lieux de mémoire* in France. Today, in Nantes, along the banks of the Loire River on the Quai de la Fosse now stands the Mémorial de l'abolition de l'esclavage (Memorial to the Abolition of Slavery), opened to public in 2012. One of the nearly two thousand green glass bricks set into the paved river esplanade of the memorial bears the name of Mosnier's ship *Le Soleil* and the year of its departure from Nantes (figure 1.1), while an abridged and modernized excerpt from his report about the women's leap is nestled among the philosophical, literary, and legal texts featured on the panels in the memorial's lower level.[85] Delgrès's memory, meanwhile, is honored by a symbolically empty plinth in vault 26 of the crypt of the Panthéon in Paris—one of the most sacred sites of French national identity—along with a commemorative plaque on the entrance to the crypt (figure 1.2) that entextualizes the collective suicide of Delgrès and his followers in terms that effectively efface suicide from the text of history:

A LA MÉMOIRE DE LOUIS DELGRÈS
HÉROS DE LA LUTTE CONTRE LE RÉTABLISSEMENT DE L'ESCLA-
   VAGE A LA GUADELOUPE
MORT SANS CAPITULER AVEC TROIS CENTS COMBATTANTS AU
   MATOUBA EN 1802
POUR QUE VIVE LA LIBERTÉ

(To the memory of Louis Delgrès
Hero in the struggle against the reestablishment of slavery in Guadeloupe
Dead without surrendering with three hundred fighters at Matouba in 1802
So that freedom may live)

FIGURE 1.1. Glass brick embedded in the esplanade of the Mémorial de l'abolition de l'esclavage on Quai de La Fosse in Nantes, France. Photo by author.

FIGURE 1.2. Entrance to Caveau XXVI in the crypt of the Panthéon with plaques commemorating Toussaint Louverture and Louis Delgrès. Photo by author.

The language of the plaque assimilates Delgrès's act to an expression of French Republican values. Its final clause, *pour que vive la liberté*, is a well-known citation from the Marquis de Lafayette as he set off in 1780 to help Americans liberate themselves from the "slavery" of British rule.

Even as certain aspects, narratives, and figures of colonial history seem, finally, to be making their way slowly into collective memory in France through various forms and under different guises, suicide remains a stumbling block for mainstream historical accounts—remains in many ways "unfit" for history.[86] This returns us to some of the questions raised in my introduction (about whether suicide can ever be "recovered" to historical consciousness, about the problems suicide poses for historical memory) as well as the psychoanalytic meanings of "resistance" as deferral, repressed content, and opposition to the work of memory. In this latter aspect, the resistance to suicide is also a resistance to grappling fully with the deathscape of empire.

II

Waxi dee bu taxawee, dund yaa tax.
(If the words of the dead live on, it is due to the living.)

WOLOF PROVERB

II

· 2 ·

ORAL ARCHIVES

The "Talaatay Nder" Narrative
in Wolof and French

Know that in my country, every time an
elder dies, a library has burned.

AMADOU HAMPÂTÉ BÂ,
in a speech before UNESCO, 1962

A Tuesday in Nder

"Asalaamalekum mbokki Senegaal, asalaamalekum mbokki Waalo" (Greetings, people of Senegal, people of Waalo).[1] Speaking in the village of Nder in the Waalo region of northern Senegal in March 2020, Diawdine Amadou Bakhaw Diaw addressed his *mbokk* (kin, compatriots) in Wolof on the two hundredth anniversary of an event known as Talaatay Nder, or the "Tuesday of Nder." Diaw is a local *boroom xam-xam* (wise man) and a *lamaan* of Waalo: a cultural custodian and descendent of the landed nobility who first occupied this region along the banks of the Senegal River.[2] Over the next hour, Diaw narrated the Talaatay Nder in Wolof, reconstructing the event in detail.[3] Early in his narration, he interrupted himself to clarify the generic status of the oral history he was transmitting: "Nettali bi sax am nañu koy nettali ndax ñu bari dañuy wax ci talaatay nder ndax du léep" (In fact, this story, there are many accounts of it, so many who speak of the Tuesday of Nder, that it is not merely a fable). Drawing a distinction between the traditional Wolof *léep* (a fable or fanciful tale) and the more general *nettali* (a "story" in the sense of a narrative account or report), Diaw ardently affirms the status of the Talaatay Nder *as history*.[4]

The two-hundred-year-old history that Diaw reactivates in the present is grim. Diaw tells how, on 7 March 1820, a Tuesday, a group of North African raiders—so-called Moors from the Trarza emirates in present-day Mauritania—crossed the Senegal River into Waalo.[5] Led by Emir Amar Ould Mokhtar, the Trarzas headed toward Nder, the capital, planning to raze the village and capture and enslave its citizens. In the absence of the *brak* or king of Waalo, who had been evacuated to Saint-Louis months earlier to be treated for injuries sustained in battle, the wife of the *brak*, the *lingeer-awo* Fatim Yamar Xuuri Yaay Mbooj Téejeg, and her entourage presided.[6]

At the village of Thiaggar, the Trarzas swiftly overcame the forces of *briok* Yerim Mbañik, the *lingeer*'s nephew and the last line of defense before reaching Nder.[7] Warned of her nephew's defeat, Fatim Yamar donned battle gear, took up arms, and rode into battle, followed by the royal guard and her female attendants. They successfully fought back the Trarzas, who began to retreat. Local *géwél* (griots) suggest the women killed three hundred raiders that day. Spurred on by her entourage, a triumphant Fatim Yamar removed her helmet and loosed her braids. Upon hearing the exultant *youyous* of the women of Nder and glimpsing Fatim Yamar's uncovered tresses, the Trarzas—furious to learn their enemies were led by a woman—turned back and redoubled their efforts, encircling the village.[8]

Faced with imminent defeat and the certainty of being captured, raped, and enslaved, Fatim Yamar and her entourage chose death. "Bës bi ñaaw na te xeejuma ci gàcce" (It's over, I will not fight in shame), the *lingeer* is said to have declared to her court.[9] Counseled by her attendant and confidante Mbarka Ja, Fatim Yamar called on a young girl, Sadani, whom she charged with an impossible task: flee the besieged village and tell the world what happened in Nder on this day. After blanketing the royal hut in gunpowder, the women of Nder set it alight, entered, and began to sing traditional Téejeg hymns as the fire raged. On a Tuesday, Nder went up in flames.

THIS IS A STORY that has been told many times and in many ways. In Senegal it is a very well-known story. If you ask anyone on the street in Dakar or

Saint-Louis about the Talaatay Nder, they will tell you, often in rich detail, about a village emptied of men, where women and children, led by a courageous princess, fought back against slavers before burning themselves alive. In this, the story of the women of Nder contrasts with that of the women of *Le Soleil*, who would have to wait over 230 years for a story to circulate in their name. But outside Senegal, the Talaatay Nder is virtually unknown.

The Talaatay Nder is not the only episode of suicidal resistance in Senegalese history. A number of other individual and collective suicides—whether responses to territorial expansion by neighboring African states, to the transatlantic and trans-Saharan slave trades, or to French conquest and colonizing violence—haunt the historical record.[10] Only a few decades after the resistance of Nder, the Peul women and children of Goundiour in modern-day Koumpentoum in eastern Senegal drowned themselves in a communal well to escape enslavement at the hands of the conquering Djolof when the village was massacred. In Wolof, the event is known as Thioural Goundiour.[11]

Under French occupation, the most celebrated Senegalese resistance leaders—such as Sidya "Léon" Diop (ca. 1850–78) and Samba Yaya Fall—died by suicide in final gestures of refusal that highlighted French cruelty while asserting Senegalese agency.[12] Sidya Diop, whose maternal grandmother died at Nder, led a fierce resistance campaign against colonizing French forces—turning against Louis Faidherbe, who initially had groomed him into the colonial administration and even sponsored his baptism. He eventually was captured and exiled to Gabon at the age of twenty-eight. After a failed attempt to return to his native Waalo, he shot himself in the chest, dying on 26 June 1878 at the age of thirty.[13] Fall, meanwhile, was deposed, exiled, and placed under house arrest by French forces in Saint-Louis, where he remained under constant surveillance. Refused permission to leave Saint-Louis to attend his mother's funeral, and no longer able to support the humiliation of captivity and exile, Fall leaped from the Pont Faidherbe, drowning himself in the Senegal River. In Wolof, the terms most often used to characterize their acts are not the typical periphrasis associated with suicide (*xaru*) but the verbs *bañ* (to refuse) and *siggi* (to straighten up). Their suicides are seen as examples of Wolof *jom*, or "dignity" (also "self-esteem," "courage," "honor"). *Jom*, Felwine Sarr writes in *Afrotopia* (2016, trans. 2019), is one of "those cultural values" that "we must rehabilitate [...] to exhume and revive the profound humanism of [African] cultures."[14] In the context of suicide, *jom* designates a specific kind of honorable self-killing to avoid personal shame (*gàcce*).[15] Popular tales in Wolof centrally represent suicides and suicide-like deaths in ways that uphold *jom* or other gendered social values (purity, virginity, etc.) that contribute to a Wolof code of honor, such as *sutura*, a Wolofized

Arabic word with various connotations including "discretion, tact, privacy, modesty, secrets."[16] Perhaps the best-known example of this is *Xaru Xanju* (*The Suicide of Xanju*), which tells the story of a female friendship that ends in the suicides of two young women, the titular Xanju and her friend Ndaté, who drown themselves in a well to protect one another's honor and to keep the other's secret.[17] Modern medical studies on suicide and parasuicide in Senegal frequently note the cultural resonances of suicide in the Senegalese oral tradition, especially the resistance of the women of Nder.[18]

Local histories of suicide recede from view in settler-colonial accounts of French colonization in West Africa and disappear in the scriptural archive. But they fall out of frame equally in more recent historiographical work. In *Reines d'Afrique et héroïnes de la diaspora noire* (2004)—one of the few written historical texts to mention the Talaatay Nder—Senegalese-born Antillean writer Sylvia Serbin suggests that the story of Nder, as well as the village itself, have fallen into total obscurity. "Today," she writes, "I am told this small village of Walo is abandoned and abandoned by nature, like memory. No commemoration comes to remember the page of history that was written there."[19]

The village of Nder is not abandoned, and the legacy of the women who died there remains very much alive. Oral tradition and aesthetic works conserve a rich, alternative archive of suicidal resistance.[20] In Nder, no physical memorial to the women exists. Although the site of the collective suicide is known, it is not marked. And in contrast to the rest of the country, people are relatively reticent to discuss the Talaatay Nder. Elsewhere in Senegal, however—throughout Waalo and in the capital, Dakar—the event is commemorated regularly through oral performances by *géwél* and retellings by *boroom xam-xam* like Diaw. The anniversary of the Talaatay Nder is celebrated annually on 7 March, the day before International Women's Day. Since 2008, feminist scholars such as Fatou Sow Sarr have campaigned to make 7 March a national holiday, mobilizing the message of the Talaatay Nder to various progressivist ends—such as arguing for the inclusion of women in governance and highlighting gender-based violence in Senegal.[21] The resistance of the women of Nder also has an afterlife in the form of an immensely varied, ever-expanding archive of imaginative retellings that revisit the Talaatay Nder as literature, music, and film, in Wolof and French—most dating from the past two decades.[22] In their turn toward the aesthetic, these works re-cite and rewrite the text of collective suicide. They renew and repurpose the Talaatay Nder narrative, drawing on the heretofore unrealized "potential" of a historical past by conjugating it in the present.[23]

As with the suicides of the women of *Le Soleil* and of Delgrès and his followers, the resistance of Nder becomes a crucible for thinking through the limits of existing archives and a means of exploring other, narrative, dialogic, and polyvocal forms of historical knowledge. This is the crux of Diaw's generic distinction (Talaatay Nder "*du léep*"), which pinpoints a problem of historical memory and narrative authority: What textual forms appear recognizable as history, and to whom? In the absence of a scriptural archive, imaginative re-tellings of the resistance of Nder restage and enact the logical and narrative paradox of the Talaatay Nder, and of collective suicide more generally. How does a story—indeed, a national epic of resistance—emerge from an event that a priori should leave no survivors? How might we learn to read a text written in flame and effaced in ash?

To answer these questions, this chapter adumbrates a translingual literary prehistory and recessed genealogy of suicidal resistance in Senegalese literature in Wolof and French. Reading across languages and between oral, scriptural, and visual suicide archives, I excavate the history of the suicidal resistance of the women of Nder and trace its reinscription into narrative. Specifically, I examine three examples of how Senegalese writers have represented and repurposed—both entextualized and narrativized—the Talaatay Nder in literature. The first is Alioune Badara Bèye's historical tragedy *Nder en flammes* (1988), initially staged by Seyba Lamine Traoré in 1990 at the Théâtre National Daniel Sorano in Dakar.[24] The second is Boubacar Boris Diop's first Wolof-language novel, *Doomi Golo: Nettali* (2003), which embeds the Talaatay Nder story within a broader dialogic structure concerned with cultural patrimony: the narrator-grandfather's framing address to his absent émigré grandson. Finally, in the conclusion to this chapter, I turn to Mohamed Mbougar Sarr's Goncourt-winning novel *La plus secrète mémoire des hommes* (2021). Sarr's text brings the suicide archive of the Talaatay Nder into contact with another, more recent suicide archive: the public self-immolation of Mohamed Bouazizi in 2010. All three texts activate the literary "potential" of historical suicide through their re-entextualizations of the resistance of Nder. Across modes (performance, prose), genres (tragedy, novel), and languages (French, Wolof), Bèye, Diop, and Sarr revive the Talaatay Nder in Senegal's post-Independence literary landscape as an enduring message of Senegalese resistance, refusal, and resilience. In my reading of Bèye's and Diop's works, I focus on representations of the designated survivor-witness, Saydané/Seydani/Sadani (her name varies across oral and scriptural traditions), who lives on to tell the story of the other women's bravery and sacrifice. Though absent from colonial-imperial accounts of the Talaatay Nder, she is ubiquitous in oral histories, where she appears as a highly fungible character—at times a young girl, at others an old woman. I read her as a subversive, resistant figure of translation and transmission. An allegory of narration and an embodiment of archive, Sadani marks the moment suicide shades into literature. She is the memory, the medium, and the messenger of the Talaatay Nder.

Whither the (Suicide) Archive?

One of the earliest published accounts of the Talaatay Nder comes from the notebooks of Yoro Booli Diaw (1847–1919). The son of Fara Penda, a *brak* of Waalo, Diaw was the first Wolof to document and compile the oral histories of his people in French.[25] He followed in the footsteps of Abbé David Boilat, the *métis* Catholic priest whose *Esquisses sénégalaises* (1853) inaugurated what David Murphy has called a hybrid Franco-African "paraliterature": texts situated between the genres of historiography, literature, ethnography, and travel writing. In this way, Diaw's chronicles are an important precursor to a national Senegalese literature in French.[26]

Conserved in several turn-of-the-century manuscripts, Diaw's notebooks were published piecemeal beginning in 1864, often with substantial emendations and explanatory paratexts.[27] In 1929, Raymond Rousseau, an instructor at the Lycée Faidherbe in Saint-Louis, published what is believed to be the remainder of Diaw's writings.[28] Diaw's account of the resistance of Nder occurs in a description of the "War against the Trarzas," where he details incursions and raids by neighboring Berber tribes, which were in frequent conflict with rulers of the Senegalese River Valley states and colonizing French forces.[29]

The conflict between the Trarzas and Waalo, the resistance of Nder, Diaw's account of it, and its subsequent iterations in literature must be understood in the context of France's colonizing expeditions in Senegal during the first half of the nineteenth century. French machinations in the Cayor region, in particular financial support for France's colonial "experiment" in the Senegal River basin, depended on alternatively managing and escalating tensions between the Trarza emirates and the precolonial kingdoms of northern Senegal.[30] The resistance of Nder occurred against this backdrop. Leaders of African states and colonizing French forces vied for power, formed and dissolved alliances, and entered into conflicts that frequently erupted in violence. This "atmosphere of generalized violence," as described by historians, was caused by the economic repression of the Senegalese River states, the social and political disruptions of domestic African slavery, and a highly unstable political landscape.[31]

These historical tensions had developed in relationship with Atlantic commerce and, later, with French experiments with agricultural colonization in West Africa.[32] Following the Congress of Vienna, France officially regained Senegal from British control. However, it was only in 1817 that the French were able to reoccupy Saint-Louis under Governor Julien Désiré Schmaltz (1771–1826). Schmaltz was tasked with spearheading France's politics of "agricultural colonization" (*la colonisation agricole*) in the region, intended to supplement and then replace France's increasingly untenable reliance on enslaved labor in the wake of the revolution in Saint-Domingue and the interdiction of the Atlantic slave trade (although *la traite clandestine*, or illegal slave trade, continued well into the mid-nineteenth century in some regions). Schmaltz chose Waalo as the site for testing out France's experiment with agricultural colonization, hoping the region would become a model for an expansive plantation economy based on the continent, namely for the cultivation of peanuts and the harvesting of gum arabic. On 8 May 1819, Schmaltz signed the Treaty of Ndiaw with the *brak* Amar Fatim Mborso, making Waalo an economic protectorate of France and acquiring large swaths of land in northern Senegal for agricultural development. For France, the treaty of Ndiaw constituted a legally documented purchase of land in return for annual *coutumes*, taxes paid in the form of money or merchandise to the *brak* and local chiefs, in addition to protection from the razzias of the neighboring Trarzas. For the Trarza emirates and the river states of Fuuta Tooro, the treaty was a provocation and casus belli.

In his written account published by Rousseau, Diaw describes how the *brak* of Waalo, wounded in an earlier battle against the Trarzas at Thiaggar, retreated to Saint-Louis to receive medical treatment, leaving Nder momentarily "defenseless" and vulnerable to attack. In contrast to most oral accounts, which date the Talaatay Nder to the spring of 1819 or 1820, Diaw places the event in November 1818. The women's resistance occupies a single sentence:

> In November of the same year 1818, in the absence of the *Brack* who was still in Saint-Louis, the Trarzas destroyed N'Der, the capital of Oualo, under the leadership of Ahma-Ould-El-Mokhtar, and with help from their allies the Toucouleurs of Almamy. Many warriors were killed by the victors. To the shame of falling into the hands of the Moors and Toucouleurs, a large number of the women under the *Linguère-Aouo* Fahty-Yamar preferred to burn themselves alive, in a large hut, on the suggestion of one of them, M'Barka, the favorite of the princess.[33]

Despite the processes of transmission, selective erasure, and reframing at work in Diaw's account—from an original oral source to Diaw, whose text is mediated and redacted further by Rousseau—a human drama of epic scale and a striking episode of collective female suicidal resistance remain legible. Not unlike the way Fabienne Kanor explodes a meager written trace—a few lines in the archive of Atlantic slavery—into a polyphonic text, Alioune Badara Bèye and Boubacar

Boris Diop demonstrate in their separate literary works that this single sentence contains the germ of a historical tragedy (Bèye) and a novel (Diop). Unlike Kanor, however, Diop and Bèye had a rich oral archive to draw on.

In the colonial-imperial archive, the story goes underground. French sources from this period contain references to the Talaatay Nder that are even more elliptical than Diaw's account, often subsuming the events under the generalized military aggression of the Trarza nations toward French and Waalo forces and eliding the women's resistance entirely.[34] Captain Adjutant Major H. Azan's expansive "Notice sur le Oualo" is emblematic in this respect. Azan simply notes that in 1819 "Nder was captured and burned," then later razed again by the French in 1855 before being rebuilt in 1857.[35] He makes no mention of collective suicide or of the fates of the *lingeer* and her entourage. The elision is surprising, given that Azan claims to have consulted the same oral sources as Yoro Diaw, including *brak* Fara Penda, during his travels through the Senegalese River states.[36] However, Azan refuses to accept the word of his various oral sources at face value: "It's thus in combining all of these accounts [*récits*], in comparing them to one another, in taking an average, so to speak, of these notes [*en prenant pour ainsi dire une moyenne de ces notes*], that I wrote the following article."[37]

A letter dated 27 March 1820 from Saint-Louis now conserved in the National Archives in Dakar gives a more complete report of the sack of Nder.[38] In a subsection titled "Causes présumées des événements survenus depuis 1819" (Alleged causes of events since 1819), the *directeur des colonies* (Schmaltz at the time) describes being alerted to the Trarzas' initial incursion into Waalo on 5 March 1820.[39] Schmaltz mentions the absence of the *brak* and of most men from the village. He also mentions—and seems surprised by—the fierce resistance of the women (*les femmes mêmes montrèrent beaucoup d'énergie*), but does not allude to a collective suicide, suggesting instead that the wife of the *brak* escaped to the safety of a nearby village under French control:

> They [= the Moors] spread throughout the country; they burned down every abandoned hut without however damaging the crops, as they had resolved in principle; finally, based on the information they gathered, they came in droves to assemble before Nder, the Brack's usual abode. The men were almost entirely absent. Under the leadership of the Briok, the hereditary prince of Wallo, they had left the village to go to Dagana where they thought the larger battle would be.
>
> The Brack still being detained in St. Louis by the wound received last September at the battle of Ntiagar, the enemies encountered no opposition except for a group of Moors loyal to the Brack and a few men who

had remained in the villages and who fought back with great vigor. Even the women showed much energy. However, after a long resistance, the village was captured. The wife of the Brack, her son, and her people, retreated to Ngniass, which was protected by two of our ships.

Schmaltz goes on to state that earlier accounts of the attack were exaggerated. He attempts to set the record straight by providing—in his view—a more precise body count: "The exaggeration of early accounts of this event initially gave reason to fear the loss of a large number of inhabitants of Wallo; it follows from more accurate reports that twenty men and thirty women were killed; and that around one hundred were taken prisoner and transported to Fanaye by the Moorish and Fouta riders." Schmaltz's misgivings about "exaggerated" reports, like Azan's textual "calculus," mean jettisoning an episode of suicidal resistance that even Diaw's relatively slim account preserves. One must wonder whether Schmaltz, Azan, and others did hear the story of the women's suicide but simply dismissed it as "incredible," as something pertaining to the realms of fable, myth, legend, or "rumor" rather than the stuff of history.[40] Recall Diaw's insistence that Talaatay Nder "du léep": the Talaatay Nder is not a fable, is not fiction. What details Schmaltz's and Azan's accounts *do* retain reveal more about the limits of colonial-imperial discursive frames, a desire to maintain focus on French control in the region, and gendered expectations around female agency, that render suicidal resistance illegible. Paradoxically, in their ostensibly "fictional" and self-consciously *literary* accounts, authors such as Bèye, Diop, and Sarr get us closer to something like historical "truth."

Nder en flammes (1988)

Nder en flammes was staged for the first time in Dakar in August 1990 at the Daniel Sorano National Theater, Senegal's most prestigious stage, opened in 1965 to serve as the main stage for the first Festival Mondial des Arts Nègres (World Festival of Black Arts) held in Dakar the following year. In the decade leading up to the first performance of *Nder en flammes*, various other historical plays were staged there, including Ibrahima Sall's *Le choix de Madior* (1981) and Thierno Bâ's *Lat-Dior, le chemin de l'honneur* (1987).[41] Since 1990, the numerous revivals of *Nder en flammes* have featured performances by some of the best-known Senegalese actors in African theater and cinema, including Coly Mbaye and Marie Auguste Diatta, known for their roles in Ousmane Sembène's *Guelwaar* (1992) and Joseph Gai Ramaka's *Karmen Gei* (2001), and Charles Foster, who appears in Moussa Sène Absa's *Teranga Blues* (2006). Versions of the play have incorporated percussion and lyrical performances in Wolof by local artists from Dakar, Pikine, and Guédiawaye, and by griots such as the Waalo-Waalo *géwél* Samba Seck.[42] More recently, Bèye's play has been revived as a means of memorializing another, more contemporary tragedy: serving to honor Marie Auguste Diatta, who, along with over 1,800 others, perished in one of the deadliest accidents in maritime history, the sinking of the *Joola* ferry off the coast of the Gambia in 2002.[43] Such commemorative functions of *Nder en flammes* add yet another dimension to the myriad ways the "tragedy of Nder" continues to signify in Senegalese culture.

Nder en flammes is the final installment in a cycle of three interlocking historical tragedies in Bèye's oeuvre, preceded by *Le sacre du Ceddo* (1982) and *Dialawali, terre de feu* (1984), which revisit the history of Waalo and Fuuta during the nineteenth and twentieth centuries. It heralds Bèye's shift toward political theater, with productions such as *Demain la fin du monde* (1993) and *Les larmes de la patrie* (2003). Because it stages an episode of local Senegalese history by incorporating traditional music and dance, making limited use of Wolof terms and formulas, *Nder en flammes* deviates in important ways from the classical French-language repertoire of colonial drama, exemplified by the theatrical productions of the William Ponty School during the first half of the twentieth century.[44] At the same time, the play cannot be considered a straightforward example of what Cheik Aliou Ndao calls a *theater of exposition*—early twentieth-century productions that presented Indigenous cultures in theatrical form as ethnographic information to "explain the African civilization to a foreign eye."[45] Bèye's play also comes before the advent of a truly Afrophone national drama, which began to emerge in Dakar in the early 2000s with the Wolof-language productions of Ndao and El Hadji Momar Samb.[46] The liminal position of *Nder en flammes*—somewhere between French colonial drama and contemporary Wolof theater, between Bèye's "historical" and "political" theater—is perhaps one explanation for why Bèye's play is so understudied.[47] Although Bèye's *Nder en flammes* often is mentioned in encyclopedic accounts of West African theater, scholars have consistently overlooked the aesthetic, literary, and performative dimensions of Bèye's play.[48] This oversight is true of Bèye's oeuvre more broadly, given that he is notably absent in major recent studies of Senegalese theater such as Brian Valente-Quinn's *Senegalese Stagecraft* (2021).[49]

Specialists of West African theater characterize the rise of Wolof drama at the turn of the twenty-first century as marking a critical stage in Senegalese postcolonial literary production and mounting a decisive challenge to the "linguistic hegemony" of French as the privileged language of literary expression in Senegal, a country long considered a bastion of the French language and a success story for France's imperial projects of *mission civilisatrice* and *mise en valeur* in West Africa.⁵⁰ From the colonial education policies of Georges Hardy and the French-language repertoire of the William Ponty School to the poet-president Léopold Sédar Senghor's *francophilie*, theatrical creation in Senegal, as Valente-Quinn writes, "went hand-in-hand with the conceptual configuration of a transnational *Francophonie*, or a community of nations united by their attachment to the French language and French culture."⁵¹

The turn away from French and toward theater in Wolof and other Indigenous languages (Sereer, Pulaar) in recent decades has contributed to the transformation of Dakar into an "Afrophone literary capital." Diop's *Doomi Golo* (2003), discussed in the following section, is an example of this trend. As Bojana Coulibaly notes, Senegal's nascent Wolof theater represents an "innovative creative tool of *resistance* to the former colonial dramatic tradition," participating, on the level of aesthetic production, in the project of Senegalese cultural liberation.⁵² For Coulibaly, historical plays are especially important, as they "are written in order to restore the dignity of Senegalese people whose epic figures have been misrepresented in the colonial epistemology."⁵³ Valente-Quinn underscores this point with respect to the Ponty School's *pièces historiques*, which "would operate to a far more pointed and political effect in the post-Independence years," becoming "a performative tool to re-adjudicate the historical roles, and restore the dignity, of nineteenth-century African chiefs and leaders."⁵⁴ Bèye's *Nder en flammes* makes good on this promise of historical tragedy to both "restore dignity" and correct "colonial epistemology" with respect to the Talaatay Nder. Though written in a former colonial language, Bèye's play nonetheless contributes to a national project of Senegalese theater as cultural "resistance" and "liberation." *Nder en flammes* returns to a historical moment at the dawn of French colonizing expeditions in West Africa and restages it for an independent, neoliberal Senegalese public in the twentieth century. The play is a mise-en-scène of historical resistance and a call for resistant community in the present, rehabilitating precolonial history as the worthy subject of contemporary aesthetic production. In the wake of national tragedy, from the literal ashes of Nder, arises a resistant spark of solidarity that, in the words of Fatou Sow Sarr, becomes an "eternal flame" burning in the dark.⁵⁵

In entextualizing the Talaatay Nder as historical tragedy, Bèye draws on both oral and written accounts from various sources: historians of Waalo, the Douane Sénégalaise, and members of his maternal family, who were half Waalo-Waalo.⁵⁶ He revisits and reconstitutes in remarkable detail not only the sack of Nder and the women's self-immolation but also the events preceding and following the episode of collective suicide, including the negotiation of the Treaty of Ndiaw, the battles of Thiaggar and Dialawali, and French experiments with agricultural colonization in the Senegal River valley. In this way, Bèye situates the Talaatay Nder narrative within a broader historical context, depicting French machinations in West Africa and military conflict with the neighboring Trarza nations. This makes Bèye's play one of the most complete French-language accounts of the resistance of Nder to date, despite the author's own claims of taking creative liberties with the story.[57] A literary work that doubles as a historical document, it is often cited as such in the absence of widely available historiographical sources on the Talaatay Nder.[58]

Nder en flammes begins and ends at twilight. Rather than relying on conventional dramaturgical unities such as "act" or "scene," Bèye structures his play in a series of tableaux distributed over five days, using divisions that are temporal (*minuit*, "midnight"; *matinée*, "morning"; *mi-journée*, "midday"; *soir*, "evening"), solar (*crépuscule*, "twilight"; *aube*, "dawn"; *aurore*, "first light"), and spatial (the play cycles between the courts of Waalo and the Trarzas, the river state Fuuta, and colonial headquarters in Saint-Louis).[59] Early performances of the play staged by Seyba Traoré featured a spare set consisting of a backdrop divided into three sections, each representing one of the spatial divisions of the play: the first in the shape of a minaret (the Trarza emirates), the second depicting a map of Senegal beneath a French flag (colonial headquarters in Saint-Louis), and the third showing a platform with two wooden pikes (the royal court of Waalo). All three were visible throughout the play. Shifts in setting were emphasized using lighting and smoke effects.[60] The revival of *Nder en flammes* in 2016 projected historical images onto a backdrop to delineate the play's different settings. Although written and performed in French, Bèye's play closely resembles traditional Wolof theatrical forms in its mise-en-scène. These typically are arranged in tableaux taking place in different locations and in different temporalities and are performed by *mbandkat* (traveling troupe). Specifically, Bèye's *Nder en flammes* recalls *nawetaan* performances, which typically are "used to highlight local folklore or to pay tribute to key figures in local or national history."[61]

A majority of *Nder en flammes* takes place in shadow—in near total darkness, beneath a sliver of moon, in the dim half-light of a fading sun, or at dawn. Only two episodes occur in broad daylight, at midday, and these have structural and thematic significance. First, there is a prescient scene in which Governor Schmaltz and the "mulatto" Pellegrin, *maître des colonies*, debate France's *mission civilisatrice* and discuss an increasingly "explosive" situation in Waalo, which risks setting ablaze (*embraser*) the entire region ("fire smolders at our doors," says Schmaltz).[62] In reality, as Georges Hardy writes in *La mise en valeur du Sénégal* (1921), it was Pellegrin who was responsible for escalating tensions between Waalo and Trarza and provoking the attack on Thiaggar:

> In response to maneuvers attributed to a mulatto [*mulâtre*] from Saint-Louis, named Pellegrin, a party of Trarzas invaded [*faire une irruption*] Oualo; as a result of this attack, the *brak* and his minister were wounded, the former quite seriously, many Black chiefs were killed, the village of Antiaga burned to the ground, and a large number of captives were taken away by the Moors, etc.[63]

The second daytime scene of *Nder en flammes* is the collective suicide—the "explosion" or "irruption" itself—in which the women of Nder, besieged on all sides, decide to take their own lives: the Linguère Fatim Yamar, a torch raised high, addresses her entourage before ushering them into the royal hut, setting it alight, and finally stepping into the flames herself (figure 2.1). The structural parallel between Schmaltz's and Pellegrin's conversation "between men" at the colonial headquarters in Saint-Louis and the self-immolation of the women of Nder is a provocative one. It speaks to Bèye's larger project in *Nder en flammes* of presenting the Talaatay Nder as contiguous with the long history of colonizing violence in West Africa, not an isolated episode of animosity between African states. Indeed, Nder would be burned to the ground again in 1855, this time by the French.

That the word *suicide* occurs only once in Bèye's play is instructive in this respect. The term never names the collective resistance of the women of Nder; their final act always is referred to as a "sacrifice" or "tragedy," or explained through periphrasis ("they burned themselves alive"). Rather, "suicide" in *Nder en flammes* characterizes the stakes of succumbing to France's "civilizing" mission, which is the real annihilating danger. In one scene, Pellegrin, accompanied by several *tirailleurs*, visits the court of Waalo to persuade the Brack to accept French presence in West Africa and to favor their efforts of agricultural colonization. Prince Yérim Mbagnick rejects Pellegrin's appeals, suggesting that *France*, not the Trarzas, will cause the suicide of Waalo:

> PELLEGRIN: But God dammit! In the name of the republic, you have the Governor's sworn word.
>
> YÉRIM: This word of honor does not suffice! In the name of whom and of what does France demand the suicide of Walo? In the name of what cause? [...] Walo shall never be a chosen land for any colonial experiment. (41–42)

In Bèye's retelling, France's "colonial experiment" augurs the suicide of a nation. Yérim's analogy recalls the warning of Samba Diallo's father, Le Chevalier, in

FIGURE 2.1. Performance of *Nder en flammes* in 2016. The *linguère* (right) holds a torch and addresses her compatriots before their collective suicide. Source: Archives of the National Theater Daniel-Sorano.

Cheikh Hamidou Kane's *L'aventure ambiguë* (1961): Le Chevalier frames submitting to the French colonial educational system as a suicide ("leur course est un suicide").[64] Waalo is impossibly positioned between the threats of jihad and slavery (the intrusion of the Trarzas and their Fuuta allies), and France's *mission civilisatrice*, which spells both real violence and "cultural slavery": that is, relinquishing their "desire to remain free for eternity" (40). In the words of the Brack, Waalo must live free or die (76).

In *Nder en flammes*, Bèye transforms the tragedy of Nder into an epic gesture of national resistance and resilience: an act of patriotic self-determination that refuses culturicide and heralds future glory. The women of Nder are heroines whose decision to die rather than surrender is a final expression of their devotion to the nation: "My sisters, there is no death more beautiful than that which consists in offering up one's life for the sake of the nation [*la cause nationale*]" (68). That they choose to die by fire enshrines them as purified martyrs, vestal daughters: "Our assailants must not see or touch our corpses. To protect our chastity and our purity, to avoid the defilement of our land and our skirts, I have chosen fire as a weapon of retaliation [*arme de riposte*], of deliverance, of dignity, and of refusal" (68). *Nder en flammes* allows us to expand Church's observation that fire was the last resort of the slave in the French Caribbean to the wider Atlantic world. Here, too, fire becomes a weapon of patriotic resistance brandished at a dire moment and a purifying element: a transformational tool of deliverance that allows the women to protect their land (*terre*), a synecdoche for the nation, and their skirts (*pagnes*), a marker of their femininity and sexual purity. Whereas Diop in *Doomi Golo* will reframe the women's suicide as feminist militancy, a final act intended to preserve their honor *as warriors*, Bèye's women of Nder are linked more closely to patriarchal and allegorical conceptions of the female body as a metonym for the nation-state. The women desire to preserve their chastity, a symbol of masculine honor, at all costs—in the manner of the "virgin" *sutura* suicides of Xanju and Ndaté.

In Bèye's retelling, the women are also, crucially, *historians*. At the very moment of their death, they become self-conscious "writers," engaging in a narrative project to determine how the "tragedy of Nder" will be transmitted to the Senegal of tomorrow. Fatim Yamar frames the women's collective suicide in writerly terms, as a necessary sacrifice in the service of collective memory:

> The history of Waalo now rests between the absolute lines of your hands which will engrave [*graver*] the most beautiful pages of the people of the cool breezes [*des fraîcheurs*]. Women of Nder, are you ready to immortalize this day of truth? [. . .] To you who say yes to death, may you be thanked for the exultant memory [*souvenir*] that you will leave to the youth of Waalo and to that of the Senegal of tomorrow. (67–68)

In the *lingeer's* formulation, voluntary death becomes a decisive act of writing that will inscribe (*graver*) a proper name and date onto the pages of Waalo's history. Her attendant Mbarka Dia reiterates the princess's words moments before stepping into the flames: "This day of Tuesday will stand out from the records of the everyday [*sortira des tablettes du commun*] to become the 'Tuesday of Nder,' the most glorious day of our country" (70). Reduced to ash, the women's bodies nevertheless leave behind a memorial trace for the future generations of Waalo to read.

The "text" of collective suicide, written and effaced in fire and ash, is displaced in the figure of the survivor-witness, the "Beuk Nek" Seydani Ba. A figure drawn not from the colonial-imperial archive but from the oral history surrounding the Talaatay Nder, Seydani emerges at a pivotal moment in Bèye's play as an allegorical figure of transmission in the wake of an act that she witnessed but could not partake in. Before ushering the rest of her entourage into the hut, the *lingeer* charges Seydani with telling the world of "the tragedy of Nder": "'Beuk Nek,' while the embers mingle with the ribbons of our flesh, you will go hide behind the great canary tree so that the tragedy of Nder has a witness [*un témoin*] and will be known by the nationalist forces of Walo and by the historians" (69). Through Seydani Ba, collective suicide has an afterlife. She simultaneously enacts and explains the possibility of collective suicide to reproduce itself as narrative.

When the curtain rises after the women's self-immolation, Seydani alone remains onstage, reckoning with the impossible "mission" confided to her: to tell the story. In the play's only soliloquy, she addresses her dead compatriots directly: "What mission have you entrusted to me? To tell [*raconter*] of your death, your sacrifice, your suffering to those who are most dear to you. To tell of this supreme sacrifice which I would have like to share in with you so as to forever nourish the consciousness of future generations" (71). The stage directions indicate that Seydani's soliloquy is pronounced "with her arms in the air, staggering about [*titubant*]" and almost "delirious" (*presque en délire*), aligning the text of survivor testimony with the sorcerer's trance or the ravings of the madman—a move we will see again, though framed rather differently, in Diop's novel. Verging on delirium and swaying as though under a spell, she continues: "Here I am, witness to your ultimate sacrifice, may the purified voice of the women of Waalo spring [*jaillir*] from your heroic death" (71). Channeled by the impossible witness, a purified voice springs from death. Seydani lets out one last cry—the toponym "Walo!," her final utterance of the play—before collapsing to the ground, where she waits amid the ruins and burned bodies ("I shall wait here among the cadavers, the charred corpses, until Yérim Mbagnick arrives") (72).

Seydani's "mission" to narrate the women's death to posterity contrasts with the other military and masculine missions structuring the action of Bèye's play. These include the Brack's "mission" to protect Waalo's independence against encroaching French and Islamist forces (39); Yérim Mbagnick's nationalist "divine mission" (*mission divine*) to propagate the house of Tedjeck and extend the borders of Waalo (35); France's "civilizing mission" (*mission civilisatrice*; 29); and "the Moorish cause" (*la cause maure*) of the Trarza and Fuuta to extend Islam into the Senegal River valley (27). Seydani's narrative mission is a *mission* in the truest, etymological sense (from the Latin *mittere*, "to send"): a "sending out" of the message of Nder. But we never actually hear Seydani recount the women's fate. After her soliloquy, female voices recede entirely from the stage.

The scene that follows transports us to the governor's residence in Saint-Louis, where the wounded Brack is recuperating after the battle of Thiaggar. The messenger Malicoumba, who presumably has learned of the events from Yérim Mbagnick, who heard them firsthand from Seydani, arrives from Waalo at dawn and transmits the message:

THE BRACK: Malicoumba, what happened in Walo?

MALICOUMBA: Brack, a tragedy! I've just come from Nder.

THE BRACK: Nder?

MALICOUMBA: Yes, Brack, Nder is no more! And with it the Linguères of Walo!

THE BRACK: But what happened to our brave Linguères, Fatim Yamar, Mbarka Dia, Makane Bâ?

MALICOUMBA: All dead!

THE BRACK: How did they die, Malicoumba! How one dies is more important than the death itself. How did they die?

MALICOUMBA: Brack, with bravery, honor, and greatness [*grandeur*]! They refused to have their bodies dirtied [*souillés*] by impure hands. They wanted to preserve their chastity, their land, and their skirts [*pagnes*] to raise up the image of our people. They burned themselves alive. The purifying flames welcomed their souls with mercy [*compassion*] and bitterness.

THE BRACK: So those brave women chose the redness of embers over the impure hands of Moorish slavers. (73–74)

In this scene, Bèye shows the story of Nder traveling *as text*: from Seydani to Yérim Mbagnick to Malicoumba to the Brack; from Nder to Saint-Louis; from being a narrative-in-progress in the mouths of women to a fait accompli recounted—ventriloquized—in the past tense by men. Bèye positions his audience as the inadvertent recipients of an "original" text: silent observers made privy to a conversation between women, as Seydani converses with the cadavers of her compatriots. The messenger Malicoumba displaces Seydani's account of the women's death in turn by reciting it, producing a new text that the Brack glosses in a recuperative act of interpretation: reclaiming the women's suicide for the nation by ascribing meaning to it. Bèye repeats this process of re-entextualization.

In the mouths of men, the "message" of the women's suicide is overdetermined, framed as a means of preserving their chastity and protecting masculine honor. Indeed, the Brack transforms the *lingeer* Fatim Yamar from historical agent into national symbol: "Linguère Fatim Yamar belonged to a whole people. She was a symbol for all of Waalo" (75). He converts the women's death into a rallying cry for military retaliation, for the scene concludes with a reference to the battle of Dialawali, 22 July 1820, where the princes of Waalo pursued and defeated the Trarzas. It ends on the Wolof phrase *Dialawali fayna Nder*: literally, "Dialawali has paid (for) Nder."

In Bèye's framing, order is restored by a textual calculus that accounts for female suicide with male revenge and reads female resistance in terms of masculine honor. This is perhaps one explanation for how a play about collective female suicidal resistance—the story of "sister-martyrs" (*des sœurs martyres*)—can end, paradoxically, with the word *brotherhood* (*fraternité*; 88). Diop's novel, which I examine next, arranges the events rather differently to more overtly progressivist and feminist ends.

Doomi Golo (2003)

As Jonathon Repinecz has pointed out, part of the enduring significance of the Talaatay Nder story, and its attractiveness as an intertext, lies "in its ready usability by twentieth- and twenty-first-century feminist discourses."[65] In the women of Nder, contemporary writers find "emblem[s] of female resistance," which they can transform into vectors of feminist and generational critiques: young, androgynous African female warriors, like Sembène's militant Dior Yacine in *Ceddo* (1977) or the "Amazons" of Dahomey, who seize and wield forms of power traditionally reserved for men.[66]

Boubacar Boris Diop's first Wolof-language novel, *Doomi Golo*, is one such example of literary repurposing of the Talaatay Nder story. In *Doomi Golo*, Diop clearly positions the legacy of the women of Nder as a feminist alternative to the traditional wisdom represented by the overtly masculinist and gerontocratic proverbs of the Wolof sage Kocc Barma.[67] In *Doomi Golo*, the women of Nder disguise themselves as men, take up arms, and ride into battle to fight back against the Trarzas. Diop reframes the women's "martyrdom" as female militancy and positions the survivor-witness's testimony as a kind of subversive subaltern speech that flies in the face of a gerontocratic masculinist tradition. The tragic frame of female suicide shifts from honorable sacrifice to a usurpation of male power. Like Bèye, Diop makes the Talaatay Nder story speak to broader questions concerning narration and the transmission of history, positing the subversive survivor-witness, Sadani Caam, as a means to call into question all claims to absolute narrative authority.

In reading *Doomi Golo*, specialists of Senegalese literature have focused on the ideological significance of Diop's decision to compose a literary work in a "minor" language (Wolof)—and in a highly literate, even scholarly register—only later to loosely adapt the text into French.[68] Given its circulation in Wolof,

French, and English, and across national borders, *Doomi Golo* has become a complex example of African literature as "world literature," and a rare example of a Wolof-language original to circulate widely outside Senegal in translation.[69] Ousmane Ngom suggests that Diop's turning toward Wolof and away from French in the early 2000s was an act of "linguistic militancy."[70] In this, it would align with Kenyan writer Ngũgĩ wa Thiong'o's injunction in *Decolonising the Mind* (1981) to reject former colonial languages in favor of developing literature in Indigenous African languages.[71] Since the publication of *Doomi Golo* in 2003, Diop has created the Wolof-language imprint Céytu at Éditions Zulma in Paris and launched the Wolof-language weekly newspaper *Lu Defu Waxu*, and in 2016 he opened the Dakar-based imprint Ejo Editions, which specializes in publishing new works and works in translation in the national languages of Senegal—including Diop's most recent novels, *Malaanum lëndëm* (*The Cloak of Darkness*, 2022) and *Bàmmeelu Kocc Barma* (*The Grave of Kocc Barma*, 2017) as well as a republication of *Doomi Golo* in 2019.[72] In *The Tongue-Tied Imagination* (2019), Tobias Warner echoes many of the claims about the significance of Diop's choice to write in Wolof but emphasizes that Diop's first novel, *Doomi Golo*, envisions and addresses a future Wolof-language readership, a "public yet to come," given that literary readerships in Wolof remain small.[73] In some senses, Diop's Wolof-language novel can be seen to extend and, to an extent, fulfill Ousmane Sembène's hope of developing a truly Afrophone cinema and national literature in Wolof. At the same time, its rewriting into French bears witness to some of the same neocolonial pressures for extroversion that Sembène faced in making his films, including *La Noire de . . .* (1966), the focus of the next chapter. Such pressures are powerful in Senegal, where French remains the official language and the medium of formal education (except in the Koranic *daara*), even though only around a third of the population speak and understand it, mostly as a second language (by contrast, Wolof is spoken as a first or second language by as much as four-fifths of the population).[74]

In *Subversive Traditions* (2019), Repinecz argues for a reading of *Doomi Golo* that moves beyond the language question and more fully takes into account Diop's creative reworkings of traditional oral narratives in Wolof, which, Repinecz suggests, are strategically reimagined and remade within a "futurist" vein as "tales for tomorrow": stories from the past that can help us envision possible, more equitable futures.[75] The general narrative framing of *Doomi Golo* supports this interpretation; its structure reflects a clear concern for the transmission and transformation of tradition. Diop's text is composed of two parts (*xaaj*). The first consists of a series of seven dialogic *téereb* (notebooks) written by the aging *mag* (elder) Ngiraan Fay and addressed to his émigré grandson, Badu Taal, whom he hopes will return to Senegal one day to dig up the chronicles that have been buried in the courtyard of the grandfather's home in Ñarelaa, a fictitious neighborhood in Dakar.[76] Part II follows the grandfather's death, when the narration is taken up by the figure of the local *dof* or madman, Aali Këbooy, who has been designated as Ngiraan Fay's successor and who emerges as an unlikely truth-telling sage by the novel's end. Viewed within this larger dialogic structure (namely, the grandfather's framing second-person address to his absent grandson) and the asynchrony of *Doomi Golo*'s narration, which cuts across time and space, Diop's twenty-first-century retelling of an episode of resistance from the nineteenth century can be seen to participate in the book's overall project of staging the cross-generational transmission and transformation of local histories by mining a shared oral archive.

In the first notebook of *Doomi Golo*, *Téereb dóom* (the Book of Ashes), the cross-generational exchange between Ngiraan and Badu centers on a retelling of the Talaatay Nder, which the grandfather leverages in favor of a feminist critique of traditional figures of patriarchal and gerontocratic authority in Senegalese culture, including Kocc Barma.[77] The *dóom yi* (ashes) of this notebook's title evoke the cinders and scorched ruins of the village of Nder in the wake of an act of collective suicide. But the "ashes" of this notebook also speak to a broader concern in *Doomi Golo*, and in Diop's oeuvre more generally, for the remains, for the remainder: What traces are left behind after disaster, and how might posterity endeavor to read them?[78] In *Doomi Golo*, the retelling of the Talaatay Nder becomes the pretext for exploring questions about narrative authority and the transmission of local histories (*Who tells the story?*) as well as a way of thinking through a logical and literary impasse: In the wake of collective suicide, a tragic act that by definition should leave no survivors, how does a story emerge?

IN *DOOMI GOLO*, Nder is left open to attack one Tuesday morning while the men are working in the fields and the *brak* and his retinue are absent.[79] The Trarzas ford the river and descend on the village. Led by the *lingeer*'s attendant and confidante Mbarka Ja, the women of Nder don men's clothing, mount their horses, and ride into battle, successfully fighting off the enemy:

Mu [=Mbarka Ja] neeti leen:
—Su noon yi xamee ne ay jigéen lanu, dafa leen di gën a jox fit! Kon, na kenn ku nekk ci nun sol ay yëre goor!
Ñu def la mu leen sant, war seeni fas, jàkkaarlook noon ya, won leen njàmbaar gu matt sëkk.[80]

(She said to them:

"If the enemy knows we are women, it will give them even more courage, so for this reason each of us must wear men's clothes."

They did what was asked of them, mounted their horses, faced the enemy, and showed great bravery until the very end.)

As the Trarzas retreat, they glimpse one of the woman's braids when her cap tumbles to the ground. Incensed at the idea of being bested by women, they turn back, and the fighting resumes:

Ñu dàq noon ya, noon ya daw! Waaye ba ñuy génn Waalo, la am ca jigéeni Waalo ya ku mbaxanaam rot, létt ya feeñ! Noon ya sog a xam ne ay jigéen lañu doon xareel. Kenn ci ñoom woo ña doon daw: Dellusileen! Sañ ngeen a taxaw ci kanamu Buuru Tararsaa naan ko ay jigéen a leen dàqe Ndeer?

Xeex bi neeti kur.[81]

(They had chased off the enemy, the enemy has fled! But as they [= the enemy] went out of Waalo, one of the women's caps fell to the ground, revealing her braids. It's then that the enemy realized that they had been fighting with women. One among them called out to the others as they fled: "Come back! Do you dare say before the king of the Trarzas that it was women who chased you out of Nder?"

The battle began anew.)

The textual moment is one of dramatic revelation, combining the erotic charge of an unveiling and the threat of pseudo-castration or unmanning.[82] It is also an instance of pure *hasard*. As Diop writes in the French translation, it is "one of those small incidents that changes the course of History."[83] The exposed braids of the unhelmed warrior of Nder disclose her sex and provoke the ire of the male onlooker, leaving her vulnerable to attack.

When defeat seems inevitable, the women of Nder retreat to the royal hut and decide to burn themselves alive, preferring a collective death by fire (*safara si*) to capture and enslavement:

Dafa ne: Jomb nanoo nekki jaam ginnaaw Barag. Nanu dugg ci néegu ñax bu mag bii, taal ko ci sunu kow.

Na mu ko santaanee la ko jineeni waalo ya defe. Néegu ñax ba jàpp, di tàkk, noon ya wër leen, jigeeni Waalo yay woy ca biir safara sa ba sedd ñoom ñépp.[84]

(She said, "Our dignity [*jomb*] does not permit us to become slaves in the absence of the *Brak*. We shall enter into the great straw hut, set it alight above us."

The women of Waalo did what she proposed. The straw hut caught fire and went up in flames; the enemy surrounded them as the women of Waalo sang from the center of the blaze until death overcame them.)

For Diop, the decision to self-immolate extends the usurpation of male power that began on the battlefield—indeed earlier, when the women disguised themselves as men. The women will not be captured and sold as slaves (*jaam*), preempting the violence of the raiders by taking their own lives. Reduced to ash and bone, their corpses will not be defiled.

As was the case in Bèye's play—and, as we will see, in Sembène's text and film—suicide becomes a radical means of maintaining *narrative* control. By designating one member of the group as survivor and witness, the women ensure that someone lives on to tell of their bravery and self-immolation. Whereas in Bèye's text this role is fulfilled by the character Seydina Ba, who is only identified as a "Beuk Nek" (*bëkk-néég*) of Waalo and whose age remains unspecified, in *Doomi Golo* the one who lives on to narrate the resistance of Nder, Sadani Caam, is clearly a young girl (*benn gone gu jigéen*): a child of only eight years old. Mbarka Ja tasks her with being the first to tell the world of the women's sacrifice:

> Mbarka Ja ma doon seen njiit nag, jotoon naa rawale benn gone gu jigéen gu ñuy wax Sadani Caam.
> Dafa ni ko:
> —Yow Sadani, bu nu taalee néegu ñax bi, soo jaaree fii, dinga mucc! Demal Sadani, su Barag dellusee, nga nettali Waalo naka la jigeeni Ndeer yi bàyyee fii seen bakkan, ci jom ak fit ak ngor. Demal, Sadani, man Mbarka Ja maa la ko sant! Sadani Caam ma jëkk a nettali Talaatay Nder, ñaata at la amoon? Am na ñu ne juroom-ñetti at doŋŋ la amoon. Dara wooru ma ci, waaye lii moom boroom xam-xam yépp ànd nañu ci: Sadani Caam ma jëkk a netaali Talaatay Nder, xale bu ndaw la woon.[85]

(Mbarka Ja, their leader, managed to have a young girl by the name of Sadani Caam escape.

She said to her:

"You, Sadani, when we set the great straw hut alight, if you pass this way, you will be saved. Go, Sadani, and when the *Brak* returns you will tell all of Waalo how the women of Nder gave their lives on this day, in dignity, courage, and honor. Go, Sadani, I Mbarka Ja ask this of you!

Sadani Caam, the first to tell of Talaatay Nder, how old was she on that day? There are some who say she was only eight. I am not sure, but what is certain it that all the *boroom xam-xam* agree on this point: Sadani Caam, the first to tell the story of Talaatay Nder, was a young girl.")

Mbarka Ja's directive to Sadani Caam (*maa la ko sant!*, "I ask *this* of *you*"), framed as a string of imperatives (*demal*, "go forth") and injunctives (*dinga mucc*, "you will survive"; *nga nettali*, "you shall tell"), lays out in no uncertain terms how the women of Nder will make their message of honor and resistance sound from beyond the grave, long after the flames have consumed them and their bodies have turned to ash. These women died not as slaves or martyrs but as warriors, with dignity, courage, and honor (*ci jom ak fit ak ngor*). Their suicide is a final, devastating assertion of their *jom* (dignity) and a refusal of *gàcce* (shame).

The key term in this passage, and throughout the entire embedded Talaatay Nder narrative, is the verb *nettali/netalli/netaali*, which might be translated as "to tell" but also carries the meanings of to narrate, report, recount, or tell the details of something: *to tell the whole story*. The term appears in its nominal form on the title page of *Doomi Golo*, designating Diop's text as a narrative account or chronical and inscribing its origins as oral text. When Diop adapted *Doomi Golo* into French, the book would be labeled a *roman* or "novel," not a *récit* or narration, a category that better approximates the Wolof *nettali*. This is one of numerous changes, suppressions, or additions characterizing the transposition of *Doomi Golo* into French and, later, English.[86] Such slippage is particularly noticeable in the text proper, where the dialogic structure of address and markers of orality in the Wolof are effaced or flattened in the French, often rendered as third-person narration.[87] The disappearance of *nettali* in translation is especially significant. The term is central to understanding the stakes of Diop's literary repurposing of local histories and oral narrative traditions in *Doomi Golo* and his reframing of the resistance of Nder in the Book of Ashes.

Crucially, *nettali* has another meaning in Wolof. While this meaning is not typically found in dictionaries, it is perhaps the most frequent one, at least in everyday speech: *nettali* has the connotations of "snitching," of telling something that should remain secret. The grandfather's *nettali* positions his grandson—and readers—as nosy eavesdroppers since his narrative makes us privy to local neighborhood scandals and family dramas but also to national oral histories, such as the Talaatay Nder. In *Doomi Golo*, Diop is setting down stories that should remain oral texts, that should remain secret. Indeed, the last of the grandfather's notebooks, *Téereb ndéey* (the Book of Secrets), is only mentioned, not included in the novel, as if didactically pointing out the importance of keeping some secrets secret.

The term *nettali* appears throughout the Wolof original in verbal and nominal forms to designate the action of telling and the (oral) texts that result. *Nettali* connects the various speech acts and narrative projects that structure *Doomi Golo* at every level—from the paratext and frame narrative to embedded tales such as the retelling of the Tuesday of Nder. Beyond the title page of *Doomi Golo*, *nettali* characterizes the first-person narration of the grandfather's framing address to his absent grandson (*Badu xew-xew yi ma la fas yééné nettali...*, "Badu, the events I have decided to narrate/recount to you..."). The grandfather's *nettali* is an address to an absent other. Through writing, he "speaks" from beyond his own death across a fissure in the text's filiation that is both generational (at the time of writing, the grandfather has already buried his own son, Badu's father) and spatiotemporal (the dead grandfather's buried notebooks await a distant, future reader in his émigré grandson).

As the grandfather suggests at the outset of *Doomi Golo*, writing is not a perfect substitute for recounting his chronicles to Badu in person but a fallible technology of memory and transmission enabling him to address his grandson across absence. Drawing a contrast between orality and writing, between words that come straight from his mouth (*sama gémmiñ gii*) and those that flow from his pen (*sama xalima*), he promises to set down (*jaaxan*) a written record that awaits a future reader in his grandson:

> Dinaa la xamal tey lu tax ma fonke nii bind ak xalaat. Li ma lay waxis, guléet bésu tey mu génne sama gémmiñ gii, jaar ci sama xalima, jaaxaan ci téere bi nga yor, di la xaar fii ci Ñarelaa...[88]
>
> (Today I will let you know why I write and think with such love and care. What I am saying to you is that today is the very first time that my words [*gémmiñ gii*] are going out into the world, passing through my pen [*xalima*], to be set down in the notebooks that you have in your possession, they will await you here, in Ñarelaa...)

Like the impossible testimony of the survivor-witness who speaks in the name of the dead, the grandfather's *nettali* stands in for a disappeared voice. In the final section of *Doomi Golo*, following the grandfather's death, *nettali* also characterizes the subversive *baat*, the "speech" or "word," of the lucid madman Aali Këbooy, who takes up the narrative project initiated by the grandfather: "Dénk naa la Aali Këbooy. Li des ci nettali bi, mooy boroom" (I entrust you, Aali Këbooy. He is the owner of what remains of this narrative).

In the embedded Talaatay Nder narrative, the terms *nettali/netaali* name Sadani Caam's narrative mission: to tell the story of Nder. They equally participate in a series of phonic and graphic resonances that disappear completely in translation. Across the Wolof text, the syllables *tal/taal* scatter and spread like ashes in the wind, creating an elaborate paronomasia that links the act of narration (*nettali/netaali*) to the proper name designating the resistance of the women of Nder (Talaatay Nder) to the mechanism of collective suicide (*taal*, "to light a fire"), to what remains in its wake (*dóómu taal*, "ashes"), and even to the text's addressee—the grandson, Badu Taal, who encodes "fire" in his surname. Moreover, in Wolof, the term for "ashes," *dóóm gi/yi* or *dóómu taal gi/yi*, is nearly homophonous with the phrase "child of the fire" (*doomu taal*). The signifier *dóómu taal* emerges as a suggestive image of ash, of cinders—the gray offspring of the flame—but also for the figure of Sadani Caam, who arises from the aftermath of a deadly fire to tell an impossible story.[89]

In Diop's retelling, *nettali* ultimately names the enduring literary force of collective suicide. Long after the fire has died out and the women's *dóómu taal yi* (ashes) have dispersed, the story (*nettali*) of collective suicide lives on, continuing to signify "like a scar which remains after the great blaze."[90] Although Tuesday is simply a "day among others" (*bés a ngoog ci bés yi*), as the grandfather says, the Tuesday of Nder stands out as a day *unlike* any other, as absolutely singular.[91] Bèye's Mbarka Dia had voiced a similar claim in *Nder en flammes*, about the singularity of the proper name "the Tuesday of Nder," when addressing the survivor-witness Seydani before the suicide: "Thanks to you, this day of Tuesday will stand out from the records of the everyday [*sortira des tablettes du commun*] to become the 'Tuesday of Nder,' the most glorious day of our country."[92] The "resistance" of the women of Nder resides not only in the act of collective suicide itself but also in their decision to make a message of their suicide: to ensure that, in the child Sadani Caam, their bravery and self-sacrifice have an afterlife as (oral) text, as *nettali*.

Like Bèye's *Nder en flammes*, Diop's *Doomi Golo* represents and enacts this imperative to *tell the story* of suicidal resistance, both restaging and extending a long chain of re-entextualizations that originates with Seydani/Sadani. Sadani Caam emerges as the urtext of suicidal resistance, the original figure of transmission and translation: the small girl who escapes a burning village surrounded by marauders and lives to tell a story of collective suicide that will become a national epic of female resistance. In this, the *nettali* of Sadani Caam repeats and responds to the narrative project of the grandfather Ngiraan Fay—and ultimately Diop—who tells of a distant past and asks to be listened to on an act of faith, a fact made even more emphatic in the French translation: "But you will ask me, Badou, with the suspicious mind of young people today, 'Nguirane, if everyone died that Tuesday in Nder, how do you know the story you are telling me? Or should I believe you just because you are my grandfather?'"[93]

The *nettali* of Sadani Caam finds a corollary in the vagrant *dof* (madman) Aali Këbooy, whose unlikely speech contains a grain of truth. The epigraphs to the Book of Ashes (the first notebook of *Doomi Golo*, which contains the embedded Talaatay Nder narrative) and the final "notebook" (simply labeled *Ñaareelu xaaj*, or part II), in which Aali Këbooy's narration dominates, explicitly link these two unconventional narrators. As Repinecz points out, the epigraph of this first notebook (*Gone mat naa bàyyi cim réew*, "Children are worth keeping in the country/community") rewrites Kocc Barma's well-known proverb *Mag mat naa bàyyi cim réew* (Elders are worth keeping in the country/community) in favor of the figure of the *xale bu ndaw* (small child), notably Sadani Caam.[94]

The juxtaposition between the narrative authority of Kocc Barma and that of Sadani Caam becomes explicit when, returning to the framing address to his grandson after recounting the story of Nder, the grandfather presents Badu with the following choice between masculine gerontocratic tradition and the feminist alternative presented by the women of Nder:

> Ni Mbarka Ja doxalee de, safaanoo na bu baax ak kàddu yu siiw yooyu. Mbarka Ja, Yàlla mayoon na ko fit, may ko xel. Dékku na saay-saay ya songoon Ndeer. Te ba dara desul lu dul génn àddina, sooru na Kocc Barma Faal, boroom xam-xam bi kenn mësul a sañ a weddi. Ndax ni Mbarka Ja rawalee Sadani Caam, lii rekk la tekki:
> —Gone mat naa bàyyi cim réew....
> Lu cee sa xalaat, Badu? Sunu ñaari ponkal yooyu, koo ci àndal? Mbarka Ja walla Kocc Barma Faal?[95]

(The way in which Mbarka Ja acted is consistent with this famous account [*kàddu*]. Mbarka Ja, god gave her an unwavering force, and cunning. She confronted the bandits who attacked Nder. When all that was left was for her to die, she confronted Kocc Barma Faal, a *boroom xam-xam* whose wisdom no one could contest. The way in which Mbarka Ja saved Sadani Caam, it can be explained [*tekki*] thus: *Children are worth keeping in the community*....

What are your thoughts on this, Badu? Our two great thinkers Mbarka Ja and Kocca Barma Faal—which one are you for?)

Kocc Barma's proverb reappears as the epigraph to part II, this time with the substitution of *dof* (madman) for Kocc Barma's *mag* (elder) and the earlier *gone* (child): *Dof mat naa bàyyi cim réew* (Lunatics are worth keeping in the country/community). In this way, the epigraphs of *Doomi Golo* posit the voices of two subaltern and subversive figures—the young girl, the madman—as alternatives to traditional forms of narrative authority. Mbarka Ja places the responsibility of transmission not with the *boroom xam-xam* or *géwél*, but in the hands, or rather in the *mouth*, of a young child (*xale bu ndaw*), the small girl Sadani Caam. *They* will speak of *her*. Diop similarly presents Badu, and the reader, with a narrative paradox, leaving the last word to the madman who speaks in riddles.

In *Doomi Golo*, the survivor-witness Sadani Caam, the militant *bëkk-néég* Mbarka Ja, and the vagrant *dof* Aali Këbooy emerge as progressive alternatives to a masculinist, gerontocratic oral tradition exemplified by Kocc Barma. They allow Diop to repurpose "traditional" oral narratives as broadscale arguments for the participation of women, children, and the dispossessed in society and in the making of history.[96] At the same time, these characters point to larger questions about the status of the witness, the nature of narrative authority, and the conditions of literary production out of oral traditions, especially in the wake of suicide. The ashen figure of Sadani Caam is emblematic in this respect: through her, the Talaatay Nder gains an afterlife as oral text.

Ashes, Ashes

As if by a lexical sleight of hand, the Wolof phrase *dóómu Nder* flickers between two meanings: "the ashes of Nder" (*dóómu Nder*) and "the *child* of Nder" (*doomu Nder*). A figure of ash (*dóómu taal*), a "child of the flame" (*doomu taal*), Saydané/Seydani/Sadani responds to both meanings. She is the remnant or remainder of Nder: "what names one thing in the place of another [...] one thing while figuring another from which nothing figurable remains";[97] the one who miraculously lives on to tell the story that should not be able to be told, the story reduced to ash. She is an allegory of archive, of storytelling itself.

In the ashen figure of Sadani, made to signify the Talaatay Nder even as she is displaced from it, collective suicide and impossible testimony *become* literature. Doubly marked by age and gender as unreliable, she flees a burning village and asks to be believed on an act of faith. The mobile—and mutable—figure of Sadani throws into crisis the kinds of masculinist, gerontocratic wisdom represented by Kocc Barma. This conservative, consolidated notion of the embodied oral archive is exemplified by Amadou Hampâté Bâ's dictum, "Each time an elder dies, a library has burned down," cited as an epigraph to this chapter

ORAL ARCHIVES · 103

and versions of which abound. A fungible figure whose age and identity vary across oral accounts, Sadani provides a decisive challenge and compelling alternative to such modes of knowledge: when a city burns, a young girl rises. She carries the suicide archive with her, disperses it, and allows it to unfurl.

A translational figure of dissemination—of *cendre-semence*—Sadani bears witness to self-annihilation, to holocaust, and lives to tell the tale. She is a martyr in the truest sense: both the "witness" and the "proof" (*martus, marturos*).[98] Hers is a singular message of testimony and survival that risks "not being able to cross the frontier of its singularity, if only to deliver its meaning."[99] Yet it *must* be translated and transmitted to become testimony, to survive as (oral) text. Sadani embodies what Mary Ann Doane calls the "index" of the event—an assurance of its existence.[100] Through her, the Talaatay Nder is made present to us.[101] We receive her *nettali* not merely as "rumor" in the archive but as a story handed down across the centuries. Sadani functions as a cenotaph, figuring Nder's ground zero while marking the moment that the story of Nder rises from the ashes and begins to travel as text.

In becoming ash (*dóóm*) and leaving ash and only ash behind, the women of Nder stand to destroy any readily decipherable trace of the circumstances of their own death; they risk their message of resistance being consumed by the flames. "Ash," as Jacques Derrida reminds us, names what "annihilates or threatens to destroy even the possibility of bearing witness to annihilation."[102] It is the "figure of annihilation without remainder, without memory, or without a readable or decipherable archive."[103] A historical moment of *becoming-ash*, the "burning up or incineration of *a date*,"[104] the Tuesday of Nder should by its very nature preclude the possibility of its own remembrance and iteration as proper name, as Talaatay Nder. Collective suicide is an unreadable and self-sealing text, an absolute crypt. It should only leave behind a Book of Ashes (*téereb dóóm*), to recall the title of the first of the grandfather's notebooks in *Doomi Golo*.

Sadani responds to this paradox. The potentially unreadable traces of collective suicide find their cipher in the designated survivor. In the translational, disseminal figure of Sadani, the women of Nder set loose the *nettali* of collective suicide, sealing and unsealing the unreadable text of their suicide for future generations in a single movement. Sadani sutures a breach in the oral text's filiation. Both the message and its medium, she enables us—the text's belated readers—to decipher what was written in flame and effaced as ash. Bèye and Diop each repeat her gesture: reading suicide by re-citing it.

Conclusion: Fatima in Flames

I shall speak of ghost, of flame, and of ashes.
JACQUES DERRIDA, *De l'esprit: Heidegger et la question* (1987)

Through contemporary aesthetic works, the Talaatay Nder continues to signify and accumulate meanings in the present. In the wake of Bèye's and Diop's entextualizations of the Talaatay Nder, Senegalese author Mohamed Mbougar Sarr has contributed to the extensive literary afterlife of this event by reinscribing the Talaatay Nder in surprising terms near the end of his labyrinthine novel *La plus secrète mémoire des hommes* (2021). Like Bèye and Diop, Sarr makes the Talaatay Nder speak to present-day political concerns while staging a powerful confrontation between suicide and literature, memory and oblivion, history and fiction. In his novel, Sarr connects the women's collective suicide in 1820 to the myriad public self-burnings that spread throughout Senegal in the wake of Mohamed Bouazizi's widely mediatized self-immolation in Sidi Bouzid, Tunisia, in 2010. Rerouting conventional genealogies of fire protests through transhistorical and transnational links, Sarr connects Bouazizi's North African suicide archive to a preexisting local genealogy of self-immolation in Senegal, beginning with the Talaatay Nder.

The rhetorical force of Bouazizi's suicide in 2010 quickly spread beyond the so-called Arab world, sparking a "copycat" effect and a dramatic uptick in suicides by public self-burning across the globe, including in Senegal.[105] These self-immolations all draw their rhetorical and political force from their legibility in relation to an established suicidal idiom of self-burning as protest made more recognizable through Bouazizi's suicide archive. In February 2011, only a month after Bouazizi had died in the hospital from burn wounds, a Senegalese man set himself on fire on a sidewalk in Dakar while holding up a scrap of paper. Bystanders could not make out what was written on it, but the message of his suicide seemed clear: Bouazizi's suicide had begun to travel.[106] The same year, two men set themselves on fire outside the residence of the then-president, Abdoulaye Wade; in 2013, another man did the same under the presidency of the newly elected Macky Sall.[107] In the spring of 2013, three more individuals—young students from the Université Cheikh Anta Diop (UCAD)—set themselves on fire.[108] On 2 November 2018, Cheikh Diop lit himself on fire in front of President Sall's residence.[109] Before his self-immolation, he filmed a video recounting a painful history of imprisonment, house arrest, and amputation after a botched forced injection. A day later, a second fire protest occurred when a thirty-year-old carpenter named Baye Pouye self-immolated in Ndayane, near Popenguine.

This charged political context might not be immediately recognizable to readers as the backdrop of Sarr's novel. None of these public self-burnings in Senegal were reported widely by the foreign press. Moreover, much of Sarr's novel takes place in Paris, not Senegal. The novel follows the efforts of the narrator-protagonist, the budding writer Diégane Latyr Faye, to make sense of a highly public self-disappearance, a professional suicide of sorts: that of a mysterious Senegalese author, T. C. Elimane, who rose to the greatest heights of the French publishing world in the late 1930s before becoming embroiled in scandal, including accusations of plagiarism, and disappearing from public view.[110] While Sarr's novel is mostly set in Paris during the interwar years, the frame narrative centers on Faye's life in 2018. Near the end of the novel, in what appears initially as a somewhat unexpected interlude in the literary-historical investigation, political suicide by public self-burning suddenly erupts, and the narrative veers off course.

As Faye flies from home to Senegal for the first time in years, Dakar erupts in antigovernment protests and popular anger over the corruption of Macky Sall's government, increased police brutality, and widespread unemployment (I return to a reiteration of this scene in my conclusion, since demonstrations—and fires—broke out again in Dakar in summer 2023). In Sarr's novel, a young activist, Fatima Diop, captures the attention of the entire nation. In front of the Assemblée nationale—at a busy intersection in the Plateau area of Dakar, not far from the presidential palace—she props up her smartphone, presses "record," and steps into frame. She then douses herself in lighter fluid and sets herself on fire. Her death is live-streamed on social media from her phone, the video of her burning body seen across Senegal and around the globe.

By the time Faye lands in Dakar, Fatima has died. Mere hours after her death, she is being hailed as a West African Bouazizi—both a martyr and a terrifying "mirror" of a Senegalese society on the brink of revolution: "They look at her photo, they remember the images of her death, and right away they say to themselves: that could have been my daughter, my sister, my niece, my cousin, my wife, but above all, that could have been me."[111] For Sarr, the figure of Fatima in flames is terrible and paradigmatic. The fire that made her body a human torch channels the rage of an entire nation: "It is a fire of anger and humiliation, but also of extreme dignity." In Sarr's use of the word *dignity* (*dignité*) here, we should read the Wolof *jom*: the value the women of Nder sought, failing all else, to protect and uphold in their suicides.

Like Bouazizi, whose death almost immediately was assigned sacrificial and political connotations—as with the suicide of the women of Nder, whose "message" was swiftly redirected toward nationalist and masculinist ends—members of Senegalese society attempt to assign Fatima's suicide a stable meaning and control its signification. Imams and local religious leaders call for prayer and peace, while government officials say her death must not be politicized, deeming it an invitation for collective responsibility, not collective anger. Fatima's image and story begin to circulate. Widescale protests are organized in her honor.

For one character, Fatima's suicide is a signal and a call to action. In Sarr's novel, her suicide is followed by a second fire protest: that of Diop's former philosophy professor at UCAD, Chérif Ngaïdé, a childhood friend of the narrator who feels personally responsible for the young woman's death. The self-immolation of an African philosophy professor offers a harrowing counterpoint to Jackson's "philosophical suicide," discussed in my introduction.[112] Far from a lonely, contemplative, private death, Chérif's suicide is a violent public response to his student's impossible "lesson."

As the city marches in honor of Fatima's "sacrifice," Chérif prepares to honor her by repeating her gesture: "There is only one way to atone [*payer*]," he writes to Faye. "It's to carry out exactly the same gesture."[113] Fearing the worst, Faye rushes to his friend's apartment in Liberté 6 to discover a scene of horror: roiling smoke, the smell of burning flesh, screams made inhuman with pain. Like Fatima, Chérif broadcasted his self-immolation, having opened Facebook Live and pressed "record." On the live-stream, the horror of a body on fire is augmented by the tragedy of Faye, along with Chérif's neighbors, trying to recover his burning body and put out the flames.

The Talaatay Nder is evoked in Chérif's digital suicide note. In the text message sent to Faye shortly before his self-immolation, Chérif recalls a conversation with Fatima and lays out a genealogy of suicidal resistance spanning the last two centuries, connecting the self-immolations of Bouazizi, Jan Palach (the Czech student who burned himself during the Prague Spring), and the Vietnamese monk Thích Quảng Đức to the women of Nder:

> In a country like ours, suicide was a horrible but effective mode of political action, effective because horrible, perhaps the only protest still audible to our rulers. Suicide sometimes changes the course of history: look at Mohamed Bouazizi in Tunisia in 2011, look at Jan Palach in Czechoslovakia in '69, Thích Quảng Đức in Vietnam in '63, not to mention the mythic suicide of the women of Nder, who preferred to kill themselves by fire in a hut rather than surrender to the colonizers. All of these suicides provoked an effect [*un retentissement*], shook the spirits, had a political signification. Maybe that is all that remains for the populations of our desperate countries. Maybe that is what the youth must do: kill themselves [*se suicider*], because their life is not a life . . .[114]

Chérif's expansive genealogy of suicidal resistance articulated near the end of Sarr's novel models the associative drift, fungible nature, and subversive potential of suicide archives. In Sarr's rewriting, the Talaatay Nder is framed as an act of anticolonial resistance and as a political language in extremis: a "horrible but effective" idiom available to desperate countries and young people betrayed and abandoned by their governments.

It is ultimately the figure of the writer-narrator, Faye, who has the last word on suicide in Sarr's novel. He must bear witness in writing to the deaths of Fatima and Chérif in a way that is both necessary and terribly inadequate. In the novel, Faye is confronted virtually by activists and protesters. His utility as a writer and public intellectual is questioned in the face of widespread social unrest. An incensed activist writes to him on Facebook: "*What do you think of all this? What are the writers doing? You are the voices of the voiceless! Why this silence?*"[115] Faye is plagued by the futility of his own project in the face of actual suffering and haunted by the reality that the obscene spectacle of a body on fire has voiced a message more powerfully than any text he might write. The disgraced and shadowy writer Elimane suddenly pales in comparison to the figure of Fatima in flames: "Faced with what was happening[,] ... what was the question of writing worth before that of the suffering of a nation? The quest for the essential book before the aspiration to essential dignity? Literature before politics? Elimane before Fatima?"[116] Fatima's public and viral suicide contrasts starkly with Elimane's covert gesture of refusal, his disappearance from public view. Her death, like the deaths of the women of Nder, throws into crisis the very project of literature, of writing. When individuals are prepared to burn themselves alive, what is there left to say? Their suicides would seem to be proof that articulate language is not enough.

THE COLLECTIVE SUICIDE OF the women of Nder haunts the following chapter, which recasts and rereads two well-known portrayals of suicide in African literature and cinema, Ousmane Sembène's black-and-white film *La Noire de . . .* (1966) and the short story "La Noire de . . ." (1962) on which it was based. At a juncture between a colonial and postcolonial moment in this study, Sembène's text and film form the midpoint of this book. Indeed, Sembène's short story, set in 1958, and his film, which takes place in the 1960s, straddle Senegalese Independence (1960).

These works mark a transition in *The Suicide Archive* from a focus on collective to individual suicide and the immediate historical contexts of French slavery and colonization to their afterlives and enduring legacies. Chapter 3 deals with a suicide in France on the eve of Senegalese Independence and its reverberations in the following decades. The world of Sembène's protagonist, Diouana, is one with which we have become familiar: a transnational space of migration. Much like Fatou Diome's Salie, Diouana finds herself torn between her native Senegal and France, which is both the "promised land" and the kingdom of her exile. Like Kanor and Diome, Sembène gestures carefully to the imbrication of Diouana's story with other histories—past and present. These include histories of Atlantic and African slavery—narratives of resistance exemplified by the suicides of the women of *Le Soleil* and Nder—as well as the Algerian War of Independence, which, as Sembène was writing, had reached hallucinatory levels of violence. The opening lines of his 1962 short story make a pointed reference to the intertwined fates of Algeria and Senegal; in 1962, Senegal had only just gained independence, and Algeria's future was far from certain.

The oral archive of the resistance of Nder, the specter of slave suicide, and the cultural-historical space of the Black Atlantic all continue to shadow this inquiry as both afterimage and aftereffect. They remain especially powerful intertexts in Sembène's text and film. Long after the flames have died down and the ashes have scattered in the wind, ghosts remain.

III

The promiscuity of the archive begets a wide array
of reading, but none [...] are capable of resuscitating the girl.

SAIDIYA HARTMAN, "Venus in Two Acts" (2008)

III

· 3 ·

SCREEN MEMORIES

Ousmane Sembène's *Black Girl* between
Image, Icon, and Archive

How do we reckon with what modern history has rendered ghostly?

AVERY GORDON, *Ghostly Matters* (1997)

Arrivals

The opening frames of Senegalese author and filmmaker Ousmane Sembène's black-and-white film *La Noire de . . .* (1966) quickly home in on the protagonist and title character Diouana (played by Mbissine Thérèse Diop, b. 1949) as she arrives in the Port of Marseille on the French liner MV *Ancerville*.[1] The first four minutes of *La Noire de . . .* are a masterclass in efficient portraiture as the camera tracks Diouana/Diop in a high-wire shot crossing the ship's narrow gangway, gliding through customs, and navigating a crowded baggage claim area. At this point, we do not yet know her name, but already we are invested in who she is and where she is going. Within seconds, this character has our focus, attention, and empathy. She will hold these throughout the film.

By contrast, Sembène's original short story "La Noire de..." (1962), on which his film was based, opens with a trove of dispassionate male officials and onlookers descending on a crime scene at a shabby villa in the resort town of Antibes, in the south of France. This group of white men—the magistrate, medical examiners, detectives and police officers, a photographer, three journalists—converges at Villa Le Bonheur Vert to observe and record traces of a grisly death: a ladder leaned against the house; a shattered windowpane; two sobbing women; a pool of blood.

As detectives and police begin asking questions and taking notes, two stretcher-bearers appear carrying a body covered in cloth. For a moment, the investigators stop writing and simply look: "Blood dripped onto the steps. The examining judge lifted a fold of cloth, furrowed his brow. A Black woman [*une Noire*] lay on the stretcher, her throat slit from one ear to the other."[2] In the short story, the image of Diouana's body on a stretcher beneath a pall is the only image of her in the narrative present. Her story comes to us as an extended flashback, recounted from the perspective of her employer, the "Madame," one of the two sobbing women who, prompted by the detectives' questions, "little by little, sank into her memories."[3] Diouana appears in the first pages of the story as a dead woman hidden beneath a shroud. When Sembène returns us to the frame narrative at the end of the story, Diouana's case is closed, and she has been reduced to a mere bit of text tucked away in the back pages of the local newspaper:

> The detectives concluded "suicide." The case was closed.
> The next day, the dailies published on page four, column six, barely visible:
> "In Antibes, a nostalgic Black woman [*une Noire nostalgique*] slits her throat."[4]

From a narrative standpoint, this structure is effective. By beginning at the end, so to speak—with the discovery of a body—Sembène's text, as Dominic Thomas writes, makes the reader "responsible for *recovering* the narrative and locating the suicidal impulse."[5] And as Reij M. Rosello suggests, Sembène "invites us to take the place of those 'investigators' and of the 'journalists' who did not know how to tell the story."[6] But will we know how to tell the story?

This chapter reopens the case of Sembène's Diouana in text and on-screen. It examines a complex instance of the "screening" of suicidal resistance in African literature and cinema by offering a forensic reading of Sembène's short story, "La Noire de...," first published in the collection *Voltaïque* (1962) and translated into English as "The Promised Land" in *Tribal Scars* (1974), and its film adaptation as *La Noire de...* (1966) / *Black Girl* (2017). Sembène's text and film are suicide archives hiding in plain sight: records of the real life and death of a Senegalese woman, Diouana Gomis (1927–58), whose suicide paradoxically has been screened (projected) across the globe and screened (blocked) from view—buried in the colonial archive. Reading between literature, film, and archive, I show how Sembène's text and film trouble and preserve access to an unimaged history that has remained off-screen and out of frame.

Extending the theoretical reflection and critical imperative developed in chapters 1 and 2, I argue for the need to take seriously the capacity of aesthetic works to recover, however imperfectly, stories of resistance that have been "screened" out of history. By tracking the multiform processes of forgetting that have accompanied Sembène's text and film, I highlight how acts of recovery can also *cover over*, demonstrating how these works function variously as cipher, sepulcher, cenotaph, and screen. I read these much-discussed works as crypto or covert genres: both coded, "encrypted" versions of a history that otherwise recedes from view and works that partake of the crypt (*crypta, kruptos*). Sembène's *La Noire de...* is the burial place for a body that was never buried. His text and film are lamentations for the dead.

Silver Screen Memories

Few early African films have exerted the same enduring influence on African and Afro-diasporic visual culture as *La Noire de....* First screened at Cannes in 1966, the film won the Prix Jean Vigo as well as best feature at the Festival of Black Arts the year it was released. Typically hailed as the first *long métrage* or feature-length film by a sub-Saharan African director, and the first to be screened widely outside Africa, it is with *La Noire de...* that Sembène—previously known for his novels and short films, *Borom Sarret* (1963) and *Niaye* (1964)—began to cement his status as the father of African cinema.[7]

Sembène's text and film stage a Black African woman's response to conditions of neoslavery, portraying a young and initially idealistic Senegalese woman named Diouana (played by a seventeen-year-old Diop in the film) who is hired in Dakar by a white French family to work as a maid and nanny. When the family returns to their home in Antibes, Diouana goes with them—only to find herself isolated, mistreated, and subjected to racism, psychological abuse, and pervasive anti-Blackness. As she says in both the textual and cinematic versions, her employers treat her "like a slave." Unwilling to tolerate her degrading "enslavement" in France, Diouana slits her throat in the bathroom of her employers' home and dies. The text and film ironize how, the following day, the suicide of "a young Negress from Dakar" is reported coldly by local newspapers, buried among other *faits divers*—which, in French, designates a short, often sensational news item, though not one of particular importance (figures 3.1 and 3.2).

Sembène's text and film comment explicitly on the screening of Black death by the French press, nodding to how the suicide of the protagonist, Diouana, is back-page news. But few people, besides scholars and biographers of Sembène, are aware that his text and film were inspired by a real newspaper report about the death of a young Senegalese woman named Diouana Gomis living in France in the 1950s, a fact Sembène acknowledged in interviews.[8] Early press around the film—even if it considered Sembène's film visually compelling and found Diop's performance as Diouana moving—tended to view *La Noire de . . .* as a neorealist parable and allegory of postcolony. Reviewing the film in 1967 in the left-wing Paris daily edited by Albert Camus, *Combat*, Henry Chapier deemed it "sentimental and naive." In terms that recall the callousness and racism Sembène associates with the French press in his own text and film, Chapier concluded flippantly, "It's up to the audience to glean the moral of the sad adventure of Douana [*sic*], who kills herself in the bathtub of an HLM in Antibes because they asked her to make the coffee in a coarse tone of voice."[9] A year after its debut at Cannes, less than a decade after the real death of Diouana Gomis, Sembène's film already was received—and reviewed—as a "purely" aesthetic object, such that the real tragedy it brought to view either was already forgotten or was deemed a bit of cinephile trivia of little consequence for the film's reception and of little relevance to its public. The power of the "screen" had taken hold.

Of course, Sembène's text and film succeed *as* aesthetic works largely for their managing of distance between representation and historical subject, between "content" and "screen." At the same time, to read Sembène within a Black radical and Black feminist tradition and to read his works as suicide archives—as this chapter proposes to do—is to attend to how Sembène's text and film perform the work of recuperation and mourning against the grain of colonial discourses that, on the one hand, cause Black death to disappear from view or, on the other hand, make death the condition of visibility for Black subjectivity. This does not mean instrumentalizing the aesthetic as a straightforward historical record of suicidal resistance; rather, it involves grappling with how the aesthetic remakes history—*puts pressure on the making of history*—by way of suicidal resistance.

Until 2022—six decades after the appearance of Sembène's short story—scholars had not tracked down a copy of the original report that inspired the film or excavated the backstory of African cinema's best-known suicide.[10] My

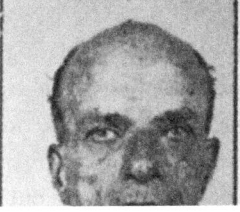

FIGURES 3.1 AND 3.2. Stills from *Black Girl* (2017) (*les faits divers*). Source: Criterion Collection.

own path to uncovering the "hard facts" behind Sembène's *La Noire de . . .* and trying to learn something about the life and death of Gomis meant reconciling evidentiary traces of a real tragedy with its powerful "screen memory." This gap in scholarship on Sembène's text and film cannot easily be attributed to a dearth of information. The story of Diouana Gomis has always been there. At least some details have been decipherable in Sembène's text since its publication and available on-screen since the film's release. The *fait divers* that Sembène shows briefly, and only partially, in a close-up shot near the end of his film, is no ordinary prop: it is a copy of the original newspaper report from the 1950s that inspired the film and that Sembène kept for almost a decade before filming. Contextual details—dates, toponyms, names—included in the short story are enough to enable anyone, given a little detective work, to unravel Sembène's process and follow *La Noire de . . .* back to its source. But the lacuna in scholarship on *La Noire de . . .* cannot be written off as the result of sheer critical lassitude and oversight. Such a gap is better explained by the pervasive and persistent forgetting that accompanies the production and circulation of what media historian Marita Sturken calls the "single-image icon."[11] It is symptomatic of the workings of what I will term a "(silver) screen memory" to describe how a widely available and visually accessible cinematic work has become a mnemic image and cover for something else—in this case, a real tragedy buried in French archives.

The (silver) screen memory limns the ways images produce forgetting. This may appear paradoxical. Images are technologies of memory. They serve as an *aide-mémoire*. But as Sturken suggests, the relationship of the image—especially the camera image—to memory and to history is one of contradiction and, occasionally, interference. "On the one hand," Sturken writes, "camera images can embody and create memories; on the other hand, they have the capacity, through the power of their presence, to obliterate other, unphotographed memories."[12] Iconic, widely recognizable images such as Sembène's film can obscure, block, or displace less well-known images. As Sturken puts it, a "single-image icon can *screen out* images of a historical event."[13] The screen becomes the memory, becomes history.

The term *screen memory* itself comes from psychoanalysis, originating in the early work of Sigmund Freud. It relates directly to the meanings of "resistance" (as opposition to recovery and to analysis) discussed in my introduction and taken up again in chapter 4. Shortly before the appearance of *The Interpretation of Dreams* (1900), during a period of intense self-analysis, Freud published a short text about the dubious nature of childhood memory formation. In "Screen Memories" (1899), Freud questions whether we have access to childhood memory at all, suggesting that the memories available to our consciousness are mere "screens," records of another psychical element that become associated with the original event:

> What is recorded as a mnemic image is not the relevant experience itself—in this respect the resistance gets in the way; what is recorded is another psychical element closely associated with the objectionable one. [...] Instead of the mnemic image which would have been justified by the original event, another is produced which has been to some degree associatively *displaced* from the former one.[14]

Freud continues: "A number of motives, *with no concern for historical accuracy*, had a part in forming [the screen memories], as well as in the selection of the memories themselves."[15] Freud's concept of "screen memories," or *Deckerinnerungen* (literally, "cover memories"), is essentially defensive: a screen memory displaces the record of an original event to protect the psyche from "objectionable" content. In comparison to the raw material from which it was forged, the screen memory is extremely well-remembered and unusually vivid. There is much to be said about Freud's early formulation of screen memories, but two aspects are especially relevant here: first, the idea that the screen is yet another example of how resistance always *gets in the way* and poses problems for analysis, in this case by blocking access to the record of an earlier event; second, the fact that the psychical forces involved in producing the screen are not beholden to "historical accuracy" but respond to other motives.

In his work on postwar memory in France during the age of decolonization, Michael Rothberg argues for an expansion of traditional uses of Freud's notion, suggesting that rereading Freud invites us to consider how screen memories operate "multi-directionally," continuing to provide indirect access to the content of an original event and laying bare the multilayered forms of forgetting implicit in processes of remembering. For Rothberg, a screen memory "illustrates concretely how a *kind of forgetting accompanies acts of remembrance*, but this kind of forgetting is subject to recall."[16] Screen memories "provide access to truths [...] that produce insight about individual and collective processes of meaning-making."[17] Following Rothberg, scholars such as Kristen Ross and Lia Brozgal point to how "screen memories" operate on national scales, showing that less visible memories often underwrite official, state-sanctioned narratives in French imperial history.[18] The insights of Rothberg, Ross, and Brozgal further align with philosopher Avishai Margalit's observation in *The Ethics of Memory* that *shared memory* "is built on a division of mnemonic labor," requiring consensus and convergence within and across mediascapes.[19]

Consensus and convergence necessarily imply elements of distortion and loss. As a shared "screen memory," Sembène's *La Noire de...* enters into a very peculiar relation to memory, history, and archive, because it both documents and displaces an unimaged event. The text and film have become such "iconic," widely circulated works—the former a masterpiece of African literature in French, the latter a hallmark of African and Afro-diasporic visual culture—that they ceased to be viewed as bearing witness to a real tragedy. The figure of Diouana has become thoroughly synonymous with Sembène's literary and cinematic character. This has meant that the real woman whose death Sembène's text and film attempted to rescue from silence and insignificance has remained hidden from view—screened by the very images intended to keep her memory alive. But Sembène's "Noire de..." is not Léopold Sédar Senghor's allegorical "Femme Noire."[20] She is not—or at least, was not initially—a symbol or icon, the object of someone else's discourse. She most certainly could not have known her suicide would change the face of African cinema.

The Diouana we see on-screen is the memory-trace of a real person: a thirty-one-year-old Senegalese woman named Diouana Gomis. Born in 1927 in Boutoupa, in the Ziguinchor region of Senegal where Sembène was born four years earlier, she was hired in Dakar as a maid for a family of white French colonists. Gomis could not read or write, spoke little French, and had never received any professional training or formal education. When her employers, the Petit family, left Dakar for an extended stay in Antibes, she went with them. She arrived in Antibes in April 1958 and died by suicide only a few months later, on 22 June 1958. Her death was reported the following day in the *faits divers* section of the local newspaper, *Le Nice-Matin*.

Although Sembène's *La Noire de...* functions as a screen memory for the real life and death of Gomis, the film furnishes the interpretive tools necessary to keep her memory alive and to engage it in the present. To echo Rothberg's observation, the forgotten or repressed content is "subject to recall": screens might obscure, but they might also become "levers" for evoking other, less visible histories.[21] Indeed, in modern (medical) usage, "to screen" means to examine, investigate, or test. *Screening* Sembène's *La Noire de...* invites us to search and scrutinize the archive of colonization—to try to glean from it what Jessica Marie Johnson calls "a black feminine presence."[22] What is screened need not be forgotten.

An illiterate maid seduced by the chimeric "promised land" of France seems an unlikely successor to the female warriors of Nder or the highly public political suicide of Fatima Diop in *La plus secrète mémoire des hommes*. However, like the *lingeers* Fatim Yamar and Mbarka Ja—as well as the anonymous women of *Le Soleil*—Diouana resists and rejects captivity by exercising the power to die. Like the women of Nder and the women of *Le Soleil*, Diouana's suicide also gave rise to multiple "texts"—as *fait divers*, short story, and film— that signify surreptitiously long after her death. In the case of the Talaatay Nder, although the women destroy all physical trace of their death in becoming ash, they ensure that their suicide has an afterlife as oral text in the figure of the impossible witness and *conteuse* (storyteller), Seydani. For Diouana, her body *is* the text. Her suicide figures an opaque message of resistance and refusal when no other means will get through. Though illiterate, at the moment of her death Diouana, paradoxically, becomes a *writer* and a historical subject. While her final act takes the form of a radical self-silencing, severing the very organs of speech, Sembène helps us to read her suicide—*hear* her silence—as a scream.

Marseille, 1958

The story of how a real suicide in June 1958 became the basis for an iconic early African film begins in the South of France in the late 1950s. At the time, Sembène was living in Marseille, where he had arrived a decade earlier at the age of twenty-three as a stowaway aboard the packing ship *Pasteur* after being discharged from the French Free Forces.[23] For years, Sembène worked as a docker in the Old Port of Marseille, unloading ships at the Place de la Joliette, Quay J3, Gate 25—an experience chronicled in his first novel, *Le docker noir* (*The Black Docker*, 1956).[24] By day, he performed the dehumanizing work of a *chien des quais*, or wharf rat (literally, "wharf dog"), lifting heavy ropes, anchor chains, sacks, and crates in difficult conditions.[25] By night and on the weekends, Sembène was educating himself and honing a burgeoning political consciousness. He joined the Confédération Générale du Travail (CGT) and devoured Marxist and antiracist texts.

During the postwar years, the labor of a docker in Marseille was synonymous with racism, exploitation, and abject poverty—if not outright neoslavery, in which predominantly Black African workers were compelled to work inhuman hours.[26] The work was backbreaking. In 1951, a heavy sack landed on Sembène, breaking several of his vertebrae.[27] He never fully recovered from the injury. No longer able to work as a docker, Sembène was transferred to the post of *aiguilleur* (switchman). The position allowed him to dedicate more time to his education and political activism, especially his militancy for the CGT. He joined the French Communist Party as well as the Mouvement contre le racisme et pour l'amitié entre les peuples and began regularly attending their meetings and workshops. He borrowed books from the libraries of the CGT, agitated for the Algerian National Liberation Front (Front de Liberation Nationale, FLN), and organized for other decolonial and antiracist causes.[28] Sembène's political activism in Marseille in the 1950s occurred against the backdrop of the independence movements sweeping the African continent and the anticolonial war raging in Algeria (1954–62).

In the aftermath of his injury, Sembène also began to write. In 1956, he published the panegyric "Liberté" in a special issue of the local militant workers' journal, *Action Poétique*, and drafted his first novel, *Le docker noir* (1956), which he published at his own expense.[29] The following year, he published his second novel, *Ô pays, mon beau peuple* (1957), about a Senegalese soldier who returns from France to Casamance (the region in southern Senegal where Sembène was born) with a white French wife. He was already at work on his third novel, *Les bouts de bois de Dieu* (1960), about the 1947–48 miner strikes along the railroad connecting Dakar and Bamako, as well as several short stories for the collection *Voltaïque* (1962), in which "La Noire de..." first appeared. Sembène would not make his first films—the shorts *Borom Sarret* (1963) and *Niaye* (1964)—until returning to Senegal after Independence (1960), when he eventually opened his own production company, Filmi Doomi Reew (Films of the Country's Children).

The summer of 1958 was a key moment in the history of French-colonized Africa and for Pan-African movements more generally. In France, the "May 1958 crisis" restored Charles De Gaulle to power as the Algerian War of Independence reached catastrophic levels of violence. Months later, the fate of French West Africa would be debated as part of the "1958 Referendum," during which president Léopold Sédar Senghor campaigned for Senegal to maintain its ties with France and remain French-speaking, an option Sembène vehemently opposed. Independence would have to wait another two years.[30]

In the opening lines of his short story, Sembène makes direct reference to this highly charged political context, connecting multiple histories of resistance and colonizing violence by evoking the entangled fates of France, Algeria, and African nations on the verge of Independence: "On the Croisette, neither the destiny of the French Republic, nor the future of Algeria, any more than territories under the thumb of the colonists, worried those who, early that morning, invaded the beach of Antibes."[31] By beginning his short story with these transnational links and insisting on the disinterestedness of the unsuspecting French coastal city of Antibes, Sembène positions Diouana's suicide as a fissure in the façade of French empire.

It was during this period of creative production and political militancy that Sembène came across a short but striking news item in the regional daily newspaper *Le Nice-Matin*. Above the fold, on page 3 of the Tuesday, 24 June 1958, issue,

FIGURE 3.3. The original *fait divers* report from the Tuesday, 24 June 1958, issue of *Le Nice-Matin*. Source: Bibliothèque nationale de France (GR FOL-JO-4126, 1958/06/17-1958/08).

among other *faits divers*, Sembène found a report about the apparent suicide of a young Senegalese woman, Gomis Diouana (her name was cited as Sembène's often was, with the surname first) (figure 3.3). The headline read: "In Antibes, a young Negress slits her throat in her employers' bathroom." This *fait divers* about a suicide on the eve of Independence was Sembène's "rumor in the archive."[32]

From Fait Divers to Fiction

The suicide of Diouana Gomis, as originally reported in a *fait divers* of the *Nice-Matin*, became the basis for Sembène's short story, "La Noire de . . ." (1962), the text he later adapted as his first feature film *La Noire de . . .* (1966). Based in Marseille, just a few hours west of Antibes along the coast, Sembène could only have come across the report of Gomis's death in the *Nice-Matin*, which served as the daily newspaper for the entire Nice and Provence-Alpes-Côte-d'Azur region in southeast France. The local press in Antibes and neighboring Grasse, as well as smaller papers closer to Marseille, did not pick up the story.

As a journalistic rubric and something of a catchall category, the *fait divers* lacks a perfect equivalent in the English-speaking press.[33] These short news items document all manner of accidents, disasters, crimes, and tragedies. Often sensational or scandalous in nature, they frequently border on the grisly and macabre. For Roland Barthes, the *fait divers* is "monstrous information"— anomic *varia* that cannot be accommodated under other categories.[34] For Pierre Bourdieu, the genre is, true to its etymology, a form of *diversion*: sensationalist and depoliticized news items—"omnibus facts"—that simultaneously attract and divert notice.[35]

One of the defining features of this journalistic genre that defies definition is its proximity to literature. As Sandrine Boudana writes, the *fait divers* "shares many characteristics with fictional, and especially literary, genres."[36] Indeed, the *fait divers* is always already a kind of fiction. The genre has frequently given rise to fiction—serving as the inspiration for novels such as Stendhal's *Le rouge et le noir* (1830), Gustave Flaubert's *Madame Bovary* (1857), and Leo Tolstoy's *Anna Karenina* (1877).[37] Sembène's *La Noire de . . .* offers an African take on this literary tradition.

The *fait divers* from the *Nice-Matin* that inspired *La Noire de . . .* is, in other words, a protoliterary document. It is where the entextualization and *mise-en-fiction* of the suicide of Diouana Gomis begins. Transcribed in full, the original report reads as follows:

In Antibes

A young negress slits her throat in her employers' bathroom.

Gomis Diouana, a young negress from Dakar, ended her days on Sunday, around 1 p.m., by slitting her throat in her employer's bathroom [*de sa patronne*].

When colonists returning to France had secured the services of the young Gomis Diouana, who was born in Boutoupa, Senegal, they certainly did not think their maid would be homesick [*aurait le mal du pays*] to the point of slitting her throat one melancholic day [*un jour de cafard*]. Speaking little French and therefore avoiding sharing her fatal [*funeste*] decision with them, they were the first to be pained and surprised by her gesture.

It was 1 p.m. and all was calm at the Villa "Le Bonheur vert" on Chemin de l'Ermitage. In Antibes, a calm before the storm it would seem, since Mme Petit, not finding her maid in the villa, went to the bathroom, which she found locked. Sensing some misfortune, Mme Petit called on a neighbor who, using a ladder, was able to see what was happening in the bathroom from outside. A grisly scene [*un spectacle macabre*] presented itself to him: Gomis Diouana lay on the ground, bathed in her own blood. Beside her was a large blade, with which she had slit her throat.

Police commissioner Tessier [*sic*], assisted by the O.P.A. Alavena [*sic*], summoned in haste, could merely confirm the death of the young negress who had passed away far from her native bush [*sa brousse natale*].

Never before had she displayed such nostalgia [*une nostalgie*] to resort to this last extreme. She could have returned to her home, her ticket being in accordance with the laws, purchased in her name, and at her disposal.

Sembène's text and film inscribe their origins in this real news article. The short story concludes by alluding to the entextualization of Diouana's suicide as *fait divers*, adapting the headline of the original report: "The next day, the dailies published on page four, column six, barely visible 'In Antibes, a nostalgic Black woman [*une Noire nostalgique*] slits her throat.'"[38] The specific *fait divers* referenced in Sembène's short story ("page four, column six") corresponds to a different report of another mysterious death in the bath in the same issue.[39] In the film, Sembène shows a brief close-up of the original broadsheet, although the date of the issue is not visible and only the first half of the *fait divers* is somewhat legible.

Reading the original *fait divers* of Diouana Gomis's suicide allows us to appreciate how closely Sembène hews to the details—and the language—of the original report in his story. Sembène follows the timeline outlined in the *fait divers* almost exactly, beginning his short story on 23 June 1958, the day after the actual suicide and the day before the death was reported in the paper. He reiterates the same details of how Diouana's body was discovered: a neighbor called to assist with a ladder glimpsed Gomis through the bathroom window (a "macabre spectacle," the journalist writes in the *Nice-Matin*). Sembène even partially includes the real family's surname—blanked out in the short story as "P . . ."—as well as the names of the villa (Le Bonheur Vert) and street (Chemin de l'Ermitage) where they lived.

In Sembène's short story, such proper names and toponyms take on an evident literary quality. The elided surnames ("Mme P . . ." and "Mlle D . . . ," Madame's sister) recall the ellipsis of the title, "La Noire de . . . ," but also the tradition of eliding names in many nineteenth- and eighteenth-century texts. In this respect, an obvious intertext would be Claire de Duras's novella *Ourika* (1823)—also based on a true story—about an enslaved Senegalese girl brought to France and given as a "gift" to a certain "Madame de B.," whose friend is "La marquise de . . ." Moreover, when we first meet Ourika, she is being treated for

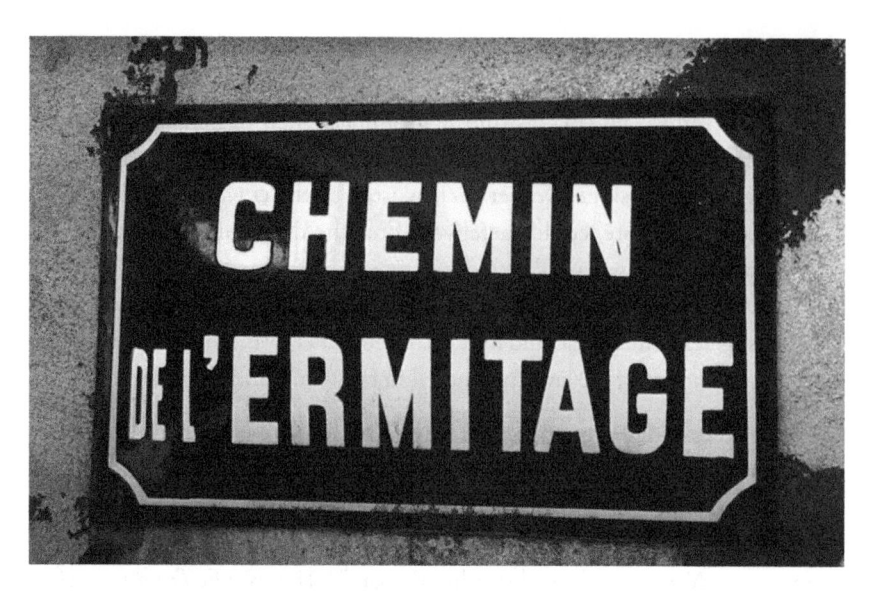

FIGURE 3.4. Still from *Black Girl* (2017) (*street sign*). Source: Criterion Collection.

"melancholia" (Diouana's diagnosis is "nostalgia" and *cafard*, or depression/melancholy).[40] The names of the villa (Le Bonheur Vert) and the street (Chemin de l'Ermitage) dramatize, on the one hand, Diouana's naive vision of the verdant "promised land" of France and, on the other hand, the isolated, "hermetic" nature of her existence in Antibes. They prepare her eventual deception and disenchantment when France proves a mirage: as Sembène writes, "The villa 'Le Bonheur Vert' had nothing green about it except its name."[41] In the film, we glimpse an enamel street sign that reads "Chemin de l'Ermitage," shortly before Diouana becomes cloistered in a sterile, white-walled apartment (figure 3.4).

These names are not, in fact, of Sembène's own invention; they are evidence of his forensic attention to real-life detail. Along with the term *nostalgie*—which Sembène uses in the short story and as the title for the poem appended to it—the various toponyms come directly from the text of the *fait divers*. The villa and street exist in the La Salis neighborhood of Antibes to this day, down a narrow gravel path between the Impasse des Œillets and the Traverse Rinaudo (figures 3.5 and 3.6).

According to architectural plans conserved in the Archives municipales in Antibes, the real Villa Le Bonheur Vert was built in the 1930s by a certain Jean Petit, presumably the father of Gomis's eventual employer.[42] Renderings drawn up by a local architectural firm, the *frères* Bartoletti, show a first floor containing the Petit family's living quarters (two bedrooms, a dining room, kitchen,

FIGURES 3.5 AND 3.6. Images of the Chemin de l'Ermitage (*top*) and Villa Le Bonheur Vert (*bottom*) (Antibes, France, 2021). Photos by author.

and bathroom) and a lower level consisting of a laundry room and cellar. It is likely that Diouana shared a bedroom with the Petit children since one of the bedrooms would have been occupied by Mme Petit. Sembène suggests as much in his short story. Implying Diouana was part of the family, Madame tells the detective, "I don't know why she killed herself. She was treated well [*bien traitée*] here, ate the same food, shared my children's bedroom."[43] In Madame's words, we should not miss an ironic play on *traiter*, which means both "to treat" and, in the case of slavery, "to trade." The reality is that Diouana was most likely anything but "well treated." The bathroom in which she died was probably the only room in the house where she had access to some fleeting semblance of privacy. If she were trying to escape any kind of abuse, it was perhaps the only door she could lock.

The Petit family sold the villa in the 1960s, shortly after Gomis's death. The new owners, a certain Monsieur and Madame Jean Valézy, renovated the existing structure, nearly doubling the square footage on one side. Today the house is well maintained. The cream-colored stucco is bright, the terra-cotta roof tiles look almost new; a pool has been added on the grounds, behind manicured hedges. Only the imposing gatepost, the name "Le Bonheur Vert" scrawled into cracked cement, shows visible signs of wear. Despite the many renovations, the bathroom in which Diouana Gomis died is still visible on the south-facing façade.

The *fait divers* ultimately sheds light on Sembène's many transpositions in moving from *fait divers* to short story to film. The film rewrites the short story, which rewrites the *fait divers*. For instance, in the film, Sembène retains the street name, which we see in a close-up shot early on, but abandons the villa setting, opting for a white-walled apartment that better dramatizes the carceral confines of Diouana's life in Antibes, where blinding whiteness surrounds her on all sides. In the film, Sembène avoids the voyeuristic spectacle of a neighbor peering in through the bathroom window but makes the suicide scene—a high-angle shot of Diouana in the bathtub—the film's striking visual climax.

Reading the original report of Diouana Gomis's suicide in context also brings into focus the ethical stakes of Sembène's project in *La Noire de....* In the same issue of *Nice-Matin*, other tragedies were reported. To the right of the *fait divers* describing the suicide of Diouana Gomis—and visible in the close-up shot of the report in Sembène's film—is another apparent suicide of an immigrant worker: the death by hanging of an Italian laborer, Magno Durbano, found suspended from a tree in the Bois d'Antibes with his working papers in his pocket. The reported suicide of Durbano resonates eerily with the grisly history of lynching by public hanging in Europe and America. Read together, the suicides of Gomis and Durbano appear as part of a more pervasive problem, not limited to anti-Blackness. This would support the broader Marxist critique made by Sembène's cinema and fiction, which highlight the racism experienced by immigrant laborers and the exploitation of the subjugated working classes. It corresponds to Thomas's observation about the way Sembène constantly "mediates" between the rhetoric of migration labor and slavery, a point I return to later in this chapter.[44]

The other suicides, accidents, and crimes reported in the same issue of the *Nice-Matin* nearly all have a "suite," however. They are followed up on, their intrigues reprised and expanded in subsequent issues. Even the case of Durbano is left "open," the title containing a suggestive ellipsis: "Hanged man discovered in the woods of Antibes ... but we still don't know the cause of the suicide." The story of the drowning of a two-year-old French boy, Yves Guillaume, tracked across at least three issues, is a further case in point. In the same issue as the *fait divers* recounting Diouana's suicide, the discovery of his body along the coast is reported on the front page, above the fold, with a portrait. By contrast, Gomis—identified merely as "a young negress" (*une jeune négresse*) in the title of the *fait divers* and in the text of the article—is barely a blip on the radar of the French press. Her story immediately falls out of frame, screened by the front-page focus on the drowning of a white child. The *Nice-Matin* published no follow-up. As Sembène writes in the short story, "The case was closed" (*On classa le dossier*).

In its genesis as *fait divers*, Sembène's *La Noire de*... can be considered a result of what Marcel Proust memorably termed "that abominable and voluptuous act that is called *reading the paper*."[45] Sembène evidently inscribes himself within a rich French literary tradition of the *fait divers*—one that connects him to nineteenth-century writers like Gustave Flaubert, Émile Zola, Stendhal, and Proust as well to more contemporary writers such as Albert Camus and Marguerite Duras.[46] A likely intertextual reference here is Jean Genet's play *Les bonnes* (*The Maids*, 1947), about two housemaids who carry out sadomasochistic rituals, playing at murdering their mistress (Madame). Genet's play was based on *faits divers* and other reports related to the widely mediatized case of Christine and Léa Papin, two sisters working as live-in housemaids in the same home in Le Mans, France, who murdered their employer's wife and her daughter in 1933. A case close to the intrigue of *La Noire de*... was reported only a few years later, in *Paris-Dakar*: the story of a young Senegalese man named Deba, who murdered his employer's wife while working as a houseboy (*un boy*, the male equivalent of Diouana's role) in their home in Quéray, France. Deba's arrest and trial was widely publicized, and a front-page photo in the Tuesday, 24 December 1935, issue of *Paris-Dakar* shows a sober Deba in handcuffs flanked by two white police officers.[47] The *fait divers* recounting the suicide of Diouana Gomis was less sensational and less visible—perhaps because her death did not play into gender- and race-based fears and there were no white victims. It was not "sensational material."

Sembène's gesture of reading-writing, which counters the discursive conditions that relegate Gomis's death to "back-page" news, also participates in a different literary tradition and literary-historical genealogy: one that seeks to retrieve traces of Black subjectivities at the points in dominant discourses— here, the popular press—where they are violently disappeared. Sembène's intervention is reminiscent of that of the abolitionist writer Thomas Day, one author of the poetic epistle *The Dying Negro* (1773) discussed in my introduction and chapter 1, based on the report of the suicide of an enslaved man in a British newspaper, the *Morning Chronicle and London Advertiser*. It bears similarities to Toni Morrison's novel *Beloved* (1987), inspired by an 1856 newspaper article, originally published in the *American Baptist*, about an enslaved woman, Margaret Garner, who killed her child. Like Sembène's *La Noire de . . .*, these works transform the meager written traces of Black death legible in the white press into haunting and humanizing antislavery narratives. Like Kanor's *Humus*, *La Noire de . . .* provides a powerful aesthetic response to what Fuentes, in *Dispossessed Lives*, poses as a historical problem with respect to writing on Atlantic slavery, and one that remains a central preoccupation for Black studies today: How can one narrate "the fleeting glimpses" of enslaved subjects within traditional archives?[48] Sembène's text and film draw on the aesthetic to accomplish something akin to what Johnson calls "accountable historical practice": a way of doing history that "challenges the known and unknowable, particularly when attending to the lives of black women and girls."[49]

Through its sensitive and moving portrayal of Diouana's interiority, Sembène's film to an extent refuses the sensationalist, hypervisible depictions of suicide in the white press, of the type exemplified by Georges Lemoine's 1886 engraving of an enslaved man crushing his own skull or by the illustration of Anna's leap in Jessey Torrey's *A Portraiture of Domestic Slavery* (1817). Sembène does not—as Lemoine's and Torrey's engravings do—show the act of suicide itself, only its aftermath. At the same time, the inclusion in the film of high-angle shots of Diouana's naked, lifeless body after her suicide is shocking and harrowing. They are "obscene" images of Black death that occur not offstage (*ob skene*) but at the film's climax. The mise-en-scène, which I analyze later in this chapter, borders on spectacle.

Summoning

As obituary notice or necrology, the *fait divers* of Diouana Gomis's suicide is a record of what Michel Foucault would have called the "contact" or "collision" with power: a chance encounter that "illuminated," however enigmatically, a life otherwise "destined to pass beneath any discourse and disappear without ever having been told."[50] In this case, the *fait divers* is a sign or symptom of colonial necropower.[51] But for Sembène, the public record is also a talisman and memento mori. It opens the way for necromancy not as resurrection or resuscitation but as summoning—a bringing to view and bringing to mind. In his essay "Debt Collecting, Disappearance, Necromancy," Nicholas R. Jones suggests that necromancy might be invoked as critical practice in the study of slavery and sub-Saharan Blackness: a way to "awaken the memory" of Black Africans and their descendants by "return[ing], on the one hand, and [animating], on the other hand, an inherent agential voice to the persons bureaucratically filtered, silenced, and regularized in slave owner's inventories."[52] The critic-as-necromancer accepts the task of "reimagin[ing] a concealed past as a reparative starting point."[53] In the context of Sembène's *La Noire de . . .* , which is a meditation on Black death, necromancing takes on additional resonances. *Necromancy* (originally from *nigromantia*, from *niger*, *nigr-* meaning "black") collapses—in fact confuses—Blackness and death in its very etymology. In the case of Sembène's text and film, what is at stake is both "dead (girl) magic" and "black (girl) magic."[54]

Like Saidiya Hartman's "Venus," Diouana Gomis appears in the archive of colonization as a *dead girl*. In the *fait divers*, she is simply "a young Negress [*Négresse*]" who decided to slit her throat "one melancholic day [*un jour de cafard*]." *Négresse*, of course, was the term in French used to refer to enslaved African and African-descended women. Hartman asks of Venus, "What else is there to know?": "Hers is the same fate as every other Black Venus: no one remembered her name or recorded the things she said, or observed that she refused to say anything at all. Hers is an untimely story told by a failed witness. It would be centuries before she would be allowed to 'try her tongue.'"[55] Although she may be in the lineage of Venus, it is in fact possible to know something of Gomis—to "screen" a dispersed suicide archive for her traces and (re)awaken her memory. In addition to the original *fait divers* reporting her suicide, several archival documents conserved in the Bibliothèque nationale in Paris, the Archives départementales des Alpes-Maritimes in Nice, and the Archives municipales in Antibes offer fleeting glimpses into Gomis's life and death and allow us to counter some of the silence surrounding her suicide.

From her official death certificate (*acte de décès*), we learn that Diouana was born in 1927 in Boutoupa, a small village in modern-day Ziguinchor (Siggcoor), on the southwest border separating Casamance and Guinea-Bissau. In his short story, Sembène also suggests that Diouana was born in 1927, according to her identity card:

—How old was she?
—Exactly, I don't know.
—She was born in 1927, according to her identity card.
—Oh! The "natives" [*indigènes*] don't know their date of birth, suggested the retiree as he plunged his hands into his pockets.[56]

This is one of several details that are not included in the *fait divers* but appear in Sembène's account, suggesting that he consulted Diouana's *acte de décès* or spoke to someone familiar with the case. Diouana was the daughter of Sabelle Da Silva and Longa Gomis, both deceased at the time of her death.[57] In Sembène's literary and cinematic imaginary, by contrast, Diouana still has family back in Dakar. This fact makes her *dépaysement* or "disorientation" in France more poignant and forms the pretext for some of the film's most powerful scenes, such as when Madame and Monsieur ghostwrite a letter to Diouana's mother for her, which she shreds—or the film's coda, in which Monsieur returns Diouana's affairs (notably her traditional mask) to Dakar and offers her family money. Like Sembène's character, the real Diouana Gomis appears to have been unmarried, or never mentioned being married to her employers, since her marital status is noted as being "without other information" in the death certificate.

We learn the most about Gomis in the text of the procès-verbal. Her case is classified as a "suicide by blade" (*suicide à l'aide d'une arme blanche*) and was overseen by Michel Teissier, the Commissaire de Police of Antibes, and the Police Adjoint Allavena.[58] In the top right-hand corner of the file's yellowed cover page, the word *suicide* is scrawled in green pencil along with the letters *Cl*, perhaps for *clos*, as in "case closed." In red ink, another hand has written "Gomis" in a loose cursive script (figure 3.7). The procès-verbal includes a typewritten and signed statement from Teissier dated 22 June 1958, when police first arrived on scene; a signed handwritten statement from the examining coroner, Dr. Herry, also dated 22 June 1958; typewritten and signed witness statements from Jeannine Petit née O'Kelly (Diouana's employer) and Jean Giraud (Petit's next-door neighbor), dated 23 June 1958; and, finally, a "bulletin de décès" filled out by hand and filed on 23 June 1958.

The statement by Teissier describes arriving at the Villa Le Bonheur Vert on the afternoon of 22 June. He was greeted by Jeannine Petit, identified as

Diouana's employer and the occupant of the villa. No mention is made of her husband. Once again, Sembène seems to have had access to someone familiar with the case—a neighbor, journalist, or detective—since in the short story the husband is similarly absent: his wife tells police he left for Paris two days earlier.[59]

Michel Teissier describes finding Diouana's body stretched out face-down in a pool of blood on the floor of the upstairs bathroom, a kitchen knife beneath her right leg and a large gash visible across her throat. Her death was confirmed by the coroner Dr. Herry, whose statement reiterates the same details, concluding that the cause of death appeared to be a suicide. Diouana's body then was transferred to the morgue of the Antibes Hospital, although no record of her seems to remain there. Nor does Gomis appear in the registers of Le Rabiac, the only cemetery active in Antibes at the time, where members of the Petit family are buried. On the following day, the police returned to the villa and took statements from both Petit and her neighbor Giraud, whom Petit had called over from his residence next door, the Villa Tour Rose, when she realized Diouana had locked herself in the bathroom and was unresponsive.

Diouana's employer, Jeannine Lucie Renée Petit (née O'Kelly), was a Frenchwoman born on 24 February 1928 in Haiphong, Indochina. Her birth is recorded in the *Bulletin administratif du Tonkin* (1928). Her mother, Yvonne O'Kelly, was a telephone operator.[60] Her father was the captain of the colonial infantry in French Indochina.[61] At the time of the suicide, Jeannine was only a year younger than Diouana herself. In his film, Sembène capitalizes on the inherent rivalry between two women around the same age in his presentation of the hostile dynamic between Madame and Diouana, pitting them against each other to underscore that theirs is a relation not of employer to employee but of master to enslaved. In the procès-verbal, Petit is identified as being unemployed and having her primary residence in Dakar, at km 4.500 on the Route de Rufisque. Jeannine's husband, who is not mentioned in the procès-verbal, most likely was Roger Petit, who, birth records show, was born in Antibes on 9 March 1928 and lived in Dakar, where he perhaps worked for the Overseas Mining Bureau or a petrol company.[62]

According to Petit's statement, the family arrived in Antibes on 7 April 1958 for a six-month vacation; Diouana arrived about a week later, presumably by boat, as in the film and short story, given the delay. Whereas, in the film, we can assume Diouana's journey from Dakar to Marseille took six days based on the regular route of the *Ancerville*, in the short story Diouana spends exactly eight days at sea. This can be explained by the fact that, in 1958, the speedy *Ancerville*, which could reach over twenty knots at sea, was not yet in service. The real

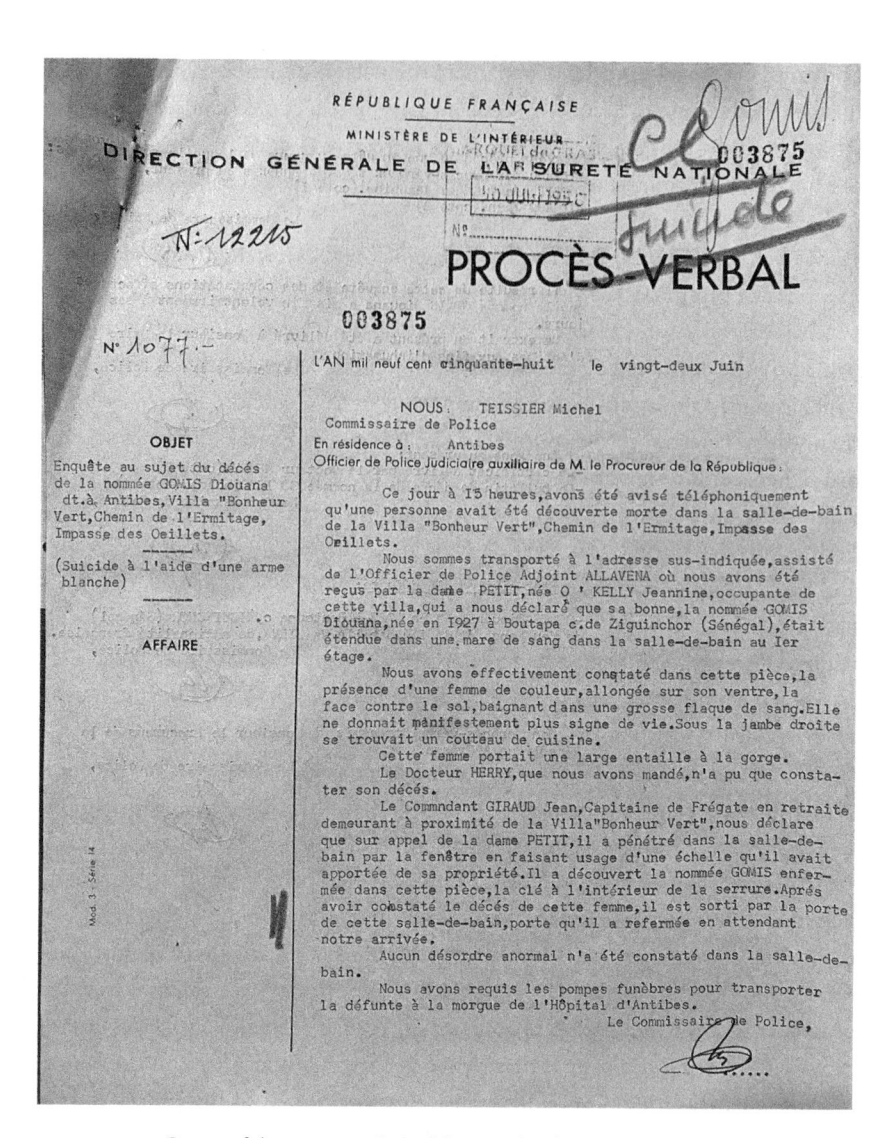

FIGURE 3.7. Page 1 of the procès-verbal of the suicide of Diouana Gomis (1927–58). Source: Archives départementales des Alpes-Maritimes (0052W0012).

Diouana Gomis and the Diouana of the short story would have traveled on a slower steamship, such as the *Azrou*, *Azemmour*, *Djenné*, *Koutoubia*, or *Lyautey*.

On the afternoon of 22 June 1958, around 12:50, Petit noticed that Diouana was taking longer than usual in the upstairs bathroom and knocked on the door, which had been locked from the inside. Receiving no response, she called on her neighbor, Giraud, who leaned a ladder against the house and peered in

134 · CHAPTER 3

through the bathroom window, glimpsing Diouana lying face-down in a pool of blood. Petit says she called the police immediately.

According to Petit, Diouana had worked for her since 1956. She was hired while the family was living in Dakar. Petit's comments about Diouana's life in Antibes are revealing. Above all, they provide a sense of Diouana's total social and linguistic isolation:

> I was always satisfied with her work and always considered her a good employee. She seemed normal to me, but she never confided in me since I did not speak her language. And as for her, she did not speak French. I was shocked when I discovered that she had killed herself using a kitchen knife. I think she did so in a moment of nervous depression. I did not know her to have any company. She only went out with me and my children.

While in the short story Diouana speaks a version of the invented colonial contact language *petit nègre*, Petit's witness statement suggests that the real Diouana's linguistic isolation in France was more pronounced—that she did not speak French at all. This is possible, even likely, since at the time less than 1 percent of women in Senegal could write or speak French.[63]

The statement given by Jean Giraud corresponds to the account given by Petit, although the timeline he provides differs slightly from hers. Giraud was born on 17 November 1896 in Antibes; at the time of Diouana's death, he was sixty-two and retired, having served previously as a naval captain and Officier de la Légion d'Honneur. In his statement, he recalls being alerted by Petit at 14:55 (over two hours after Petit says she first checked on Diouana) that the "native maid" had been locked in the bathroom and was not responding. Giraud took a ladder over to the Petit residence and climbed through the bathroom window, which he says was propped open (in Sembène's story, the neighbor shatters the windowpane). He stepped over Diouana's body and unlocked the door, closing it behind him and keeping the key, which he handed over to the police when they arrived, as happens in the short story.[64]

Like Petit, Giraud suggests that Diouana, for all intents and purposes, seemed "perfectly normal" (*tout-à-fait normale*) but admits never actually having spoken to her:

> I knew the maid by sight, and she seemed perfectly normal to me. As far as I could tell, she was at home in this family as if in her own. She took care of the Petit family's children. There's no doubt that this woman killed herself, seemingly in a crisis of nervous depression. I cannot give

any sense of the reasons that might have led this woman to kill herself. I never had the opportunity to speak to her directly.

In Sembène's short story, Giraud's literary double, "the Captain" (*le Commandant*), knows more than he lets on to police. He is a "regular" among the family's social group and attends the dinners at which Diouana is paraded about as an exotic object.[65]

In *La Noire de...*, Sembène masterfully and poignantly brings into view Diouana's isolation, suffering, and resistance. Sembène's aesthetic project provides what the French *fait divers* fails to and what, in the procès-verbal, emerges under erasure: a richly detailed and visually striking imaginative account of a Black African woman's life in Antibes during the 1950s. In this white, bourgeois neighborhood, even before her death, Diouana Gomis was a ghost: a spectral presence, at once "hypervisible," in Hartman's sense, and totally invisible.[66]

This tension between hypervisibility and invisibility has also structured the reception and circulation of Sembène's text and film, and thus the shadow-memory of Diouana Gomis. The power and popularity of Sembène's film especially are such that the unimaged history it documents has been displaced by its glossy, well-known screen memory. The film's status as canon seems to have precluded any interest in recovering the "unconscious," resistant content of the original suicide, which has remained off-screen. The restoration of *La Noire de... / Black Girl* by the Criterion Collection in 2017—which has given the work new life and increased circulation in the Anglo-American world—has paradoxically contributed to this broadscale forgetting. Sembène's "Black Girl" is simultaneously everywhere and nowhere to be found. Screening Sembène's text and film for the ciphered traces of this unimaged history help bring the story of Diouana Gomis back into view.

I now want to turn more fully to the aesthetic works at hand—not to leave behind archival traces of the real-life incident but, rather, to expand the exploration of archive to encompass Sembène's text and film. To put it a different way, now that we have tracked how Sembène responds to and transforms the "rumor" of Gomis's suicide in the archive, the goal here is to read, listen, and look for the *rumeurs* available in Sembène's own text and film. I'll do this by attending to various resonances of suicidal resistance, especially resistance to slavery, in *La Noire de....* Reading for resistance allows me to establish more capacious, diasporic, transnational, and transhistorical links and to put Sembène's text and film in dialogue with other literary and visual "texts."

Visions of France

Sembène is well known for his portrayals of African women.[67] One thinks especially of Dior Yacine in *Ceddo* (1977), who saves her village from Islamists by shooting an imam at point-blank range, or Rama in *Xala* (1973/1974), a "modern-day Amazon" who advocates for Africanization.[68] Compared with these characters, Diouana appears as something of an outlier. In the short story, her character is not especially well developed, and her defining gesture in both the story and the film—her suicide—is neither a spectacular act of insurrectional militancy nor an obvious usurpation of masculine authority. It could be tempting to read Diouana as a melancholic, pessimistic body—as an abject victim. The charge of "nostalgia" in the *fait divers* urges us in this direction, pathologizing Diouana's victimhood rather than recognizing her suicide as a response to psychological trauma. Perhaps this is what Dorothy Blair has in mind when she suggests that Sembène's earliest attempts to craft multidimensional female "heroines—Black or White" were largely "unsuccessful."[69]

On the surface, Sembène's *La Noire de . . .* is a straightforward narrative of displacement and disenchantment: a tragic bildungsroman ending in suicide. In this, Diouana's story resonates readily with the France-obsessed, suicidal trajectories portrayed in other works of Senegalese fiction published before or shortly after Independence. These include the suicide of Fara in Ousmane Socé Diop's *Mirages de Paris* (1937) and the ambiguous death of Samba Diallo in Cheikh Hamidou Kane's *L'aventure ambiguë* (1961), discussed in chapter 1 in connection to Maximin's *L'isolé soleil*.[70] Such fateful journeys to the metropole, which lead to experiences of racialization and racism and often end in death, disappointment, or disappearance, evidently inspire and inform a more contemporary corpus: that of migration narratives in which African protagonists travel to Europe in hopes of pursuing education or work and emerge from the experience in a nebulous intercultural space. Fatou Diome's *Le ventre de l'Atlantique* (2003), discussed in chapter 1 in connection to Kanor's *Humus*, and Alain Gomis's film *L'Afrance* (2001), in which the protagonist El Hadj contemplates suicide, are examples of this trend.[71] Such works belong to what French literary critic Jacques Chevrier terms *migritude* literature (a neologism formed from *négritude* and *migration*), referring to "extracontinental" Francophone African cultural production that deals centrally with the experiences of migration, and especially to literary texts produced by young Francophone African writers, such as Diome, living and working abroad.[72] In their transposition and transformation of earlier literary suicidal itineraries, Diome's novel and Gomis's film allude to works from this earlier generation: in Diome's novel, we find references to the "mirages" of "un nègre à Paris," and at one point in Gomis's film, El Hadj recites entire passages from *L'aventure ambiguë*.[73]

Other works, set in post-Independence Senegal and involving subjugated female protagonists who die by suicide, seem inspired by Sembène's "La Noire de . . ." This is especially true of Aminata Maïga Ka's tragic novellas about female oppression, *La voie du salut* (1985) and *Le miroir de la vie* (1985).[74] In *Le miroir de la vie*, Fatou Fane, a Sereer maid who has been impregnated and abandoned by her lover, hangs herself in a jail cell after being arrested for disposing of her stillborn baby. In *La voie du salut*, the suicide of the character Sokhna is reported the following day by national newspapers in terms that closely recall Sembène's short story: "The next day [*le lendemain*], the national dailies wrote: 'A young girl by the name of Sokhna Sow was recovered [*retirée*] from a well, into which she had thrown herself last night.'"[75] These texts are rarely discussed in connection with Sembène.

More recent work has emerged in the lineage of Sembène's text and film. Khalid Lyamlahy's haunting novel *Évocation d'un mémorial à Venise* (2023) is a case in point.[76] As its title suggests, Lyamlahy's novel erects, or rather evokes, a textual memorial: to Pateh Sabally, a twenty-two-year-old Gambian man who drowned in Venice in January 2017 after jumping into the Grand Canal. His death was witnessed by hundreds of bystanders, many of whom recorded the drowning on their cell phones. No one entered the water to save him. More than the bungling detectives and male onlookers with which Sembène opens his shorty, these "failed witnesses," to borrow Hartman's term, push the notion of witnessing beyond its referential limits. Is a suicide attended by many but prevented by none, and encouraged by some, a suicide? Perhaps it is a lynching. Somewhere between Sembène's "La Noire de . . ." and Sarr's *La plus secrète mémoire des hommes*, Lyamlahy's *Évocation* follows the *enquête* of a young writer to make sense of Sabally's death by following its textual, digital, and (audio)visual footprints. Like Sembène and Sarr, Lyamlahy connects a singular suicide to a long history of loss, that of so many Africans whose journey to Europe ends in death: the novel is dedicated to "the memory of Africans dead far from their countries, buried [*ensevelis*] in silence and oblivion."[77]

Critics have tended to read the suicides or suicide-like deaths portrayed in pre- and post-Independence works as straightforward acts that fulfill thinly veiled *romans à thèse*, analyzing voluntary death through exclusively Eurocentric frameworks.[78] In this view, literary characters such as Diouana, Fara, and Samba are all cautionary tales about the annihilating danger of embracing the metropole. Their suicides serve as grim but logical end points for iterations of the trope of the African in Paris, sardonic indictments of the (post)colonial subject's Bovarysme, or evidence of their failure to reconcile a split identity—the ultimate sign of a failed assimilation or *assimilation manquée*.

This reading is available, even foregrounded, in Sembène's text and film. Like Socé's Fara and Kane's Samba—and like Diome's Moussa and Madické—Sembène's Diouana falls under the spell of France and its culture, and this violent disillusionment precipitates her downfall. But there are important differences. Whereas Fara's and Samba's enchantment with France is linguistic—Fara is seduced by French romantic novels, Samba by the writings of thinkers like Pascal—the illiterate Diouana falls in love with a *vision* of France. She is seduced by the France she sees *on-screen*: "the beautiful cities she had seen on the silver screens [*écrans de cinéma*] of Dakar."[79]

In Dakar, as she walks her daily route to work along the Avenue Gambetta, Diouana dreams of expensive clothes and expansive villas, thrumming the word "France" like the name of a lover.[80] Once in Marseille, she speeds along the Côte d'Azur to Antibes in the passenger seat of Monsieur's car, enamored by a spectacle that spoils her not-so-distant memory of Africa: "She devoured everything with her eyes, marveled, was astonished. She was furnishing her mind's eye [*elle se meublait l'esprit*]. It's beautiful! All of Africa seemed to her like a sordid hovel."[81] Sembène's film further dramatizes this mythologized vision of the metropole through selective use of color. Although widely available versions of *La Noire de . . .* , including the recently restored Criterion Collection version, *Black Girl*, are in black-and-white, the original film included a color sequence in which the camera follows Diouana's journey from the Port of Marseille along the French Riviera to the family's apartment in Antibes.[82] The effect is an inversion of Dorothy Gale's journey from black-and-white Kansas to the technicolor world of Oz in *The Wizard of Oz* (1939).[83] In this sense, the best-known versions of Sembène's film are themselves "screen memories"—single, monolithic images of what is really a dispersed cinematic text, including an original color sequence now existing as excised footage in the French Film Archives (AFDF CNC).[84]

Diouana's path toward suicide thus takes the form of a violent *disillusionment*. Her visual "awakening" is consistent with what Christopher L. Miller considers a trend in early novelistic depictions of Africans in France, which "stage the encounter between Africans and French as a matter of *hallucination, mirage, anesthesia,* or *fantasm*"—that is, as a matter of blurred, screened, or fogged *vision*.[85] Diouana—like Socé's Fara—*goes to see France*.[86] But "la France" proves a chimera.

As Diouana enters her third month in Antibes, her visual appetite—like her physical appetite—declines: "Her eyes sunk, her gaze was less alert, it no longer lingered on small details. [. . .] Having become almost unrecognizable, she was worn down. Of France . . . Beautiful France [*la Belle France*] . . . she had only a vague idea, a fleeting vision [*une vision fugitive*]."[87] In the film, she bemoans how her expansive, dreamlike vision of the metropole has been reduced to the narrow confines of her employers' apartment: "Is France this black hole? [...] Here my life is spent between the bedroom and the kitchen. Is that what it is to live in France?"[88]

To read Diouana's suicide in this light—as a tragic, but ultimately predictable, pessimistic response to disenchantment, displacement, and deception—is to fall prey to a surface reading of Sembène's text and film. Such a reading mimes the violence of the original *fait divers*, which dismisses her act as evidence of "nostalgia," homesickness, and melancholic longing for her "native bush" (*sa brousse natale*). It means failing to reckon with the white supremacist structures her death lays bare and violently contests. It ignores the specific resonances of suicide within Senegalese culture and Wolof philosophy. Suicide, in this context, could serve to uphold values such as *sutura* (discretion) or *jom* (dignity). To return briefly to Freud's psychoanalytic notion of screen memory by way of Wolof philosophy, *sutura* comes from the Arabic word *satara*, meaning to screen, cover, or veil. As an act of *sutura*, suicide protects or conceals something that should remain hidden. But as a manifestation of *jom*, suicide is ultimately a means of *affirming* and *protecting* the self in extremis. As Léopold Sédar Senghor writes: "Occasionally, Fate denies us all effective riposte. We have only one solution then: to abandon our vital breath to save our personal life, our soul. Suicide is the final demand [*l'exigence dernière*] of Susceptibility, daughter of honor."[89] As Sembène himself has said, "In all times, refusal has been the sign of a fundamental dignity."[90] Reducing Diouana's suicide to a state of victimhood requires bracketing local (Senegalese) and pan-African histories and ontologies of suicidal resistance, including the collective suicide by self-immolation of the women of Nder discussed in the previous chapter. Such histories are equally available as intertexts for Socé's and Kane's novels.[91] They help us to recognize suicide as, on the one hand, a complex and deeply ambivalent act, about which we can make no sure claims, and, on the other, a well-established practice of anticolonial and antislavery resistance with local (Senegalese) and transnational (Atlantic) genealogies. These historical and cultural intertexts shift the frames for reading suicide toward an Afrocentric reading.

Reading for Resistance

Sembène's text and film invite us to understand Diouana's suicide otherwise: as a decisive and devastating gesture that rehearses and reactivates a pan-African genealogy of suicide as a form of resistance to injustice, oppression, slavery, colonization, and exile. Diouana is not a pessimistic suicidal body but a resistant one, in multiple senses. Despite evident parallels between their life stories, Sembène's Diouana is *not* a postcolonial Ourika—the young Senegalese woman brought to France and who resigned herself to a slow and sentimental *lent suicide*, suffering of melancholia in a French convent. Her story more closely resembles that of Aliin Sitooye Jaata—the young queen and former housemaid from Casamance who incarnated the popular anticolonial resistance in Casamance during the 1940s—or the Waalo-Waalo women of Nder, who chose a violent death over slavery.

Diouana's suicide by cutting in *La Noire de...* occurs off-screen and, in the short story, "offstage," but this should not prevent us from recognizing the sheer violence of her death and the unusualness of its method. Medical studies suggest that suicide by cutting the throat is by far "the least frequent suicidal method."[92] A single, decisive gash—as noted in the coroner's report of the real suicide of Diouana Gomis ("a large and deep gash across the throat") and in Sembène's story (her throat is slit "from one ear to the other")—is most atypical. Whereas "tentative cut marks are common in suicidal deaths," throat-cutting "without hesitation marks is a very rare occurrence."[93] Fatal cutthroat injuries are more likely to be the result of murder than suicide.[94] This brings Diouana's suicide in *La Noire de...*, as in real life, into an altogether different register—one that shares less with a romantic or sentimental tradition of suicide and more with the horrorscape of chattel slavery, in which the most extreme forms of self-violence and self-destruction became viable modes of resistance and practices of freedom. It raises the question whether she committed suicide at all or, instead, was brutally murdered by her employers.

That Diouana enacts her suicide on her throat further aligns her death with the myriad acts of self-destruction under slavery, especially aboard the slave ship, by which enslaved persons committed suicide by swallowing their tongues, tearing at their throats, or using their hands to choke themselves. Diouana's suicide might be read as a form of what Johnson, writing about the everyday resistance practices of enslaved African and African-descended women, calls "black femme freedom" to refer to the creative, sometimes violent, ways enslaved women practiced freedom even when they could not call themselves free.[95] Her suicide flips the script, challenging her captors' understanding of "what, where, and how [her body] should be used, [her] labor expended, and [her life] lived"[96]—or, in this case, ended.

The subtext of resistance under Atlantic slavery is an important one in *La Noire de....* The shadow of slave suicide, a silenced history explored in previous chapters, looms large in Sembène's text and film. As Thomas has shown, much of the enduring power and relevance of *La Noire de . . .* comes from Sembène's careful "mediation" of two discursive and historical orders in telling the story of Diouana: slavery and colonialism on the one hand, economic migration and globalization on the other.[97] Sembène shows how the latter is indebted to the former. This is a rhetorical trend we have come to recognize in the authors examined in *The Suicide Archive*, who all insist on the fact that the experiences of colonization and slavery persist in the present not as vestige but as organizing structure and continuum. In addition to being a story about the perils and vicissitudes of transnational migration, Sembène's *La Noire de . . .* is also a study of the afterlives of Atlantic slavery and empire—a story about how older forms of labor, displacement, dispossession, and injustice survive in the present.

In both the short story and the film, the comparison of Diouana's domestic "enslavement" in France to the history of Atlantic and African slavery is explicit. In the short story, she understands her deception as a "purchase" in bad faith: "Sold . . . sold . . . purchased . . . purchased, she repeated to herself. They purchased me. [. . .] They lured me, tied me up [*ficelée*] and I am tethered [*rivée*] here, like a slave."[98] Whereas, in the short story, Diouana is hired by responding to a newspaper ad, in the film she is chosen by Madame at a "maid market" in Dakar: a modern-day *marché des esclaves* (figure 3.8). And unlike the white family, who travel to the south of France by aircraft, in both the text and the film Diouana travels from Dakar by boat, repeating Sembène's own clandestine journey aboard the *Pasteur* and evoking centuries of transatlantic and Mediterranean crossings.[99]

Even before Diouana's fateful crossing, Sembène gestures at the imbrication of these two trajectories—Diouana's neocolonial domestic enslavement in France and Atlantic slavery—in the short story by including a spectral image of Gorée Island, a site infamous for its role in the slave trade and known for its "door of no return": "There, leaning out of the large window overlooking the sea, Diouana, transported [*transportée*], tracked the flight of the birds, high up on the immense blue expanse; far away, Gorée Island was barely visible. She had her ID card in her hand, she turned it, turned it over, examined it and smiled inwardly to herself."[100] As Thomas writes, "Through the invocation of the island of Gorée, Sembene offers the reader an ominous metaphor that foreshadows Diouana's experience in France, but also engages in [. . .] mediation [. . .] as a mechanism for establishing a transhistorical connection to the question of slavery."[101] On the level of wordplay, *transportée* captures Diouana's mental reverie but also points to her looming conversion into commodity: human cargo soon to be ferried across the sea.[102] Her identity card is a death sentence and a one-way ticket.

FIGURE 3.8. Still from *Black Girl* (2017) (the maid market). Source: Criterion Collection.

In the film, Sembène's staging of suicide draws on a provocative visual grammar that imbues Diouana's death with historical significance, inscribing it within a transatlantic genealogy that superimposes onto the death of a Senegalese maid the horrorscape of the *cale* (hold). As a fluid, maritime, and quasi-nomadic space transformed into a site of self-actualizing violence and metempsychosis, the bathtub in which Diouana kills herself becomes a metonym for the Middle Passage. Sembène's framing of Diouana's lifeless body underscores this point. The oblong, vessel shape of the bath enclosing Diouana's Black body provocatively parallels famous cross-section illustrations of slave ships (figures 3.9 and 3.10).[103] Moreover, Diouana is accompanied in her suicide by a suitcase, and her death is observed by a mute witness: her mask, an object that makes the Mediterranean and Atlantic crossing twice in the film. She is preparing for a journey, a reincarnation: this is her final "departure"—both a "return" and a voyage *sans retour*. As Fabienne Kanor writes, Sembène's image of "[Diouana's] Black body, submerged and inert, sends us back to this treacherous place: this sea which is neither flat nor liquid,

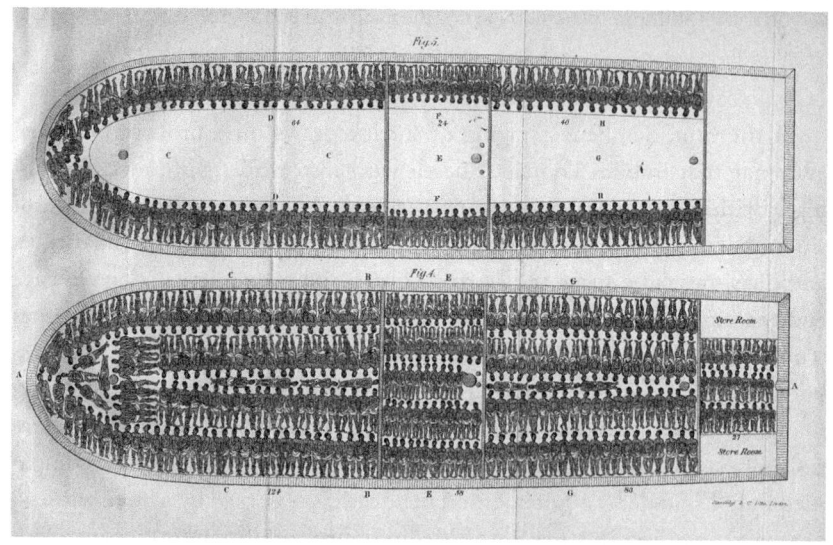

FIGURES 3.9 AND 3.10. *Top*, still from *Black Girl* (2017). Source: Criterion Collection. *Above*, cross section of a slave ship. Source: Carl Bernhard Wadström, *Plan and Sections of a Slave Ship* (Darton & Harvey, 1794–95), Yale Beinecke Rare Book and Manuscript Library (brSides f° 2012.9).

but a wall to bash one's head against, a solid sea that is only crossed in one direction."[104]

The maritime resonances of the bath are complicated when we consider that the bathtub in which she dies is also a highly bounded, protective amniotic vessel. This recalls the various resonances of *ventre/ventrem* (as womb, as "belly" of the Atlantic, as *partus sequitur ventrem*) discussed in chapter 1. The womb-like nature of the bath—and the bath as a typical place of *accouchement*, of labor and childbirth—is significant if we endeavor to read Diouana's suicide not solely as an act of resistance vis-à-vis an oppressive neocolonial condition (domestic slavery) but also as reflecting a desire to remove herself from a patriarchal economy of bodies. Her suicide rejects enslavement in Antibes while refusing to participate in an oppressive nationalist, hetero-reproductive script that would have required her to remain in Dakar, marry, and have children rather than pursuing an impossible union with *La Belle France*.

In the film, Sembène clearly dramatizes Diouana's rejection of hetero-reproductivity by introducing the character of Diouana's brawny (and mostly shirtless) boyfriend, whose political leanings are announced through his visual association with Patrice Lumumba and "Uhuru," and who cautions Diouana against what he perceives to be an unconventional lifestyle (figure 3.11). Diouana's boyfriend becomes a symbol of a nationalist, anticolonialist heteronormative narrative—one that pays little attention to sexual difference—of the type championed by the African Renaissance Monument in Dakar (2010). He might be read as an embodiment of the pressures of what Gayatri Spivak calls "reproductive heteronormativity," which Diouana rejects by taking on work in France. Her suicide, in this sense, would encode a message of "unrecognizable refusal of victimage by reproductive heteronormativity," revealing the extent to which she finds herself impossibly positioned at the untenable intersection of two oppressive regimes that make overlapping claims on her body.[105] In *La Noire de . . .* , the bathtub becomes a gendered technology of Black bodily defiance. It is where Diouana asserts herself as a thoroughly unmanageable and *intractable* Black body and simultaneously makes herself legible, if not intelligible.

That Diouana's suicide occurs in a space dedicated to daily care of the body—a site of ritual purification, cleansing, or baptism—lends a further charge to her act. Most obviously the bathtub captures a racialized discourse on hygiene, figuring the notions of degeneration, Blackness, and Indigeneity that subtend Sembène's text and film.[106] Sembène presents Diouana's suicide as a direct response, at least chronologically speaking, to an altercation with Madame over the tidiness of the bath during which Madame not only cathects the charge of dirtiness from the physical condition of the bathroom onto Diouana ("how

FIGURE 3.11. Still from *Black Girl* (2017), featuring Diouana's lover (*foreground*) and flag with Patrice Lumumba and Uhuru (*background*). Source: Criterion Collection.

filthy you are," *tu es sale quand même*) but also accuses Diouana of lying. If lying is a sin, a stain, then the bath signals the possibility of ablution and purification.[107] This fact further aligns Diouana's death with the collective suicide of the women of Nder, whose fiery deaths typically are referred to as a purifying "sacrifice" rather than as "suicide." Indeed, Diouana's decision to die in the bathtub makes her body an object of ritual sacrifice. Her death directly recalls the practice of Senegalese and French Muslims in HLM (*habitation à loyer modéré*) killing sacrificial sheep by slitting their throats in bathtubs during the celebration of aïd al-Adha or aïd el-Kebir, annual rites known in Wolof as Korité and Tabaski.

Sembène's framing of the suicide scene also clearly alludes to Jacques-Louis David's canonical 1793 painting portraying the death of the murdered French revolutionary Jean-Paul Marat (1743–93), *La mort de Marat* or *Marat assassiné* (figures 3.12 and 3.13). Scholars have tended to read Sembène's visual citation of David's work as an ironic commentary on Enlightenment thinking and republican values, which professed the revolutionary ideals of *liberté, égalité, fraternité* even as the institutions of French slavery and colonialism persisted, but David's painting is also a reflection on revolutionary writing.[108] David depicts Marat, the radical journalist and editor of the revolutionary periodical *L'ami du peuple*, lying dead in his bath after being stabbed by Charlotte Corday: killed while writing.

In *La Noire de* . . . Sembène re-creates this painting as moving image. His cinematic eye lingers on the bathtub in a medium shot long enough for us to watch the razor slip from Diouana's extended, lifeless right hand before panning to a close-up of the bloodied blade—mirroring David's composition, which uses Marat's elongated arm to draw the viewer's eye to both the quill and the blade. In Sembène's staging, the articulation between death and writing is compressed even further than is the case in David's painting. Whereas Marat is depicted in the process of writing on a piece of paper or parchment, Diouana transforms her own body into the surface of inscription. In David's painting, the instruments of writing and death (the quill, the blade) are visually equated (both rendered in white/light paint) but separate; in Sembène's film, they eerily coincide. And while Marat's left hand holds a piece of paper with legible writing on it, Diouana's left hand is invisible, submerged in the bath. Instead, her blood has made an abstract, dysgraphic "writing"—an indecipherable inky smear—on the gleaming white side of the tub: a *B*, perhaps for Boutoupa, her native village. Her braids even seem to form the letter *X*. This is the archetypal mark of (ab)negation, but also the mark used in place of a signature for people, like Diouana, who cannot write—most notably, in the history of French colonization, enslaved persons.

Considered within a transatlantic and West African genealogy of violent resistance, Diouana's suicide becomes much more clearly a radical—and revolutionary—rejection of the status of commodity ascribed to her and a refutation of her social death in France. Purchased "like a slave," she decides to take her own life, destroying the "property" of her employers and negating the idea that her body is a source of extractive labor. Her death resonates strongly with the genealogy of antislavery suicide in the Atlantic world unearthed earlier in *The Suicide Archive*.

"Nostalgia"

Sembène's poem "Nostalgie," appended to the short story in the original version published in *Voltaïque* in 1962, provides a further gloss on the subtext of slavery in "La Noire de . . ." "Nostalgie" has received surprisingly little scholarly attention in the criticism on *La Noire de* . . . , despite its powerful argument that Diouana's death is part of a long history of resistance to Black capture, deportation, and enslavement. The poem's title itself is "ripped from the headlines," appearing in both the fictionalized *fait divers* that Sembène includes at

FIGURE 3.12. Still from *Black Girl* (2017). Source: Criterion Collection.

the end of his short story and in the original newspaper report from 1958.¹⁰⁹ The term *nostalgie*, or nostalgia, appeared first in the nascent medical literature of the seventeenth century as a clinical diagnosis for a dangerous (and deadly) disease before spreading to other, namely colonial-imperial contexts during the Napoleonic wars.¹¹⁰ As Thomas Dodman writes, "Though [nostalgia] was thought of primarily as a soldiers' (and, to a lesser extent, sailors') disorder—almost like an occupational disease—clinical nostalgia assembled a long cast of occasional victims [. . .] from permanent emigrants and colonial settlers to exiles and chattel slaves."¹¹¹ In the world of French empire, nostalgia came to describe and diagnose the nervous conditions of soldiers, sailors, and convicts, as well as African slaves. It was one of many "maladies des nègres" that supposedly afflicted captive Africans aboard the slave ship and on the plantation.¹¹² As we saw in the introduction, it was often mobilized as a pathology in the "diagnosis" of suicidal slaves—a way of sidestepping the question of routinized violence and psychological trauma of colonization and enslavement.

The title prepares the overarching message of the poem, since in "Nostalgie," Sembène directly connects Diouana's fate to the history of the French

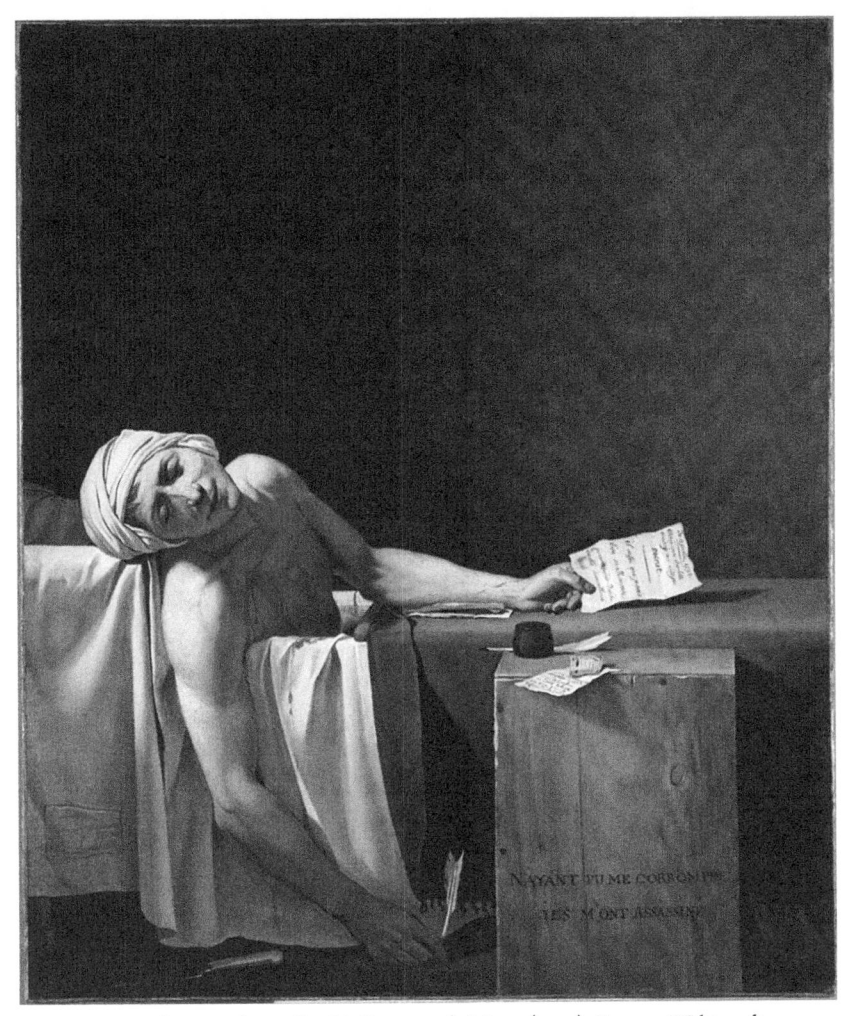

FIGURE 3.13. Jacques-Louis David, *La mort de Marat* (1793). Source: Wikimedia Commons.

slave trade on the African coast, framing her death as proof of the ways the afterlives of slavery continue to structure and haunt our present. The poem opens by evoking the pitch of slave ships on the open sea and the spectral cries of the enslaved:

> Diouana.
> Notre Sœur
> Sur la barre ne tanguent plus les négriers

L'épouvante, le désespoir, la course éperdue
Les cris, les hurlements se sont tus
Dans nos mémoires résonnent les échos
Diouana[113]

(Diouana
Our Sister
Slave ships no longer pitch in the shallows
The terror, the despair, the frantic course
The cries, the screams have died down
In our memories, the echoes resound
Diouana)

"Nostalgie" continues in an ostensibly "postslavery" moment, enumerating the ways Atlantic history signifies in the present. In "Nostalgie," the slave palaces dotting the African littoral are indelible scars—monuments to a grisly history:

Les siècles sont ajoutés aux siècles
Les chaînes sont brisées
Les carcans dévorés par les termites
Sur les flancs de notre Mère
Afrique
Se dressent les maisons d'esclaves
(Ces maisons sont des monuments à notre histoire)[114]

(Centuries are added onto the centuries
The chains are broken
The shackles devoured by termites
On the flanks of our Mother
Africa
Stand the slave castles
[These houses are monuments to our history])

Sembène's suggestion here, as throughout his text and film, is that the past of slavery is not past. Diouana, like so many before her, died not from melancholic longing but from a fatal "exchange"—the forced displacement of enslavement, which in the present has only taken on a new guise:

Tu es victime comme nos ancêtres
Du troc
Tu meurs de l'implantation
Tels les cocotiers et les bananiers

Meublant les rives d'Antibes
Ces arbres implantés et stériles.[115]

(You are a victim like our ancestors
Of the traffic
You die from implantation
Like the coconut and banana palms
Furnishing the shores of Antibes
Those implanted and sterile trees.)

Despite its recourse to a poetic voice, "Nostalgie" is not a lyric poem. It lacks rhyme or an obvious metrical scheme. It bears little similarity to any French poetic form. Rather, Sembène's "Nostalgie" should be read as intervening in the colonial-authoritative racist discourse of the original *fait divers* report. Recall that the term *nostalgie* comes directly from the text of the French *fait divers*: "Never before had she displayed such nostalgia to resort to this last extreme." The poem thus recites one of the key terms of that report—along with others, such as *brousse*—to resignify it. Sembène suggests that Diouana's death was not the result of a melancholic disposition or *mal du pays* but an expression of freedom.

Perhaps most significantly, the fugue-like poem "Nostalgie" is a requiem. Like Kanor's ghostly chorus of drowned voices in *Humus*, "Nostalgie" offers a symbolic means of reclaiming Diouana as a "proud African woman" (*une fière Africaine*), a "mother" and "sister" ("Diouana / Our Sister," "You are our / Mother / Diouana") from Sembène's native Casamance.[116] The poem's iterative structure allows the proper name "Diouana"—which, in the short story, is constantly disfigured by Madame and Monsieur[117]—to resound, repeated eight times in the poem. It is a "summoning" and a dignifying memorial attempt to bring Diouana home.

In the film, a similar effect—a kind of elegy and homecoming—is achieved in the striking (and much discussed) final sequence during which Monsieur travels back to Dakar alone to return Diouana's belongings and wages to her family. After Diouana's mother refuses to accept Monsieur's "blood money"— her daughter's unclaimed wages—a young boy follows Monsieur with Diouana's mask held to his face and flanked by ghostly shadows, chasing the Frenchman out of the city. (This mask, it is worth pointing out, seems to be a version of a Bamana initiation mask; the origins of the term *Bamana*, from *ban-mâna*, "to refuse the master," surely would not be lost on Sembène.)

The extradiegetic music playing throughout the sequence is a corollary to Sembène's concluding ode to Diouana in "Nostalgie." Simultaneously haunting, mournful, and menacing, the track throbs with a drum that pulses steadily like a heartbeat, gradually gaining power and urgency as Monsieur rushes out of the village. Few critics, however, have acknowledged the lyrics. Playing in the background, overlaid with the insistent drumbeat, are the strains of a popular Sereer song from the early 1960s by the singer Khady Diouf. A kind of call and response between Diouf and a mixed chorus, the song, "Ndey wassanaam" (literally, "Ndey or 'mother' forgive me") is about the death of *another* Diouana: the singer's cousin, Diouana Sarr.[118] Her name is repeated with each refrain. Through this audiovisual graft, another faceless Diouana is added to the strange palimpsest of *La Noire de . . .*

Split Figures, Absent Voices

The poem "Nostalgie" to an extent rescues Diouana's disappeared voice—so often ventriloquized or co-opted in the short story—recuperating her death for collective memory. Sembène's film takes the recovery of Diouana's voice a step further, because in the film, unlike the short story, she narrates her own experiences in the first person and in fluent French. We are given intimate access to her subjectivity through the extensive use of voice-over (*voix-off*). Often, Sembène pairs Diouana's monologues in the voice-over with extreme close-up shots as if to visually underscore how closely *La Noire de . . .* hews to the protagonist's subjectivity (figures 3.14 and 3.15).

Many scholars read Sembène's use of voice-over generously, as a form of "contestatory voicing" by which the "neo-colonised African 'I' can be said to predominate."[119] For critic Sheila Petty, Diouana speaks "for herself" from "within herself" on-screen.[120] But Diouana's interior monologue is not a straightforward use of voice-over. There is something "off" about this *voix-off*: an odd estrangement between voice and action in the film, the commentary seeming to sail over, or float above, the events taking place on-screen.

Like many early films, *La Noire de . . .* was shot silently, with the speech of actors dubbed in postproduction in France. But this postproduction dubbing does not account entirely for uncanniness of the voice-over. The dubbing is also a doubling, yet another example of neocolonial silencing by which Diouana's *for intérieur* is overwritten or covered over by someone else—and not voiced by Mbissine Thérèse Diop. Sembène's limited budget prevented him from bringing Diop to France to record her character's lines, so Diouana's speech and thoughts were dubbed instead in a more standard, non-African metropolitan French by the Haitian-born actress and singer Toto Bissainthe (1934–94), who lived for most of her life in France.[121] The result is an uncomfortable disjuncture between the Diouana we see on-screen and her voice,

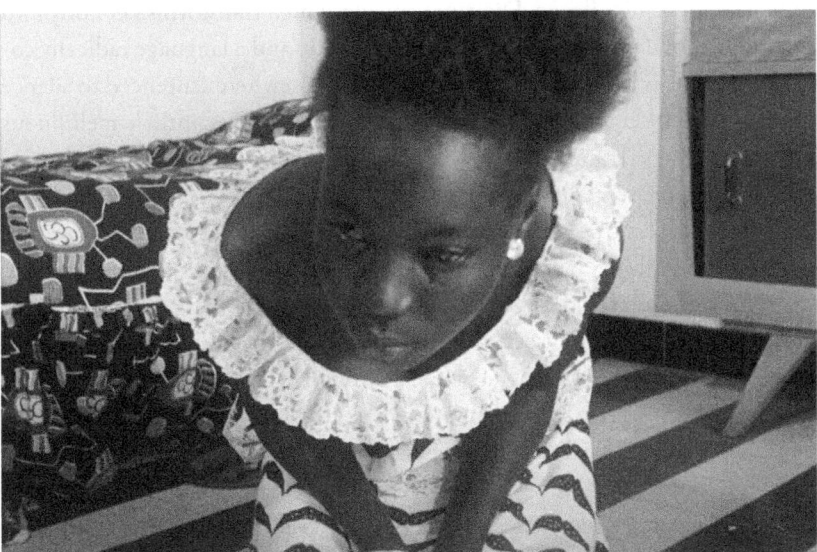

FIGURES 3.14 AND 3.15. Stills from *Black Girl* (2017): close-up shots of Diop as Diouana. Source: Criterion Collection.

which is not hers, in the voice-over: a troubling separation between Diouana/Diop's body and the language grafted onto it. From the very first lines she speaks, the Diouana we see on-screen is a split, uncanny being. This fact takes on greater significance when we consider that the periphrasis used in Wolof to refer to suicide is the verb *xaru,* which literally means "to split the self" or "to self-split."[122] The superimposition of Bissainthe's voice onto Diop's silent body brings the split figure of Diouana into a strangely diasporic and translational time-space—that of "the wake." Reminiscent of the way Haiti erupts suddenly in Sissako's *Timbuktu* (2014) whenever the flamboyant Zabou speaks, summoning Port-au-Prince from the Sahara, Bissainthe's melodic French opens a seam in the film and in history. Like Sissako's Zabou, Sembène's Diouana is *fissurée*: "What is time?" Zabou says. "I am cracked [*fissurée*]." Diouana's grafted and split language open onto the myriad disruptions, displacements, and "ruptures of the transatlantic and trans-Arab slave trades."[123]

Bissainthe's French can be read—or heard—in Sembène's film as a sign of absence, such that Diouana/Diop's own language—whether Wolof, Senegalese French, Manjak, Sereer, or any combination of these—remains legible, audible, only as it is effaced. Diouana's suicide, which transforms her body into a signifier, is one point in the film where her body and a language radically coincide. Suicide is the moment when Diouana—elsewhere sentenced to silence and servitude, her own language receding beneath Bissainthe's mellifluous French—"speaks" from within and *through* her own body in a fatal and silent idiom. The sonic screening of Diop's voice by Bissainthe's is another reminder of the many layers of remembering and forgetting, presence and absence, visibility and invisibility, audibility and silence, structuring Sembène's aesthetic intervention in text and on-screen. In the figure of Diouana, Sembène's film thus gives us the image of one woman (Diop) and the voice of another (Bissainthe). He conjures another Diouana through Khady Diouf's Sereer lyric. Simultaneously screened and summoned by this uncanny configuration is a fourth woman: the faceless and voiceless Gomis.

When Gomis died, she was over a decade older than Diop, who was just seventeen when she incarnated Diouana, and seven years older than Bissainthe when she voiced her. This is worth lingering on. Part of the commercial success and visual power of *La Noire de . . .* —its efficacy as icon and "screen memory"—is due to Diop's radiant, youthful presence on-screen. From the film's first frames, spectators—and, palpably, Sembène's camera—are in thrall to Diop's luminous and expressive gaze, her young unblemished skin, and shining eyes. We are buffeted along by the contours of Bissainthe's melodious voice. It is the voice of a singer in her prime.

The seventeen-year-old Diop is both ingenue and muse. At once statuesque and girlish, she inspires our pity and commands our respect. She is as elegant and captivating in a stylish housedress and smooth hairpiece as she is wrapped in a simple white peignoir with her hair in twists. As if to amplify her tragedy, Sembène makes his suicidal heroine young. Above all, he makes her beautiful. But perhaps the real Diouana was portly or limped. Perhaps her skin was rough and weathered, her features worn down and tired. Perhaps her voice was gravely and terse. She would have spoken Wolof, and likely several other languages—Pulaar, Sereer, Manjak, Arabic. At the very least, we know that she did not speak French.

We have no way of knowing what the real Diouana Gomis looked or sounded like. No photo of her exists in the dispersed archive of her suicide. No record in her own words, in her own name. We have only "rumor": a slim account of her encounter with power.

Conclusion: Departures

> My account replicates the very order of violence that it writes against by placing yet another demand upon the girl, by requiring that her life be made useful or instructive, by finding in it a lesson for our future or a hope for our history. We all know better.
> SAIDIYA HARTMAN, "Venus in Two Acts" (2008)

The real Diouana Gomis persists in the archive of colonization as an unimaged presence, glimpsed through the structures of silencing and ventriloquism that conditioned her disappearance and condition her appearance as trace years later. Hers was a violent departure that inscribed an otherwise invisible and "faceless" existence onto the ledger of history. Like the suicides of Azor and the women of *Le Soleil*, the suicide of Gomis creates a sudden and horrible flash of visibility in the traditional archive. As Hartman writes of Venus,

> An act of chance or disaster produced a divergence or aberration from the expected and usual course of invisibility and catapulted her from the underground to the surface of discourse. We stumble upon her in the exorbitant circumstances that yield no picture of the everyday life, no pathway to her thoughts, no glimpse of the vulnerability of her face or of what looking at such a face might demand. We only know what can be extrapolated from an analysis of the ledger or borrowed from the world of her captors and masters and applied to her.[124]

Faced with the facelessness of Venus in the archive, Hartman says it becomes impossible to say anything about her at all beyond describing the conditions of her silence. Any act of narrating her existence risks committing further violence. This is true of Sembène's text and film. It is equally true of my own critical gesture, which exposes the life and death of a woman who perhaps desired above all *not* to be seen, perhaps wanted to stay dead. Let us recall Stephen Best's assertion in *None like Us* that "no one wants to be erased from history.... Obliterated. Snuffed out."[125] It is easy, and important, for us—the living—to believe that. Among other things, it allows for a positivist model of history. But suicide does not answer to positivism or to history. Suicide is the undoing of the positivist historical subject. Suicide responds otherwise: erase me. Let me vanish.

To tell the story of Diouana Gomis—to tell the story of suicidal resistance—is an impossible task. A history of her can only emerge as failure. To attempt to look on her face is to know that we have *already* failed her. Aesthetic forms—which offer no clear answers and make no absolute claims—provide a way forward. Sembène's text and film perform a powerful work of rehabilitation with respect to the story of Diouana Gomis. But they do not "resuscitate the girl" or give voice to her in any straightforward, unmediated way, not without a self-consciousness around the violence and trespass of their own gesture. Instead, and above all, his text and film offer modes of attending to what Hartman calls "black noise," the *rumeurs* of the underground: "the shrieks, the moans, the non-sense, and the opacity, which are always in excess of legibility and of the law and which hint at embodied aspirations that are wildly utopian."[126] Sembène's narrative accounts read, re-sound, and reckon with the suicide of Diouana Gomis *as* black noise, as utopian vision. Like Kanor's *Humus*, his project consists in trying to hear a disappeared voice. He attends to an unheard message of resistance—dysgraphic letters traced in blood, a silent scream—and renders it recognizable as such by reinscribing it in his text and film, allowing its traces to multiply. He both transforms and amplifies this impossible speech.

Sembène positions us as belated readers and requires that we interrogate our belatedness. Like the detectives and journalists with which the story opens—metonyms for the colonial-imperial apparatus that will allow traces of Gomis's death to remain legible decades later—we arrive too late to a scene of violence we could not prevent. Sembène's *La Noire de...* insists that it will always be too late, so long as the discursive conditions that relegate the suicide of a Black woman to "back-page news" and the unlivable structural violence her death contests remain intact. Whatever narrative we "recover" in our reading will not bring Diouana back to life.

Nor does Sembène let the ghost of Diouana Gomis rest, however. The sepulcher that *La Noire de...* affords her is an uneasy one—a form of constant virtual reanimation. He gives her suicide a second act, in text and on-screen, for which she did not ask. To return to Hartman's Venus, Sembène places *yet another demand on the girl*: "that her life be made useful or instructive," that we find in it "a lesson for our future or a hope for our history."[127] Sembène makes the dead girl in the archive speak in spite of herself and in a voice that is not her own. He enlists her suicide in the "as-yet-incomplete project of freedom."[128] Even as they preserve the ciphered traces of the real life and death of Diouana Gomis and give her the sepulcher she was denied, Sembène's text and film function as cenotaphs, visual and sonic screens, signs of absence. We still do not know where (or if) the real Diouana Gomis was buried, or if her remains were returned to her extended family in Senegal. As both sepulcher and screen, lamentation and scream, *La Noire de . . .* finds a form for "the dead girl"—years later and far too late—to finally try her tongue. Sembène's text and film remain beautiful records of a voice we will never hear and a face we can never know.

IV

The Photograph belongs to that class of laminated objects
whose two leaves cannot be separated without
destroying them both.

ROLAND BARTHES, *Camera Lucida* (1980)

VI

· 4 ·

MULTIPLE EXPOSURES

Geologies of Suicidal Resistance

> The calm,
> Cool face of the river
> Asked me for a kiss.
>
> LANGSTON HUGHES,
> "Suicide's Note" (1926)

Hidden Scenes

In the mid-nineteenth century, the French-born American Egyptologist John Beasley Greene (1832–56) took perhaps the earliest known photographs of the Rhummel River. The Rhummel snakes through a vertiginous gorge traversing the limestone plateau on which the ancient city of Constantine in northeastern Algeria is perched (figures 4.1 and 4.2). Between 1855 and 1856, shortly before his premature death, the twenty-four-year-old Greene produced a series of calotype negatives on silver chloride paper, using an exposure technique he had learned from one of the founding fathers of photography in France, Gustave

FIGURES 4.1 AND 4.2. John Beasley Greene, *Views of Constantine and the Rhummel* (1855–56). *Top*, riverbed, near Constantine, Algeria (84.XM.813.2); *above*, waterfall, near Constantine, Algeria (84.XM.361.37). Source: Getty Museum.

Le Gray.¹ Greene's calotypes and the salt prints created from his negatives are spare, modern images: tightly cropped, unpeopled landscapes that home in on the ravine, riverbed, cascades, and craggy rock faces of the Rhummel Gorge.² Apparently disinterested in Constantine's human history and French colonizing presence in the city, their compositions are dominated by a concern for deep time and geological scale.

In their stark focus on geological features, Greene's images differ noticeably from better-known, state-sponsored photographs of Constantine produced during the same period.³ Throughout the mid- to late nineteenth century, French military photographers created panoramic cityscapes, boudoir interiors, and controversial figure studies of Algerians that were commercialized as souvenir albums and postcards—making Constantine one of the most photographed cities in the world at the time. Greene's work, by contrast, remained almost entirely unknown until the end of the twentieth century.⁴

For all their spareness, Greene's calotypes of the Rhummel are not timeless or straightforward records of the landscapes they capture. Taken less than two decades after the Siege of Constantine (1837), his photographs are haunted images in which hidden scenes of violence remain active and stirring as latent, translucent images that never fully developed on the silver chloride paper. If, as Mark Sealy suggests, the archival photograph always encodes a "message from the past" that might be "put to work in the present," Greene's calotypes can be seen to conceal and disclose simultaneously "the slippery, ghost-like nature of the colonial in photography."⁵ They are examples of what Tina M. Campt considers "haptic" objects: images that emit a low-frequency hum or a sensorial buzz attuning us to the presence of something else.⁶ This invisible, ghostly presence corresponds to what Roland Barthes terms the "blind field" (*champ aveugle*) of the photograph or, as Avery Gordon writes, "precisely what is pressing in from the other side of the fullness of the image displayed within the frame."⁷

Campt's "haptic" register, Sealy's ghostlike "message" from the past, and Barthes's "blind field" are ways of naming something stirring but not visible in Greene's seemingly fixed images of the Rhummel—something that orders and disorders what Ariella Azoulay has called the "glossy emulsion" and serene stasis of the photograph in the colonial-imperial archive.⁸ It is a phantom exposure, a hidden scene that is excised by the camera's shutter but shadows and haunts the resultant image.⁹

In 1855, Greene captured an unmarked mass grave—a natural tomb vaster than any of the man-made mausoleums or pyramids he photographed during his travels. More than a *lieu* or *nœud de mémoire*, the Rhummel is an immense riverine burial ground.¹⁰ It is a fluvial "seametary," to return to Hakim Abderrezak's terminology evoked in earlier chapters.[11] Like the Atlantic and the Mediterranean, the bed of the Rhummel harbors countless unidentified deaths. It is a rocky crypt whose ghosts are not victims of precarious ocean crossings but examples of what Durkheim termed *les suicides obsidionaux:* desperate acts of self-killing by the besieged, for which only biblical examples are given, despite the fact that the long nineteenth century abounded with instances of Algerians destroying themselves and their cities in deadly acts of resistance against French conquest.[12] Greene's images of the Rhummel are suicide archives of their own.

Since at least the second century AD, beginning with the suicide of Sophonisba, a Carthaginian princess who poisoned herself to avoid enslavement by the Romans, Constantine and the Rhummel Gorge have been a locus of human tragedies and storied sites of suicidal resistance.[13] Over the centuries, the ravine has served as executioner's block, sacrificial altar, resistance monument, and impenetrable crypt. This history preceded and succeeded Greene. Under Ottoman rule up until the period of French occupation, criminals and women suspected of adultery were precipitated from the cliffs pictured in Greene's calotypes, notably at a rocky outcropping known as the *rocher des femmes adultères* or the *rocher du sac* (*Kef Chekara* in Arabic), since victims were placed into burlap sacks before being tossed over the edge.[14]

During the Siege of Constantine (1837), the riverbed and gorge became a veritable horrorscape. Families seeking to protect their daughters from being raped by French soldiers lowered the young women into the ravine from the cliffs on ropes, many of which gave way, plunging the women into the jagged chasm below; others simply jumped.[15] As the French poured into the city, several hundred combatants died by suicide, throwing themselves from the same staggering heights to avoid falling into the hands of invading French forces.[16] After the siege, military surgeons descended into the ravine to treat anyone who had survived the fall. Their eyewitness accounts describe the riverbed littered with broken bodies—mostly of women and children, some paralyzed or mutilated but still alive—the limestone stained red with blood and strewn with contorted, shattered limbs.[17]

This history did not end with French conquest. During the Algerian War of Independence, French soldiers used this same river as a mass grave to deposit the bodies of countless Algerians, many of whom died while being tortured at a notoriously violent CRA (*centre de renseignement et d'action*) on the outskirts of the city: the Améziane Farmhouse.[18] Occasionally these bodies surfaced, washing up on the banks with cords tied to heavy rocks still around their necks. Constantine remains officially classified as one of several "high-rate suicide zones" in the region. Since 1993, the city has seen an alarming increase in civil suicides, many of whom throw themselves into the abyss from the city's numerous bridges—part of what specialists now characterize as a "suicide epidemic" in Algeria, a phenomenon I return to in this chapter's conclusion.[19] In the past decade, in the wake of Bouazizi's suicide, self-immolation has become increasingly widespread.[20] Constantine and the Rhummel are where this unimaged history of loss accumulates, where it is obscured and preserved.[21]

Multiple Exposures

Accessing an excised suicide archive of the Rhummel—the hidden scenes or "blind field" of Greene's images—necessitates other tools of capture and reference and demands other technologies of making visible than those employed by the young photographer (the camera, the calotype). To echo Campt and Gordon, such a project requires a perceptual sensibility that is not only visual but also "haptic" and "hauntological." This chapter explores the capacity of literary texts to provide such tools and to perform this kind of work.[22] The previous chapter's notion of a "(silver) screen memory," referring to the ways images repress, displace, or cover over unimaged histories, remains useful. As the "screen memory" of Diouana Gomis suggests, a repressed memory might be reawakened—summoned in the present. This chapter builds on that reflection by developing a literary hermeneutic informed by the photographic to attend more fully to sedimented histories of suicidal resistance.

What I will call a literary technique of *double* or *multiple exposure* names an "anarchival" technology of making-visible.[23] The metaphor and materiality of the multiple exposure allow access to something akin to—yet distinct from—what Maxim Silverman has called "palimpsestic memory," in reference to the layered structure of historical memory related to French colonization and the Holocaust, an idea that now has become a dominant paradigm for reading "postwar" and "postcolonial" literature.[24] Palimpsestic memory implies a disrupted *textual* temporality in which "the present is shown to be shadowed or haunted by a past which is not immediately visible but is progressively brought into view."[25]

Because it captures a subject (or different subjects) at various points in time, the dialectical image produced through the technique of multiple exposures might be considered a kind of palimpsest. It is, in fact, something different. Whereas a palimpsest preserves the legible traces of a past event—an earlier scene of writing, only partially effaced—the multiple exposure accesses the other side, or the underside, of the image. It activates something stirring just beyond the pale of the visible or, to return to Campt's sonic lexicon, something vibrating just below the frequency of the audible. The temporality of the multiple exposure is that of a present continually ruptured, contaminated, or shadowed by the past *as well as* that of a present pregnant with invisible, future potential. The technique of multiple exposure leaves open always the possibility of repetition: the accumulation of additional, subsequent exposures on the same surface. In this, it is oriented toward a past process and future gesture. It suggests that earlier, latent images might surface belatedly in the present, but also invites the grafting of new images, new associations, onto an existing composite structure.

I focus here on how the Constantine-born writer Nourredine Saadi (1944–2017) excavates and exposes historical and literary examples of suicidal resistance. Like the other works discussed throughout *The Suicide Archive*, Saadi's novels are preoccupied with how the colonial (and precolonial) past fails to remain "past" and with how suicide becomes a complex sign or symptom of histories of violence repeating in the present. To echo Michel-Rolph Trouillot's words, such works strive not for "fidelity" vis-à-vis a historical past but for "authenticity" and honesty with respect to how that past continues to make itself seen and felt.[26] Saadi's final two novels, *La nuit des origines* (2005) and *Boulevard de l'abîme* (2017), both set between Constantine and Paris, are my focus here because they take on one of the central tasks of *The Suicide Archive*—to hold the multiple, competing resonances of "historical" suicide in tension—as an organizing principle. His entextualizations of suicide in both novels dissolve hermetic distinctions between "Europe" and "Africa," between historical memory and fiction, between a colonial past and postcolonial present. They enjoin us to read across time and space, hazarding new associations and establishing different signifying chains. Saadi's novels are of interest for how they further develop the interrelation of suicide, historical memory, (post)colonial violence, and experiences of exile and displacement explored in earlier chapters. In Saadi's novels, Constantine and Paris become superimposed memoryscapes, such that the roar of the Rhummel remains audible in the slow-moving waters of the Seine and Constantine's deep and recent past continually breaks through into the narrative present. Read through the lens of the multiple exposure, Saadi's fiction constructs other models for writing history by way of points of suicidal resistance—allowing competing histories of loss to emerge and remain legible simultaneously as if translucent images overlaid within a single frame.

Saadi's novels share much with Ousmane Sembène's portrayal of suicide in text and on-screen in *La Noire de . . .* , discussed in the previous chapter. In fact, Saadi's novels circle around the same year, 1958: the year of Diouana Gomis's suicide and the moment of intense violence in French-colonized Algeria evoked at the outset of Sembène's short story. More than chronology,

Saadi's novels and Sembène's text and film share formal concerns in how they entextualize women's suicides. Like Sembène's *La Noire de . . .*, Saadi's texts traffic in a literary ventriloquism of the *suicidée*. In *La nuit des origines*, the protagonist Abla's *crise* consistently is misconstrued and misread by men— labeled as *hystérie, illuminisme, folie*. Her official diagnosis, a bout of tetany provoked by the ingestion of barbiturates, highlights the abject failure of the disciplines of psychiatry and medicine to account for what Saadi presents as a deeply historical and historicized act and as something totally outside history as we know it: an ahistorical *mal* that shares the recurrent structure of trauma. In *Boulevard*, as in Sembène's *La Noire de . . .*, access to the "inscription" of female suicide is heavily mediated (represented through police reports, newspaper articles, male-authored texts). The meaning of suicide emerges through the poetics of multiple exposure, glimpsed through layered discursive frames. But Saadi, like Sembène, provides skeleton keys within his works that make it possible to discern his own authorial hand in restaging, and reframing, female suicide in ways that open up suicide to other significations.

Saadi's writing of suicide and French Algerian history together does not emerge in a vacuum; rather, it participates in a robust literary genealogy predating Independence. Political and historical suicides are ubiquitous in the Algerian novel in French and Arabic, so I will limit myself to a few especially salient examples here. The first is the suicide of Amer in Mouloud Feraoun's *Les chemins qui montent* (1957). Saadi's *La nuit des origines* regenders and reverses the plot of Feraoun's novel, and *Boulevard* takes up some of its major narrative conceits (a personal diary, a fictitious news article).[27] Saadi's preoccupation with ancient Algerian history in the figure of the Numidian princess Sophonisba finds common ground with literary rewritings of the militant suicide of the Berber queen Dihya "la Kahina" (al-Kāhina), in works such as Kateb Yacine's play *La Kahina ou Dihya* (1972) and more contemporary novels such as Gisèle Halimi's *La Kahina* (2006) and Isaure de Saint Pierre's *La Kahina, reine des Aurès* (2011).[28] Constantine's suicidal geography is equally explored in the Arabic-language works of Algerian writers. For instance, al-Ṭāhir Waṭṭār's novel *al-Zilzāl* (*The Earthquake*, 1974) begins much like Saadi's short text "Retour à Constantine," discussed next in this chapter, with a hallucinatory walk through Constantine and Algerian history (it ends with the narrator attempting to throw himself into the Rhummel before he is seized by police).[29] And in Ahlam Mosteghanemi's *Dhākirat al-jasad* (*Memory in the Flesh*, 1993), a former FLN fighter constantly fights back the urge to throw himself off one of the city's many bridges.[30] Related scenes play out in Algiers in novels such as Waçiny al-A'radj's *Sayyidatu al-maqam* (1993), translated into French as *Les ailes de la reine* (2009), and Samir

Kacimi's *Yaum Rai'a lil-Mawt* (2009), recently translated as *Un jour idéal pour mourir* (2020).[31] As in Saadi's work, suicide becomes a means of staging intergenerational trauma in Michael Haneke's well-known film *Caché* (2005), set in Paris, and Kaouther Adimi's novel *Des ballerines de Papicha* (2010), set in Algiers.[32] In creating transhistorical and transnational links between Algeria and France through displaced protagonists, Saadi's work evidently shares the concerns of the *migritude* narratives discussed in previous chapters. But whereas works like Fatou Diome's *Le ventre de l'Atlantique* (2003) or Mati Diop's *Atlantics* (2009/2019) deal with ocean crossings and exiles haunted by Atlantic history in the *longue durée*, North African narratives have, understandably, tended to take the Mediterranean as their geographic, cultural, and historical focus.[33] The theme of the Mediterranean as a site for precarious, even suicidal aquatic journeys—as "seametary," in Abderrezak's sense—is taken up again in the following chapter in a discussion of Mahi Binebine's novel about crossing the Strait of Gibraltar from Tangiers, *Cannibales* (1999).[34] In this sense, Saadi's novels about Algeria's "city of bridges" form a thematic and formal bridge to the final chapter of *The Suicide Archive*, in which "exposure" becomes an explosion.

In order to show what and how, exactly, the metaphor and materiality of the multiple exposure surfaces or "exposes" in literature, I examine Saadi's poetics of multiple exposure in a short prose text, "Retour à Constantine" ("Return to Constantine," 2003).[35] Written in the wake of Algeria's civil war, typically called the *décennie noire* or Black Decade (1991–2002), "Retour à Constantine" develops in miniature the themes and questions that centrally occupy Saadi in his subsequent novels—not least, the long suicidal history of his native city. I use the text of "Retour" to identify and lay out the poetics of multiple exposure as an aesthetic principle in Saadi's work before tracing its operation across *La nuit des origines* and *Boulevard de l'abîme*. These novels unfold in constant reference to one another and to the text of "Retour." Saadi's oeuvre—like Sembène's *La Noire de . . .* —itself emerges as multiple exposure: composite, multiply grafted works that iteratively return to, redevelop, rewrite, and "reexpose" images introduced in earlier texts. In Saadi's works, the technique of multiple exposure allows for the articulation of alternative genealogies and expansive geographies of colonizing violence.

"Retour à Constantine" (2003)

Like Greene's calotypes and Sembène's *La Noire de . . .*, Saadi's "Retour à Constantine" is structured by signs of absence and peopled by the ghosts of dead women. The text unfurls as an apostrophe of the self, staging a paradoxical return to a childhood home that perhaps never existed in the first place but, rather, was hallucinated or invented:

> You dreamt so much about this return, ever since you hallucinated that house in a novel, on the couch, in reinvented stories you ended up believing. You needed its reality—7 Baghdad Street—written in brown ink on a yellowed birth certificate that you had slid under the same glass as the sepia photo of your mother, tethered [*accroché*] to your exile.[36]

The address, a street in the medina of Constantine, has disappeared from modern maps of the city.[37] Returning after a long absence to this narrow street perched above the Rhummel, or perhaps arriving there for the first time, the speaker of "Retour" finds only the skeleton of a building. The doorframe opens onto rubble—wreckage from one of the many earthquakes that have shaken the city over the years—framing only the abyss: "Now, in the doorway [*l'encadrement*] which strangely only guards old stones, from high up in the medina, you look down onto the emptiness, the tragedy, the excess [*démesure*] of your city."[38] It is from this vantage point in a doorframe above the Rhummel that the speaker of "Retour" scans the city and revisits its past.

"Retour" follows the speaker's circuitous descent into personal, urban, and national history, inching over the topography of a city that no longer appears familiar. During this mental and visual flânerie, he encounters the ghosts of suicides (*les fantômes des suicidés*): specters of the countless individuals who have flung themselves from the city's heights into the Rhummel. One phantom retains his attention: the face of a young girl he witnessed being dredged up from the ravine by firemen. It is a memory he associates swiftly with another image—the famous death mask of a suspected suicide recovered from the Seine and her depiction in Louis Aragon's surrealist novel *Aurélien* (1944): "(You still remember the face of that young woman whom firefighters had recovered and whom you later associated with *L'inconnue de la Seine* in *Aurélien*)."[39] The move is subtle but emblematic of how Saadi excavates and "multiply exposes" suicidal geologies, geographies, and genealogies in his texts. As an example of what I am calling a double or multiple "exposure," this memory graft overlays the image of an unidentified Algerian girl retrieved from the Rhummel Gorge with the iconography of the "Unknown" woman of the Seine (figure 4.3): an unnamed woman who had many names, known as the "Ophelia of the Seine," the "Drowned Mona Lisa," or the "Mona Lisa of suicide."[40] Saadi exhumes the bodies of two drowned women simultaneously, seeing two faces in one.

This nameless Algerian girl dredged up from the Rhummel and the Inconnue de la Seine appear in "Retour" as figures of absence, but also as sites for cathexis and the associative work of memory. Saadi's multiple exposure repeats the technologies of reproduction and superimposition that made the Inconnue so famous: her image became the "negative" for countless "positives"—photographs, sketches, and pale plaster death masks modeled (and molded) on her lifeless face.[41] Saadi reproduces the Inconnue in his own text, grafting her image onto a memory of witnessing a young suicide brought up from the ravine. His superimposition is such that neither girl is fully masked, neither death entirely effaced.

Following the anarchival logic of Saadi's superimposition, it becomes possible to make a subsequent exposure and to discern a third, translucent image: another death mask, another drowned girl, not mentioned explicitly in "Retour," but known to generations of Algerians in both Algeria and France. This time we can give her a name: Fatima Bedar (figure 4.4), a fifteen-year-old French Algerian high school student who defied her parents' wishes and attended the protests of Algerians in the streets of Paris on 17 October 1961—a night when the Seine ran red with Algerian blood after Maurice Papon's police massacred some two hundred Algerians and dumped their bodies into the river from bridges across the city (figure 4.5).[42] Police later fished Fatima's drowned body out of the Seine and, like the Inconnue before her, displayed her corpse in a Paris morgue. Her father, who identified the body, was forced to sign a procès-verbal that officially classified his daughter's death—a brutal murder at the hands of Papon's police—as a suicide.[43]

The ghosts of three drowned women thus surface in Saadi's "Retour à Constantine." The first two are "Inconnues": unnamed women, one French, one Algerian; one dredged up from the Seine, the other recovered from the Rhummel. The first became famous despite her anonymity; the second remained unknown, perhaps never to be identified. She finds an afterlife in Saadi's text, her image shadowed by the first. We can make these ghostly death masks intersect in a third figure, discerning another face not quite visible and overlaying yet another exposure in the same frame: that of a French Algerian girl, Fatima Bedar, whose "suicide" in the Seine on the eve of Independence was made to "mask" a mass murder by French police.

This is the permissive logic of the multiple exposure at work. Saadi provocatively superimposes Algerian and French female suicides, historical and literary deaths. He exposes the suicidal history of the Rhummel while smuggling into his text another river, the Seine, through the image of the Inconnue. Both are fluvial "seametaries" at the bottom of which lie so many drowned Algerians.[44] One is reminded of Siméa's assertion in Maximin's *L'isolé soleil*, discussed in chapter 1, that "there are many suicides among the colonized" and that, in Paris, the Seine is their burial ground. Saadi's poetics of multiple exposure makes it possible to read, *see* and *hear*, the Seine and the Rhummel together as geological features that harbor deep genealogies of loss. Like the exiled speaker of Baudelaire's "Le cygne," who looks at the Seine and thinks of the grieving Andromaque (herself contemplating another river, the Simoïs), for the speaker of "Retour" the Rhummel becomes a "sign" pointing to disparate histories of displacement.

The logic of the multiple exposure invites us to constellate other rivers and other bodies of water. To this layered geography, we might add the Grand Canal in Venice, in which Pateh Sallaby drowned. Evoked in the previous chapter in connection to Lyamlahy's novel *Évocation d'un mémorial à Venise*, this "river" is conjured in Paul Maheke's haunting installation *The River Asked for a Kiss (to Pateh Sabally)* (2017), which draws its title from Langston Hughes's poem "Suicide's Note," used as an epigraph to this chapter (figure 4.6).[45]

In addition to this "unknown woman of the Rhummel," another ghost haunts the river in Saadi's "Retour à Constantine": Sophonisba, the Carthaginian princess whose suicide around 203 CE at the battle of Cirta is one of Constantine's founding myths. Sophonisba's phantom haunts Saadi's novels in significant ways, but she appears first in "Retour à Constantine"—a text that plays on the multiple significations of *revenant*. In "Retour," the speaker identifies Sophonisba with Constantine's long history of resistance and resilience but also—in a parenthetical aside—with an ineluctable destiny:

> Your city was not well. [...] Crushed under three thousand years of events and by the two million residents today who cling to their rock, it still resists [...]. (It will always bring into the world a Sophonisba—the beautiful woman who will always love a Syphax while she marries a Massinissa, vassal to the outsider, before committing suicide).[46]

For the speaker of "Retour," Constantine always will have a Sophonisba: a suicidal heroine torn between allegiances and suspended between nations. This is the dark legacy that the unnamed woman dredged up from the Rhummel and each of the female protagonists of Saadi's subsequent novels confirm and extend.

Toward the end of "Retour à Constantine," the speaker formulates this pulsion to rehearse Constantine's original suicide in precise terms, as a feature of the city's precipitous landscape—a "genealogy of nature":

> One must be born above its verticals to feel the weight of a destiny, a genealogy of nature that brings you into the world on the edge of a chasm, under the roar of a ferocious and grandiose torrent rolling in this gigantic corridor of vertiginous vertical rocks—impregnable walls pockmarked with giant crypts where so many civilizations have ended [*échouées*].[47]

FIGURES 4.3 AND 4.4. *Top*, L'inconnue de la Seine. Source: Wikimedia Commons (L'Inconnue de la Seine, masque mortuaire). *Bottom*, Fatima Bedar. Source: Mémoires d'Humanité / Archives départementales de la Seine-Saint-Denis.

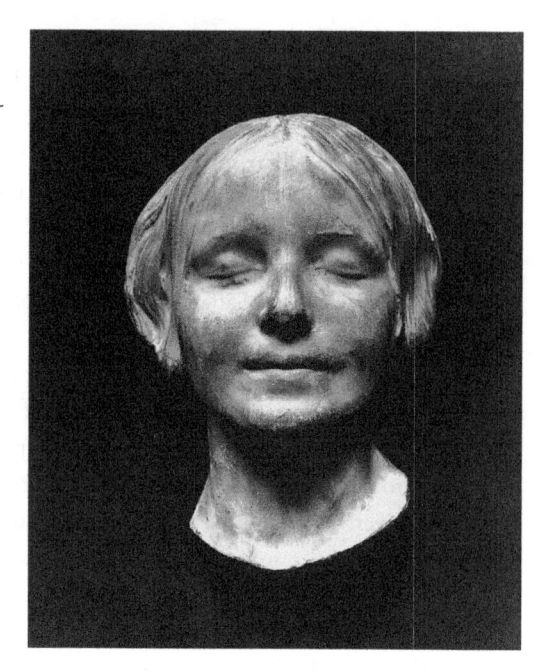

FIGURE 4.5. Photo taken by Jean Texier following the 17 October 1961 massacre and originally published in *L'Humanité*. Source: Mémoires d'Humanité / Archives départementales de la Seine-Saint-Denis ("Ici on noie les Algériens").

What Saadi calls a "genealogy of nature" names a gravitational pull that is geological and genealogical, geographic as well as historic: "the weight of a destiny" shared by all born above the abyss. This destiny is a shared genealogy of suicidal resistance whose point of origin is Sophonisba, the princess who made the bed of the Rhummel both a *lit de noces* (marriage bed) and *lit de mort* (deathbed). For Saadi, the Rhummel continues to accrue loss and signify absence in the present. The tense of Sophonisba's ghost is the future (*La très belle qui aimera toujours . . .*): her image shadows all past, present, and future suicides at the Rhummel Gorge.

The full signifying range of the kind of nonlinear, layered memory activated by Saadi's multiple exposure in "Retour à Constantine" comes into focus at the

FIGURE 4.6. Paul Maheke, *The River Asked for a Kiss (to Pateh Sabally)* (2017), part of Diaspora Pavilion, during the Fifty-Eighth Venice Biennale. Source: Francesco Allegretto and Paul Maheke.

very end of the text, after the speaker has retraced in his mind's eye a trajectory through the city and revisited its founding myths. At this point, Saadi abruptly reframes the narrative's scene of address, returning the reader to the moment with which he opened the text: the destabilizing pitch of opening a door and stumbling onto absence. He repeats the text's incipit almost verbatim ("you push open the door of the house you were born in and you stumble—stupefied, stunned, speechless—into the void")[48] before effecting sudden, multiple displacements in the final paragraph, which consists of two sentences in italics:

> *Dazed leaving his analyst's office, he headed down the street toward the quays along the Seine, wondering, confused, why he had come up with that dream during the session and telling himself, like someone whispering truths to themself, that the sacred rocks like the others come crashing down during earthquakes. The birth city will always come to mind for the exiled* [se déplacera toujours dans la tête de l'exilé].[49]

In this shift from second to third person, from present to anterior past, we realize now that the speaker of "Retour" is not in Constantine but in Paris, exiting his therapist's practice rather than entering his childhood home, wandering the banks of the Seine but remembering the Rhummel. The entire "address" of "Retour" now must be reframed, in terms of not only its scene of enunciation (Paris, along the Seine) but also its generic status: a dream conjured during a session of psychoanalysis (*séance*), a fiction masquerading as memory.

As the text closes, it opens again, reexposed, a new meaning grafted onto it. Now "Retour" becomes more clearly about the conditions of exile and melancholic longing—about the impossibility of the very "return" it stages.[50] A return *to* Constantine remains possible only as reverie, but the ghostly return *of* Constantine (*Retour de Constantine*)—as repressed memory, as *revenant*—is unavoidable. Constantine's suicidal history resurfaces in the present, in Paris, along the banks of the Seine. These twin rivers and twin cities become ways of staging the absolute entanglement of Algérie-Française.

The emergent frame of psychoanalysis introduced at the end of "Retour" anticipates *La nuit des origines* and *Boulevard de l'abîme*—interior, "psychological" novels that draw on psychoanalysis and psychoanalytic resistance in substantial ways. Like the speaker of "Retour," the protagonists of Saadi's novels are "displaced" Constantinians living in exile in Paris. They walk the streets of the metropole but have the uncanny sense that their native city continues to make itself visible and felt beneath their feet. The pasts of both cities wash up, over and over again—resurfacing on the banks of memory in the present, like the rivers' drowned. As in "Retour à Constantine," suicide serves as a conduit for historical memory and a privileged site for Saadi's poetics of multiple exposure. In these novels, the logic of the multiple exposure becomes an organizing principle, and the increasingly frequent irruption of the past in the present—of Constantine in Paris—drives the narratives toward their denouements and the respective protagonists, Abla and A., to their own unraveling. For the displaced protagonists of Saadi's final two novels, suicide becomes the only release from histories they cannot seem to repress and a compulsion to remember they cannot resist.

La nuit des origines (2005)

The final image of Saadi's *La nuit des origines* (2005) is a photograph of a dead woman from Constantine. The face of the deceased protagonist, Abla, appears in the epilogue, in the form of an ID photo in the hand of her ex-lover Alain or Ali-Alain, who imagines enlarging and framing the image alongside a portrait of the Romantic poet Gérard de Nerval (1808–55):

He held her ID photo in his palm for a long time, staring at it as though he were reading the lines of his hand: I will enlarge it, then frame it in an old, gold Marie-Louise, and I will hang it across from the portrait of Nerval. C'est l'Autre... I will simply sign in pen Abla—Alba, rather, as I called her the first time.[51]

The overlay of memorial, photographic, and scriptural procedures evoked at the end of *La nuit des origines* is characteristic of Saadi's poetics of multiple exposure. In this final scene, Alain finds himself on a plane "returning" to Constantine for the first time since his birth to deliver Abla's remains and affairs to her family and attend her funeral. A native of Constantine living in Paris, Alain works as a picture framer in an old photography studio in the Puces of Saint-Ouen, the northern suburb of Paris where much of the novel takes place. He inherited the building from an eccentric daguerreotypist known for his technique of capturing a subject's expression at the precise moment of exposure, just as the magnesium flash ignited.[52] So it seems especially fitting that Saadi frames his novel, and Abla's suicide, with the narrative "frame" of this talented *encadreur* imagining a suitable frame for a portrait of the woman he loved.

Alain's fantasy of framing at the end of *La nuit des origines* is also one of countersigning since he imagines forging Abla's name, signing the name he gave her, "Alba," in his own hand. The move replicates the playful inscription made by Nerval, who famously wrote beneath a daguerreotype of himself, "Je suis l'autre" (this is the portrait, *C'est l'Autre*, to which Alain alludes).[53] A citation from Nerval's *Aurélia* (1855), published posthumously after the author's suicide, closes Saadi's novel: "'*Besides, she belonged to me more in death than she did in life.*'"[54] Saadi's novel unspools very much like one of Nerval's novellas—or perhaps like a morbid variation on Baudelaire's "À une passante," giving the *fugitive beauté* of the female passerby a tragic denouement.[55]

Like the narrator of *Aurélia*, who obsessively mourns and reifies an enigmatic woman already lost to him, Alain spends the novel "try[ing] to understand her, to grasp [*saisir*] this woman..." (144). He wishes to still Abla's flight and render her legible. "I hold on [*je m'accroche*], but I suffer from her living so elusively [*insaisissable*]," Alain bemoans, in terms that closely recall his métier (143). It is a stasis and feat of possession that he only manages in death, like pinning a butterfly in an album.

Abla's doubled proper name, which Alain imagines signing after her suicide, and which he along with several other characters mispronounce for the first time as "Alba" or "white," enacts the instability that Alain found so unsettling about her. Subject to a constant metathesis throughout the novel, even in these final lines, her name oscillates between forms and meanings: "Abla... Alba, it's beautiful. Abla, she corrected, annoyed, bla, blah, I'm tired of my name always being mispronounced since I've been in France" (25).⁵⁶ This fugitive Algerian woman, Abla/Alba, shifts constantly beneath our eyes, like the flickering image on a tilt card: a human *tabula scalata*. Only in death does Alain "fix" Abla's name and image, the legible features of her identity.

Alain's fiction of legibility, however, comes at a high cost since he never manages to grasp Abla's motivations for leaving Constantine or for her suicide. He never succeeds in understanding her past. He never makes sense of her final act. As she warns him early in the novel, "You don't understand.... You cannot understand!" (40). Especially in her death, she remains enigmatic. Her suicide becomes the ultimate self-sealing text, something no one can fully witness or access.

Alain's fantasy of capture and reference is also a fantasy of restoration: a creative act of genealogy that attempts to repair a fractured filiation through a series of grafts and superimpositions. Throughout the novel, Alain progressively assimilates Abla as the allegorical *femme-nation* or *femme-patrie*. He cathects onto her his place of origin: Algeria and the city of Constantine, places he has no memory of and knows only through images on postcards (27). He assigns her a language, Arabic, which he no longer speaks nor understands (112). Ultimately, he overlays her image with that of his dead mother, of whom he has only a single photograph and whose tomb he visits with Abla in the Muslim cemetery of Thiais.⁵⁷

Abla flatly rejects Alain's multiple forms of "transference" of a fantasy of origins (native city, mother tongue, maternal figure). She actively resists Alain's desire to (super)impose onto her a geography and a genealogy. "But I'm not a country, not Constantine, not your mother...," she exclaims in a moment of frustration, desiring instead total rupture and freedom: "That might be what I want to rid myself of [*me défaire*], free myself from... a country. A parable..." (191). Her suicide charts a double movement in this sense. It provides the pretext for Alain's long-dreamed-of "return to Constantine," restoring his Algerian identity. At the same time, it constitutes a permanent severance. The opposite but entangled journeys of these twinned lovers, Abla and Alain, give the narrative its chiastic structure: the novel begins with Abla having arrived in Paris from Constantine, seeking rupture from a past that haunts her, and ends with Alain leaving Paris to return to Constantine. Abla's suicide enables Alain to reconnect with his origins, but it is equally a desperate attempt to reject, betray, negate, or erase her own.

That Alain plans to hang Abla's photo next to a framed portrait of Nerval in his photography studio reflects his desire to cathect onto her the weight of a genealogy, since Abla will hang alongside an image of the substituted father, Nerval, the first *encadrement* (frame/framing) Alain made: "He had found the copy of the enlarged photo by Nadar, a portrait of Gérard de Nerval, signed in pen 'C'est l'Autre,' the first thing he had framed in the studio, whom he had presented to visitors as his late father" (45–46). These reproductions of portraits signed by individuals who died by suicide, framed alongside each other, stand in for a dead mother and faceless father. Alain's real father is a mystery, a blank space in his family tree: a French conscript who died before he was born, of whom his mother never spoke and Alain possesses no image or memory. Like Alain, Abla carries the burden of a "memory full of holes" (102): an absent father, a dead mother. But she strives in vain to rid herself (*se défaire, se libérer*) of the kinds of associations, genealogies, and origins that Alain so desperately seeks to recuperate or, all else failing, invent for himself.

Whereas Alain desires to recover a past he never fully experienced, Abla tries to forget a past she remembers all too well. Her ocean crossing, traveling from Algeria across the Mediterranean to Paris, is a desire for amnesia: "I crossed the sea to forget, forget that city, the shadows from childhood, forget everything, forget that cursed country . . ." (141). But Abla's desire to free herself of the past is frustrated at every turn—up until the moment of her suicide—by images and objects recalling her origins and causing Algerian history to erupt suddenly in the present. This is true from the first page of the novel, when Abla ducks into an antique shop in the Puces during a rainstorm and stumbles upon an immense four-poster bed: an exact duplicate of her childhood bed in her grandfather's home in Constantine.[58] For Abla, the *lit d'or* immediately brings to mind the riverbed of the Rhummel and an embodied memory of sleeping above Constantine's abyss: "Scenes from childhood passed through her head, when she lay, afraid, in that bed atop the rumbling of the Rhummel, with the fear that to fall asleep was to fall into the abyss" (12).

In Abla's memory, the *lit d'or* and the *lit du Rummel* are evoked simultaneously as multiple exposure. One conjures the other, and two genealogies surge up in the present. The first is an unconventional "filiation": memories of Abla's grandfather, who we later learn has chosen her as his heir in a subversive rerouting of genealogy. The second corresponds to what Saadi, in "Retour à Constantine," terms a "genealogy of nature," a phrase reformulated in *La nuit des origines* in even more precise terms as an embodied genealogy of geology: "To be born above its abysses, you are bequeathed the darkest of legacies [*la plus obscure des ascendances*], a genealogy of geology [*une généalogie de géologie*], of geography as much as of history, and that vertigo you will keep in your eyes everywhere" (204). This "darkest of legacies" (*la plus obscure des as-*

cendances) is the strange inheritance of a bed perched above a river, now separated by a sea, whose double Abla finds "washed up" on the banks of another river, the Seine. The original French might equally be parsed as "the darkest of descents" and thus would name a precipitous fall, or leap, into the abyss.

As was the case in "Retour," the Rhummel River, called to mind in *La nuit des origines* by the sight of the *lit d'or*, becomes a privileged site for Saadi's poetics of multiple exposure, which overlays Algerian and French geographies. In *La nuit des origines*, Saadi's poetics of multiple exposure effectively becomes the motor of the text. Recollections of the Rhummel become increasingly frequent and unsettling for Abla, and she begins to see—or hallucinate—Paris as a riverbed. From the moment the Rhummel is conjured, Saadi's text is awash with aquatic images and fluvial metaphors. Exiting the Puces after the storm subsides, Abla floats downstream like Ophelia: "Carried away by the crowd, she let herself slip into the human tide, protected under the mass of umbrellas which formed great black water lilies" (14). Once back at her lodging—the Palais de la Femme, a refuge for displaced women—she looks out at the slick of asphalt and sees a river: "Below, the street formed a luminous river" (21). Later, peering out the window at a construction site in the street, she compares the scene below to the aftermath of an earthquake and a war zone in terms that recall the refuse depicted at the opening of "Retour": the wreckage of one of the Algerian city's many quakes—detritus clustered on the cliffs above the Rhummel.

The superimposition of French and Algerian rivers at the Palais de la Femme takes on more pointed historical significance when we consider its location: on the Rue de Charonne, steps from the Charonne metro stop—a seemingly anodyne detail mentioned numerous times in the text. More than an inconsequential geographic marker, an *effet du réel*, the signifier "Charonne" opens onto a recessed genealogy of state violence: the "Charonne massacre." On 8 February 1962, French police brutally suppressed protesting Algerians in Paris, as in October 1961, hurling manhole covers at demonstrators who had taken shelter in the entry of the Charonne metro station and killing between thirty-two and two hundred men and women.[59] Read as multiple exposure, Saadi's memory-image allows us to discern these complex layers and to attend to this overlay of geological features and state violence. When Abla looks out onto the Rue de Charonne, she sees a river—*Ici on noie les Algériens*, "Here we drown Algerians"—she sees Constantine, she sees war.[60]

The multiple exposure characterizes the structure of historical memory relating to the Charonne and October massacres in very real, even material ways. Photographs and footage of the Charonne massacre—an event that quickly superseded the October 1961 massacre in terms of media coverage, commemorative attention, and general visibility—became the "screen memory" of October 1961, an event for which scant visual traces remained.[61] In fact, Jacques Panijel's film *Octobre à Paris* superimposed archival images and collated film footage from the massacre at the Charonne metro stop onto content related to the October massacre a year prior. The poetics of multiple exposure invites us to attend to the historical potential remaining active and accessible even in fixtures of landscapes we assume to be familiar, providing skeleton keys for discerning the layered, mediatized structure of historical memory produced, as Lia Brozgal puts it, "in the absence of archive."[62]

Saadi's poetics of multiple exposure comes into sharpest focus in *La nuit des origines* in the moments before Abla's suicide. Like Diouana's death in *La Noire de . . .* , Abla's suicide is a hypervisual event that overlays multiple images of suffering and activates disparate genealogies of violence simultaneously. Following a psychotic break, Abla awakens for the last time in a vaguely carceral iteration of her *lit d'or*: restrained in an iron bed in the psychiatric ward of a Paris hospital. The treating psychiatrist, Professor Katz, attempts to understand Abla's *crise* through the lens of the violence of the *décennie noire* (Black Decade), the period that serves as the historical backdrop to the novel:

> Don't fall asleep, talk to me, what led you to leave Algeria, those events [*événements*], those killings [*tueries*]? I saw in *Match*, you know, that photo of the Madonna mourning her children, I understand you . . .
>
> She slowly propped herself up on her elbow, seemed to speak but no sound came out of her mouth; looking him straight in his eyes, fixedly, coldly, she yelled: You want me to tell you what, when the fetus came out of its mother's womb it was to be slaughtered? You want to know what, when the slaughterer kills believing he still deserves heaven? What do you want to know about me, about Algeria, when there are no more words, no more vocabulary with which to speak of it? (197–98)

Dr. Katz's desire to understand Abla's suffering—or, rather, his suggestion that he already does—is based on a visual equivalency: "I saw. [. . .] I understand you." Evoking one of the only press images to circulate outside Algeria during the "information blackout" of the "invisible war" of the *décennie noire,* he connects Abla's image to Hocine Zaourar's photograph of the "Madonna of Bentalha" (figure 4.7).[63]

Zaourar's photograph depicts an Algerian woman slumped against the wall of a hospital in the village of Bentalha in the aftermath of the massacre of hundreds of civilians by insurgents. Her mouth agape, her eyes pained, she is captured in frozen, silent anguish. Reminiscent of the way the speaker of

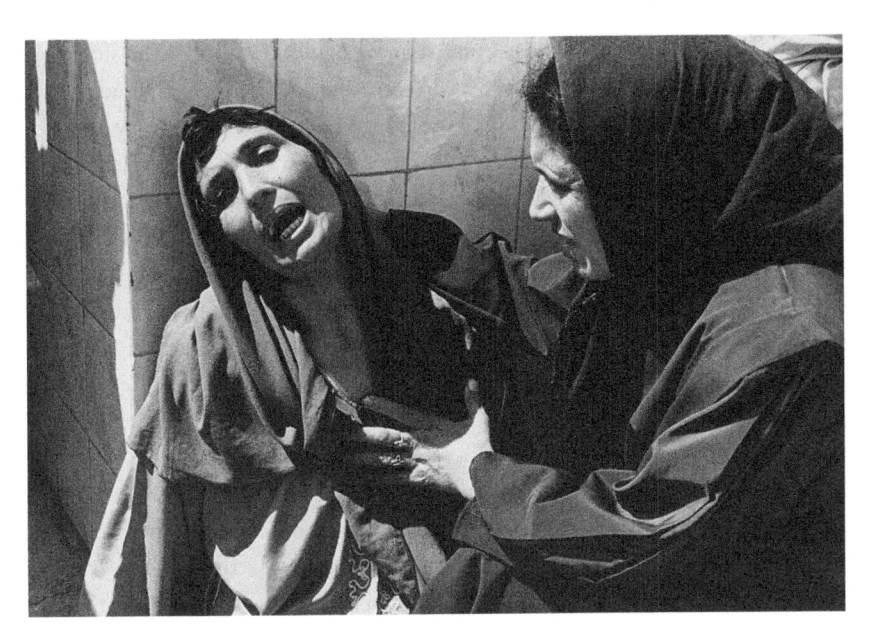

FIGURE 4.7. Hocine Zaourar, "Madonna of Bentalha" (1997). Source: Hocine Zaourar, "Madonna of Bentalha" (1997), World Press Photo.

"Retour" overlays the death mask of the Iconnue de la Seine onto the face of an unnamed woman recovered from the Rhummel, this is the image Katz sees shadowing the "real" Algerian woman before him: an Algerian pietà, propped up on her elbow in a Paris hospital bed.

For Abla, the visual equation masks more than it reveals. Katz's grafting of images rehearses the essentializing logic on which Saadi's characters have relied throughout the novel to "make sense" of this displaced Algerian woman. In France, Abla carries what Rose, writing about psychoanalytic displacement, calls "the burden of a past that is not easily recognized."[64] The doctor's periphrases (*ces événements, ces tueries*) obscure violence even as they attempt to name it. They bring to mind the myriad euphemisms used decades earlier in France to avoid naming the Algerian War of Independence as such.[65] They reiterate the vague allusions repeatedly ascribed to Abla's "flight" from Constantine and her arrival in Paris, leading Abla to wonder, "How to explain to them why she fled the country, her mental, intimate, personal breakdown?" (50). They rely on imposing a particular fiction and image of Algerian identity to render Abla's suffering legible—visible—within the terms of the metropole.

To borrow Walid Benkhaled's and Natalya Vince's phrasing, Abla must "perform" her Algerianness as an identity in and *of* crisis wherever she goes.[66]

She cannot suffer as an individual but must be made a symbol of the suffering of an entire nation: a portrait of victimhood during the Black Decade. Saadi's novel exposes the identarian pressures placed on Abla in France by (mostly male) French authorities, doctors, administrators, friends, and strangers, as well as other Algerians, such as Ali, who project their fantasy of origins onto her. The flattening of Abla's identity and constant (mis)translation of her motives for coming to France operate on a broader scale in the transnational discourse concerning the Black Decade. As Joseph Ford suggests, rather than illuminating the complex sociopolitical realities of the period, much Algerian literature in French—as well as literary criticism focused on this literature—has contributed to obscuring and simplifying the Black Decade for foreign audiences by relying exclusively on a language of conflict and crisis.[67] Saadi's novel to an extent bypasses these discursive circuits: in *La nuit des origines*, the violence of the Black Decade is almost entirely offstage, gestured to elliptically or mentioned in passing. Despite Dr. Katz's assertion, "I understand you . . . ," characters' references to the Black Decade typically reveal a total lack of understanding.

Zaourar's "Madonna" was subject to similar misinterpretations and made to appear in certain overdetermined frames. The image circulated widely, gaining acclaim among Western audiences in part because of its ostensible legibility within a Christian iconography of maternal suffering.[68] The woman was reported to have been grieving the eight sons she lost in the massacre (in Saadi's novel, Katz repeats this claim). In reality, her maternal status was invented, and this woman, like Abla, was childless.[69] For the doctor, Abla's suicidality and her inexplicable presence in Paris are conceivable—translatable—only through the frame of the contemporary violence of the Algerian civil war. She is visible to him as a type, understandable through an affective register of victimhood prepared by Zaourar's photograph. Her silence frustrates him—"speak to me," the doctor pleads—so he ascribes to her a story (and an image) of his own fashioning. For Abla, there is no language, or perhaps no *longer* a language, that can communicate the past she carries with her—"there are no more words, no more vocabulary with which to speak of it," she exclaims—save, perhaps, the dysgraphic language of suicide.

Even death fails to free her from the Algerian identity she so desperately seeks to efface and leave behind. The "failure" of Abla's suicide to undo (*défaire*) her allegiance to Constantine even in her own undoing (*défaire*) becomes apparent when, after her suicide, the doctors find on her person a family heirloom—her maternal grandfather's eleventh-century Arabic manuscript: "We found against her, on her body, this thing, Arabic writing, it looks like a parchment, I don't know, look, a talisman maybe" (199).[70] One is reminded of Sembène's Diouana, who is accompanied in her suicide by her traditional mask. But whereas Diouana reclaims the mask for herself shortly before her death, throughout the novel Abla has tried repeatedly to renounce her grandfather's manuscript by selling it to the Bibliothèque nationale, interrupting its line of transmission through transaction. After her death, the manuscript clings to her body as it did in life—"like a skin she couldn't manage to rid herself of [*défaire*]" (134).

Beyond the doctor's associations and her grandfather's manuscript, Abla dies, in a sense, already having "returned to Constantine"—where her remains eventually will be delivered—falling asleep one last time in her childhood bed perched above the suicidal landscape of the Rhummel Gorge: "Little by little, her eyelids slowly closed on those haunting images [...] two terrifying precipices on either side of the turbulent bubbling of the Rhummel in which she was drowning her tears" (197). As she expires in a hospital bed in Paris, the logic of the multiple exposure is such that her death is haunted by Constantine's original suicide, that of Sophonisba, and her face shadowed by the photograph-cum-icon of Our Lady of Bentalha.

Saadi's final novel, *Boulevard de l'abîme*, extends and repeats the suicidal imagery of *La nuit des origines* but leads us back in time, before the contemporary violence of the *décennie noire* which formed the backdrop to his earlier novel. In *Boulevard*, Saadi suggests that the tragic end of an Algerian woman in a Paris apartment in the 1980s has its beginning several decades earlier, in Constantine, in the traumatic violence of the late 1950s during the War for Independence. In this, the novel is both an investigation into suicide and a genealogy of colonial violence.

Boulevard de l'abîme (2017)

Saadi's final novel, *Boulevard de l'abîme* (2017), begins much like Sembène's 1962 short story, with a police investigation into a woman's suicide. At the beginning of the novel, the protagonist, an unidentified Algerian woman, is already dead—found lifeless in her Paris apartment. All that remains is for the inspector assigned to the case to sort through the woman's affairs to determine whether her death really is a suicide or a murder masquerading as one. In terms that precisely recall the incipit and excipit of "Retour"—as the speaker opened the door of his childhood home and later stumbled out of his therapist's practice (*stupéfait, ébaubi*)—*Boulevard de l'abîme* opens with the opening of a door. This time the door opened in the text is to the wardrobe of a deceased woman:

The inspector, stupefied, dumbfounded by such a wardrobe, opened up, one by one, the cupboards, the cabinets, drawers, chest, shelving units, rummaging, rifling, looking for a sign, a trace, proof, something!

"Confirm it was a suicide," the chief had ordered, "it's almost certain, but there have been so many disguised murders. [...] A report, as soon as possible to close the case."[71]

This textual "opening," coinciding with a frenzied opening of doors, drawers, cabinets, cupboards, and chests, is already a fantasy of closure: a desire to "close the case," as the chief orders. But closure, in this case, can only come about by multiple acts of opening and unsealing—by uncovering evidence that might help explain how, and why, this woman ended her life:

She must have left a note somewhere, a goodbye letter to a man, to her family, what do I know? [...] Suicides always leave a trace, a letter, a scribble, a final message at the last moment. [...] I don't understand how such a woman could voluntarily end her life, I don't understand.[72]

Like Sembène, Saadi gives us the end at the beginning. He also requires us to read until the end—until the very end, to the final page, in fact—to understand the beginning.

In a note on the last page, signed with his initials, "N. S.," Saadi explains that the events of his novel were inspired by a real *enquête:* a report on an infamous torture center on the outskirts of Constantine, the Améziane Farmhouse—a text that first circulated in the clandestine journal *Vérité-Liberté* (1961) under the title "Rapport sur la ferme Améziane" in Pierre Vidal-Naquet's *La raison d'état* (1962).[73] Saadi's note reads:

The Report on the Farm, which figures on page 138, is partly inspired by the book *La Raison d'Etat* published in 1962, in which Pierre Emmanuel Vidal-Naquet reproduces a report on the tortures in Constantine that originally appeared in the newspaper "Vérité-Liberté." *I imagined it was written by characters from the novel.* (A friendly nod to the memory of Jean-Luc Einaudi, a gone-too-soon anticolonial historian friend who sanctioned an investigation into the Constantine torture center during the Algerian war, which I have called here: the Torture Farm [*la Ferme des supplices*].)

Boulevard de l'abîme begins as a seemingly straightforward investigation into an apparent suicide in Paris: "It's so obvious," the inspector thinks, examining the empty bottles of barbiturates and psychotropics, "she couldn't fail, the suicide is proven."[74] However, it swiftly becomes a deeply unsettling and far from obvious descent into the past of the Améziane farmhouse. The search for answers to one woman's mysterious death unearths far more than the detective intended: namely, the troubling memory of his own time as a French conscript in the Algerian War of Independence—a past he thought he long had buried—and the point where this history intersects with the fate of a woman whose body now is proving impossible to bury, whose case refuses to close, and whose past cannot be laid to rest.

The narrative frame of the police investigation (*enquête*) of a suicide opens the door in *Boulevard de l'abîme* for an inquiry into the history of the Améziane farmhouse. This is a site Jim House and Neil MacMaster have characterized as "the most terrible of all Algerian interrogation centers," where some 108,175 people were detained, "of which an untold number died from torture or summary execution."[75] The report by Pierre Vidal-Naquet's mentioned by Saadi had called attention to the torture center as early as the 1960s, but the full scope of the horrors that took place at the Améziane farm only came to light gradually, as survivor testimonies surfaced. In his *Enquête*, Jean-Luc Einaudi presents in painstaking detail the testimonies of Algerians, such as Djamila Guellal, Zéléïkha Boukadoum, Hachemi Zitouni, and Omar Zemmoura, among many others, who survived brutal torture, rape, and sexual degradation at the hands of French police and soldiers. Though most survivors bore indelible marks and scars from their *séances* (the term used by police and soldiers to describe torture sessions), the farm was designed to leave behind no written trace, no paper trail, since upon their release detainees were made to sign a document declaring that they had been well treated and merely questioned.[76] In this sense, the Améziane farm figures a specific kind of French Algerian *non*-history since the site was constructed as an "administrative black hole": a place with "no recognized official existence" and of which the Prefect of Police Maurice Papon famously denied having any knowledge.[77] The farm was where hundreds of people disappeared without a trace—until their bodies surfaced on the banks of the Rhummel. As Saadi writes, "In the morning, we more and more frequently found anonymous bodies drowned in the Rhummel, a stone tied around their necks."[78] In *Boulevard*, Saadi excavates and exposes the imbricated histories of the Améziane farmhouse and Rhummel as multiple exposure and by way of suicide. The Parisian suicide of an Algerian woman—an enigmatic figure identified only by the initial, "A.," ascribed to her—becomes the textual flashpoint where layered histories of suicide, resistance, and colonial violence converge and overlap in the present.

Saadi's novel has at least two beginnings. The first chapter, labeled "1," which opens with the detective opening up a dead woman's wardrobe in an attempt to close the case, is preceded by a short, italicized paratext: an omniscient, extradiegetic address to a feminine *vous*, the figure of *l'absente* or *la disparue*, that additionally interpolates an *il*—the man who loved her, who wrote to her, and who, after her death, tries to render her in writing. In a constant slippage between being (*l'être*) and writing (*lettre*), Saadi begins at the beginning of the alphabet, with the woman's initial:

> *A, like . . . We begin by changing, masking, veiling your name, reducing it to an initial, disembodying* [désincarner] *you into a letter of the alphabet—why not the first?—concealing your identity, inventing for you a civil status, a legend, you become a fictional character.* [. . .] *Your story is stolen, your life is veiled, as if you never existed and you are thus reduced, transformed into writing, into sepia ink, dark, dispossessed of what you were, stripped of yourself.* [. . .] *Whoever disappears by their own hands, at will, carries with them the enigma of their death, leaving the questions to the living.*[79]

This disembodied address corresponds to the novel's scene of writing: an effort by an ex-lover to reconstitute and reinvent the past of the woman he loved and whom he lost to suicide—an attempt to make sense of her final, fatal gesture. The task of the writer at the outset of the novel is to find a suitable form, in writing, for absence. He settles on the letter (*lettre*), as both epistle ("he began to unravel the story [. . .] in this long letter you will never read") and graph. Part investigation, part letter to the dead, *Boulevard* is an address to the absent other who is represented by the first letter of the alphabet: *à A*—a tautology. At the end of the novel, the letter *A* is a cenotaph, marking an otherwise unadorned tombstone in the cemetery of Thiais where the *suicidée*, A., is buried: "No date in parentheses, no trace of time. [. . .] Simply engraved was a letter, an enigmatic initial: A."[80] This trace—both sigil and sign, enigma and emblem—is the cipher that both A.'s lover and the detective spend the novel trying to decode: the unreadable text of her suicide.

Saadi's evocation of the letter *A* at the outset of the novel leads us to other letters, both orthographic and epistolary in a manner reminiscent of the almost hallucinatory play of letters, anagrams, and homonyms in Maximin's epistolary *L'isolé soleil* analyzed in chapter 1. Formally, the novels resemble each other: both are composed in multiple voices, in multiple scripts, and framed as myriad texts in progress (letters, journals, articles, investigations). Part I of *Boulevard de l'abîme* is titled "Lettre à la disparue" or "Letter to the Disappeared." In French, there is a double sounding: "lettre A, la disparue" (letter "A," the disappeared) or "lettre à l'A disparue" (letter to the disappeared "A"). Part II of the novel is labeled simply with the letter *A* followed by an epigraph: an excerpt from a letter from Gustave Flaubert to George Sand assuring Sand that his "poor [Emma] Bovary" did indeed kill herself and that anyone who thinks otherwise grossly misunderstood her character.[81] Part III, "La ferme des supplices" (The torture farm), deviates from this scheme and from the motif of the "letter"— though perhaps with good reason. This final section focuses on the horrors of the Améziane farm, a place where articulate language was given over to brutal acts of disarticulation, to torture so horrific that it shattered all language.[82]

The extradiegetic, italicized narration that opens the novel with its apostrophe of the dead is one of several narrative strands that structure *Boulevard de l'abîme*. The italicized address (*à A.*) threads throughout, providing access to the novel's scene of writing and offering glimpses into A.'s past in the form of recollections focalized through the perspective of her ex-lover. To this, Saadi joins other texts in other hands: embedded narratives and memories stacked like Russian dolls, layered like sedimented histories. The result is that Saadi's poetics of multiple exposure functions on a macrostructural level, operating across the novel, such that the text's dominant geological feature, Constantine's *abîme*, also becomes its organizing principle: a narratological *mise en abîme*.

The third-person narration focalized on the detective's *enquête* subsumes correspondences with A.'s lover, transcribed depositions related to the investigation, as well as newspaper articles. Its most distinctive feature, however, is that its narrative present frequently is interrupted by the work of memory, giving way to another embedded, past-tense narrative that is distinguished by a smaller typeface and broader margins, as though receding from the page—a typographic *mise en abîme*. This embedded narration corresponds to the detective's memory of the Algerian War, when he served as a member of the SAS (Sections Administratives Spécialisées).[83] In the detective's narrative, Saadi reproduces the "Rapport sur la ferme":[84] a yellowed, typewritten document that the detective unearths sorting through an old briefcase, "a trunk brought back from the army that he had kept like a funeral urn for his memories of Algeria," and that he proceeds to scan "like someone slowly rereading a letter they know by heart."[85] This report, which emerges from the detective's past as if from beyond the grave and reads like an intimate letter, documents in clinical detail the workings of the Améziane farm and the torture techniques employed and perfected there (*gégènes, supplice de l'eau, pendaisons, brûlures*). It attempts to account for hundreds of thousands of victims and disappeared persons.

In Saadi's retelling, the detective investigating A.'s suicide and attempting to file his own report is returned to this other report from decades earlier, to which he contributed. During the war, the detective, then an SAS officer, helped hide a draft of the "Rapport sur la ferme" under a prostitute's bed in a brothel frequented by the French military before transmitting it to the clandestine journal *Vérité-Liberté*.[86] Like Sembène's *La Noire de...*, Saadi's novel becomes very much a story about newspapers: an investigative documentary narrative that constantly blurs divisions between history and fiction. Saadi takes the *mise en abîme* further by associating the brothel where the detective hides the report with an address that readers of Saadi's other works will recognize: "around Bab-el-Jabia, number 7," that is, a house marked "7" near the Sidi Rached (Bab Jabia, or Bab el Jabia) bridge in Constantine. This is the same brothel alluded to in Saadi's "Retour."[87] Like *L'isolé soleil*, whose final lines furnish the incipit of Maximin's subsequent novel, *Soufrières*, Saadi texts are spliced together in intricate ways, traversed by intertextual borrowings and repetitions that mimic the way memory itself operates in these novels: where images, words, and sounds are constantly, often unexpectedly, subject to recall, association, and anagrammatic play.

The final narrative strand that structures *Boulevard de l'abîme* is labeled "(Carnet noir)." Its title evokes another infamous report, published decades after the "Rapport sur la ferme," concerning postcolonial state violence: the "Cahier noir d'octobre" (1988) by the Comité national contre la torture, which documented the torture and abuses perpetrated by Algerian police against protesters in October 1988.[88] The "Carnet noir" constitutes the only extended first-person narration of Saadi's novel. It corresponds to the *for intérieur* of A., to which we have access through the contents of a dog-eared leather notebook (*carnet*) discovered by the detective as he searched through her possessions. Initially characterized by frenzied, dysgraphic writing, the "Carnet noir" gradually gives way to something more regular, more readable—namely, A.'s transcribed sessions (*séances*) with her psychoanalyst:

> [The detective] thought of the black notebook with a clasp which he opened abruptly, scattering the pages: the first crumpled, smeared with wine stains, sentences thrown together messily, without punctuation or crossing-outs, only a few removed, illegible words, which must have being violently erased, no doubt names, a trembling penmanship, thrown down on the paper, one would have said words of distress or drunken writing, enigmatic; then, in the middle of the notebook, a title: SESSIONS [*séances*].[89]

Saadi's recourse to psychoanalysis as a narrative device builds on themes already explored in "Retour à Constantine" and *La nuit des origines*. In *Boulevard de l'abîme*, however, the stakes are somewhat higher, given the affinity not only between A.'s "Carnet noir" and Algeria's "Cahier noir" but also between *séances de psychanalyse* (psychoanalytic sessions) and *séances de torture* (torture sessions), the former serving as a way of "working through" the recurrent trauma of the latter. Indeed, *séance* traverses the various historical and narrative threads of the novel, becoming a transhistorical link by which the violence of colonial torture during the 1950s is connected to the postcolonial torture of the 1980s. Both find their way into the present. Saadi's novel shows the *séances* of torture and analysis at work as techniques of "exposure" to the past and to pain. While the *séance* of psychoanalysis aims at a therapeutic release through language, the *séance* of torture inflicts pain to produce a confession. Both are technologies of exposition and extraction: attempts to make the body speak. Both are directed at kinds of "resistance" (to analysis, to capitulation).

It is only through the superimposition of the novel's narrative strands as multiple exposure that we gradually make sense of the death of A. Her story emerges glimpsed at the points of overlap and convergence in Saadi's richly layered textual configuration. Like Sembène's short story, Saadi's *Boulevard* makes us, along with the detective, responsible for "recovering the narrative and locating the suicidal impulse."[90] We finally come to understand that *A* stands for Améziane, A.'s surname and the name of her childhood home: the farmhouse that became a torture center during the war, where her brother was detained and tortured, and where Saadi's own father was tortured in 1958. The novel bears a dedication to this effect: "To the memory of my father, tortured in March 1958 at the Torture Farm, Constantine."

In *Boulevard*, Saadi uses A.'s suicide to reinvent and restage the history of the Améziane farm and of its original proprietors, the Améziane family. It is a history he imagines can end only in the suicide of the woman made to carry the burden of this past—a history of torture that continues to torture (*taurade*) her in the present:

> I'm tired, exhausted, I've really had enough, enough of all this, with this past that gnaws at me, sticks to my skin, that comes back to me, in my face, it's a part of my life however, so distant, over [*close*], I threw the keys into the Rhummel, I've paid, paid terribly with my suffering, I try to forget this story but it keeps coming back, harassing me.[91]

Like Abla in *La nuit des origines* and the narrator of "Retour à Constantine," A. is pursued by a history that seems to have no end, that follows her wherever she goes. A.'s frustration closely recalls the words of the detective in Sembène's short story: "C'est un boomerang, cette histoire" (This story/history is a boomerang).[92]

Against this historical backdrop, the details evoked at the very beginning of Saadi's novel take on a different significance. An initially unidentified woman, an "Inconnue," A. resembles a drowned woman in her death, lying naked in the corridor, with vitreous eyes and a frozen stare; spittle collects like seafoam (*une écume jaunie*) at the corners of her mouth.[93] Her body bears strange traces of physical trauma: faded bruises and red marks revealed during her autopsy.[94] These injuries mirror (almost verbatim) the telltale signs of time spent at the Améziane farm, as described in Saadi's fictionalized "Rapport sur la ferme" and in Einaudi's *Enquête*.[95] The female suicide victim, whose death in Paris at the beginning of the novel overlays the imagery of the drowned and the tortured, is the flashpoint for Saadi's excavation and multiple exposure of a history of (post)colonial violence centered on Constantine and the Rhummel. This excavation is the "exposure" of a crime for which there has been no reckoning: it serves as a damning indictment of Papon and his forces since it reveals how the Rhummel, like the Seine in 1961, had served as a fluvial burial ground for so many victims of French state terror.

Saadi hews closely to the history of the Améziane farm as presented by Vidal-Naquet, and to the biography of the Améziane family as presented by Einaudi—down to the name of A.'s dog, Athos, which is the same as that of the Améziane family's dog, a detail mentioned in passing in Einaudi's *Enquête*. Like Sembène, who grafts toponyms, names, and dates from the real-life death of Diouana Gomis into his short story, Saadi exhibits a near-forensic level of attention to detail. Like Diouana, A. is a historical double for a real woman, Monique Améziane: the daughter of the original proprietor of the farm, a wealthy, pro-French *bachagha* of Constantine, who later entrusted the grounds to the care of his son, Mouloud Améziane, in the early 1950s when he fled to France.[96] Mouloud, Monique's half-brother, gave his father's property to the FLN before French troops made it a torture center during the war.[97]

Despite its basis in a carefully documented family history, *Boulevard* is no more a "historical novel" than, say, Kanor's *Humus* or Maximin's *L'isolé soleil*. Like these novels, *Boulevard* throws the writing of history itself into crisis. Saadi's poetics of multiple exposure more closely resembles that of A.'s ex-lover, who cannot "recount the facts in chronological order" and instead allows scenes and images to accumulate "as they would come back to him in his imagination."[98] The historical focus that organizes *Boulevard* is a particular episode in Monique's adolescence in May 1958—an event replayed by A., and by other characters, again and again. It is an especially striking example of the poetics of multiple exposure at work: a point of convergence and refraction where the various narrative strands of the novel spectacularly overlap.

On 8 May 1958, Monique's brother Mouloud was arrested and tortured at the family farm. A few weeks after his disappearance, Monique, a lycée student of only seventeen or eighteen at the time, agreed to participate in a public demonstration of loyalty to France on the condition of her brother's release; she had been told her cooperation was the only way her brother would be spared death.[99] This demonstration took the form of one of the many unveiling rituals orchestrated by the French as part of an "emancipation" campaign: a ceremony during which Algerian women embraced Western "modernity" by removing and burning their *haïks*.[100] This spectacle, which Frantz Fanon analyzes in his pioneering essay "L'Algérie se dévoile," adds another valance to our notion of "exposure."[101]

At the theater in Place de la Brèche, Constantine's most iconic square, surrounded by military officials and in front of an enormous crowd, Monique read a prepared speech that announced the "emancipation" of Algerian women. She then dramatically removed her veil—in Saadi's text a black *melaya*, in reality a white face veil and *haïk*—exposing her hair and baring her face, tossing the coverings into the crowd.[102] Underneath, she was styled as an Algerian Marianne, in a blue dress with a Republican *cocarde tricolore*.[103] The scene was reported in the newspaper *La Dépêche de Constantine* on 27 May 1958, along with a photo of Monique (figure 4.8) and the caption, "A young Muslim woman, Mademoiselle Améziane, daughter of bachagha, has just spontaneously removed her veil and invited all Arab women to follow her example."[104] The "spontaneity" of Monique/A.'s unveiling was pure fiction. One of the great ironies of Monique's coercive unveiling, explored by Saadi in *Boulevard*, was the fact that she never had worn a veil prior to the ceremony because she was raised in a generally Francophile family by her mother (Mouloud's stepmother), a French Jew. On the balcony of the municipal theater, the young Constantinian thus becomes a tragedienne in an impossible role, one she did not choose, like Corneille's Sophonisbe. As Saadi writes, "She looked like an actress in a tragedy taking off her costume, her ancient double from which she had freed herself to the cheers of the spectators."[105]

In his novel, Saadi describes the photograph of Monique and imagines the text of an accompanying article in the *Dépêche* describing her unveiling.[106] Saadi's imagined newspaper text is at least partially based on the text of the "real" article, a passage from the 27 May issue describing Jacques Soustelle's reception at the Place de la Brèche:

> Sheikh Lakhdari Abdellell, imam of the Sidi-El Ketani mosque, then shows, in a message addressed to Muslims, that integration does not affect the free exercise of religious practices. The Sheikh also declares that ancestral customs, such as the wearing of the veil to which Arab women are subjected, have nothing to do with the Islamic religion.

FIGURE 4.8. Monique Améziane reading the "emancipation" text in Constantine, Place du Théâtre, 1958, printed in the *Dépêche de Constantine*. Source: *Dépêche de Constantine*, 27 May 1958, 10 (Bibliothèque nationale de France, L 1.15–MFM MICR D-314 1958/04-1958/06).

"Woman, break your chains!" he cried. "And you, man, lean on your wife, your equal!"

Immediately, this great authoritative voice's advice was followed. A young Muslim woman, Mademoiselle Améziane, daughter of the bachagha, tears off her veil and invites all Muslim women to follow her example. A tremendous ovation greets this gesture, and the "Marseillaise," hymn of freedom—therefore of emancipation—resounds, sung by the crowd.[107]

Saadi initially focalizes the episode of A.'s unveiling through the perspective of the detective, who finds a folded copy of the original newsprint nestled among the pages of A.'s *carnet noir*. Her fateful performance then is evoked in detail in each of the narrative strands—a parallax effect whereby the moment of A.'s unveiling is multiply captured and refracted.

Each time, Saadi makes a revealing substitution, preferring a black *melaya* to Monique's white *haïk* pictured in the newspaper article. For A., this "sinister fabric" renders her unrecognizable and links her fate to that of Sophonisba:

Where was my father, in his bachagha splendor, when I was led to the courtyard in front of the theater as on the trestles of a stage, dressed in a black *melaya*—an actress who did not know her lines—asking me what

I was doing there in front of that crowd of screaming French-Algerians, hidden under that sinister fabric, that black rag in which I had been concealed?... As Sophonisbe shouted to the inhabitants of the city before ingesting poison out of her love for Massinissa: "For what crime could I deserve your hatred?" Sophonisbe of Cirta is a bit like my Numidian ancestor, isn't she?[108]

Sophonisba's exclamation, "For what crime could I deserve your hatred?" (Par quel crime ai-je pu mériter votre haine?), which A. imagines being the princess's final words, her spoken suicide note, are the result of another substitution and superimposition made by Saadi. Sophonisba never speaks these lines in Corneille's tragedy (or in any other versions of the play). They belong to Racine's *Esther*—"Par quel crime ai-je pu mériter mon malheur?"—the Jewish queen who saves her people from one massacre by causing another: another image, another tragedy, another history of disrupted genealogies overlaid as multiple exposure.[109]

Saadi's vestimentary and textual substitutions activate a feminine genealogy of the veil centered on Constantine, where, in contrast to other Algerian cities, the black *melaya* or *m'laya* became "the mourning symbol for occupied Algeria" after the defeat of Ahmed Bey and later "a ritual passed down from mother to daughter, generation to generation."[110] A sign of mourning specific to Constantine, the black *melaya* is a metonym for a genealogy of grief and colonial violence transmitted among women over the centuries. Saadi's substitution, in this way, is also a literary "correction" of history since women in Constantine to this day wear black, not white, veils—a fact French authorities overlooked in their last-minute staging of Monique's spectacular unveiling.

Crucially, A.'s black *melaya* returns us to the theme of photography as a technology of capture and reference: a tool of colonizing war. It evokes the "camera covered with a black veil" that haunts the detective's memories of the Algerian revolution: a cloth-covered camera wielded by a military photographer, before which Algerian women were paraded and forced to remove their veils so they could be photographed and assigned identity cards.[111] During the revolution, entire communities were rounded up, and Algerian women were forcibly unveiled, so as to render them "visible and 'legible'" to French authorities.[112] The detective parses this dark irony, in which the various valences of "exposure" (photographic process, unveiling) converge: "It's comical, this veiled device facing unveiled women!"[113]

In Saadi's novel, the photograph of Monique/A. in the black *melaya* enables the detective to fit together the pieces of this puzzling case with his own history. The detective uncovers a clipping of the photograph supposedly printed in the *Dépêche* among the pages of the "Carnet noir." He recalls standing in the crowd, looking up at the young *lycéenne*, and witnessing her staged unveiling in 1958 without realizing its full significance. The image from the *Dépêche* prompts the detective to rummage for another photograph, one of A. that he had slipped out of its frame and into his pocket at the beginning of the novel as he sorted through her belongings. He recognizes the *lycéenne* in the woman whose suicide in Paris is under investigation. This unmasking of a veiled identity comes about through the comparison of two photographs—a superimposition of faces and multiple exposure:

> And suddenly he took the photo of the woman who had committed suicide from his drawer and began to compare the two faces . . .
> "No, not possible, my God, it can't be her, this story [*cette histoire*] is going to drive me crazy . . ."
> It took so many years, so many events in his life, so many oversights to be overtaken by this scene printed in the photograph of a yellowed newspaper, hidden between the pages of a diary of a woman who committed suicide in Paris. The inspector, stupefied, dumbfounded, perplexed, kept repeating to himself as if lamenting: "No, it can't be her, it's not possible, it's my delirious imagination, the spell [*l'envoûtement*], this damn country that overwhelms me [*m'envahit*]," comparing again and again the two photographs, scrutinizing the faces as if looking for signs.[114]

The ability to "close the case"—that is, to identify this suicide victim and the traumatic past her death conceals—depends on an openness to seeing multiple images and multiple histories simultaneously: the capacity to discern two faces in one, or rather the same face at two different points in time, as ghostly images shadowing each other. This is the vertiginous logic of the multiple exposure at work: a visual and textual *mise en abîme* that dramatically collapses histories and geographies into a single, dizzying frame. It is mad history, or history that risks madness: *Cette histoire va me rendre fou . . .*

In the end, A.'s suicide becomes a fiction: another effect of *mise en abîme*, a fiction within a fiction. Despite the detective's careful investigative work, he will be forced to classify this suicide as an "AVC," a hemorrhaging of the brain; it is the only explanation for her mother's death that A.'s distressed daughter will accept.[115] This suicide of memory thus becomes an insult to memory ("You insult her memory, doctor," the daughter says), and must be masked, covered up.[116] For the detective, this is a hard pill to swallow, despite his supervisor's suggestion that it is merely "part of the job":

"But chief, I'm a sworn police officer, should I lie and invent a version that does not correspond with the truth?"

"Oh, it's nothing, you must have swallowed other lies, right? It doesn't change anything you know, it's only that in the case of suicide that the murderer also happens to be the victim, right?"[117]

The biting irony in the officer's reluctance to call this suicide something other than voluntary death is the fact that so many murders of Algerians—in Paris as in Constantine, most notably at the hands of Papon's police—have been covered up by the state-sponsored fiction of suicide. This was the case, as we saw, with the "disappearance" of Fatima Bedar. Until recently, her murder by police remained legible in the state archive as a fiction: a procès-verbal in which a "little story" (*une petite histoire*) about suicide by drowning had been told.[118] It was the case, too, of the fifteen or so bodies, other drowned Algerians, recovered along with Fatima.[119] These are the dangerous historical fictions, intended to occlude colonial and state violence, that Saadi's literary fiction registers, exposes, and unmasks.

By writing suicide as multiple exposure, Saadi's work, like the other authors in *The Suicide Archive*, constantly shuttles between historical and literary suicides, "real" and literary deaths. His work explores the way suicide gives rise to fiction—to the stories we tell in suicide's wake—but as with Sembène, Saadi's novels also reveal the extent to which suicide can become a "mask" or screen in its own right: in this case, dangerous fictions layered over acts of state terror. The poetics of multiple exposure facilitates the excavation of suppressed histories of violence. Beyond a purely aesthetic principle, the multiple exposure emerges in Saadi's work as a critical imperative: to identify two faces in one, to see the Rhummel in the Seine and the Seine in the Rhummel, to remain haunted by Sophonisba, and to recognize the present as shadowed by the past as well as latent, invisible potential.

Conclusion: Sophonisba's Ghost, or The Last Exposure

> She is going to die. [...] Whether or not the subject is already dead, every photograph is this catastrophe.
> ROLAND BARTHES, *Camera Lucida* (1980)

In "Retour à Constantine," *La nuit des origines*, and *Boulevard de l'abîme*, Saadi's evocation of the suicide of Sophonisba and the suicidal history of the Rhummel is part of a broader strategy of engaging histories and fictions of suicide as "multiple exposure." In these works, Sophonisba's ghost is the figure of a suicidal past that is not past but continues to signify and have relevance in the present. Like the gorge itself, her ghost enables us to accommodate a sense of a deep time and geological scale, one that would respond to the plural chronotope of the *longue durée*.[120] Constantine's suicidal history and the ghost of Sophonisba still haunt the ravine in real ways, as additional exposures accumulate.

In contemporary Algeria suicide remains, overwhelmingly, a "feminine" phenomenon.[121] Since Independence (1962), Algeria has seen a stark rise in the rates of suicide and suicide attempts, particularly among young women between the ages of sixteen and twenty-nine, with an especially sharp increase in comparison to the rest of the Maghreb since the *décennie noire*.[122] Suicide rates continued to skyrocket in the wake of natural disasters in the early 2000s that resulted in immense human and material loss.[123] The female "tenor" of Algerian suicide has remained a consistent and defining feature. Sociologists suggest that women in Algeria are at least three times more likely than men to attempt suicide. This ratio has remained stable since the end of the 1980s and now reflects broader trends in suicidal ideation across the Maghreb, in contrast to most other parts of the world, where suicide rates for men are higher.[124]

More than participating in a long-standing tragic genealogy of female suicide, Saadi's portrayal of suicidal heroines reflects and responds to a historical reality as well as an ongoing public health crisis in contemporary Algeria. His fiction, like that of other authors examined throughout *The Suicide Archive*, offers an aesthetic response to a longtime problem in suicidology: what Philippe Besnard calls an "incompatibility between Durkheimian sociology and women."[125] Historically, the predominantly female nature of suicide in Algeria engendered a certain illegibility and was the source of a major and persistent discrepancy between official suicide reports from government and police officials and the scientific data collected and produced by sociologists and suicidologists through clinical studies and fieldwork.[126] Because the dominant referential and discursive models for recognizing, registering, and representing suicide are inherently masculinist, female suicide tends to fall out of frame.[127] In Algeria, as elsewhere, female suicides typically have been explained through "a masculine interpretation of suicides by women marked by modesty, avoidance, and honor."[128] For this reason, they are more easily dissembled, misclassified, or misconstrued. We have observed this trend throughout *The Suicide Archive*, in the coercive framings of female suicide in and out of the archive, in both colonial and postcolonial scripts, with the suicides of the women of *Le Soleil*, Delgrès's female followers, the women of Nder, and Diouana Gomis.

Literary suicides, to an extent, "write back" to the dominant discourses on suicide that historically have obscured women's suicides by bringing them into view. They provide other frames for thinking voluntary death and the history of Algérie-Française together. Saadi's novels accomplish this generative reframing through their poetics of multiple exposure: a technology of making-visible that I have additionally identified and developed here as a literary hermeneutic. By enabling disparate histories of suicide and resistance to remain legible simultaneously and surface belatedly, the operation of "multiple exposures" invites us to attend to what initially seems to escape the dialectical image. It helps us to visualize hidden scenes of violence that evade the camera's shutter. Like the suicide archive, the shadow-image of the multiple exposure is never fully fixed. As a semantic chance available in French as well as in English would have it, the "last exposure" (*la dernière pose*) is not necessarily the final (*l'ultime*) exposure; it is merely the most recent (*le dernier*) in a potentially endless chain.

V

Misery acquaints a man with strange bedfellows.

WILLIAM SHAKESPEARE, *The Tempest*

· 5 ·

STRANGE BEDFELLOWS

On Suicide Bombing and Literature

> I tried to deliver this message to them, but I couldn't find another way. Even worse, they've convinced the world and themselves that they are the victims. How can that be? How can the occupier be the victim? If they take on the role of oppressor and victim, then I have no other choice but to also be a victim and a murderer as well.
>
> KAIS NASHIF as Said in *Paradise Now* (2005)

Human Bombs, Other People

When Jacqueline Rose writes in *The Last Resistance* (2007) that "all suicides kill other people," she has in mind the living: "Anyone left behind after a loved one commits, or even attempts, suicide is likely to spend much of the rest of their life wondering whether they themselves have, or should have, survived. Suicide is rarely the singular, definitive, act it appears to be."[1] Suicide destroys lives. But to assert that suicides kill other people is also to recognize, as Rose later does, that at the moment of death, the self becomes "other." To kill oneself is to kill the self as other. Early periphrases for suicide in French, discussed in my introduction, recognize this schism: suicide is a *homicide de soi-même*, a "murder of the self." During suicide, the ego "turns onto itself the hatred it feels toward the object."[2] It turns on itself *as object*. Suicide combines "the wish to die, the wish to kill, the wish to be killed."[3] Nowhere is this truer than in the case of the suicide bomber who explodes the self as other in the process of exploding others—who dies to kill.

Although closely associated with our contemporary moment, especially the post-9/11 era, the suicide bomber is not a new figure. In histories of suicide attacks, the death of the biblical figure Samson in a Philistine temple at Gaza is often cited as an early example of a strategic willingness to die in order to kill. Suicide attacks in the contexts of slavery and colonization have received comparatively less attention. In *None like Us* (2018), Stephen Best gives an example from Willem Bosman's *New and Accurate Description of the Coast of Guinea* (1703): a report by an enslaved survivor-witness that a West African chief "blew up himself and all his Enemies at once" in 1659 amid negotiations with the Dutch.[4] In the history of French empire, the suicide of Louis Delgrès and his followers in 1802—discussed in chapter 1—seems to be the earliest example of a suicide bomb. By exploding themselves along with Napoleon's troops, Delgrès and his followers transformed their bodies into deadly weapons against French slavery. Closer to the setting of Nourredine Saadi's novels examined in the previous chapter is the history of women who carried bombs throughout Algeria's long anticolonial War of Independence. Although they did not explode themselves, they used their gendered bodies as tools of resistance, navigating security checkpoints and passing unremarked through public spaces. The "unveiling" of Algerian women allowed them to pass for Europeans. Whereas the folds of the *haïk* could be used to conceal weapons or contraband, its removal also created openings for resistance. As Frantz Fanon writes, the newly unveiled Algerian woman scrambled the colonizer's radar:

> Carrying revolvers, grenades, hundreds of fake identity cards or bombs, the unveiled Algerian woman glides like a fish in Western waters. Soldiers, French patrols smile at her as she passes by, compliments about her physical appearance ringing out here and there, but no one suspects that inside her suitcase is the machine gun which, presently, will mow down four or five members of one of the patrols.[5]

Perhaps the most famous example of an Algerian female bomb carrier is the twenty-one-year-old Zohra Drif, who disguised herself as a Frenchwoman and set off a bomb in the Milk Bar in Algiers in 1956 while working as a clandestine resistance fighter for the National Liberation Front. She and the many other Algerian women who planted bombs or smuggled weapons and information throughout the war belong to a genealogy of female agents of political violence and resistance, one that includes the suicide bomber.

Alternative genealogies and historical examples do little to change the fact that in public discourse and popular imaginaries, suicide bombing attacks continue to figure a limit to thinking on contemporary violence even as the phenomenon has become a disturbingly regular feature of today's geopolitical landscape.[6] More than other forms of violence and other forms of suicide, suicide bombing is considered "a peculiarly monstrous, indeed inhuman, aberration *that cannot—or indeed must not—be understood.*"[7] Although statistically suicide bombings claim fewer victims than acts of conventional warfare and state violence, neoliberal democracies in the West view the suicide terrorist with a special kind of dread and antipathy. Perhaps this is because suicide terrorist attacks, as Alex Houen suggests, are "experienced and expressed *as hyperbole,*" or because they provoke public responses that can only be classified in terms of sheer "horror."[8] Official discourses and public reactions to suicide attacks cordon off the act as unthinkable, unimaginable, and inhuman. But of course, suicide bombing today is *entirely* imaginable, even quotidian.

As Rose suggests, we are not encouraged to understand the actions of suicide bombers, much less identify or empathize with them. The individual who kills the self to kill others is so aberrant, so anomalous—so categorically *evil*—that their act would seem to defy comprehension, inviting only condemnation.[9] There is nothing, we are told, to be learned from suicide bombing.

To say or suggest otherwise, especially as a politician or public intellectual, is to risk censure and hostility.[10] Consider the response to comments that Jenny Tonge, a Liberal Democrat MP in the United Kingdom, made about Palestinian suicide bombers in 2004. Speaking candidly during a meeting of the Palestinian Solidarity Campaign, Tonge tried to put herself in the shoes of the suicide bomber, remarking,

> This particular brand of terrorism, the suicide bomber, is truly born out of desperation. Many people criticize, many, many people say it is just another form of terrorism, but I can understand and I am a fairly emotional person and I am a mother and a grandmother. I think if I had to live in that situation—and I say that advisedly—I might just consider becoming one myself.[11]

Tonge's gesture at "feminine" understanding led to her immediate dismissal from her party's front bench, and the Israeli embassy responded with a statement saying, "We would not expect *any human being*—and surely not a British MP—to express an understanding of such atrocities."[12] Attempting to "understand" suicide bombing, to bring the phenomenon into the realm of the human, is to sympathize with the enemy and to condone unspeakable violence—to somehow become inhuman, or antihuman.

In a talk given shortly after 9/11 titled "Responses to War" that was later published as an essay, "Terror: A Speech after 9–11," Gayatri Spivak attempted to do precisely that: to try to understand the prerequisites for murderous acts of self-destruction and to imagine the political message they might contain.[13] On the eve of the "war on terror," Spivak addressed a self-killing that slaughtered innocents, a homicidal suicide that doubled as an "act of war": when four hijacked planes crashed into the Twin Towers of the World Trade Center, the Pentagon, and a field in Pennsylvania on the morning of 11 September 2001, killing several thousand people.

The theorist's remarks on suicide bombing were met with backlash, skepticism, and outrage. Revealingly, the published essay, "Terror," incorporates a lengthy apologia in which Spivak responds to critics and attempts to nuance and attenuate some of her earlier claims. The idea that suicide bombing might be the object of literary-philosophical inquiry was—and in many ways still is—scandalizing. Even more so was Spivak's imaginative leap of identification: her expressed willingness to move toward a possible understanding of the suicide bomber. In her own words: "I believe that we must be able to imagine our opponent *as a human being*, and to understand the significance of his or her action. It is in this belief—not to endorse suicide bombing but to be on the way to its end, however remote—that I have tried to imagine what message it might contain."[14] To understand is not to condone, to imagine is not to endorse. Spivak's essay, no matter how one twists or turns it, does not suggest that suicide bombing is anything other than unequivocally wrong and universally bad. What her text does contest and resist, however, is the idea that the actions of the suicide bomber exceed human comprehension—that the suicide bomber exists beyond the scope of analytical purchase.

The outsized response to Spivak's comments on suicide bombing pinpoints a troublingly powerful paradox at the heart of neoliberal discourses surrounding the various forms of contemporary violence broadly construed under the rubric of "terrorism," and suicide terrorism in particular. To call suicide bombing attacks "terrorism"—or even "hyperterrorism," to adopt a recent coinage[15]—is to beg the question.[16] As Adriana Cavarero writes, the names we ascribe to forms of contemporary violence "supply interpretive frameworks for events and guide public opinion."[17] And as Spivak reminds us, "terror" is merely "the name loosely assigned to the flip side of social movements—extra-state collective action—when such movements use physical violence."[18] The proliferation of terms used to refer to suicide bombings themselves—suicide attack, homicidal suicide, homicide bombing, sacrifice bombing, genocide bombing—lends a sense of the challenges of naming an act that claims both perpetrator and victim and produces the perpetrator as a victim of their own violence.

The suicide bomber, in this sense, is not only a uniquely dangerous figure but also scandalous, deviant, and radically "other." This seems to be especially true when the person who carries out a suicide attack is a woman and when her victims are civilians, or when the bomber is "Arab" and the victims Europeans; these bombers consistently elicit the strongest public reactions.[19] Historically, suicide bombers have been profiled as *male* political radicals, but a significant portion of suicide bombing attacks globally are now carried out by women, and women-perpetrated suicide bombings tend to inflict greater causalities.[20] The rhetorical quarantining and particular "horror" surrounding suicide attacks carried out by women and "Arab" bombers obscure a far more complicated picture while serving to uphold fictitious dichotomies between "soldier," "civilian," and "terrorist," but also "Westerner" and "Arab," "modern" and "premodern," "victim" and "perpetrator."[21] The advent of female suicide bombers from the mid-1980s onward has forced government and national security officials, as well as terrorism experts, to profoundly rethink how women play important and active roles in political violence.

This historical trend demands that we consider how counterterrorist discourses draw substantively from discourses on gender and sexuality in addition to race. As Jasbir Puar points out, the discursive process of "discerning, othering, and quarantining terrorist bodies" is also a project of sexual othering.[22] It is part of a broader form of social control that simultaneously serves to "discipline" and "normalize" subjects "*away from* these bodies" and to enforce the "mandatory terms of patriotism," or what Puar calls "homonationalism."[23] Beyond the particular horrorism ascribed to the female suicide bomber, the Muslim/Arab terrorist frequently appears in counterterrorist discourses, especially in the West, as "a queer, nonnational, perversely radicalized *other*."[24] Terrorist attacks, moreover, often are experienced and narrated as a collective "trauma of national sexual violation."[25] The terrorist in this sense becomes a figure of sexual deviancy, failed heterosexuality, emasculation, and queerness. This stereotype extends homophobic-racist images of Muslims and Orientalist tropes that date back to the eighteenth century and are revived in contemporary global conflicts in which terrorism plays a visible role (the Gulf War, the US war on terror, the Israel-Hamas war and genocide of Palestinians).[26]

All this is to say that Western democracies have erected a mythologized version of the suicide bomber—as irredeemably inhuman and radically other—as an effective foil to and cover for "legitimate" acts of war. This sleight of hand is executed, moreover, through discourses and procedures of naming that are rhetorical if not fundamentally literary.[27] My point here is not to suggest equivalences between suicide bombing and acts of state violence, colonizing war, drone strikes, or nuclear imperialism, but to observe that certain forms of contemporary violence—such as policing—are deemed legitimate, justifiable, and ultimately "understandable," others irretrievably barbaric and unfathomable. This social and political taboo puts suicide bombing in a very peculiar relation to literature: How can something that is forbidden to understand be written about?

The final chapter of *The Suicide Archive* begins with this hermeneutical and ethical impasse. On the one hand, suicide bombing is "beyond the pale of understanding" (Rose), and efforts to understand it, to think through it—however tenuous, however speculative or "imaginative"—are taken to be callous, even treacherous and antihumanistic, intellectual exercises. On the other hand, suicide bombing is characterized by a constant suspicion about motives and a desire to assign the act a stable meaning. In the post-9/11 era, this suspicion around meaning amounts to what Talal Asad has called a form of "official hermeneutics" in reference to the massive state-sponsored intelligence-gathering efforts aimed, at least officially, at *understanding* and obstructing suicide terrorism.[28] For a phenomenon ostensibly "beyond" comprehension, it paradoxically seems taken for granted that suicide bombing demands particular analytical attention and that, given the appropriate interpretive apparatus, it can be apprehended in minute detail—as well as predicted and prevented.[29] Alongside claims that suicide bombing cannot, must not, be understood exists an immense and highly elaborate industry dedicated to modes of interpreting, explaining, profiling—in short, *theorizing*—suicide bombers and their actions, whether in terms of psychopathology, religious fanaticism, or collective ideology (in the United States, the Patriot Act and the capture, detainment, and interrogation of Muslims are examples of this).[30]

Faced with this paradox, as well as the kinds of disciplinary, discursive, and conceptual bulwarks erected around suicide terrorism, it would appear there simply is no good way to write (or speak) about suicide bombing. At the very least, writing about suicide bombing poses what Rose identifies as a "question of genre."[31] Rose writes: "It is not just [...] that every statement is liable to be contested. Nor just the disputed vocabulary. [...] *What is at issue is something more like an ethics of form.*"[32] In the conclusion to her essay, Rose goes on to reformulate this generic problem as the call for a new idiom—a "language" with which to speak about acts of contemporary violence such as suicide bombing that would not also, at the same time, be an illusory will-to-power: "We need to find a language that will allow us to recognise why, in a world of rampant inequality and injustice, people are driven to do things that we hate. Without claiming to know too much. Without condescension."[33] Rose ultimately leaves open the question "How, then, should you write about suicide bombing?"[34] Best, writing about the Black Radical tradition, echoes her query when he asks "whether self-immolation presents a problem for history *writing*; whether a suicide bombing can even be made available to historical consciousness."[35]

What Rose formulates tentatively as "an ethics of form" and the need for an adequate "language," I read as a signal for the entrance of literature, and literary criticism, into the field of inquiry. At this point, the claim that the tools of literary criticism have a role to play in moving us toward a possible understanding of the suicide bomber should not be altogether surprising. The lexical field laid out by scholars such as Rose, Asad, Houen, and others in their characterizations of suicide bombing—terms like *hermeneutics, interpretation, fiction, message*— is undeniably textual and suggestively literary. Official interpretations of and responses to suicide bombing attacks are already deeply *literary* activities, tangled up in the experience of fiction.[36] The attacks themselves are devastatingly lethal modes of writing in extremis: what Robert Pape calls a "strategic" means for nonstate actors to voice a political message through violence.[37] Moreover, as Samuel Thomas writes, suicide bombing "in all its diverse and terrible forms [...] is also the source of a significant outgrowth in discursive/creative practices."[38] This is certainly true in the case of African literature in French, which has seen the rapid growth of a "terrorist genre" dating back at least to the Black Decade in Algeria.[39] We are better prepared to recognize, read, and respond to the impossible message of suicide bombing if we first attend, as I have tried to do throughout this book, to the problems suicidal resistance poses for writing and meaning in general—to consider, in other words, its rhetorical force.

None of this is to overstate the role of aesthetics or the symbolic in the fields of (bio)politics and war, nor to attenuate the particular "horror/ism" or physical and psychological devastation of suicide bombing. Instead, I mean to show how literature and literary criticism provide powerful, necessary, and unexpected interpretive tools for thinking about contemporary violence. With respect to suicide bombing, aesthetic works articulate different modes of understanding to open up conceptual possibilities, whereas official discourses (history, geography, psychology) foreclose meaning. We have seen this at work with other forms of suicide that perhaps are more clearly read as forms of anticolonial and antiimperialist resistance. Here I want to test the boundaries of the suicide archive, as well as the notions of suicidal resistance and the rhetorical force of suicide, by taking up an act that so often is posed as a conceptual limit and a totally "other" kind of self-killing.

This final chapter sets suicide bombing within a broader landscape of political violence and violent resistance. It explores the capacity of literary texts to serve as training grounds for a specific kind of imaginative, and ethical, aesthetic practice requisite for meaningful political progress: what Spivak identifies as "an imaginative exercise in experiencing the impossible—stepping into the space of the other—without which political solutions come drearily undone into the continuation of violence."[40] Specifically, this chapter focuses on a French-language example of terrorist fiction: Moroccan writer and painter-sculptor Mahi Binebine's novel *Les étoiles de Sidi Moumen* (2010), later adapted for film by Nabil Ayouch as *Les chevaux de Dieu* (*God's Horses*, 2012).[41] Like many of the works discussed in *The Suicide Archive*, Binebine's text entextualizes a historical suicide and writes into an existing suicide archive. Inspired by the Casablanca suicide bombings of 16 May 2003, the novel recounts the childhood and adolescence from the point of view of its perpetrators, young men from the same *bidonville* (shantytown) in Morocco, Sidi Moumen, before they carry out a suicide mission. Based on the 2003 bombings but published in the wake of another series of suicide attacks by young men from the same Casablanca suburb in 2007, Binebine's novel grapples with historical specificity and a generalized structure of historical violence, staging the singularity of an event and the inevitability of its repetition only a few years later. Rather than explaining or pathologizing the perpetrators of the 2003 bombings, Binebine helps us to imagine possible conditions prerequisite for such violence, redirecting our attention to the structural violence of the state. To this end, Binebine draws parallels to another desperate act that has preoccupied us throughout this study: that of the *harragas* or individuals who try to migrate from West and North Africa to European shores through perilous ocean crossings. In the conclusion to this chapter, I take up these parallels in some detail in a discussion of Binebine's earlier novel, *Cannibales* (1999).

My analysis of *Étoiles* focuses on how Binebine's formal innovations with the terrorist genre contest the idea that there is no mode, no adequate language, for understanding suicide bombing. Binebine's novel does this in two different but related ways: first through its unconventional and unsettling mode of address, and second through its ambivalent sexual politics and "queering" of suicide terrorism. Narrated from the disembodied perspective of one of the bombers, Yachine, who tells his story from beyond the grave, *Étoiles* is a striking example of what Frédéric Weinmann, following Derrida, calls "autothanatographic narration" and what Alice Bennett terms "death writing"—

forms of postmortem narration in the first person.[42] The novel fits definitions of "unnatural" or nonnatural narrative, referring to a subset of fictional narratives involving storytelling scenarios (such as a dead narrator) that violate "physical laws, logical principles, or standard anthropomorphic limitations of knowledge."[43] The ghostly frame of *Étoiles* is part of Binebine's general subversion of the dominant discursive frames for representing suicide terrorism, which proceeds by unsettling fixities that are narratological and ontological as well as sexual. *Étoiles* is noteworthy for staging male homosocial and homosexual desire: the dead narrator-protagonist, Yachine, as well as the other young men of Sidi Moumen, frequently deviate from heterosexual norms, and gay sex acts are the only sex acts explicitly depicted in the novel. As Jean Zaganiaris shows, the presence of same-sex sex acts does not a priori make a novel "queer," since such acts often are recuperated and "reconquered" in Francophone Moroccan literature in ways that reinforce the terms of heterosexuality.[44] But Binebine's *Étoiles* also stages moments of queer intimacy, tenderness, and care that stand out against a narrative brimming with violence. Though Binebine's novel is consistently overlooked in surveys of Maghrebi literature representing nonconforming sexualities—perhaps because such surveys focus almost exclusively on Maghrebi writers who themselves identify as gay or lesbian—it offers an important reflection on queer desire and queer violence.[45]

These two features of *Étoiles*—ghostly narration on the one hand, queerness on the other—intersect in what I consider the novel's "queer voice." Following Susan Lanser, I use the term *queering* here to mean "(1) to make a claim for the non-heteronormative sex, gender, or sexuality of someone or something; (2) to disrupt or deconstruct binary categories of sex, gender, and/or sexuality; and (3) to disrupt or deconstruct any entity by rejecting its categories, binaries, or norms."[46] For Lanser, a "queer voice" is a narrative voice which—whether through textual or sexual ambiguity, *or both*—"confounds the rules for voice itself and thus baffles our categorical assumptions about narrators and narrative."[47] Binebine's unconventional and sexually ambiguous dead protagonist-narrator exists neither inside nor outside the story world—or, rather, exists in both at once—and lends the suicide bomber a "queer voice." But Binebine's novel also cultivates a kind of "queer intimacy" between reader and terrorist, bringing us into a space of understanding and ineluctable identification through language. In this, *Étoiles* cultivates what Martha Nussbaum terms *narrative imagination*: a willingness to become "an intelligent reader" of another person's story and "to understand the emotions and wishes and desires that someone so placed might have."[48] In so doing, *Étoiles* troubles official discourses that figure the suicide bomber as anonymous, monstrous, inhuman, and incommensurably other.

Fictions of Terror

Étoiles belongs to an emergent subgenre of African literature in French that can be qualified loosely as "terrorist fiction." Of course, the figuration of terrorism is a broader feature of contemporary postcolonial fiction.[49] This literary genealogy extends beyond Africa and the Middle East to the postcolonial literatures of South Asia, as exemplified by novels such as Karan Mahajan's *Association of Small Bombs* (2016).[50] In French, terrorist narratives historically have been the purview of Algerian writers. Early examples of the genre consisted almost exclusively of novels by Algerian authors who wrote during or immediately after the violence of the Black Decade and whose texts, traditionally characterized as "emergency literature" (*littérature de l'urgence*), represent Islamic fundamentalist terrorism in Algeria during this period.[51] The genre of "terrorist fiction" in film is older, dating at least to Gillo Pontecorvo's film *La Bataille d'Alger* (1966), which famously was screened at the Pentagon in 2003 in the wake of 9/11.[52] In the post-9/11 era, Algerian writers such as Boualem Sansal, Yasmina Khadra, and Salīm Bāchī have expanded the terrorist genre in scope and focus—offering literary responses to terrorism within a transnational perspective and setting their novels in the Middle East, Europe, and the United States. For instance, Boualem Sansal's novel *Le village de l'Allemand ou le journal des frères Schiller* (2008), translated into English as *The German Mujahid* (2009), connects the seemingly disparate histories of Islamist violence, the Holocaust, and totalitarianism of the postcolonial Algerian state, while Khadra's treatments of terrorism in novels such as *Les hirondelles de Kaboul* (2002), *L'attentat* (2005), and *Les sirènes de Baghdad* (2006) span Afghanistan, Tel-Aviv, and Iraq.[53] Salīm Bāchī's *Tuez-les tous* (2006), on the other hand, narrates the 9/11 attacks from the perspective of one of the hijackers, joining a predominantly Anglophone corpus of works that scholars characterize as "(post-)9/11 novel[s]," while Bāchī's later novel *Moi, Khaled Kelkal* (2012) takes place in France.[54]

In the past decade, the *mujāhid* (jihadist) has become a key figure in the literatures and cinema of West Africa and the Sahel, notably in Mauritania and Mali—Sissako's prize-winning film *Timbuktu* (2014) is a well-known example—but also in Senegal, with the publication of Mohamed Mbougar Sarr's novel *Terre ceinte* (2015). In this sense, the emergence of a terrorist genre in African literature in French has roughly followed the spread of an extremist threat across the continent, historically and cartographically. This genre responds to what Eileen Julien, writing about the African novel, calls "a singular thirst for the sensational": namely, a taste or desire in the Global North for stories from the Global South, especially from Africa, about "autocracy, multiple forms of patriarchy, violence, abuse of 'human rights,' child soldiers, alienation, the quest for identity."[55] To her list, we might now add "suicide terrorism."

Before the 2003 Casablanca bombings, many Moroccans considered their country relatively insulated from the threat of terrorist attacks, despite having witnessed the violence of the Black Decade in neighboring Algeria.[56] As Binebine notes, before 2003 terrorism was a foreign problem: "We used to think that [terrorism] existed in Algeria, in Chechnya, in the Middle East, everywhere else but here, at home."[57] This all changed around 9:30 p.m. on the evening of Friday, 16 May 2003, when five explosions ripped through the Casablanca night in less than an hour and within a one-mile radius of each other.[58] Eyewitnesses crowding to the scene of the first explosions near Place Verdun in the city center later described what they saw in the language of suicidal horrorism—as a total shock to the senses, a sudden and almost unimaginable intrusion of the grotesque into daily life:

> *Horror on Verdun Square*—Casablanca is in shock. Before the television begin to transmit the first images of the attacks carried out Friday evening at five different sites in the economic capital, citizens of the city could hardly imagine what was really happening. [...] Those who were able to get close to the sites of the attack [...] discovered horrific, monstrous scenes: hair and flesh clinging to a satellite antenna, exploded bodies there as well, blood everywhere.[59]

The following morning, Moroccans woke to the continuing drone of ambulance sirens and to grim reports broadcasted across every major radio and television outlet. World leaders—from George W. Bush and Jacques Chirac to Pope John Paul II—were swift to denounce the attacks, much as they had done after 9/11, and in much the same terms. The news cycle for regional papers such as *Le Matin du Sahara et du Maghreb*, *Al Bayane*, and *La Vie Eco* was given over to documenting the bombings, condemning terrorist activity, and commemorating the victims.[60]

In the days following the bombings, more details emerged. The synchronized attacks were masterminded by the Jordanian radical Abu Musab al-Zarqawi and executed by the Salafia Jihadia, a Salafi jihadist militant network with links to the Groupe islamique combattant marocain and Al-Qaeda.[61] The bombers all came from the same bidonvilles or *karians* (slums) on the outskirts of Casablanca, namely Sidi Moumen, Carrière Thomas, and Thomasville. For some Moroccans, including Binebine, this was the first time they had heard these toponyms, which designated the country's invisible cities: sprawling zones of single-story dwellings with insecure land tenure inhabited by Morocco's urban poor, most without access to electricity or running water.[62] "It's at that moment," notes Binebine, recalling listening to news reports of the bombings, "that I first heard of the bidonville of Sidi Moumen."[63]

The sudden encroachment—indeed, explosion—of the bidonville into the heart of Casablanca would have major implications for Morocco's urban planning and counterterrorist policies in subsequent years. Long considered spaces of urban and social deviance—especially under the French Protectorate (1912–56)—the bidonvilles now were the sites of an unprecedented local terrorist threat and insurrectional potential.[64] As early as 2004, the Ministry of Housing announced the program Villes Sans Bidonvilles (VSB), based on the United Nations' "Cities without Slums" initiative, aimed at eradicating Morocco's bidonvilles and other forms of precarious or informal housing.[65] The program gained renewed urgency in 2007, when young men from Sidi Moumen once again were identified as the perpetrators of a series of suicide bombings in Casablanca: one in March (when a man blew himself up at an internet café) and two in April (when three suspected militants exploded themselves during a police raid and two people exploded near the US consulate a few days later).[66] Today one of the lines of the Casablanca Tramway has Sidi Moumen as its terminus—an urban renewal and reform effort to link the once peripheral and impoverished neighborhood directly to the city proper. The year 2003 thus marked the beginning of Morocco's own ongoing and, for many Moroccans, deeply "misguided" war on terror. In addition to the destruction of the country's bidonvilles, this war involved a wide-ranging "Countering Violent Extremism" government strategy that targeted the Salafist population and led to a deterioration of human rights conditions in Morocco.[67]

Not surprisingly, 2003 also saw an outgrowth of creative production and new forms of literary "engagement": the first experiments with the terrorist genre in Moroccan literature.[68] In the wake of bombings in Casablanca (2003, 2007) and Marrakesh (2011), Moroccan writers and filmmakers responded with a proliferation of aesthetic works—largely novels, many published by local presses, but also films in French and Arabic—that take terrorism and Islamist fundamentalism as central themes and inflect the terrorist genre in important ways.[69] Several novels deal directly with the May 2003 bombings and are characterized by their extreme topicality. The journalist Ahmed Beroho's thriller *Le 16 Mai* (2003), for instance, was written in the twenty-two days immediately following the bombings and published shortly thereafter.[70] Ahmed Bouchikhi's *Les jumeaux de Sidi Moumen* (2011), published in the wake of the second Casablanca bombing, circulated briefly in French and Arabic but is now out of print.

Among literary responses to the Casablanca bombings, Binebine's *Étoiles* is the most widely read outside Morocco. The novel won the Prix Littéraire de la Mamounia in 2010 and has been translated into almost a dozen languages. Later, in collaboration with Binebine, the Moroccan filmmaker Nabil Ayouch adapted the novel for screen as *Les chevaux de Dieu* (2012), nominated for an Academy Award in 2013. Binebine and Ayouch's collaboration led to an ongoing engagement with the youth of Morocco's remaining bidonvilles and poorer urban neighborhoods. Using revenue from the film and novel, they founded the Fondation Ali Zaoua and the "Les étoiles" Youth Cultural Center in Sidi Moumen, which has expanded to satellite locations in Tangier (2017), Agadir (2019), Fès (2021), and Marrakech (2021).[71]

Although Binebine began work on *Étoiles* immediately after the 2003 bombings, it would be nearly eight years before he published the novel. At one point he considered abandoning the text entirely, and in the interim he wrote another novel, *Le griot de Marrakech* (2008). But the story, and the space of the bidonville, continued to "haunt" him, Binebine says.[72] For Binebine, the major difficulty of writing about suicide terrorism hinged on a question of understanding and form: "In fact, I was writing a book that scared me, because *if I understood these kids, how was I to say it in a story—me, someone who opposes terrorism with all my might?*"[73] This returns us to Rose's question: "How, then, should you write about suicide bombing?" Binebine's novel offers a formal solution to this impasse, bringing us into the space of the other, the suicide bomber—access that official discourses simultaneously desire and forbid.

During the genesis of the novel, Binebine learned to inhabit the space of the suicide bomber in quite literal terms. A journalist friend from the outskirts of Casablanca brought Binebine to Sidi Moumen shortly after the 2003 bombings, and he returned over a dozen times while writing. He met the families and friends of the bombers, ate in their *baraques*, and spoke with the people who call Sidi Moumen home. He sat at their tables, occupying the empty seats their sons and brothers had left behind. Like Spivak's imaginative leap of empathetic identification, Binebine's text—in both its process and narrative praxis—models a willingness to move toward the suicide bomber. In *Étoiles*, Binebine makes the ultimate leap of identification, fusing his narrative "I" with the bomber's own. In inhabiting this impossible subject position, he challenges us to understand the suicide bomber. He suggests we might even learn to *love* him: "Finally I found and came to terms with the key to the book—I found a way out by allowing myself to make my readers love these kids."[74] This is the queer intimacy and textual complicity that the ghostly narration of *Étoiles* cultivates.

Dead Narrators

Étoiles is, above all, a ghost story. More precisely, it is an autothanatography and extended use of prosopopoeia: a fiction of "the voice-from-beyond-the-grave."[75] From beginning to end, the novel follows the spectral roaming of a dead man, adopting the perspective of the spirit of an eighteen-year-old suicide bomber, Yachine, who tells his story in the first person, addressing the reader from the hereafter. His flesh reduced to dust by the blast that killed him and many others, his head "blown into a thousand pieces,"[76] and his bones mingled in a shallow grave with those of another bomber named Khalil, Yachine now exists in a nebulous limbo, a "purgatory" (85) from which he haunts and narrates the scenes of his childhood and adolescence:

> I won't describe for you the place where I currently find myself since I myself don't know what it is. All I can say is that I am reduced to an entity that, to use the words of the world below [*d'en bas*], I will call a consciousness. That is to say, the peaceful consequence of a myriad of lucid thoughts. Not those thoughts, obscure and poor, that punctuated my short existence, but thoughts with infinite facets, iridescent thoughts, blinding thoughts even. (11)

Persisting as an expansive and lucid consciousness, Yachine speaks to us from beyond death, from the *barzakh*—in Islamic eschatology, the liminal zone separating the dead from the living.

In life, Yachine had led an almost invisible existence in Sidi Moumen, cut off from "the other world" (*l'autre monde*) of Casablanca by an immense, crenelated wall that hid the bidonville from view, a vaguely military barrier in which Yachine and his friends bored holes to gain surreptitious glimpses of the outside world (9). In his "new condition of specter" (10), Yachine remains similarly invisible, "confined [*cantonné*] in his purgatory" and eclipsed by a gossamer partition he occasionally perforates when called on, slipping silently into the realm of the living: "When the living think of me, they open a portal [*un soupirail*] for me into their world. So, I slip in delicately, without making the smallest of noises" (85).

From the ghostly perspective and in the otherworldly voice of Yachine, Binebine painstakingly crafts a backstory for six of the fourteen Casablanca bombers. In Binebine's retelling, nearly half of the bombers are childhood friends who come of age together playing on the bidonville's soccer team, the Étoiles de Sidi Moumen (the Stars of Sidi Moumen), whose name lends the novel its title. Focalized through Yachine's postmortem narration, Binebine follows the childhood and adolescence of six friends growing up in abject poverty playing soccer on a dump heap, surrounded by drugs, crime, sexual violence, and death. These are Yachine and Hamid, brothers who largely fend for themselves and try to assist their overburdened mother; Nabil, the son of a local sex worker, Tamou, whose androgynous looks and pale eyes make him a troubling source of attention and an object of desire; Fouad, the son of the muezzin and the only *étoile* to receive some kind of formal education, who later drops out and becomes addicted to sniffing glue; Azzi or Youssef, the son of a coalman, whose father renames him "Ali" after his dead younger brother, who drowned while entrusted to Youssef's care; Khalil, the son of a coachman, who gets work as a shoeshine boy and dreams of migrating clandestinely to Europe. Through the perspective of his dead narrator, Yachine, Binebine plots the devastating, and ultimately fatal, metamorphosis of these six boys into human bombs as their "religion of soccer" (72) gradually is replaced by something far more sinister.

Yachine describes how the boys' "slide" into suicide terrorism—what he calls "a somber slide into a world that was not our own" (104)—occurs gradually, as the Étoiles are brought, one after another, into the fold of "the Garage," a community of extremists masquerading as mechanics led by the charismatic Abou Zoubeïr. Yachine's older brother, Hamid, introduces the other boys to the Garage and finds them work among Zoubeïr's followers. They memorize the Quran, pray rigorously, learn martial arts, and are encouraged to give up alcohol and other substances. They develop mechanical expertise that will turn deadly, repairing motorbikes and appliances as a precursor to gaining familiarity with explosives. They screen videos of Palestinians being massacred and listen to dissertations on the perfidy of the West. From his perspective in the hereafter, Yachine recounts how the grip of Abou Zoubeïr and his teachings slowly but surely tightens: the boys grow long beards and urge their mothers and sisters to veil themselves; they distance themselves from their childhood pastimes, including soccer.

Binebine's emphasis in *Étoiles* on radicalization as a gradual process of socialization (even fraternization) and his depiction of the kinds of conditions (socioeconomic desperation, routinized violence, lack of access to formal education) that might favor the growth of an extremist threat in Morocco's bidonvilles are not in themselves especially remarkable. Nor are such observations the exclusive purview of literary representations of suicide terrorism; sociological studies, historical accounts, and political analyses all do this too. Rather, the originality of Binebine's literary treatment of the Casablanca bombings as well as its theoretical importance reside in the novel's ghostly narrative frame. Binebine's voicing of the dead terrorist makes an important contribution to the genre of terrorist fiction and to a literary history of posthumous utterance by restless spirits and spectral voices who speak back from beyond their own deaths.

The dead narrator, Yachine, is an example of a trend in contemporary fiction, what Bennett identifies as "a proliferation of dead fictional characters narrating their lives and deaths."[77] This narrative technique has made major inroads in the terrorist genre, particularly in the wake of Yasmina Khadra's wildly popular novel *Attentat* (2005). Khadra's narrator, Amine—who, we gather from the novel's paratexts, has already died, killed in a separate terrorist attack—tries to understand his wife's decision to explode herself in a crowded café. This trend of postmortem narration has continued after the success of Binebine's novel, with texts such as Salīm Bāchī's *Moi, Khaled Kelkal* (2012) and Bashīr Muftī's *Ashbāḥ al-Madīnah al-Maqtūlah* (*The Ghosts of the Murdered City*, 2012), novels in which terrorists also tell their stories from beyond the grave.[78]

Through his exploded narrator, Yachine, Binebine confronts us with a mode of otherworldly literary utterance that disrupts boundaries that are ontological (between the living and the dead) and narratological (between a narrating self and a narrated self).[79] By taking the autothanatographic as its narrative mode and the ghost story as its form of emplotment, *Étoiles* blends features of self-narration and ordinary omniscient narration. Like the narrator-protagonists Nina in Neil Jordan's *Shade* (2004) or Susie Salmon in Alice Sebold's *The Lovely Bones* (2002), Yachine is "everywhere and nowhere," both "immanently present within the narrative" and inhabiting a space and time that "is enough of a nowhere to be unnarrated, and presumably unnarratable."[80] His roaming spectral "I" telescopes between diegetic levels and shuttles between his past among the living, a historical present on the earth he haunts, and his own ambiguous position in the hereafter. The sheer narratological range of Binebine's dead protagonist perhaps comes into sharpest focus when Yachine shifts from relaying an admittedly "condensed" summary of violent scenes from his childhood and adolescence to witnessing his own burial, funeral, and mourning after the bombings:

> There were not just acts of violence in Sidi Moumen. What I'm telling you here is a summary of eighteen years in an anthill. So, obviously, it's a little rough. These sad episodes marked a young existence. And a young death, too. A death practically without a cadaver, because mine was collected by the spoonful. The irony is that they buried me with Khalil's remains: a toothless jaw, two fingers from his right hand, the hand that had activated the device, and one foot with his ankle because we had had the horrible idea of buying matching sandals. [...] So here we are, lying together in the same square of shade under the jujube tree in the back of

> the cemetery. [...] We were not granted any prayer, since you don't pray over the tombs of suicides. I see again still my father, my brothers, and the bravest of the Stars of Sidi Moumen encircling the hole into which they had just slid me. (63)

Anchored in a narrative present reinforced by deictic markers ("What I'm telling you here..."), Yachine seems deeply aware of the peculiar perspective afforded by death and self-conscious in his newfound role as a phantom storyteller who now is responsible for arranging the events (*épisodes*) of his life, unspooling and unpicking his past: as he later intimates, "Now that I'm up here [*là-haut*], I unfurl my past like a ball of yarn studded with knots" (115).

At first glance, the unconventional narrative configuration of *Étoiles* allows Binebine to fulfill what Francis Blessington, writing about Khadra's novel *L'attentat* (2005), considers one of the major functions of terrorist fiction: bringing us inside the mind of the terrorist. Blessington writes, "What we want most from the terrorist novel is to know and experience why someone chooses terror. We want to be inside the mind of the terrorist."[81] We can recognize this as the space of desire and deferred understanding to which the lover of the dead protagonist in Saadi's *Boulevard de l'abîme* aspired through writing: literature responds to a desire to be inside the mind of a suicide, to know why. It is the forbidden, taboo space of identification with which the "official hermeneutics" around suicide bombing is obsessed and which public discourse positions beyond understanding, beyond imagining. But Binebine's novel does not provide us with easy answers. We do not come away, as Blessington suggests often is the case, with a clear understanding of *why* Yachine and the other boys "chose" terror or with a clear "judgment" about their actions. Instead, we are left to wonder—about the conditions that give rise to acts of (self-)destruction—and to confront the ultimate taboo of suicide bombing: Might we have done the same?

Yachine not only is a dead narrator but also a potentially unreliable one. On the first page of the novel, he admits, "since the day a rock [...] struck me on the skull, my head is gone [*je n'ai plus ma tête*]" (9). As he narrates, he literally "no longer has his head" because the explosion that killed him blasted his brain into "a thousand pieces" (10). Like the ghostly narration of the women of *Le Soleil* in Kanor's *Humus*, Yachine's narrative perspective is suspect and necessarily incomplete and fragmentary from the outset. Indeed, his own postmortem narration raises the possibility of countless other stories—or different versions of the same story—recounted by the unquiet spirits of his fellow bombers as well as their victims. This undercuts the narrative authority of any single account of an event that claimed forty-five lives and attunes us to yet another valance of

Binebine's calling the boys "stars": suggestive of a constellation of fragmented stories blasted into space.

In addition to psychological introspection, Yachine's autothanatographic narration in the novel enables Binebine to invest his dead protagonist with critical distance and to treat his improbable ghost status with a touch of acerbic humor. For instance, when Yachine says he refrains insofar as possible from interfering with the affairs of the living, he cheekily adds, "It surprises you, doesn't it, that a restless spirit [*une âme errante*] can interfere with the world of the living? But you have no other choice than to take me at my word" (85). Although Yachine claims to harbor little regret for departing the world of the living—"And I'll say it outright: I don't regret ending it all. Not the least bit of nostalgia for the eighteen hellish years I was given to live" (10)—his obsessive revisiting of the past and the spaces of his childhood, as well as his own narrative tics (scathing asides, sudden lapses into direct address), suggest otherwise. From his (non)position in the hereafter, he looks back on his short life with nostalgia, remorse, guilt, disillusionment, and mordent bitterness. Despite his spectral state, his past continues to weigh on him. This perhaps is why he remains trapped, forced to haunt the bidonville:

> From the very depths of my solitude, when the memories of my shipwreck [*naufrage*] assail and torment me, when the weight of my errors becomes too heavy to carry and my spirit, already old and tired, begins to wheel about like some infernal merry-go-round, [. . .] I go off to roam around in the sky of my childhood. (153)

Yachine reserves a special disdain in the afterlife for the architects of the 16 May attacks, whom he imagines gleefully sending six young men to their deaths:

> Abou Zoubeïr, the Emir Zaïd and his followers must be rubbing their hands together in front of their television screens. [. . .] As for us, we were dead, very dead.
>
> And I'm still waiting on the angels. (152)

By situating his narrator beyond the grave, Binebine gives the terrorist the last word but in a deeply ambivalent way—as a restless phantom condemned to haunt the earthly world he so desperately sought to escape.

In its voicing of the dead, *Étoiles* finds a formal solution to the major logical and narratological impasses of narrating suicide bombing, and suicide in general, in the first person: How to access an event whose only true witness can no longer speak for themselves? The text provides a spectral "supplement" to the Casablanca bombings, registering ghostly voices and ghosted stories—those of the young men of Sidi Moumen—even as it deconstructs its own narrative authority.[82] Through the dead narrator, Binebine finds a suitably uncanny textual form for representing an act (suicide bombing) that so often is considered to exist beyond the pale of understanding and language. Without a claim to absolute knowledge, Binebine's novel creates an unsettling textual intimacy, even complicity, between bomber and reader, performing an ineluctable identification through language that allows for the kinds of imaginative and ethical modes of understanding envisioned by thinkers like Spivak, Rose, or Nussbaum. In the following section, I focus on a second, related aspect of the strange intimacy that *Étoiles* cultivates: Binebine's "queering" of the suicide bomber.

Queer Terrorists

In addition to Binebine's "queering" of voice through the novel's autothanatographic narrative configuration, *Étoiles* reads as queer or queerish in other ways: as a deeply homosocial novel in which the figure of the suicide bomber is noticeably "queered."[83] From its earliest pages, *Étoiles* is rife with homosocial overtones, homoerotic undertones, and homophobic violence (in the film adaptation, one of the first lines we hear is the Arabic slur for "fag").[84] Although the young men occasionally fantasize about sex with women, this always takes place in a homosocial setting. In one such scene, in the homey *baraque* of Yachine and Nabil, Khalil narrates his fantasy of intercourse with a European woman, "pull[ing] out his thick hard cock and slap[ping] it on the table" (101–2) in front of the other boys. Apart from Yachine reminiscing a chaste kiss between him and Ghizlane (83), only same-sex sex acts are depicted explicitly in the novel. The novel, moreover, is patterned by male bonding. The sites it predominantly depicts—the dump heap, the soccer pitch, the Garage—are all spaces dominated by boys and men and from which girls and women are excluded or altogether absent. Binebine ultimately portrays suicide bombing as an act carried out "between men," to borrow Eve Sedgwick's phrasing.[85] The novel thus would seem to align with overstated claims that terrorism emerges in a world without women and that it exploits the volatility of repressed male sexuality.[86]

In Binebine's novel, extremist Wahhabism—a reform movement within Sunni Islam—takes hold in the absence of father figures and despite the influence of women. The boys' fathers are all ineffective, impotent, aloof, abusive, or absent. The other men of Sidi Moumen—the "Doberman," a vampiric policeman whose post is burned to the ground by the inhabitants of the bidonville, and the lecherous mechanic Ba Moussa, who molests Nabil and ends up buried in the dump heap after Nabil strikes him dead—are treacherous, self-serving, and perverse. Yachine and Hamid's father, a former quarry worker, is a shadow of a man who rarely speaks or moves from the corner of their *baraque*; Nabil's father is a mystery, and the circumstances of Nabil's birth precipitate a family drama that ends with a taximan driving himself off a cliff; Khalil's father was a coachman whose fortunes swiftly dissipate after his only horse breaks its foot; Fouad's father, the muezzin, is struck by paralysis and dies; Youssef/Ali/Azzi's father, a miserly and physically abusive coalman (*charbonnier*), officially buries his only living son, renaming Youssef for his drowned younger brother.

By contrast, the women of *Étoiles* are characterized by kindness, grit, and enterprising spirit: their capacity to carve out forms of dignity and connection in the face of rampant inequality and immense suffering. Yachine and Hamid's mother, the warm and generous Yemma, maintains a meticulous household, singlehandedly supporting her two youngest sons, a physically incapacitated father, and an older son, Saïd, who struggles with some unspecified mental illness. The beautiful and seductive Tamou earns the begrudging respect of Sidi Moumen despite her profession, radiating in her musical performances at marriages and other ceremonies. Yachine's childhood crush, Fouad's sister Ghizlane, goes to school and becomes a talented seamstress and embroiderer. Her grandmother, the compassionate widow Mi-Lalla, belongs to the "aristocracy" of neighboring Douar Scouila, where she lives comfortably off her late husband's military pension and the money she makes as a bailiff, later taking in Fouad and Ghizlane when their mother remarries. Though relegated to the fringes of the novel's action, the female characters of *Étoiles* form an organizing and humanizing presence—one that offsets the masculine cohort, led by Abou Zoubeïr, responsible for radicalizing the young men. In juxtaposing the women's resistant self-sufficiency and self-sacrifice to the murderous "martyrdom" of men, Binebine offers a gendered critique of, and alternative to, the boys' descent into darkness. At the same time, he upholds certain patriarchal gendered stereotypes that reduce terrorism to a pathology or crisis of failed heterosexual masculinity: one that might be avoided through the "rehabilitating" influence of women and the presence of appropriate male role models. Indeed, the boys' gradual radicalization and the increasing authority of Abou Zoubeïr, who fills the void of the absent father, are indexed in the novel by how female characters progressively recede from view: Yachine and Nabil move out of their mothers' homes and into a *baraque* together; Azzi later moves in with them; Fouad spends more and more time away from his grandmother's home and urges Ghizlane to cover her hair and go about fully veiled.

In addition to the broader homosocial framing of *Étoiles*, Binebine's young male protagonists frequently deviate from or subvert standards of heteronormative masculinity. This is especially true of the twinned figures of the narrator Yachine (who struggles to reconcile his *faiblesses* [weaknesses] and *lâchetés* [cowardices], presumably nonheteronormative desires), and his friend Nabil (whose androgynous beauty attracts attention from women and men). The two emerge as an unconventional couple over the course of the novel, which stages both queer violence and queer desire—and, often, the intersection of the two.

Early in the novel, we are attuned to the routinized violence and banality of death in the bidonville through a scene of homoerotic play turned deadly, as Yachine and his childhood friend Morad affectionately wrestle behind the *décharge*:

> We were merely playing at imitating the heroes of Hindu films. Morad took pleasure in biting at my ears and whispering strange words into them. His coarse tongue made me tremble. He had taken me prisoner by pinning my arms to the ground. His curls smelled of olive oil. They tasted of it, too, for my mouth was full of them. (15)

Yachine's brother Hamid, witnessing the scene from afar, is filled with rage and homosexual panic at the sight of the two boys on top of one another. He bashes Morad's head in with a heavy stone, sneers *pédale* (queer, faggot) and other epithets at Yachine, then unceremoniously buries the boy's body in the dump heap. True to its etymology, the *décharge* becomes a morbid figure for nonnormative sexualities and queer violence—a repository for deviance and excess. Later in the novel, the lecherous mechanic Ba Moussa is buried there, practically next to Morad, after he drunkenly molests Nabil, who fights back and kills him in self-defense. The bidonvilles of Casablanca were apparently notorious for such clandestine or unauthorized burials. In his sociological study, J. Ratier notes that one of two principal "clandestine cemeteries" in Casablanca was in Sidi Moumen, where "dubious deaths" escaped official channels through secretive nighttime burials.[87]

Nabil eventually replaces Yachine's murdered companion Morad, and the two become fast friends: "It's in that way, after the disappearance of Morad, that Nabil and I had become inseparable" (20). In a classic Girardian "triangle," Nabil rivals (and usurps) Yachine's heterosexual crush, Ghizlane, when he and Yachine move into a *baraque* together: "I really think she was jealous," recalls Yachine, "She would have liked to be in his place" (97).[88] On the literal refuse of Sidi Moumen, Nabil and Yachine transform their *baraque* into a domestic "nest" (98) and queer family unit—a heterotopic space where they welcome, cook for, and shelter the other boys: "With boys like Khalil the shoe-shine boy, Nabil son of Tamou, Ali (or Youssef) alias Azzi, Fouad or my brother Hamid, we ended up making in spite of everything and against all odds a whole family" (55). Such configurations of two or more bachelors sharing a *baraque* were not uncommon. Ratier notes that Moroccans referred pejoratively to young men leading such a communal lifestyle as *rouassa*, from the Darija word for "Russian."[89] As an alternative and resilient, if fragile, haven, this unlikely homosocial community of Yachine, Nabil, and the other boys emerges amid and despite the surrounding suffering, violence, and squalor. It contrasts with the failed heteronormative family units from which the young men progressively distance themselves and the dangerous homosocial space of extremist violence (the Garage) to which they are increasingly drawn.

The juxtaposition of two episodes in particular troubles a heteronormative reading of *Étoiles*, allowing us to further appreciate Binebine's innovation with the terrorist genre in French. The first occurs when Nabil is gang-raped by the other boys during a drunken celebration after winning a soccer match against their rivals. Intoxicated by victory, the sweltering August heat, and an "explosive" concoction of alcohol and hashish, the boys drink, smoke, and dance in a circle as Nabil, dressed in a belted white gandoura, turns in the center before passing out, "like a parachutist amidst his cloth" (58–59). Hamid proceeds to kiss and then rape the unconscious Nabil in front of his teammates with a facility and casualness that surprises only Yachine:

> He was kissing him, or rather devouring him with kisses as if he had desired him forever and finally had the chance to avail himself. [...] Then, pausing, he cast his gaze over the horny horde and, very gently, without any embarrassment over our presence, he undressed Nabil, took out his own cock stiff as a stick and planted it into the plump, pinkish behind that was offered up to him. He did it with a naturalness that disconcerted me. Besides me, it didn't seem to shock anyone. (59)

The other boys—some hesitant, others impatient—follow suit, taking turns at "mounting the sleeper" (*enfourcher le dormeur*; 59). Yachine is the only one not to participate actively in the rape. When the others have finished and it becomes Yachine's turn, Hamid—as if out of fraternal modesty—leaves the *baraque* while his brother tries to prove his heteronormative masculinity through same-sex rape: "I needed to prove to them that I wasn't a queer, a faggot" (60). As Yachine hesitates before the naked, unconscious body of his best friend, Nabil comes to, and Yachine helps him to cover himself, pulling down the folds of the white gandoura "on his nudity, on his distress and his humiliation, like lowering the curtain of a theater where a macabre play has just been staged" (60).

The sexual politics of this chilling gang rape scene, as well as the fact that the narrator witnesses but not does participate in or try to stop it, are difficult to discern. Whereas Hamid's earlier outrage at seeing his brother tumbling with another boy behind the dump heap seems a straightforward example of homosexual panic converted into antigay violence (queerbashing, murder), the gang rape he initiates is so disconcertingly casual as to appear second nature. The only panic the rape produces is in the bystander Yachine, for whom the scene activates attendant anxieties around his own unresolved sexuality (of his brother leaving the room, Yachine remarks, "He knew my weaknesses, my cowardices" [60]). For the other boys, the instance is one of sexual violence but also unbridled and apparently unproblematic same-sex desire—through which sodomy and rape become forms of homosocial bonding for the participatory perpetrators. The rape further relies on an environment of generalized misogyny and homophobia, given that the victim, Nabil, is the most overtly "feminine," "passive," and "queer" of the group.

The second scene forms a coda to the first and occurs immediately before the 16 May attacks, when Abou Zoubeïr's followers take the soon-to-be bombers to a campsite in the Atlas Mountains for a final intensive training episode. The trip is intended to discipline their bodies through strenuous exercise and purify their souls through rigorous prayer as well as to familiarize them with the explosive devices they will use during the bombings, including the long-awaited *ceintures de paradis* (suicide belts). Despite the sanctity and seriousness of their mission, the trip into the mountains only heightens the young men's male homosocial desire. Just as their earlier physical training frequently had devolved into "orgiastic struggles" (107), their phallogocentric knife fights in the mountains arouse: "It was so arousing [*excitant*]. There were a few scrapes, but nothing serious" (128).

The queer subtext of *Étoiles* comes to a head when, on their last night in the mountains, Nabil and Yachine have sex in the tent they are sharing. Earlier criticism on *Étoiles* has read Nabil and Yachine's coupling near the end of the novel in terms of "repressed sexualities": a moment of the profane that highlights the total failure of the boys' spiritual purification through radicalization and trivializes the "religious grandiosity of the mission," given that they can be seen to submit to their "most base" human desires shortly before carrying out the attacks.[90]

I read this scene differently. In a novel brimming with violence, including sexual violence and queerbashing, the scene is strikingly tender. It contrasts markedly with the rape scene, which Yachine observes and is complicit in but in which he does not actively participate. In this earlier scene, the unconscious Nabil, dressed in a white gandoura and called by his mother's name, is assimilated to a female sex object and violently penetrated by the other boys "like a cadaver." The rape reinforces the terms of heteronormativity and misogyny in evidence throughout the novel. In the mountains, by contrast, Yachine and Nabil draw near to one another to keep warm and sleepily make love in the only instance of consensual sex depicted in the entire novel—a fact that would seem underscored by the proliferation of reciprocal verbs in this passage:

> I ask God for forgiveness because Nabil and I made love to each other. I'm not quite sure how it happened. We hadn't planned it, but it was so. To warm ourselves, we huddled against one another in that tent with a roof low like a grave. I don't know if we were asleep, but our drowsy minds were elsewhere. The mountain air had something to do with it. Nabil's body brushing up against mine caused my penis to become terribly erect. He took it in his hand quite naturally and we kissed each other. We undressed and made love [*nous nous aimâmes*]. In silence. There, it's said. (128)

While Yachine struggles to reconcile the act with his recent spiritual training ("I let my guard down before the devil's ruses," he confesses earlier), his poignant narrative description undercuts performative utterances of remorse. The "naturalness" with which the boys have sex and kiss is far from the "disconcerting" ease with which Hamid initiates the rape of Nabil.

This love scene in a tent resembling a tomb hauntingly anticipates the bombers' coupling with Death—a grotesque wedding night for which they prepare like virgins, collectively bathing and shaving together before dressing all in white:

> We washed ourselves and shaved our bodies closely, preparing for death as if for a marriage. We made a few jokes about Nabil's ass, Nabil who was refusing to let himself be rubbed down. [...] Zaïd brought us the clothes for the final night. Perfectly clean, totally white linen such as our bodies thus purified of defilement demanded. (138)

More directly, the love scene prefigures Nabil and Yachine's fatal "union" to one another. At the end of the novel, the two make eye contact before exploding themselves simultaneously, alongside each other in a restaurant, surrounded by dining heterosexual couples. While the other boys run up against obstacles, botch their detonations, or abandon the mission, Nabil and Yachine seal their fates together in a final, "deadly embrace." Even the language used to describe the instant before their deaths is laden with double entendre: "I turned toward him and nodded. A nod that chilled my blood because it meant that we had to do it [*passer à l'acte*]. When he entered the restaurant, my heart started pounding [*battre à tout rompre*]" (150). Shortly before they explode, Binebine has us imagine affection, reciprocity, and queer intimacy in ways that amplify the tragic. In another context, in another world, these boys were lovers.

Binebine's queer(ed) suicide bomber—though, to my knowledge, a first in the Francophone terrorist genre—does not emerge in a vacuum. As Puar reminds us, there is an important historical and rhetorical connection between anxieties around terrorism and anxieties around queer or marginal sexualities. Often, as the infamous "fag bomb" demonstrates, there is a direct line drawn between the two: a powerful equation between the figures of "the terrorist" and "the queer."[91]

Binebine's queering of the Casablanca bombers rejects such discourses, which queer and sexualize terrorists in order to other and distance them as nonnational, perverse entities—that is, to equate "monster," "terrorist," and "fag" (Puar). Binebine's project in *Étoiles* consists in moving *toward*—not away from— the suicide bomber, inhabiting his subject position and inviting his readers to do the same. This identification through language is an invitation to recognize these characters and their struggles as fundamentally human. Far from pathologizing terrorist bodies, Binebine challenges us to understand, if not like and love, the young men of Sidi Moumen—and to imagine that they might have loved each other, too.

God's Horses

One of the notable formal differences between Binebine's text and Ayouch's film adaptation, *Les chevaux de Dieu* (2013), is the absence of any autothanatographic slant. The ghostly frame of Yachine's restless narrating spirit disappears completely, and in contrast to the novel, the film does not pretend to have even limited access to the protagonists' mental states or motivations, in life or in death. Although there is a gesture at prolepsis in the film—as the opening credits roll, we hear a conversation between Yachine and Nabil that is replayed later, shortly before their suicide—the narrative plotted by Ayouch is linear, even teleological. Rather than Yachine unspooling and selectively arranging events from the hereafter with varying degrees of attention and detail, Ayouch follows a strict chronology: from children to adolescents to bombers. Devoid of the critical distance and mordent irony afforded by Yachine's spectral commentary from the hereafter, and without the complicity and identification created by extended first-person narration, we are positioned instead as interested but ultimately detached witnesses to the story unfolding before us. In this, the film more closely resembles the discourses around suicide bombing to which we are accustomed. Such discourses inspire "horror," but do not train the narrative imagination toward understanding in the ways envisioned by Spivak or Nussbaum. The effect is chilling, but not especially unsettling: our own subject position is never threatened, our own gaze never questioned.

Ayouch's reframing of Binebine's novel along these lines cannot simply be attributed to differences or limitations in media: the film adaptation of Alice Sebold's novel *The Lovely Bones*, for instance, retains its otherworldly first-person narration through an effective and haunting use of voice-over whereby the dead protagonist-narrator, Susie Salmon, revisits the scenes of her rape and murder as she does in the novel. Even more relevant is Julie Loktev's tightly shot film *Day Night Day Night* (2006), which focuses on the last forty-eight hours in the life of a nineteen-year-old female suicide bomber as she prepares to explode herself in Times Square. Loktev manages to achieve a proximity and intimacy—even "empathy"[92]—not unlike that cultivated in Binebine's novel. We hew so closely to the protagonist's sole perspective, and the camera centers so tightly on her movements, that we feel implicated in her every action. In *Les chevaux de Dieu*, by contrast, the "terrorist" remains at arm's length—at a distance comfortable enough to be observed.

Ayouch's reframing is part of a more general streamlining of the novel's plot, which also flattens the queer subtext of Binebine's novel. The novel's complex and nuanced subtext of homosocial desire, same-sex attraction, homophobic violence, and queer intimacy becomes, in the film, a highly ambivalent and inconsistent portrayal of queerness. Ayouch entirely abandons the earlier episode involving Morad and Yachine as well as the later love scene between Nabil and Yachine. Instead, Yachine's attraction to Ghizlane is foregrounded, organizing Binebine's protagonist away from a potential queer reading. In Ayouch's portrayal, Nabil is more overtly feminized and more closely assimilated to the image of his mother, Tamou: he wears earrings and tight clothes, and in one scene we see him trying on his mother's lipstick shortly after she moves away from the bidonville. Yachine and Nabil take over Tamou's home, rather than finding a *baraque* of their own, and the rape scene occurs here, after Nabil dances in one of his mother's scarves. The charge of the rape scene in Ayouch's film adaptation is even more uncertain than in the novel, since only Hamid rapes Nabil, and the rape is overlaid with a spliced-in montage of Tamou performing at a party. The moments of queerness that Ayouch retains from the novel are its instances of antiqueer violence (Nabil's rape and molestation) rather than its moments of queer intimacy, tenderness, and reciprocity (Morad and Yachine's affectionate wrestling, Nabil and Yachine's love scene).

The title of Ayouch's film, *God's Horses* (in French, *Les chevaux de Dieu*, and in Arabic, *Ya khayl Allah*)—an expression that never occurs in Binebine's novel—is a further indication of how Ayouch focuses on the boys' religious formation and conversion into martyrs. While Binebine's *Étoiles* preserves a sense of tragedy as a reminder and affirmation of the boy's identity before they become suicide bombers, Ayouch's title—which also is how the title of Binebine's novel has been translated into English—frames them purely as jihadists, faithful servants of a religious cause, and agents of destruction.[93]

In the film, the boys' "radicalization" is far more complete. Whereas Yachine's ghostly narration in the novel undercuts the seriousness of their religious undertaking, in the film he becomes the favorite of Abou Zoubeïr and the most outspoken proponent of his teachings. In the case of Yachine's wayward brother Hamid, the transformation is total, and it occurs completely off-screen, in jail, after his work as a drug mule gets him into trouble. In a clear gesture of "extroversion" in Julien's sense, Hamid is released the day after the 9/11 attacks and returns to the bidonville a changed man: suddenly soft-spoken and pious, his beard grown out, the bike chain he used to carry to defend himself replaced by a string of prayer beads. Such a portrayal maps more easily onto official discourses surrounding terrorism and responds more readily to our expectations and attendant anxieties around suicide bombing, reifying the "terrorist" as a cultish fanatic and radical other, positioned at the far edges of—or, better, beyond—humanity.

Binebine's novel erodes complacency: we come away troubled, not reassured. Our own humanity hangs in the balance. In the conclusion to this chapter, I want to focus on how Binebine further deconstructs and transgresses discourses around suicide terrorism by contextualizing the act against a broader historical and political backdrop. Binebine accomplishes this (re)contextualization in part by connecting the rise of suicide bombing to the phenomenon of irregular migration, the topic of an earlier novel, *Cannibales* (1999), published near the end of the Black Decade.

Conclusion: Mahi Binebine's *Cannibales* (1999)

> Clandestine emigrants impose on the world their right to a better life: by refusing the status quo, they jostle the geopolitical order [. . .] and thus contribute to moving the lines.
>
> FELWINE SARR, *Afrotopia* (2016)

In *Étoiles*, Binebine redirects focus away from pathologized conceptions of the suicide bomber as a perverse religious radical and toward myriad forms of oppression, socioeconomic precarity, and biopolitical exclusion. The most "monstrous" figure in *Étoiles* proves not to be what Puar identifies as the "terrorist-fag" but the state: the novel's ultimate absent father figure, whose total abdication of responsibility creates the conditions of deprivation and desperation in which radicalism takes hold.[94] Part of Binebine's point in *Étoiles*—and his impetus for later creating the "Étoiles" cultural centers with Ayouch—is that Wahhabism fulfills basic human needs not otherwise met in Morocco's bidonvilles. The suicide mission with which Yachine and his friends are charged paradoxically gives the young men a sense of their intrinsic humanity, supplying an identity and a purpose before they carry out an "inhuman" act. "We were no longer parasites," Yachine says of the boys' time at the Garage, "scraps of humanity, good-for-nothings. We were clean and dignified, and our aspirations resonated with healthy minds. We were listened to, guided" (110).

Binebine situates suicide terrorism—so often taken to be a singular, exceptional phenomenon—within a broader landscape of structural violence. He posits it as one of two possible outcomes for young men the state has abandoned. In fact, *Étoiles* draws clear parallels between suicide bombing and what Binebine portrays as a similarly desperate act, motivated by a related desire for escape: irregular migration. Khalil in particular dreams of migrating clandestinely to Europe despite his cousin's efforts to dissuade him with a sobering example, that of the body of a Black African migrant washed ashore with the tide (100). It is telling in this sense that Yachine's spectral condition is often expressed in terms that evoke the figure of the drowned *harraga*: he refers to his demise as a "shipwreck" (*mon naufrage*; 153), and he haunts the "dunes of detritus" of Sidi Moumen like "infinite beaches" (24).

This is the other, parallel history that is the focus of Binebine's earlier novel *Cannibales* (1999), and to which the author, in a later interview, directly compares *Étoiles*. Binebine notes, "This story about the attack presented itself as identical, with the same type of helpless youths, without any dream of a future. [...] In these two parallel realities, we find the same business that sends children to their death."[95] Such parallels add another valence to the kinds of "intimacies" and relations of proximity and identification that Binebine's novel cultivates, making homicidal suicide and clandestine migration two sides of the same coin. Binebine's imbrication of clandestine migration and suicide terrorism as "parallel realities" is revealing insofar as he identifies both phenomena as psychologically extreme acts that are, nonetheless and contra hyperbolic rhetoric, "understandable" when viewed through the lenses of systemic structural and state violence.

Although published over a decade apart, Binebine's *Cannibales* (1999) and *Les étoiles de Sidi Moumen* (2010) are twin narratives. They trace related responses to histories of destitution and desperation: parallel attempts by a group of young people to secure one-way tickets to "paradise." The English title of *Cannibales*, *Welcome to Paradise*, plays directly on the various meanings of *paradis* in the context of migration and perilous ocean crossings: as the chimeric "promised land" of Europe, to recall the English title of Sembène's story, and as the afterlife, since so few candidates survey the journey. J. R. Essomba's earlier novel *Le paradis du nord* (1996), about two men trying to reach France from Africa, exploits a similar ambivalence in its title.[96] Of course, even fewer individuals make the journey safely multiple times. In *Cannibales*, this is part of the mystique of the *rabatteur* (recruiter), Morad/Momo, who has been expelled from Europe three times and is an expert in shuttling between "Paradise" and Earth/Hell—not unlike Yachine. But does this make him a god or a ghost? The expression *barça ou barzakh* (Barcelona or death) limns this razor-thin edge between the fulfillment of dreams and death. In *Étoiles*, of course, the "paradise" promised is not that of Europe, as is the case for the *harraga* who "burns" the sea to reach foreign shores, but a heroic martyrdom or *istishhad* through a fiery self-explosion. Their "tickets" are *ceintures de paradis* packed with explosives.

Binebine's portrayal of clandestine migration in *Cannibales* seems to directly prepare his later representations of suicide-bombing in *Étoiles*. Many of the names of the protagonists (Youssef, Morad, Tamou) are recycled across the narratives. Even the first-person narrators of the two novels resemble each other. Like Yachine—"What? I'm rambling! And what of it?" (25)—the narrator of *Cannibales*, Azzouz, is prone to invention and narrative digressions: "But I'm making things up. As is my habit."[97] As Yachine does, he frequently revisits scenes of his childhood and adolescence in ways that help us understand his desire to emigrate but also amplify the tragic dimensions of his story, such as when we learn that Azzouz was a promising student before trying to reach Europe. Azzouz is shadowed throughout the novel by his double, Réda, his cousin for whom he feels responsible and with whom he narrowly escapes death, resuscitating him on the beach. In *Étoiles*, this dyad is furnished by the duo of Yachine and Nabil, the narrator's chosen family. Azzouz's ambivalent narrative position as a survivor—someone who fails to make the crossing and is spared while the others drown—anticipates Yachine's spectral witnessing from beyond the grave as he recounts the other boys' lives and deaths. Both novels, moreover, occur in the wake of extremist violence in North Africa. Binebine published *Cannibales* from East Hampton, New York, at the height of violence against writers and intellectuals in Algeria during the Black Decade. Just as migration "surfaces" suddenly in Binebine's later novel through the image of a drowned Black migrant washed ashore, extremist terrorism punctures the narrative of *Cannibales* when we learn that the one Algerian character, Kacem

Djoudi, is fleeing the civil war after his family in Blida was brutally massacred by "some bearded fanatic" (86).

Between *Cannibales* and *Étoiles*, Binebine shows both deadly enterprises—clandestine migration on the one hand, suicide terrorism on the other—to be far-ranging systems of exploitation that prey on vulnerable, precarious populations by trafficking in false promises and counterfeit dreams. The rapacious men of the Garage—who prove mere marionettes of Abou Zoubeïr, the Emir Zaïd, and his followers, themselves even further removed from the suffering they both inflict and exploit—find corollaries in *Cannibales* in an elaborate network of recruitment, corruption, coercion, and abuse that includes *passeurs, rabatteurs*, truck drivers, and corrupt police officers. While the Mediterranean is the ultimate *mangeur d'hommes* in *Cannibales*, Binebine reveals the entire system of clandestine migration to be cannibalizing (and cadavarizing) at every level. Like suicide terrorism, it is a system that relies on the convergence of historical, political, and economic forces to produce, as Azzouz puts it, "humiliated" and "unpredictable" men capable of "all kinds of madness" (14). Like the boys of *Étoiles*, who are already living a kind of social death in Sidi Moumen—that is, already produced as ghosts by the state—Azzouz and his fellow *harragas* feel they have little to lose and everything to gain. As Azzouz asks himself, what "hole," what "abyss"—even that "grey vault of the sea," to borrow Walcott's words—could be "deeper, darker than that the one into which destitution had already thrown them?" (14).

The parallels between *Cannibales* and *Étoiles* become most evident in the final pages, where the narrators of both novels experience an uncanny déjà vu that exposes the seemingly endless cycle of structural violence governing their lives and deaths. In the case of *Étoiles*, Yachine observes a new generation, a potential cohort of future bombers (153–55). Already, earlier in the novel, Yachine had recognized his situation as symptomatic rather than singular. He and his fellow future bombers could be any six boys, in any bidonville, or anyone in any place where children are robbed of a future: "In another Garage in another bidonville, Abou Zoubeïr has hung up my photo alongside those of the other martyrs. [. . .] And other boys, looking up at our portraits, will dream of justice and sacrifice, just as we once had while watching the tapes of Palestinian and Chechen martyrs" (86). The end of the novel confirms this. In the wake of an explosion that has killed dozens but, in a sense, changed nothing, the haunting close of *Étoiles* presages the repetition of violence:

> The bidonville has not changed. It has even gotten larger, and the once isolated barracks now form a town. A huge city of the living dead [*morts-*

vivants]. I wait and I cry before the wheel which keeps turning. The dump heap is there—immutable, infinite. Amidst the commotion of the dumpsters [...] I see underfed children, carefree, chasing after a deflated soccer ball: The New Stars of Sidi Moumen [*les Nouvelles Étoiles de Sidi Moumen*]. (153–54)

In the case of *Cannibales*, the novel ends the day after Azzouz and his cousin Réda have been rejected by the sea. As they help launch the boat that will carry them to Spain, they are pushed back by the swells and dashed against the "cursed shore that birthed [them] and to whose agony [*affres*] [they] were forever condemned" (204). Like the bombers in *Étoiles* whose suicide belts fail to explode, sparing their lives and the lives of many others, this failure turns out to be a blessing for Azzouz and Réda, who escape death. As they walk through Tangier the day after their failed departure, they glimpse footage of a Spanish news program showing police recovering bodies from the sea. Recognizing the composition of the victims—"a man with a baby curiously strapped to him by a bit of cloth, two Black men, a White man, and a woman with undone braids"—as well as the green rain jacket of the *passeur*, they know this was the boat they had tried to leave on (214).

Like *Étoiles*, *Cannibales* ends where it began, since Azzouz and Réda "end up" at Café France, the setting of the novel's opening scene and where they first met the *rabatteur* and other potential migrants. The verb Binebine uses in the passage is *échouer*—of a boat, literally to "run aground," "wreck," or "beach": "How is it that we ended up [*échouer*] once more in front of Café France? It was the last place we wanted to find ourselves" (215–16). The latent metaphor parallels the final pages of *Étoiles*, when Yachine returns to the scene of his *naufrage* (shipwreck) and the novel returns to the status antequem. Just as Yachine observes the "Nouvelles Étoiles," Azzouz and Réda spy the recruiter Momo through the window of Café France, ensconced amid a new group of candidates for departure: "At times [Momo] laughed, and his laughter reached us, bewitching, at other times he grew serious, and his gestures assumed the same solemnity that, hanging on his every word, the new table [*la nouvelle tablée*] adopted in turn" (215). For a moment, this *mise en abîme* through the café window—both a scene of looking and of recognizing oneself in what one sees—seems like it might be a turning point. Even if the continuation of the cycle is clear (there is a *nouvelle tablée*), for Azzouz and Réda the curtain seems to have been pulled back. They are now on the outside looking in. Surely they will not try again.

But as Binebine also suggests in *Étoiles*, the wheel of oppression continues to turn, disinterestedly. The ending of *Cannibales*, like that of *Étoiles*, points only to repetition: "Silent, carefully avoiding looking at one another, we stayed contemplating the lights of the smoke-filled room. The radio crackled the listless romance of a singer tinged with despair. It started to grow cold. Réda entered the café first" (215). So long as there continue to exist entire cities of the living-dead—*morts-vivants*, as Binebine writes in *Étoiles*—there will be individuals prepared to take seemingly radical decisions to "impose on the world their right to a better life."[98]

Both *Cannibales* and *Les étoiles de Sidi Moumen* expose the wheel of oppression without lapsing into easy environmental determinism or sentimentalism, however. As we learn early in *Étoiles*, while Yachine witnesses his own funeral from the hereafter, "the bravest of the stars of Sidi Moumen"—namely, the other half of the soccer team whose names we never learn—are those who resisted radicalization and who live on to attend the other boys' burials. And while the desperation of the *harragas* emerges as analogous to suicide across *Étoiles*, *Cannibales*, and interviews with Binebine, "actual" suicide remains something "foreign" and "rare" in *Cannibales*. Individual suicide is evoked only briefly in the novel as Azzouz recalls the tragic suicide of his aunt, Réda's guilt-stricken mother, who threw herself into a well when Réda was a child (46). It is, Azzouz assures the reader, "a rare practice" (37) where he comes from. Azzouz's assertion in *Cannibales* that suicide is "rare" in Morocco will not be one that Binebine maintains in his later novel *Étoiles*; of course, in the interim, Morocco would see multiple suicide bombings. Today Morocco has the second-highest rate of suicide in the so-called Arab world.[99] Abd Rabbu al-Bakhsh, a sociologist studying suicide in northern Morocco, suggests that "the phenomenon of suicide is flourishing in Morocco, and is linked to the social, economic, political, and cultural transformations that the country is witnessing, *and to a range of other phenomena such as irregular migration, violent extremism, and crime.*"[100]

Binebine's literary response to the Casablanca bombings calls our attention to these "other phenomena." It (re)contextualizes suicide bombing within a range of historically contingent practices that emerge not as "unthinkable" acts carried out by psychopathic monsters or anonymous migrants but, rather, as desperate solutions to lives that—through structural violence and rampant inequality—are produced as precarious and unlivable. In doing so, Binebine's literary engagement with suicide bombing, especially when considered alongside his engagement with irregular migration in *Cannibales*, points less to pathology and more to cycles of dehumanizing violence, exclusion, and misery.

Within the broader homosocial framing and ambivalent sexual politics of *Étoiles*, taken together with the putative queerness of figures like Yachine and Nabil, Binebine's queering of suicide terrorism might be read as part of a broader commitment to unsettling categorical assumptions about suicide bombing and to painting a more complex picture of the social realities that exist alongside (extra)ordinary violence. Between condemnation and humanization of the suicide bomber, *Étoiles* charts a possible imaginative response. Through its queering of voice and voicing of the dead, Binebine's text models an "ethics of form" (Rose) for what Spivak calls "an imaginative exercise in experiencing the impossible—stepping into the space of the other," in this case the radical other: the "terrorist," the queer. Without condescension and without compromising his antiterrorist, pacifist message, Binebine invites us to draw closer to the suicide bomber, listen to him, and imagine him as human, as like us. This is the queer intimacy—a textual proximity—*on the way to understanding* that Binebine's novel makes possible. *Étoiles* salvages the profoundly human life that existed before the human bomb, but it also accomplishes something more subversive. For in *Étoiles*, Binebine makes "reader" and "terrorist," "literature" and "suicide bombing," *harraga* and *shuhada* strange bedfellows.

CONCLUSION

THE SUICIDE ARCHIVE: A SOCIAL DOCUMENT

> We considered the archive not as a talisman or a fetish, but as a *document*. The archive is meaningful in its context, it is not "truth," it belongs to an entire social environment.
>
> FRANÇOISE VERGÈS, "A Museum without Objects" (2016)

Disappearing Acts

I want to conclude with a missing record and an archive on fire.[1] This book has explored the challenges (and openings) that suicide poses for archival research and literary history while considering the ways that revisiting archives and aesthetic works with particular attention to suicide sheds light on colonial dynamics in the present. It has traced a long history of death, disappearance, and dispossession as responses to slavery, colonization, state terror, and their afterlives. By way of conclusion, I want to think briefly about what acts of self-destruction and self-disappearance mean for archives that themselves are occasionally destroyed or disappeared.

In 2019, when I began researching the Talaatay Nder, the episode of collective suicidal resistance discussed in chapter 2, I was eager to tether the story to a written trace, an archival document. Over the next few years, I would hear different versions of the Talaatay Nder in Wolof, French, and English from friends, teachers, colleagues, and strangers. These stories all had points of overlap and divergence; no one was identical to another. Given the vibrancy of contemporary historical memory related to the Talaatay Nder, I had hoped a Senegalese historian had sifted through the various oral versions and set them down in writing. At the time, I did not ask myself why this might not be the case, why it might be better this way, and why this, too, was part of the story.

During the summer of 2021, I searched the archives of the Université Cheikh Anta Diop (UCAD) in Dakar for an unpublished master's thesis from 1992 by Bitty Bocar Ba, "Talaatay Ndeer: Histoire du suicide collectif des femmes de Ndeer le 5 mars 1820 (Royaume du Waalo)." Ba's thesis seemed to be the only historical study dedicated to the Talaatay Nder. I hoped it might help me reconcile conflicting details and fill gaps in my knowledge by determining a definite date for the Talaatay Nder. I hoped it might lead me to other sources, other archives. I had come across references to Ba's text in different places, but no one seemed to have read it. In any case, the sources never cited the text directly.

Ba's text proved a chimera. The archivist at UCAD helped me locate a range of documents of interest, but I was told the thesis had been lost, damaged, or stolen. I went back several days in a row, hoping different archivists or librarians might have different answers. Although disappointed, I was not especially surprised or discouraged. Archival research is difficult and frustrating; it requires a high tolerance for loose or dead ends. Working in West African archives can be especially challenging: catalogs are not always digitized, searchable, or accurate; materials frequently are in fragile condition or a state of decay; collections or parts of collections often have been moved, sold, damaged, reorganized, or dispersed; microfilming and digitization initiatives are underfunded and uneven; rarely do archives and their stewards have the support or resources they need. Occasionally, entire libraries and archives are destroyed.

When I returned to Senegal in June 2023 to finish writing this book, UCAD's library had burned. A week before I arrived in Dakar, deadly clashes between protesters and Senegalese police erupted throughout the city after opposition leader Ousmane Sonko was convicted of "corrupting the youth" (*corruption de la jeunesse*) but acquitted on charges of rape and sentenced to

FIGURE C.I. Aftermath of a fire at Université Cheikh Anta Diop in Dakar, Senegal, June 2023. Source: John Wessels/Agency France Press.

two years in prison. Sonko's supporters maintain that his sentencing was part of efforts to derail his candidacy in upcoming elections by the then president, Macky Sall, who at the time seemed poised to install himself for a third term in office. Social media sites and internet access were cut in parts of the capital in response to the violent protests. Businesses and schools closed. Police fired directly on demonstrators—many just teenagers—leaving at least sixteen people dead (though likely more), killed by live ammunition. During the protests, demonstrators set fire to university buildings, including the UCAD library. The director of the archives, Lamine Diabaye, estimates that over two hundred thousand documents were destroyed. If Ba's missing thesis did in fact remain somewhere in the university collections, it surely has been burned.

In the days that followed, archivists, librarians, students, faculty, staff, and volunteers gathered at UCAD to sort through the debris and salvage what remained. The courtyard and hallways were carpeted with singed volumes, many blackened beyond recognition. Volunteers used bricks, stones, and pieces of detritus from the torched buildings to mark piles of related texts and to prevent pages from scattering in the wind (figure C.1). It is a harrowing scene: a library burned, students displaced, so much history lost. But it also inspires resolve. It bears witness to a group of people determined to rebuild an archive from the ashes.

I struggle to find a more prescient image for the kind of work the suicide archive entails, invites, and demands. It is a collective, social, and ongoing project *in the present* of sorting and sifting through fragile archives marked by irrecoverable loss—unreadable and missing traces—in the hopes of telling a new story, or new versions of an old story.

I provide this anecdote about Ba's missing thesis not to fetishize the archival "chase" but to mark a turning point in my own thinking about archives and archiving, a shift that has shaped this book. My project survived without access to Ba's elusive text. I found other sources, written and oral, published and unpublished, archived and unarchived. Importantly, I began to take these unarchived sources seriously as being central to the story I was trying to tell: as evidence of a fragmentary, fungible, dispersed, ever-shifting—though no less powerful, no less "true"—suicide archive.

Missing Traces, Phantom Limbs

Ba's disappearing thesis turned out to be an invitation to the work of the suicide archive itself: an invitation to learn to write about disappearance and destruction in the presence or absence of "actually existing archives" and in ways that inscribe loss.[2] Archives real or imagined, documents lost and found, remain central to the task of understanding how the colonial past fails to remain past—how it informs and determines contemporary dynamics in both visible and invisible ways. As Patrick Gathara writes, "The path to colonial reckoning is through archives, not museums."[3] That is, through the hundreds of thousands of records of subjugation, violence, and corruption, as well as resistance, resourcefulness, and survival, that would allow for a more complete understanding and more accurate narrative of colonial history.

But access to colonial archives, and thus to a version of colonial history, remains wildly inequitable. Most archives are consolidated in the territories of former imperial powers themselves, and most European governments have been reluctant to return official archives to the countries they previously colonized, reluctant to hand over "the power to re-frame history."[4] The societies most immediately concerned with and impacted by this history and its archives—the people who live its pernicious legacies daily—are precisely those denied access to it. Often, what these societies are left with are missing traces, phantom limbs.

This is germane to a point that Felwine Sarr and Bénédicte Savoy make throughout their *Rapport sur la restitution du patrimoine culturel africain: Vers une nouvelle éthique relationnelle* (November 2018), a document tasked both with assessing the history of France's appropriation of African art, artifacts, and archives and laying out a plan for restitution.[5] Sarr and Savoy write, "What we must begin to deal with is the work of the reconstruction and recuperation of those missing traces of history and memory—as if they were phantom limbs—*above all when history has been deprived of available archives*."[6] What I have tried to show in this book is that suicide emerges as a "phantom limb," repressed content, and missing link in the history of French empire. It continues to make its presence felt, if only as absence. As a transhistorical and transnational link—both limb and ligature—suicide helps to articulate continuities between the colonial past and our present moment. It is imperative that we recognize the ways contemporary forms of violence and violent resistance, including suicide, remain haunted by the deep genealogies of anticolonial and antislavery suicide this book has traced. To fail to do so is to postpone reckoning and to ignore the suicide archives hiding in plain sight.

But as the case of Ba's missing thesis makes clear, archives are fragile and fallible—that is, fundamentally human—institutions. Access remains unequal. Archives sometimes disappear. As Françoise Vergès reminds us, the archive is not "truth." It belongs "to an entire social environment."[7] This means that, like suicide and the literary text, the meaning, purpose, form, and value of archives are not fixed or a priori guaranteed. Archives emerge out of historically specific contexts and by way of socially embedded acts of interpretation. They occasionally must be reenvisioned, rebuilt, and remade.

The aesthetic works examined here all acknowledge and enact this. They take points of suicidal resistance in and out of the archive as sites of historical, political, and ethical potential: openings for alternate histories to surface and new forms of historical knowledge to emerge. In my deployment of the notion of the "suicide archive," I have tried not only to model a way of archiving suicidal resistance through aesthetic forms but also to explore the historical potential and interpretive yield of reading aesthetic forms *as* archives. Aesthetic works entextualize, narrativize, and novelize suicide in ways that amplify or set loose suicide's "rhetorical force." They navigate treacherous terrain, enabling us to hear the impossible speech and *rumeur* contained within a tragic, inaccessible, unaccountable act.

If we are to take seriously what Sarr and Savoy call the work of "reconstruction and recuperation" with respect to "missing traces of history and memory," then the story of suicidal resistance must be told, no longer relegated to the margins of historical accounts. A better way of saying this: we must learn to recognize how missing traces have been telling the *story* of suicidal resistance all along. After all, the suicide archive is just that: a story, a social document. The work it performs and invites is always plural and never finished. There exist many more suicide archives to uncover and many more modes of archiving suicide to explore.

ACKNOWLEDGMENTS

This book owes much to the insights, generosity, friendship, and encouragement of many people.

At Yale, I am forever grateful for the incomparable mentorship of Jill M. Jarvis, Christopher L. Miller, and Cajetan Iheka. They have read and reread versions of this manuscript at nearly every stage, provided feedback, asked questions, and made suggestions that sharpened this project—and my thinking—in inestimable and indelible ways. This book would not exist without their support. Many thanks also to Alice Kaplan, Pierre Saint-Amand, and Maurice Samuels for their encouragement and for reading early drafts. Walid Bouchakour, Alioune Badara Fall, Cheikh Thiam, and Ali Touilila have been constant interlocutors and friends throughout.

I am lucky to now have generous and brilliant interlocutors in my colleagues at the University of Cambridge. Many thanks to Charles Forsdick, Emma Gilby, and John David Rhodes. They helped see this book over the finish line. I am equally indebted to my wonderfully supportive former students and colleagues at Trinity College (CT), especially to Sara Kippur, Blase Provitola, Kifah Hanna, Karen Humphreys, and Diana Aldrete. Infinite gratitude also to Jeanne-Marie Jackson at Johns Hopkins University, who provided vital and perspicacious feedback on the final manuscript.

It has been a privilege to work with the editorial, production, and design teams at Duke University Press. My thanks and esteem to Elizabeth Ault for seeing what this project was about, as well as to Benjamin Kossak for his kindness and attention to detail. I am profoundly indebted to the two anonymous readers, whose substantial comments and precise suggestions enriched this book immeasurably. Ihsan Taylor and Christi Stanforth have been superhuman in their attention to detail. I am additionally grateful to Sam Jones and Griffin Berlin for assistance with translations as well as numerous linguistic, editorial, and bibliographic details.

This book is a testament to the expertise of archivists, librarians, and staff at over a dozen archives, libraries, and institutions in Africa, Europe, the United States, and the Caribbean. They are too numerous to name here, but they have my deep appreciation. Many thanks to the faculty and staff at the West African Research Center in Dakar, as well as Julie Diouf at the Daniel-Sorano National Theater, for help locating documentation of early stagings of Alioune Badara Bèye's play *Nder en flammes*. Much gratitude also to Amadou Bakhaw Diaw and Fatou Sow Sarr for their knowledge and insights.

I additionally wish to thank several people who had parts, big or small, in shaping this book by serving as *compagnons de route*, advocates, mentors, teachers, translators, guides, hosts, support systems, and dear friends. These include Allegra Ayida, Moctar Ba, Andrea Bongini, Riley Calhoun, Marie-Bénédicte Diethelm, Bryan Fleming, David Francis, Adrien Goetz, David Grosso, Rok Hudobivnik, Caitlin Kossmann, Thibaud Marcesse, Peter Marino, Nyuol Matiok, Farid Matuk, Aissa Mboup, Kevin Newmark, Roxanne Panchasi, Kevin Quinn, Ksenia Sidorenko, Mariame Sy, Maty Tall, Matthew Tanico, Margaret Thomas, Fatima-Ezzahrae Touilila, Kate Wysocki-Barrows, and Liesl Yamaguchi.

Research for this book received generous support from the American Institute for Maghrib Studies; the Camargo Foundation; the Bibliothèque Marmottan; the Yale Whitney and Betty MacMillan Center; the Gilder Lehrman Center for the Study of Slavery, Resistance, and Abolition; the Chateaubriand Fellowship Program; and the Phi Beta Kappa Society, as well as a Book Completion Grant from Trinity College and a Manuscript Colloquium sponsored by the Trinity Institute for Interdisciplinary Studies. Parts of chapters 1, 3, and 5 appeared in different forms in *Research in African Literatures*, *New Literary History*, the *French Review*, and *Public Books*.

My deepest thanks go to my family, especially my parents and grandparents, who throughout the writing of this book have been unwavering in their support. I am humbled by their love, reassurance, and care, which have afforded me the ability to read, write, and explore.

NOTES

PREFACE

1. Yaeger, "Consuming Trauma," 229.
2. Aranke, *Death's Futurity*, 6.
3. Brathwaite, "Jou'vert," 113.
4. Dominique Godineau suggests that by the end of the eighteenth century, political suicide was "a French specialty"; Godineau, *S'abréger les jours*, 291.
5. Terri Snyder makes a related historiographical claim about suicide in the British Atlantic; see Snyder, *Power to Die*.
6. Glissant, *Philosophie*, 19. The phrase appears originally in Glissant's formulation of "Tout-monde"; Glissant, *Une nouvelle région*, 96.
7. Mbembe, *Critique of Black Reason*, 129.
8. Lee, *Ingenious Citizenship*, 191–244.
9. In French, *décalage* refers to a gap, lag, or misalignment in space, time, or both.
10. Conan and Rousso, *Vichy*.
11. Aranke, *Death's Futurity*, 15.
12. C. Sharpe, *In the Wake*, 22.

INTRODUCTION

Epigraph: Dugoujon, *Lettres sur l'esclavage*, 88–89 (emphasis in original); also cited in Schœlcher, *Histoire de l'esclavage*, 461. Unless otherwise noted, translations are my own. In certain cases (for instance, when transcribing archival documents, oral texts, or citing poetry), I provide the original citation and an English translation.

1. My recourse to the French colonial legal archive is inspired by Frédéric Régent's observation that, lacking first-person accounts of slavery by enslaved persons, scholars of French slavery might turn to legal proceedings to recover "fragmentary" access to the voices of the enslaved; Régent, "Figures d'esclaves," 111. See also Régent, Gonfier, and Maillard, *Libres et sans fers*. Régent's approach is reflected in recent work by Sophie

White, who focuses on how the voices of enslaved men and women emerge across the records of four court cases in eighteenth-century New Orleans; White, *Voices of the Enslaved*. Régent and White draw on court cases in which the enslaved testified and had their testimonies recorded. The cases of Azor and other suicides are particularly complex, given that suicides were tried posthumously; their "voices," if they appear at all, appear only as reported speech.

2. "Azor" and its near anagram "Zamor(e)" were "hugely popular," exotic names associated with French slavery. Evocative of the Azore Islands, "Azor" is the name of one of Olympe de Gouges's characters in *Zamore et Mirza* (1788) and *L'esclavage des noirs* (1792). See "Exotic Names Associated with Slavery," in Miller, *French Atlantic Triangle*, 145, 452n15.

3. ANOM, COL C7 A 61 f° 327. The judge Louis Butel de Montgai presided over the tribunal.

4. On the legal and social history of suicide in Ancien Régime metropolitan France, see Godineau, *S'abréger les jours*, especially the first chapter on postmortem trials, "Le cadavre devant ses juges," 17–84. For an overview of the criminalization of suicide in eighteenth-century France, see Merrick, "Patterns and Prosecution."

5. Godineau, *S'abréger les jours*, 36.

6. Godineau, *S'abréger les jours*, 7.

7. Godineau, *S'abréger les jours*, 7–8. The phrase used to describe Azor's suicide, *se brûler la cervelle*—like the expressions *se faire sauter le caisson* and *se faire sauter la cervelle*—probably entered usage in the mid- to late eighteenth century, based on expressions related to death by firearm (e.g., *je vous brûle la cervelle*).

8. Godineau, *S'abréger les jours*, 7–8, 17.

9. Godineau, *S'abréger les jours*, 7–8.

10. As Montesquieu writes in *Lettres persanes* (1721), "The laws in Europe are furious against those who kill themselves. We make them die, so to speak, a second time"; Montesquieu, "Lettre LXXVI," 167.

11. Originally published by Louis XIV, the Code Noir legally designated the enslaved as property. See Farley, "Apogee of the Commodity"; Sala-Molins, *Le Code Noir*.

12. This was also the case in the British Atlantic. See Snyder, "Power to Die or the Power of the State?," chap. 4 in *Power to Die*, 82–100.

13. The natural disasters included, in Guadeloupe, the earthquake of 1843 and a fire in Pointe-à-Pitre in 1871; and in Martinique, a fire in Fort-de-France in 1890 and the eruption of Mount Pelée in 1902. Church, "Last Resort," 513.

14. "Registre des naissances et décès des esclaves, Pointe-à-Pitre, 7 octobre 1804 au 22 septembre 1805" (ADG, Series 1 E 35/95). Most of the deaths recorded are of enslaved men and women in their teens and early twenties, some are children as young as ten and four years old.

15. In his *Essai sur le suicide en Afrique noire*, Jean Marius Raynaud highlights the decalage between official reports and the widespread reality of suicide within slavery, pinpointing an ambiguity in Schœlcher's inventory of suicides in Martinique over a six-month period: "8 slaves [*noirs*] killed themselves, *or more exactly the colonial civil authorities recorded 8 suicides.*" Raynaud's monograph exists in manuscript form (ANOM, 2 ECOL 21). On the "problem" of evaluating sources and statistics related to suicide within slavery,

see Snyder, "Problem of Suicide in North American Slavery," in *Power to Die*, 7–22. See also Lester, "Suicidal Behavior."

16. The most famous case of such an insurance policy at work is the massacre of captive Africans aboard the British slave ship *Zong*. This is the subject of Fred D'Aguiar's novel *Feeding the Ghosts* (1998) and Marlene NourbeSe Philip's *Zong!* (2008). On the *Zong* massacre, see Baucom, "Specters of the Atlantic." See also Baucom, *Specters of the Atlantic*, especially chap. 3, "'Madam Death! Madam Death!': Credit, Insurance, and the Atlantic Cycle of Capital Accumulation," 80–112.

17. Émérigon, *Traité des assurances*, 394 (emphasis in original).

18. Church, "Last Resort," 531.

19. Raynaud, *Essai*, 32.

20. De Mackau, *Compte-rendu*, 32–33.

21. Fanon, *Wretched of the Earth*; Memmi, *Colonizer and the Colonized*, 146; Mbembe, *Critique of Black Reason*, 120.

22. For an overview, see Klonsky et al., "Ideation-to-Action Theories of Suicide."

23. Godineau, *S'abréger les jours*, 149–65.

24. See the chapter titled "Les 'maladies des nègres'" in Dorlin, *La matrice de la race*.

25. The efficacy of the *supplice de la claie* to serve as a suicide deterrent and form of social control was a subject of public debate throughout the nineteenth century. Consider the following excerpt from the *Mercure*: "What purpose could the horrible spectacle of a cadaver being drawn and quartered [*traîné sur la claie*] serve? In order to have a salutary effect, in order to make suicides less frequent, it is not an inanimate body that should be dragged about on an instrument designed for criminals!"; "Du suicide," 269.

26. Foucault, *History of Sexuality*, 140–41, 143–44.

27. Godineau, *S'abréger les jours*, 58–59.

28. Mbembe, "Necropolitics." See also Mbembe, *Politiques de l'inimitié*.

29. Harms, *Diligent*, 262.

30. Millet de la Girardière and Pierre Barse were condemned to be placed in an iron cage and suspended in stirrups above a sharpened blade. In the preface to *Se défendre*, Elsa Dorlin describes this specific torture scene; Dorlin, *Se défendre*, 5. In reality, Millet de la Girardière died by suicide in prison before he could be tortured, while Barse was "beaten and burned" alive. Their deaths are described in archival documents: "Barse, one of the leaders, was beaten and burned [*roué et brûlé*]. Another, Millet de la Girardière, who was supposed to suffer the same fate, killed himself in prison" (ANOM, COL C7 A57 f° 200). Oriol similarly notes, "On the evening of 6 October 1802, 23 white people were killed in Saint-Anne. Lacrosse demanded an investigation: 'it is acknowledged that two white men: Barsse [*sic*] and Millet de la Girardière, the latter 69 years old and crippled with debt, led a group of 80 slaves [*nègres*] [...] with the goal of pillaging and stealing.' Barsse was beaten and burned alive on the Place de la Victoire. De la Girardière was condemned to 'die in an iron cage, naked, straddling a sharpened blade, in the same square.' To escape this torture, he hanged himself in prison." See Oriol, *Les hommes célèbres*, 270. On Millet de la Girardière's suicide, see Lacour, *Histoire de la Guadeloupe*, 3:416–18.

31. Novels such as Beninese writer Olympe Bhêly-Quénum's *Un piège sans fin* (1960) and Congolese writer Sony Labou Tansi's *La vie et demie* (1979) are a case in point. In

the former an indentured laborer is brutally beaten and publicly humiliated by a French colonial overseer in Bénin before killing himself; the latter opens with a gruesome torture scene at the hands of a fictitious African dictatorship in which the resistance fighter Martial refuses to die despite being disemboweled and essentially cut in half.

32. Bancel et al., *Zoos humains*.

33. See Niort, *Du Code Noir*.

34. The secondary literature on slave suicide is relatively limited and overwhelmingly Anglo-American in focus. Mention of suicide typically is anecdotal and subsumed under broader studies of Atlantic slavery (e.g., Mannix and Cowley, *Black Cargoes*, 19, 120). For analyses that systematically address suicide within slavery, see Snyder, *Power to Die*; Snyder, "Suicide, Slavery, and Memory"; Bell, "Slave Suicide"; Daniel Walker, "Suicidal Tendencies"; Hall, *Social Control*, 20–23; Piersen, "White Cannibals, Black Martyrs"; Stevenson, "Jumping Overboard." See also the section "Les actes de l'auto-destruction," in Yale, "La violence dans l'esclavage," 54–59. In a recent "state of the art" on resistance studies in France, the only mention of suicide appears in a citation from Schœlcher, where it is characterized as an infrequent and undesirable alternative to marronage; Le Glaunec, "Résister à l'esclavage," 22. During the nineteenth century, Schœlcher himself wrote at length about slave suicide, dedicating a chapter to the subject in *Histoire de l'esclavage* (1847); Schœlcher, *Histoire de l'esclavage*, 455–68. For a rare French study discussing suicide as a form of resistance, see Dorlin, "Les espaces-temps." In his article on marronage, Yvan Debbasch connects marronage and suicide as two forms of resistance and escape; Debbasch, "Le marronage," 10n4.

35. In his *Nouveau voyage aux isles de l'Amérique* (1724), the Père Labat describes how the enslaved would consume dirt, ash, lime, and other non-food substances; Labat, *Nouveau voyage*, 151.

36. See Leti, "L'empoisonnement."

37. Consider Raynaud's comments on the frequency of suicide during the Middle Passage: "Their passions are violently repressed and their future closed off; thus discouraged, they kill themselves [*se suicident*]. From the beginning of the great period of the slave trade, authors observe this tendency to escape the cruelty of fate through death. The most common means of suicide is drowning. During their walks on deck, the enslaved [*les noirs*] throw themselves into the sea even if they are in the middle of the ocean with no chance of escaping by swimming"; Raynaud, *Essai*, 18. In *Les aventures d'un négrier* (1854), Théodore Canot similarly notes: "From the beginning [of the crossing], a palpable dissatisfaction was evident among the slaves. [. . .] A few days after our departure, one slave, in an excess of rage, leapt overboard and, during the night, another strangled himself to death. These two suicides in the span of twenty-four hours awakened serious concern in for the officers and lead me to make all necessary preparations in view of a possible revolt"; Canot, *Les aventures d'un négrier*, 134.

38. Savary, *Le parfait négociant*, 140.

39. Ho, *Esclavagisme et engagisme*.

40. We see this claim repeated in many eighteenth- and early nineteenth-century treatises on suicide. The medical interest in the suicide of French colonial subjects continued into the twentieth centuries. For instance, E. Jourdran and M. Fontoynont, medical

doctors in Tananarive, published their short study "Le suicide chez les malgaches" (ANOM, BIB SOM B 996) with the goal of demonstrating "the reason for the majority of suicides, otherwise relatively infrequent among the Malagasy people, and to contribute in this small way to a study of the psychoses according to race and religion"; Jourdran and Fontoynont, "Le suicide chez les malgaches," 2. Until the late twentieth century, France's overseas departments such as Guadeloupe and Martinique were entirely ignored in global studies of suicide; André Morel points this out in his doctoral medical thesis, "Suicides et tentatives de suicide à la Martinique" (1979), which examines 37 suicides and 152 parasuicides in Martinique during the year 1976 (ANOM, BIB AOM TH 508). See also Petit, "Un suicide chez les noirs"; Collomb and Collignon, "Les conduits suicidaires."

41. Liengme, "Le suicide parmi les noirs."

42. Snyder, *Power to Die*, 37–40; see also Snyder, "Suicide, Slavery, and Memory," 41.

43. The committee published a report in 1847, titled "Testimonios del expediente formado par averiguar las causas que influyen en el frecuente suicidio de los esclavos"; cited in Hall, *Social Control*, 21.

44. Raynaud, *Essai*, 31. Corre notes the same phenomenon in his *Crime en pays créoles* (1889), providing data on the alarming suicide rates of Hindu immigrant workers in Maurice after abolition—at least 476 over a ten-year period; Corre, *Le crime en pays créoles*.

45. Schœlcher writes: "What terrible arguments assembled for the cause of abolition! Such numerous suicides, a direct, immediate consequence of slavery—are they not its most striking condemnation?"; Schœlcher, *Histoire de l'esclavage*, 466.

46. These were linked to racist theories of environmental determinism. See, for instance, Levacher, *Guide médical*, 241–45. The term *nosopolitique*, combining Foucault's biopolitics with the French *nosologie*, the branch of (colonial) medicine concerned with the classification of maladies, comes from Elsa Dorlin, who points out that such medical texts aimed at producing an "interested knowledge" concerning "the psychic or physical pathologies, conditions, and afflictions resulting from the social and, stricto sensu, political tensions such as poisoning, incapacitating mutilations, suicides, insanity. [. . .] *And this, primarily to preserve the interests of the slavery and the slave trade at its height*"; Dorlin, "Naissance de la race" (my emphasis).

47. Frossard, *La cause des esclaves*, 263.

48. Raynaud, *Essai*, 19.

49. An individual suicide risked creating an "epidemic" of suicidal behavior. Raynaud notes: "Sometimes, the punishment for the slave who attempts suicide is terrible, for the slave traders fear his companions will imitate him, they fear above all else collective suicides"; Raynaud, *Essai*, 19.

50. Frossard, *La cause des esclaves*, 263.

51. Paul Barret, a medical doctor in the French navy, describes this device: "They take the precaution to gag the victims destined for sacrifices, by means of a wooden cross, of which one of the bars goes into the mouth and pushes hard down onto the tongue to prevent it from folding back on itself"; Barret, *L'Afrique occidentale*, 147.

52. Snyder, *Power to Die*, 37–40.

53. On the "irony" of suicide prevention within slavery, see Snyder, *Power to Die*, 37–40. In "Necropolitics," Mbembe writes: "The slave is therefore kept alive but in a

state of injury, in a phantomlike world of horrors and intense cruelty and profanity"; Mbembe, "Necropolitics," 21.

54. Wiredu, "Death and the Afterlife," 141.

55. Europeans leveraged the claim that certain Africans were inclined to suicide due to spiritual beliefs, cultural values, or ethnic "predispositions" to divorce suicide from the violence of enslavement. In his response to the Abbé Grégoire's *De la littérature des nègres* (1808), for instance, the planter François Richard de Tussac writes that, since enslaved Africans "believe in resurrection, they think that in killing themselves it is a means to return to their country. It is therefore not [. . .] mistreatment by their masters that leads them to this"; De Tussac, *Cri des colons*, 133. On this tendency in Anglo-American texts, see Snyder, *Power to Die*, 12–13. Harms similarly notes that the Fon of Dahomey were "thought likely to become depressed in captivity and commit suicide"; Harms, *Diligent*, 161.

56. See Commander, *Afro-Atlantic Flight*.

57. On Ebos landing, see Snyder, *Power to Die*, 161–66. On the flying African, see Young, "All God's Children Had Wings"; Powell, "Summoning the Ancestors," 259–62; Gomez, *Exchanging Our Country Marks*, 117–18. In *Sartorius*, Glissant connects the collective suicide of the Batoutos to Nigerian captives; Glissant, *Sartorius*, 50.

58. Nahli Allison, "Revisiting the Legend." The imagery of the flying African, and thus the specter of slave suicide, has a long afterlife in African American culture, evoked in mainstream visual art and performances such as Beyoncé's *Love Drought* (2016).

59. Newton writes, "By hoping and desiring, the revolutionary suicide chooses life; he is, in the words of Nietzsche, 'an arrow of longing for another shore.' Both suicides despise tyranny, but the revolutionary suicide is both a great despiser and a great adorer who longs for another shore"; Newton, *Revolutionary Suicide*, 371.

60. Senghor, *Négritude et humanisme*, 77–78.

61. Parasucide refers to a range of self-harm behaviors, including passive suicide, that may or may not be intended to result in death.

62. Harms describes an example of this aboard the *Excellent*, when some enslaved men and women profited from the confusion generated by a revolt to leap overboard: "Revolt and suicide—two ways to escape captivity—seemed to go hand in hand"; Harms, *Diligent*, 270.

63. Among the suicides in Martinique cited by Raynaud—many of which are cited in Schœlcher—we find the following: a leather strap, a cord made from strips of cloth torn from the suicide's shirt, a shard of glass, a sash from the suicide's skirts. See Raynaud, *Essai*, 16–17; Schœlcher, *Histoire de l'esclavage*, 455–68.

64. Schœlcher lists numerous cases of enslaved men and women, some as young as 15, who died by suicide in Martinique between 4 February and 12 July 1845, almost immediately after enduring severe corporal punishments or being threatened by their enslavers; Schœlcher, *Histoire de l'esclavage*, 455–68.

65. Drawing on data from the Dugoujon and Schœlcher, Rayndaud notes several instances of captured enslaved men who died by suicide in the jail cells in which they were detained before they could be tried or returned to the plantation; Raynaud, *Essai*, 26–27. A series of letters from July 1752 between Antoine Philippe Le Moyne and Gilbert

Guillouet d'Orvilliers (ANOM, COL C14 22 fº 60 and fº 165) recount similar scenarios in the context of slavery in French Guyana.

66. Régent et al., *Libres et sans fers*, 251–52, 359–60.

67. This is the image with which Snyder opens her historical study of suicide under slavery in British North America. Snyder, *Power to Die*, 1–3; see also Torrey, *Portraiture*, 42.

68. See Brown, *Art of Suicide*.

69. I am inflecting Hartman's concept of a "scene of subjection"; see Hartman, *Scenes of Subjection*. In a study of Renaissance "self-finishing," Drew Daniel evokes the notion of "self-finishing" in relation to Hartman's "scene" and "self-fashioning"; Daniel, *Joy of the Worm*, 1.

70. Schœlcher writes, "In accomplishing his suicide [*son acte de désespoir*], could this slave have wanted, beneath the very eyes of the leader of the colony, prove that the daily torture of slavery is less tolerable than death? Could he have wanted to protest, in this cruel manner, against the reports of the governors and public prosecutors, who paint a pretty picture of servitude?"; Schœlcher, *Histoire de l'esclavage*, 456.

71. Métral, *Histoire de l'expédition des Français*, 18.

72. Schœlcher lists several cases of apparent suicides and unexplained deaths in which the bodies of enslaved men and women were found in various states of decay but with no apparent signs of violence or clear evidence of the precise means of death. Schœlcher, *Histoire de l'esclavage*, 462–63. Snyder describes the "suicide-like behaviors" of enslaved men and women who were "found dead" after exposing themselves to the elements or starvation and others who "appear to have courted or sought death quite deliberately"; Snyder, *Power to Die*, 19.

73. Snyder, *Power to Die*, 18–19.

74. Schœlcher, *Histoire de l'esclavage*, 466 (emphasis in original).

75. See Woywodt and Kiss, "Geophagia."

76. See chap. 3, "Incorrigible Dirt Eaters," and chap. 4, "Of Paper Trails and Dirt Eaters," in Hogarth, *Medicalizing Blackness*.

77. Dodman, *What Nostalgia Was*, 91.

78. Labat, *Nouveau voyage*, 151.

79. Gilroy, *Postcolonial Melancholia*; Wilderson, *Afropessimism*.

80. Snyder, "Suicide, Slavery, and Memory," 50–51.

81. Levacher, *Guide médical*, 184.

82. Levacher, *Guide médical*, 96.

83. Lagercrantz, *Geophagical Customs*, 63.

84. Debret, *Voyage pittoresque*, 47.

85. Debret, *Voyage pittoresque*, 47.

86. Snyder, *Power to Die*, 17. On the concept of "slave suicide ecology," see Snyder, "Suicide, Slavery, and Memory," 42, 53–59.

87. Patterson, *Slavery and Social Death*.

88. Writing about slavery in British North America, Richard Bell asks: "Was a slave's suicide an act of principled, yet costly, resistance to tyranny that challenged the hypocrisy of the revolutionary settlement? Or was it a measure of abject victimhood that begged for humanitarian intervention?"; Bell, "Slave Suicide," 526.

89. See Miller, *French Atlantic Triangle*, 33–39.

90. Miller writes, "*There are no real slave narratives in French*—not as we know them in the Anglophone Atlantic, not that have yet been discovered. That absence, for now at least, haunts any inquiry into the history of slavery"; Miller, *French Atlantic Triangle*, 34. There also exist important Arabic-language sources, namely the texts of Omar ibn Said (1770–1864), a Fula Islamic scholar from Futa Toro in present-day Senegal, who wrote several texts in Arabic, including an autobiography, while enslaved in the United States.

91. Church, "Last Resort."

92. Sala-Molins, *Le Code Noir*, 209, cited in Miller, *French Atlantic Triangle*, 35. See also Little, "Pirouettes sur l'abîme."

93. Miller, *French Atlantic Triangle*, 34 (emphasis in original). On the status of the slave narrative as a privileged genre in Black Atlantic history and African diaspora studies, see Jensen, *Beyond the Slave Narrative*.

94. Church, "Last Resort," 514.

95. Snyder, *Power to Die*, 16.

96. Trouillot, *Silencing the Past*, 69.

97. Voltaire's *Candide* is a well-known example. Although better known for the episode involving the mutilation of the "slave of Surinam" according to punishments prescribed by the Code Noir, the narrative of North African slavery traced by La Vieille ends with a reflection on suicide.

98. Mailhol, *Le philosophe nègre*, 13–14, 39 (my emphasis).

99. See O'Connell, "Victor Séjour."

100. Hacking, "Making Up People," 234.

101. Hacking, "Making Up People," 235. Durkheim's sociological taxonomy of suicide remains a touchstone for broad-scale analyses of suicide. On a recent reevaluation of Durkheim, see Borlandi and Chakaoui, *Le suicide*.

102. Durkheim, *Le suicide*, 311.

103. Durkheim, *Le suicide*, 311.

104. Durkheim, *Le suicide*, 259.

105. Waters, *Suicide Voices*.

106. Jean Pierre Le Glaunec notes: "If you look closely, the topic of 'resistance' does not occupy the 'proper place' it deserves in French historiography. [...] While the question has not ceased to be studied in Anglo-Saxon historiography since the 1960s [...], one is struck by the rarity of works in France"; Le Glaunec, "Résister à l'esclavage," 16.

107. Daniel, *Joy of the Worm*, 7.

108. Kasahara-Kiritani et al., "Reading and Watching Films."

109. Spivak, "Rethinking Comparativism," 615.

110. Palmer, "Otherwise than Blackness," 260.

111. See Best, *None like Us*, especially his first chapter, "My Beautiful Elimination," 29–62. As Cedric Robinson, writing about the same tradition, puts it, by turning violence "inward" and defining "the terms of their destruction," Black rebels "lived on their terms, they died on their terms, they obtained freedom on their terms," rejecting "actual being" for "historical being"; Robinson, *Black Marxism*, 168–71.

112. Best, *None like Us*, 94.

113. Best, *None like Us*, 94, 26.
114. Best, *None like Us*, 95.
115. Fasolt, *Limits of History*.
116. Best, *None like Us*, 95 (emphasis in original).
117. On the "unshareability" of suicide, see Goh, "Shared Unshareability."
118. Jackson, *African Novel of Ideas*, 145–80.
119. Jackson, *African Novel of Ideas*, 147.
120. Jackson, *African Novel of Ideas*, 149.
121. Newell, "From Corpse to Corpus," 392.
122. Silverstein, "Texts, Entextualized and Artifactualized," 56.
123. Newell, "From Corpse to Corpus," 392.
124. Azim, *Colonial Rise of the Novel*, 7.
125. Jackson, *African Novel of Ideas*, 17; Bakhtin, *Dialogic Imagination*, 261.
126. Forter, "Atlantic and Other Worlds," 1329.
127. D. Scott, *Conscripts of Modernity*.
128. On "necroresistance," see Bargu, *Starve and Immolate*. The notion of the (im)possibilities of "subaltern speech" emerges in dialogue with Spivak, "Can the Subaltern Speak?"
129. Foucault, *History of Sexuality*, 95.
130. Foucault, "Interview," 12.
131. This is the kind of voyeuristic literary access that a text like the late Édouard Levé's *Suicide* (2008) promises—a novel doubling as its author's public suicide note.
132. J. C. Scott, *Weapons of the Weak*. See also J. C. Scott, *Domination*.
133. Best, *None like Us*, 123.
134. Best, *None like Us*, 123.
135. Edwards, "Taste of the Archive," 970.
136. McLaughlin, "Resistance."
137. Freud, "Inhibitions, Symptoms and Anxiety," 159.
138. Rose, *Last Resistance*, 21.
139. Rose, *Last Resistance*, 24.
140. Rose, *Last Resistance*, 31; Freud, "Inhibitions, Symptoms and Anxiety," 157–60.
141. Freud, "Inhibitions, Symptoms and Anxiety," 160.
142. Helton et al., "Question of Recovery," 1. See also Coats and Dippold, "Beyond Recovery."
143. Helton et al., "Question of Recovery," 1.
144. Hartman, "Venus," 2.
145. Fuentes, *Dispossessed Lives*, 5.
146. J. L. Morgan, *Reckoning with Slavery*, 9.
147. C. Sharpe, *Ordinary Notes*, 251 (my emphasis).
148. Best, *None like Us*, 15.
149. See, for instance, Spivak, "Scattered Speculations," "Rethinking Comparativism," and "Terror."
150. Gupta et al., *Usurping Suicide*, 9–10.
151. Gupta et al., *Usurping Suicide*, 10.
152. Gupta et al., *Usurping Suicide*, 54–109.

153. On "anarchives," see Brozgal, *Absent the Archive*. On "other-archives," see El Guabli, *Moroccan Other-Archives*.

154. Higonnet, "Suicide," 103.

155. L. T. Murphy, *Metaphor and the Slave Trade*.

156. Dominic Thomas suggests that studies of belonging and memory in the wake of French empire have no other choice but to "journey across the arbitrary lines of demarcation that distinguish the colony from the postcolony and the colonial from the postcolonial period"; D. Thomas, *Black France*, 2.

157. Werner and Zimmermann, "Beyond Comparison"; Rothberg, *Multidirectional Memory*; Rothberg, "Introduction: Between Memory and Memory"; Feindt et al., "Entangled Memory"; Lowe, "History Hesitant"; Azoulay, *Potential History*.

158. Lowe, "History Hesitant," 98.

159. Azoulay, *Potential History*, 20, 43.

1. CHORAL HISTORIES

A section of this chapter is significantly revised from a previous publication, "A Fugue for the Middle Passage? Suicidal Resistance Takes Flight in Fabienne Kanor's *Humus* (2006)," *French Review* 95, no. 2 (December 2021): 127–44, https://muse.jhu.edu/article/839848.

My subhead "Forgetting Delgrès" nods to Laurent Dubois's essay "Haunting Delgrès," which inspires my reflections on historical memory related to Delgrès and French slavery here. See also Dubois, *Colony of Citizens*, especially chap. 12, "The Road to Matouba," 317–23, and chap. 15, "Vivre libre ou mourir!," 374–401, on Delgrès.

Epigraphs: Day and Bicknell, *The Dying Negro*, 1; Glissant, *Poetics of Relation*, 5–6.

1. Nantes was the most active French city involved in the transatlantic slave trade, with 1,754 expeditions recorded between 1688 and 1830; Hourcade, "Commemorating a Guilty Past," 124. See also Pétré-Grenouilleau, *Nantes et la traite négrière*; G. Martin, *L'ère des négriers*.

2. The ship's expeditions are documented in Mettas and Martin. The transcription of Captain Mosnier's surname varies (Mosnier, Monnier), as does that of the ship's owner (Larralde, Larralda). See Mettas, *Répertoire*, 563, 574–75; G. Martin, *L'ère des négriers*, 92–93, 114; G. Martin, *Négriers et bois d'ébène*, 81.

3. Louis Mosnier is mentioned in a maritime register from 1764 (ADLA C 1401 f°23 n°24), where he is listed as being fifty-two years old, suggesting he was in his early sixties at the time of the 1773/74 voyage.

4. On the role of sharks in the transatlantic slave trade, see Rediker, "History from Below the Water Line."

5. Kanor, *Humus* (2006), translated into English under the same title (2020); Maximin, *L'isolé soleil*. Before the publication of *Humus*, Kanor adapted the text for the theatrical performances *Homo humus est* and *La grande chambre*, staged with two actors performing passages from the characters "L'amazone" and "La muette" set to music; see Herbeck, "Entretien," 968.

6. Solitude was a female resistance fighter who continued to battle French troops after the collective suicide of Delgrès and his followers at Matouba, before being imprisoned

by the French and hanged, one day after giving birth. She was called the "Mulâtresse" because of her pale skin and light eyes, having been born to an enslaved mother who was raped by a white sailor during the Middle Passage. Her story was popularized by André Schwarz-Bart's novel *La mulâtresse Solitude* (1972), and she is commemorated by statues along the Héros aux Abymes Boulevard in Guadeloupe and in Hauts-de-Seine in France. Currently, Solitude is being considered for inclusion in the Panthéon, where she would join Louis Delgrès and Toussaint Louverture. A garden in Paris was built in her honor, the "Jardin Solitude." See Gautier, *Les sœurs de Solitude*; Moitt, *Women and Slavery*.

7. See L. Thomas, "Daniel Maximin's *Lone Sun*." See also Sago, "Beyond the Headless Empress."

8. Best, *None like Us*, 115.

9. ADLA B 4595 f° 173–74.

10. Herbeck, "Entretien," 966.

11. Kanor, *La poétique de la cale*, 100.

12. These included the Port du voyage sans retour, the *zomaï*, and the tree of Agadja, a mystical site that effaced the memory of the enslaved after circling it seven times, for women, or nine times, for men. In Kanor's novel, the fire in the *zomaï* mentioned in Mosnier's report is evoked on p. 111, while the image of enslaved Africans circling a tree appears on p. 100 and again in the final section, "L'héritière," p. 247. On these symbolic sites, see Landry, "Touring the Slave Route."

13. Fuentes, *Dispossessed Lives*, 1.

14. Glissant, *Le quatrième siècle*; Chamoiseau, *L'esclave vieil homme*; Condé, *Moi, Tituba*.

15. Miano, *La saison de l'ombre*; D. Diop, *La porte*.

16. Miller, *French Atlantic Triangle*, 347.

17. Kanor, *Humus*, 13. Hereafter, citations for the novel are given parenthetically in the text. All quotations come from the 2006 edition.

18. "La mère" later echoes this analogy between slavery and hell; Kanor, *Humus*, 225.

19. Herbeck, "Entretien," 971 (my emphasis).

20. Some captives provide their own names: the Amazon is Sosi; the Slave calls herself as "La petite fille de Noupé"; the Little Girl refers to La blanche as "La grande"; the Twin who narrates her and her sister's section is Antar; the Queen is Huita; "La volante" identifies herself as Cecile.

21. See voyages 36, 38, and 1234 in Mettas, *Répertoire*.

22. As Kanor notes, "She is the only one to not physically experience slavery, to not know the whip, the sickness, the terror"; Herbeck, "Entretien," 969.

23. See Migerel, *La migration des zombis*.

24. "L'esclave," for instance, narrates her leap in the present tense. "La petite" evokes the leap hypothetically at first, before her narrative is interrupted by a section break after which her section concludes with a postmortem, past-tense narration; Kanor, *Humus*, 164. "L'employée," a conscripted worker tasked with surveilling the female captives, initially observes the women's movements as a bystander, in the third person, but then, in the seconds before their leap, joins them; Kanor, *Humus*, 150.

25. Diome, *Le ventre*.

26. Diome, *Le ventre*, 226.
27. Soumahoro, *Le Triangle et l'Hexagone*, 11.
28. Glissant, *Poétique de la relation*, 19.
29. Diome, *Le ventre*, 254–55.
30. Herbeck, "Entretien," 973.
31. D. Thomas, *Black France*, 183.
32. D. Thomas, *Black France*, 199.
33. On the term *seametery*, see Abderrezak, "Mediterranean *Seametery* and *Cementery*"; Abderrezak, "Mediterranean Spring, Sieve and Seametery."
34. See C. Sharpe, *In the Wake*; Hartman, *Lose Your Mother*.
35. For examples, see Hayet, *Chansons de bord*.
36. Jehan de Nantes is perhaps based on Jean-François de Nantes, who figures in many French sea shanties. "Jan" is also the name of the sailor with whom "La blanche" forms a sexual relationship and conceives a child; later, after being abandoned by her lover, she resolves to jump but is fished out of the sea. Then she loses her mind, and eventually she throws herself into a sugar mill.
37. Kanor, *Humus* [248] (n.p.; emphasis in original).
38. See, for instance, Costello, *Black Salt*; Putney, *Black Sailors*.
39. See Harms, *Diligent*, 296–97. The use of music as a suicide deterrent is mentioned in Des Bruslons, *Dictionnaire universel*, 2:860; see also Savary, *Le parfait négociant*, 140.
40. Herbeck, "Entretien," 973.
41. In *Humus*, several of the women form homosocial, or explicitly homosexual, bonds. "L'esclave," describes her relationship with her companion (*camarade*) her beloved (*aimée*), with whom she lies at night—a relationship, she notes, "is not sanctioned by the Law"—and who dies while awaiting embarkment on *Le Soleil* (66–67). "L'employée" is enthralled by the androgynous Amazon Sosi, who appears "man and woman at once" (145)—"this girl had a certain fascination over me" (148)—and who inspires her to leap with the other women. On homosociality, homosexuality, shipboard bonding and *matelotage* in the French Atlantic, see the following chapters in Miller, *French Atlantic Triangle*: "Homosociality, Reckoning, and Recognition in Eugène Sue's *Atar-Gull*," 274–99; and "Edouard Corbière, 'Mating,' and Maritime Adventure," 300–321.
42. Herbeck, "Entretien," 973.
43. Glissant, *Poétique de la relation*, 19.
44. Kanor, *La poétique de la cale*, 113.
45. On the reestablishment of slavery in France's colonies, see Bénot and Dorigny, *Rétablissement de l'esclavage*.
46. The decalage in historical memory and commemorative actions surrounding Louverture and Delgrès can be explained, in part, by the ways traditional accounts of French imperial history have tended to narrate the Haitian/Saint-Domingue Revolution as a "success story"—leading to the emergence of a sovereign nation, the Republic of Haiti, out of "the ashes" of the former French colony of Saint-Domingue—while portraying the resistance movement in Guadeloupe as something more ambiguous: a fatal last stand doomed to failure, given that slavery was reimposed and Guadeloupe remains a French territory to this day. See Dubois, "Road to Matouba," in *Colony of Citizens*, 320.

47. Nesbitt, "Aperçu de l'historiographie," 11.

48. Larousse, *Grand dictionnaire*, 6:353.

49. Dessalines himself invoked "the brave and immortal Delgrès" as an example of resistance to slavery in his "Proclamation aux Haïtiens" (28 April 1804). News of Delgrès's defeat "propelled" resistance in Saint-Domingue, which had weakened after Toussaint Louverture's capture; Dubois, *Colony of Citizens*, 320.

50. The passage goes on to mention "a heroic suicide" and "unprovoked death," assimilating Delgrès to a Western form of "knightly" sacrifice and courage [*courage chevaleresque*]. It reiterates the famous image of Delgrès, "a new Tyrtaeus," sitting in a canon opening playing his violin for his soldiers as Richepanse and his troops approached."

51. Dubois, "Haunting Delgrès," 167–68; Dubois, *Colony of Citizens*, 322.

52. Glissant, *Le discours antillais*, 131.

53. Glissant, *Le discours antillais*, 497.

54. Aimard, *Le chasseur de rats*.

55. Nesbitt confirms this timeline, writing that "after the Second World War, from the 1950s onward, we see Delgrès's name appear in a veritable explosion of interest, first in newspapers, and later, from the 1960s on, more and more frequently in history books"; Nesbitt, "Aperçu de l'historiographie," 22–23. The earliest physical monument to Delgrès is a small stone stele erected at Matouba in 1948.

56. See Césaire, "Mémorial de Louis Delgrès"; Daniel Radford, *Zone dangereuse*; Tirolien, "La mort de Delgrès: Poème dramatique en un acte," in *Balles d'or*, 31–36; Rupaire, "Matouba," in *Cette igname brisée*; Condé, *An tan révolisyon*; Saint-Ruf, *L'épopée Delgrès*. Saint-Ruf had revisited the Delgrès epic even earlier, in 1955, in a commemorative speech given on the anniversary of Delgrès's death on 28 May in Paris. The text of the speech later was published; Saint-Ruf, *La leçon de Delgrès*. Other historical accounts include Danquin, *Contribution à une étude sur l'insurrection*; Danquin, "Delgrès, figure du tragique"; Danquin, "La postérité de 1802"; Adélaïde-Merlande, *Delgrès, ou, La Guadeloupe en 1802*; Bangou, *La Révolution et l'esclavage*. See also Etna, "1802: La guerre de la Guadeloupe."

57. The Delgrès epic has been interpreted in film by Christian Lara, in *1802: L'épopée guadeloupéenne* and in a historical action novel by C. K. Londero, *Bonaparte et Delgrès*. For an analysis of the film alongside Maximin's novel, see Murdoch, "Locating History."

58. On Maximin's role in the commemorations, see Dubois, "Haunting Delgrès," 172–76.

59. Dubois, "Haunting Delgrès," 173.

60. Josephine Baker as well as the French resistance fighters Geneviève de Gaulle-Antonioz and Germaine Tillion, women who fought against Nazism, have been included.

61. On Maximin's approach to history, see Edlmair, *Rewriting History*; Erickson, "Maximin's *L'isolé soleil*"; Murdoch, "Locating History"; Murdoch, "*L'isolé soleil/Soufrières*," in *Creole Identity in the French Caribbean Novel*, 104–41. On Maximin's Caribbean trilogy, see Chaulet-Achour, *La trilogie caribéenne*.

62. Many characters are engaged in creative projects of transcribing, translating, or composing Creole texts of their own. Siméa is a translator-poet at work rendering the texts of Caribbean, French, and Black American writers in French and English (129–13)

and translating Creole tales ("Trois fois bel conte . . . ," 159–62); Louis-Gabriel improvises a version of the tale "Pélamanlou et Pélamanli" (194–97); Louis-Gabriel's friend Toussaint declaims a Creole translation of a poem by Damas shortly before he is shot during a protest against Vichy occupation (202).

63. Bongie, "(Un)Exploded Volcano," 629. See also "The (Un)Exploded Volcano," in Bongie, *Islands and Exiles*, 348–401; and Murdoch, "*L'isolé soleil/Soufrières*."

64. For Bongie, "intertextuality becomes, in Maximin, the privileged mode for conveying this insight into the dynamics of loss and fictive recovery that complements the process of creolization"; Bongie, "(Un)Exploded Volcano," 629.

65. L. Thomas, "Daniel Maximin's *Lone Sun*," 70.

66. In Maximin's words: "The subject of *L'isolé soleil*? Well, it's the story of someone who is questioning the historical novel. But it is not just that. It is the story of a young girl (in this regard, she is most certainly me) who is seeking a writing more than a style, a means of cobbling together language, of playing with it. [. . .] The historical novel is thus doubly present, as writing and as subject matter"; Maximin, cited in Chaulet-Achour, *La trilogie caribéenne*, 139–41.

67. Maximin, *L'isolé soleil*, 17. Hereafter, citations for the novel are given parenthetically in the text.

68. Kanor, *Humus*, 13.

69. See Chaulet-Achour's chapter "Jeux d'écriture," in *La trilogie caribéenne*, 70–101. See also Edlmair, *Rewriting History*.

70. The Soledad Brothers George Jackson, Fleeta Drumgo, and John Clutchette were three African American prisoners at the Soledad Prison in California charged with the murder of a white prison guard in retaliation for the shooting of three Black prisoners during a fight.

71. The phrase comes from Donadey, "Beyond Departmentalization," 50.

72. Rosello, *Littérature et identité créole*, 16, 44.

73. Socé, *Mirages de Paris*.

74. *Bois-d'ébène* is the title of Haitian poet Jacques Roumain's celebrated collection of poems (1945) mentioned at the end of Maximin's novel; Maximin, *L'isolé soleil*, 282. See also Roumain, *Bois-d'ébène*.

75. Raphaël Confiant's novel *Le nègre et l'amiral* (1988) also concerns this history.

76. On this silence, see Toureille, "La dissidence dans les Antilles."

77. In Guadeloupe, the day is commemorated annually in April.

78. Marie-Gabriel's ancestor Jonathan cautions Delgrès in the moments before the explosion at Matouba using these words: "We aspire to sow our seed [*semence*] in the vagina of the mount, put out the fires of the city and make nice to the hostages who are torturing us. You hope then that your *suicide* will suffice to redeem us of our errors? Your heroic death will, of course, force the memory of the centuries [*le souvenir des siècles*] but it will cause the fierce struggle of the living to fall into obscurity"; Maximin *L'isolé soleil*, 55–56 (my emphasis).

79. A famous example of this is the "branded hand" of Jonathan Walker, captured in the daguerreotype by Southworth & Hawes (1845); see O'Neill, "Rebranding of Jonathan Walker."

80. The painting by Jean-François Millet, *L'Angélus* (1857–59), which depicts two farmers stopping to pray, is mentioned in the novel as an image typically found in Antillean homes; Maximin, *L'isolé soleil*, 191.

81. Kanor, *Humus*, 225.

82. "Anti-Racism Protesters in Martinique Tear Down Statue of Napoleon's Wife."

83. Klaa, "Le Pen Says 'Colonisation Gave a Lot' to Algeria."

84. See Forsdick, "Interpreting 2004"; Forsdick, "Panthéon's Empty Plinth."

85. A complete list of citations included in the memorial is available at Mémorial de l'abolition de l'esclavage, Nantes, http://memorial.nantes.fr/wp-content/uploads/2017/03/citations_francais.pdf.

86. Best, *None like Us*, 96.

2. ORAL ARCHIVES

Epigraph: Amadou Hampâté Bâ, cited in Konaté, "Le syndrome Amadou Hampâté," 58; also discussed along with earlier iterations in Repinecz, *Subversive Traditions*, 239n3.

1. All translations are my own. For Wolof transcriptions, I use conventions roughly consistent with those in Pamela Munro and Dieynaba Gaye's dictionary *Ay Baati Wolof*. For citations from Diop's *Doomi Golo: Nettali*, I preserve the original orthography; where Wolof is transcribed in older French texts, I typically include modern transcriptions for these terms in parentheses. Unless otherwise noted, all quotations from Diop's novel are from the Wolof-language edition, *Doomi Golo: Nettali*. For consistency, I have used the French spelling (Diop) throughout.

2. *Lamaan* is a Sereer term used in Wolof meaning "master of the land." Originally, it designated landed nobility in the Senegambia region, successors of the *brak* or kings; later, it came to refer to descendants of the original *lamaan yi*, individuals like Diaw who function as guardians of traditional religion and local history.

3. Amadou Bakhaw Diaw, "Bicentenaire de la tragédie de Talatay Ndér Senegal 7 Mars 1820–7 Mars 2020 Partie 08," YouTube video, 6:52, posted 9 March 2020, https://youtu.be/CmTKlOmgdSs. In addition to details from Diaw's original oral account given on the bicentennial, my account draws on narrative interviews in Dakar; private correspondence with Diaw and Sarr in the spring of 2020; and Seye, *Walo Brack*, 152–56.

4. In *Subversive Traditions*, Jonathon Repinecz repeatedly refers to the "Tuesday of Nder" as "legend," assimilating it to other epic forms; Repinecz, *Subversive Traditions*, 79, 200.

5. By some accounts 5 March 1820, by others a Tuesday in November 1819; I retain the date 7 March 1820, given by both Diaw and Seye in their accounts.

6. In Wolof, *lingeer* is a female ruler, usually translated as "princess" or "queen"; *awo* means "first wife." I use both the Wolof transcription *lingeer* and the French spelling *linguère* interchangeably.

7. *Briok* is the Wolof term for the second in succession after the *brak*. The *kaddji* immediately follows the *brak* in the line of succession.

8. The *lingeer* evacuated her two daughters—the future *lingeers* and resistance leaders, Ndatte Yalla and Njëmbët Mbooj—to nearby Ronkh, thus preserving the royal bloodline of the Téejeg.

9. Amadou Bakhaw Diaw, in private correspondence. Literally: "The day is done, I will not lance in shame."

10. The nineteenth century in Senegal saw at least one high-profile example of French suicide: Governor Olivier died on 20 March 1846 after slitting his own throat. His death was reported as "an attack of apoplexy" and covered up, but later exposed by his successor Houbé. See Marty, "Le suicide d'un gouverneur" (ANOM, 20381 1920).

11. See the Wolof-language interview with historian Tidiane Sewane and the French-language interview with André Sarr of the Comité scientifique de Pencum for DakaractuTV, "Incursion à Koumpentoum: L'histoire méconnue du suicide collectif des femmes de Goundiour," YouTube video, 5:48, 22 January 2019, www.youtube.com/watch?v=Prx-IVwSPszo. See also Diam Sy and Seck, "'Thioural Goundiour,'" 12; "L'histoire méconnue."

12. Diouf, *Le Kajoor au XIXe siècle*, 274–77. See also Camille Sabatié, *Le Sénégal*, 156n10. Sabatié gives the erroneous date 1884 (a year after the French dethroned Samba Yaya and helped to install Samba Laobé). The correct date is given by Monteil, "Lat Dior, Damel du Kayor," 81.

13. The historical significance and symbolic resonances of Diop's act are not lost on local historians and Senegalese citizens, who claim Diop as "an heir to the princesses of Nder" (*un héritier des princesses de Nder*). On the life and death of Sidya Diop, see Saint-Martin, "Léon Diop Sidia"; Gaye, *Sidiya Joop (1848–1878)*. Contemporary accounts connect Diop's suicide to his maternal family: see "Sidya Léon Diop, fils de la Reine Ndatté Yalla Mbodj"; "Sidya Ndaté Yalla, une vie d'honneur."

14. Felwine Sarr, *Afrotopia*, 118.

15. On *jom* and voluntary death, see Ly, "L'honneur dans les sociétés Ouolof," 41. See also Legoff, "Le noirs se suicident-ils en A.O.F.?"

16. On *sutura*, see Mills, "Sutura."

17. This story is retold in Billal Fall's play *Le serment* (1979), which first was performed on 24 March 1979 by actors from the Troupe du Lycée John F. Kennedy de Dakar, directed by the author and Dominique Gomis. The story has also been told by the actors of Daaray Kocc, in a production titled *Xanju*, in Alhamdou Sy's film *Doomu Adama* (2006), and in the song "Khandiou" (1995), by the artist Le Sahel on their album *Sénégal Flash: Banjul*.

18. In his unpublished thesis on parasuicides in Dakar, Aïda Sylla suggests honor self-killings are "allowed, encouraged, even valorized," citing the story of Yacine Boubou who gave "his own life so his son could ascend the throne of Cayor" and the women of Nder who "burned themselves alive to escape slavery"; Sylla, "Les tentatives de suicide à Dakar," 3. He returns to these examples, as well as the proverb "You can kill us, but you cannot dishonor us" (a citation from Senghor that serves as the motto of the Senegalese army) under his discussion of "anomic suicide"; Sylla, "Les tentatives de suicide à Dakar," 7.

19. Serbin, *Reines d'Afrique*, 158–63.

20. On oral history in Wolof, especially in Waalo, see P. S. Diop, *Oral History*; Kanouté, *Tradition orale*; Leymarie, *Les griots wolof*; Barry, *La Sénégambie*; Fall, "Orality and Life Histories."

21. See Faye, "Fatou Sow Sarr en a marre."

22. These include narrative historical accounts by Serbin and by Tidiane N'Diaye, who reiterates Serbin's version in her chapter "Résistance africaine," in *Le génocide voilé*

(2008), as well as Chantal Durpoix's documentary film *Talaatay Nder* (2016), Marema's song "Talatay Nder" on the album *Initié* (2016), and the children's book by Fatou Sarr, *Talaatay Nder* (2010). Louis Schmaltz's historical novel based on the life and travels of Julien Désiré Schmaltz also includes a brief account of the Talaatay Nder narrative in an appendix labeled "Description of the principal events, people, and places that shaped, from 1771 to 1827, the destiny of Julien Désiré." His description of the women's armed resistance is especially literary: "That time, just like the famous gladiator Spartacus, the women chose to be massacred with weapons in their hands rather than become exploited merchandise, available and taken advantage of at will [*corvéable à merci*]. The women decided, quite simply, to end their days by setting ablaze the hut in which they were taking refuge." See Schmaltz, *Carnet de voyage*, 340–41.

23. Azoulay, *Potential History*. See also Azoulay, "Potential History."

24. Diakhate, Eyoh, and Rubin, "Senegal," 242. A press clipping from *Le Soleil* (3 August 1990) in the archives of the National Theater (ATNDS) provides a brief review of an early performance of Bèye's play, which closed the theater's season.

25. Born in Khouma (Xuma) in northern Senegal and educated at Faidherbe's École des Otages, Diaw later succeeded his father as *brak* and ruled until 1914. As early as his time at the École des Otages, Diaw began compiling notes on Senegalese history, legends, and customs. Rousseau, "Le Sénégal d'autrefois." See also Oumar Sall, "Yoro Dyao"; Boulègue, "À la naissance de l'histoire écrite sénégalaise."

26. Diaw's notebooks were preceded by works by David Boilat, a Catholic priest born to a French father and *signare* mother, such as *Mœurs et coutumes des Maures du Sénégal, en langue des Maures du pays* (1843), written in Arabic, *Voyage à Joal* (1846), *Esquisses sénégalaises* (1853), and *Grammaire de la langue woloffe* (1858). See D. Murphy, "Birth of a Nation?"

27. Encouraged by Faidherbe, Diaw first published one of his notebooks, titled "Histoire des Damels du Cayor," in 1864 in the *Moniteur du Sénégal*, a French weekly founded by Faidherbe in 1856 and published by the Imprimerie du Gouvernement in the then capital Saint-Louis. In 1912, Henri Gaden (*secrétaire général* of the colonial administration) published two notebooks accompanied by an introduction, footnotes, and appendix in the *Revue d'Ethnographie et de Sociologie*, under the title *Légendes et coutumes sénégalaises: Cahiers de Yoro Dyâo*. Gaden, "Légendes et coutumes sénégalaises."

28. Rousseau, "Le Sénégal d'autrefois." See also Irvine, "When Is Genealogy History?"

29. Colonial records dissertate at length on the military prowess, chivalric agility, and tremendous cruelty of Trarzs, as well as their "Toucouleur" (Tukolor or Haalpulaar) allies from the river states of Fuuta Tooro, who made numerous attacks on Wolof and French settlements during the first half of the nineteenth century. See Marty, *L'Émirat des Trarzas*, 99. In *Le Sénégal*, Faidherbe describes a typical scene in which mounted "Moors" ride off from razed villages in the Waalo, Cayor, and Djolof regions, with the "living spoils" of their raids in tow: infants and children in their arms or strapped to the saddle, their mother dragged behind "tethered to the tail of the horse, if she didn't perish in the fire"; Faidherbe, *Le Sénégal*, 40.

30. On this, see Hardy, *La mise en valeur*, especially "La guerre contre des Trarza," 90–92.

31. On Schmaltz, see Jore, "La vie diverse et volontaire." On the treaty of Ndiaw, see Barry, *Le royaume du Waalo*, 238–40; Roy, *Histoire des colonies françaises*, 124–25; Seye,

Walo Brack, 138–52. For the text of the treaty, see the annex in Barry, *Le royaume du Waalo*, 349.

32. See Barry, *Senegambia*, 260–62; Barry, *La Sénégambie*, 196–201. On the abolition of slavery in Senegal, see Diouf, *Le Kajoor au XIXe siècle*, 151–53. On agricultural colonization in Senegal, see also Brooks, "Peanuts and Colonialism."

33. Diao, cited in Rousseau, "Le Sénégal d'autrefois," 149 (emphasis in original). Brigaud reproduces Diaw's account from Rousseau but gives the year as 1819; Brigaud, "Le royaume du Waalo," 78.

34. Sabatié notes merely that "the Trarzas [. . .] crossed the river and burned down several villages"; Camille Sabatié, *Le Sénégal*, 45. This text reproduces P. Cultru's *Histoire du Sénégal du XVe siècle à 1870* (1910) as well as Diaw's "Histoire des damels du Cayor." Even Amadou Wade's "Chronique du Wâlo," which purports to present a French translation of the "annals" of the kingdom of Waalo (*xew-xew yi amoon ci Waalo* or "what took place in Waalo") is silent on the resistance of Nder besides mentioning that the *brak* Yërim Adaté Bubu was killed "in the famous battle of the *Talaata i Nder* or the Tuesday of Nder" and referencing Monteil; see A. Wade, "Chronique du Wâlo." Monteil notes that "the battle of Ndeer, famous in the annals of Wâlo, is commonly called *talaata-i Ndeer* or 'Tuesday of Ndeer,' from the day on which it took place"; Monteil, *Esquisses sénégalaises*, 56.

35. Azan, "Notice sur le Oualo," 10:353.

36. Azan, "Notice sur le Oualo," 10:333–34.

37. Azan, "Notice sur le Oualo," 10:334 (my emphasis).

38. ANS 2b5 f° 171.

39. This timeline aligns with current consensus, placing the Talaatay Nder on or around 7 March 1820, presuming the Trarzas' march toward Nder would take a day or two.

40. Azan draws a clear distinction between different kinds historical knowledge, eschewing a "legendary section in which historical events are found mixed up with incredible tales [*récits*]" and concluding teleologically in favor "of credible facts" and "a very true [*très-exacte*] historical section, composed of the collection [*réunion*] of information provided by people who took part in the events contained within, and official documents sourced from various government employees"; Azan, "Notice sur le Oualo," 10:338.

41. Sall, *Le choix de Madior*; Bâ, *Lat-Dior*.

42. Sankharé, *Regard sur les œuvres*, 51–54.

43. See Mbodji, "*Nder en flammes* rejouée."

44. On the history of the William Ponty School, see Sabatier, "Educating a Colonial Elite."

45. Ndao, "Abdou Anta Kâ et le théâtre africain," 204.

46. Examples include Ndao's *Guy Ndjulli* (2001) and *Bokk Afrig* (2004) as well as Alaaji Momar Samb's *Kujje* (2002).

47. See Sankharé, *Regard sur les œuvres*, 51–54.

48. Oumar Sankharé's is the only monograph dedicated to Bèye's work.

49. Valente-Quinn, *Senegalese Stagecraft*.

50. On the rise of Wolof theater, see Coulibaly, "Senegalese Theater Unabashed." On France's *mission civilisatrice* and *mise en valeur* in West Africa, see Conklin, *Mission to Civilize*.

51. Valente-Quinn, *Senegalese Stagecraft*, 4. See also Hardy, *La mise en valeur*.
52. Coulibaly, "Senegalese Theater Unabashed," 124 (my emphasis).
53. See Coulibaly, "Senegalese Theater Unabashed," 134.
54. Valente-Quinn, *Senegalese Stagecraft*, 32.
55. See Fatou Sarr, "Talaatay Nder et le message de Dialawali."
56. See the author's "Remerciements" (Bèye, *Nder*, 7). Bèye would later write the introduction to the major historical study of Waalo, Seye's *Walo Brack* (2003). All citations to *Nder en Flammes* are from the 1990 edition unless otherwise noted.
57. Bèye is cited as saying, "It's a play, not a faithful reproduction of reality. Otherwise, where would the creation be?" See "Le chef de l'État préside la soirée de gala," *Le Soleil*, 7 May 1991 (ANTDS).
58. In their medical studies, Aïda Sylla and Aby Diop cite Bèye's play as the authoritative account for the resistance of Nder; it is the only nonscientific text cited. Sylla, "Les tentatives de suicide à Dakar," 50; A. Diop, "Les suicides et tentatives de suicide à Dakar," 8. To my knowledge, Bitty Bocar Ba's unpublished master's thesis in history, "Talaatay Ndeer" (Université Cheikh Anta Diop, 1992, AUCAD), is one of the few historical studies of the Talaatay Nder. When I requested to view it in July 2021, it could not be found among the collections. I return to the search for this document in my conclusion.
59. On traditional theater in Senegal, see Ndao, "Abdou Anta Kâ et le théâtre africain."
60. The set is described in a review in the *Soleil* (Friday, 3 August 1990) (ANTDS). The most recent revival (2016) involved a slightly more elaborate set but remained true to the spareness of Traoré's design.
61. Valente-Quinn, *Senegalese Stagecraft*, 58.
62. "Le feu couve à nos portes"; Bèye, *Nder*, 30. Hereafter, citations for this work are given parenthetically in the text.
63. Hardy, *La mise en valeur*, 91–92.
64. Kane, *L'aventure ambiguë*, 80.
65. Repinecz, "'Tales of Tomorrow,'" 61. See also Repinecz, *Subversive Traditions*.
66. Repinecz, "'Tales of Tomorrow,'" 66 (my emphasis).
67. See Repinecz, "'Tales of Tomorrow,'" 59.
68. For comparisons between the Wolof original and its French adaptation, see Goldblatt, "Lëndëmtu," 66; Carré, "Between Mother Tongue."
69. African cultural production has never fit easily within world-literature frameworks. For a recent evaluation of the advantages and disadvantages of world-literary approaches to African literature, see Fyfe and Krishnan, *African Literatures*.
70. Ngom, "Militantisme linguistique."
71. Wa Thiong'o, *Decolonising the Mind*.
72. B. B. Diop, *Malaanum lëndëm*, *Bàmmeelu Kocc Barma*, and *Doomi Golo: Nettali*.
73. See Warner, *Tongue-Tied Imagination*, 84.
74. These estimates are rough and based on outdated census data from 2013. The *World Atlas* suggests that as low as 20 percent of men and 2 percent of women speak and understand French; see Pariona, "What Languages Are Spoken in Senegal?"
75. Repinecz, "'Tales of Tomorrow,'" 65.

76. These are: *téereb dóom (I–III)* "the book of ashes," *téereb ngelaw* "the book of winds," *téereb lëndëmtu (I–II)* "the book of darkness," *téereb fent* "the book of invention," *téereb wis* "the book of brief digressions" (*wis* literally means "to sprinkle" or, as a noun, "water droplets"), *téereb bu ñuul bi* "the black book." Part II is presumably the mysterious seventh notebook, the *téereb ndéey* or "book of secrets," which the grandfather mentions at the beginning of the novel.

77. See Repinecz, "'Tales of Tomorrow.'"

78. Diop is perhaps best known for his "book of bones": *Murambi, le livre des ossements* (2000), a novel that emerged out of Nocky Djedanoum's "Rwanda: Écrire par devoir de mémoire" project, a 1988 initiative that engaged a group of ten African writers to grapple with the legacy of the Rwandan genocide. *Doomi Golo* inflects and develops some of the questions about the constructedness of received histories and the positionality of the writer that Diop already began to articulate in *Murambi*. For an overview of the "Écrire par devoir de mémoire" project, see Apap, *Écrire par devoir de mémoire*; Hitchcott, "Global African Commemoration." On Diop's involvement in the "Écrire par devoir de mémoire," see Hitchcott, "Writing on Bones."

79. In *Les petits de la guenon*, Diop gives the date as Tuesday, 4 March 1820, but notes "on this particular point, the opinions of chroniclers diverge"; B. B. Diop, *Les petits*, 34.

80. B. B. Diop, *Doomi Golo: Nettali*, 34.

81. B. B. Diop, *Doomi Golo: Nettali*, 35.

82. The scene recalls Torquato Tasso's "Moorish" warrior-maid, Clorinda, whose "unconfined locks" streaming behind her on the battlefield become a privileged signifier of her femininity; Tasso, *Jerusalem Delivered*, 57.

83. B. B. Diop, *Les petits*, 35.

84. B. B. Diop, *Doomi Golo: Nettali*, 35.

85. B. B. Diop, *Doomi Golo: Nettali*, 36.

86. For instance, in the original Wolof title (and throughout the text) the gender of the titular monkey remains unspecified (Diop uses the term *golo* and never *golo bu jigéen*, "female monkey, she-ape") whereas the French title, *Les petits de la guenon: Roman*, makes the gender explicit, using *guenon* rather than *singe*.

87. On this, see Goldblatt, "Lëndëmtu."

88. B. B. Diop, *Doomi Golo: Nettali*, 78.

89. As a noun, *taal* refers to a (cooking) fire, as opposed to the more general *safara si*, but as a verb means "to light, to start a fire" and, by extension, to begin cooking (as in, placing a pot over a fire). This is the verb Diop uses for the women's final act, preferring it to the more specific *jafal*, "to set on fire."

90. B. B. Diop, *Doomi Golo: The Hidden Notebooks*, 14. In the French, "the scar after the great burning" (*la cicatrice d'après la grande brûlure*); B. B. Diop, *Les petits*, 30.

91. B. B. Diop, *Doomi Golo: Nettali*, 30.

92. Bèye, *Nder*, 70.

93. B. B. Diop, *Les petits*, 36 (my emphasis).

94. Repinecz, "'Tales of Tomorrow,'" 60. The French and English versions state this more emphatically: "Malheur au peuple qui ne sait plus écouter ses petites filles" (Shame on the nation that doesn't listen to its little girls); B. B. Diop, *Les petits*, n.p.

95. B. B. Diop, *Doomi Golo: Nettali*, 36.
96. Repinecz, "'Tales of Tomorrow.'"
97. Derrida, *Cinders*, 53. For the French original, see Derrida, *Feu la cendre*.
98. See Derrida, "Poetics and Politics," in *Sovereignties in Question*, 75, 79.
99. Derrida, "Poetics and Politics," 69.
100. Doane, *Emergence of Cinematic Time*, 69–107.
101. Doane, *Emergence of Cinematic Time*, 95.
102. Derrida, "Poetics and Politics," 68.
103. Derrida, "Poetics and Politics," 68.
104. Derrida, "Shibboleth," in *Sovereignties in Question*, 46 (my emphasis).
105. Longitudinal studies have noted a copycat effect in the wake of Bouazizi's self-immolation, showing that cases of public suicide by self-burning in Tunisia have since tripled. See Blaise, "Self-Immolation, Catalyst of the Arab Spring"; Ben Khelil et al., "Comparison of Suicidal Behavior." This trend continues at the time of this writing, with the suicide of climate scientist and activist Wynn Bruce, who set himself on fire in front of the US Supreme Court on 24 April 2022.
106. "Man Dies after Setting Himself on Fire in Senegal."
107. "Senegal Man Dies in Dakar Fire Protest."
108. "Three Students Set Fire to Themselves in Senegal."
109. A. Diop, "Sénégal, vidéo avant son immolation."
110. Sarr's novel is inspired by actual literary history, namely the rise and fall of the Malian writer Yambo Ouologuem. See Calhoun, "Putting French Literary History on Trial."
111. M. M. Sarr, *La plus secrète mémoire*, 342.
112. Jackson, *African Novel of Ideas*.
113. M. M. Sarr, *La plus secrète mémoire*, 392.
114. M. M. Sarr, *La plus secrète mémoire*, 391 (emphasis in original).
115. M. M. Sarr, *La plus secrète mémoire*, 368 (emphasis in original).
116. M. M. Sarr, *La plus secrète mémoire*, 352.

3. SCREEN MEMORIES

This chapter is significantly revised and expanded from previous publications: "(Im)possible Inscriptions: Silence, Servitude, and Suicide in Ousmane Sembène's *La Noire de . . .* ," *Research in African Literatures* 51, no. 2 (Summer 2020): 96–116, https://doi.org/10.2979/reseafrilite.51.2.06; "Looking for Diouana Gomis (1927–58): The Story behind African Cinema's Most Iconic Suicide," *Research in African Literatures* 52, no. 2 (Summer 2021): 1–28, https://doi.org/10.2979/reseafrilite.52.2.01; "Sembène's 'Black Girl' Is a Ghost Story," *Public Books*, 4 November 2021, https://www.publicbooks.org/sembenes-black-girl-is-a-ghost-story/.

Epigraphs: Hartman, "Venus," 13; Gordon, *Ghostly Matters*, 18.

1. The *Ancerville* entered service in 1962, traveling regularly between Dakar and Marseille with stops in Casablanca, Tenerife, and Las Palmas, typically spending six days at sea. See "'Ancerville' atteint 25 nœuds aux essais."
2. Sembène, "La Noire de . . . ," 152.
3. Sembène, "La Noire de . . . ," 154.

4. Sembène, "La Noire de...," 171.
5. D. Thomas, *Black France*, 125 (my emphasis).
6. Rosello, *Postcolonial Hospitality*, 122; cited in D. Thomas, *Black France*, 125.
7. See Prédal, "La Noire de...." The characterization of *La Noire de...* as a "long métrage" is somewhat misleading since Sembène cut the film from seventy to around sixty-five minutes to avoid certain production restraints imposed by the Centre national du cinéma. Sembène referred to the film as a "short feature film" or a "long short film." See Malčić, "Ousmane Sembène's Vicious Circle," 169. See also Pfaff, *Cinema of Ousmane Sembène*, 113; Virtue, "'Le film de...,'" 558; Hennebelle, "'For Me, the Cinema,'" 9.
8. Vieyra, *Ousmane Sembène*, 189.
9. Chapier, "La Noire de...," 8.
10. Calhoun, "Looking for Diouana Gomis."
11. Sturken, "Absent Images," 35.
12. Sturken, "Absent Images," 35.
13. Sturken, "Absent Images," 35.
14. Freud, "Screen Memories," 321 (emphasis in original).
15. Freud, "Screen Memories," 322 (my emphasis).
16. Rothberg, *Multidirectional Memory*, 13 (my emphasis).
17. Rothberg, *Multidirectional Memory*, 14.
18. See Ross, *Fast Cars, Clean Bodies*; Ross, *May '68 and Its Afterlives*; Brozgal, *Absent the Archive*; Rothberg, *Multidirectional Memory*, 359n22.
19. Margalit, *Ethics of Memory*, 52.
20. Senghor, "Femme Noire," in *Poèmes*, 16–17. The title of the English translation of Sembène's short story was influenced by a line from Senghor's poem: "Je te découvre, Terre promise" (I discover you, my Promised Land).
21. Rothberg, *Multidirectional Memory*, 359n22.
22. Johnson, *Wicked Flesh*, 158.
23. On Sembène's wartime participation, see "Here We Come, Marshall!," in Gadjigo, *Ousmane Sembène*, 59–62.
24. Gadjigo, *Ousmane Sembène*, 101.
25. Gadjigo, *Ousmane Sembène*, 101. See also Bertoncello and Brédeloup, "Le Marseille des marins africains."
26. Pacini and Pons, *Docker à Marseille*.
27. Gadjigo, *Ousmane Sembène*, 104.
28. Gadjigo, *Ousmane Sembène*, 107.
29. Sembène, "Liberté."
30. On Sembène's choice to set his short story prior to the 1958 referendum, see Stratton, *Contemporary African Literature*, 42.
31. Sembène, "La Noire de...," 149.
32. Best, *None like Us*, 123.
33. The literature on the *fait divers* is robust. Some well-known discussions of the genre include Merleau-Ponty, "Sur les faits divers"; Barthes, "Structure du fait divers"; Bourdieu, *Sur la télévision*. See also Barillaud, Bièque, and Dahlet, "Le fait divers"; Dubied, *Les dits et les scènes*; Chevalier, *Splendeurs et misères*.

34. Barthes, "Structure du fait divers," 188.//
35. Bourdieu, *On Television*, 17–18.
36. Boudana, "Unbearable Lightness," 203.
37. See David H. Walker, *Outrage and Insight*; Evrard, *Fait divers et littérature*; Huy, *Les écrivains et le fait divers*; and Toudoire-Surlapierre, *Le fait divers et ses fictions*.
38. Sembène, "La Noire de . . . ," 174. In this case, "le lendemain" could effectively be the day of the real *fait divers* since *Nice-Matin* did not have a Monday issue.
39. The article, "A Mother of Six Children Drowned in Her Bathtub," details how a certain M. Margue, "unfolded a newspaper" while waiting for his wife to finish her bath. When he knocked on the door to the bathroom and failed to receive a response, he broke into the bathroom and found his unconscious wife "collapsed in a half-full bath." It is possible that these details, lifted from another *fait divers* reported on the page following the report of Gomis's suicide, informed Sembène's mise-en-scène of suicide in the film, which juxtaposes the image of Diouana's partially submerged, lifeless body with a white Frenchman unfolding his newspaper.
40. Duras, *Œuvres romanesques*.
41. Sembène, "La Noire de . . . ," 150.
42. The "Table décennale des actes de naissances, mariages, décès (Antibes, 1923–1932)" (ADAM) show that a Roger Petit was born on 9 March 1928; Andrée Petit on 23 September 1926; Eugène Petit on 5 April 1931; Eugène Petit on 7 October 1931; Louis Petit on 2 March 1925; Nicolas Petit on 12 November 1932. See the Département des Alpes-Maritimes, https://www.departement06.fr/.
43. Sembène, "La Noire de . . . ," 153.
44. D. Thomas, *Black France*, 115.
45. Proust, "Filial Feelings," 115.
46. See Huy, *Les écrivains et le fait divers*.
47. "Le Sénégalais Deba comparait aux assises pour meurtre."
48. Fuentes, *Dispossessed Lives*, 1.
49. Johnson, *Wicked Flesh*, 4. See also White, *Voices of the Enslaved*.
50. Foucault, "Lives of Infamous Men," 161.
51. See Mbembe, "Necropolitics."
52. Jones, "Debt Collecting," 215.
53. Jones, "Debt Collecting," 218.
54. I am drawing here on the popular phrase and hashtag #BlackGirlMagic as a form of resistant self-expression; see Jordan-Zachery, "Resistance and Redemption Narratives."
55. Hartman, "Venus," 2; Hartman is citing M. NourbeSe Philip's text *She Tries Her Tongue, Her Silence Softly Breaks* (1993).
56. Sembène, "La Noire de . . . ," 153.
57. Sembène at least seems to have spoken to the police superintendent and examining magistrate; see Ellerson, "M'Bissine Thérèse Diop," 245–46. The surnames Da Silva and Gomis (equivalent to Gomes in Portuguese) reflect the historical influence of Portuguese in the region.
58. Both names are misspelled in the *fait divers* report.
59. Sembène, "La Noire de . . . ," 153.

60. See "Partie non officielle, état civil, ville de Haiphong," 964.

61. *Annuaire général de l'Indo-Chine*, 204.

62. "Table décennale des actes de naissances, mariages, & décès de la commune d'Antibes, 1923–1932" (ADAM), 56. Phone books from Dakar from the 1950s list Roger Petit's address in Dakar as km 5.2 route de Rufisque (BNF, *Annuaire 1956–57*, 65; BNF, *Annuaire 1958*, 69), which differs slightly from the address given by Jeannine. In the 1950s, this address corresponded to the Hann region of Dakar, and specifically to the headquarters of the Bureau Minier de la France d'Outre-Mer as well as to a petrol company (*Annuaire 1958*, 68), so it is possible Petit's phone records reflected his place of work rather than his family residence. A certain Jean Petit also was living in Dakar at the time, on the Rue Carnot in Plateau (BNF, *Annuaire 1956–57*, 33; BNF, *Annuaire 1958*, 34), although it is difficult to say whether this is the same Jean Petit, Roger's father, who built the Villa Le Bonheur Vert.

63. Pfaff, *Cinema of Ousmane Sembène*, 114.

64. Sembène, "La Noire de . . . ," 151.

65. Sembène, "La Noire de . . . ," 168.

66. On the "hypervisibility" of the Black subject, see Hartman, *Scenes of Subjection*, 4.

67. Dorothy Blair notes: "It is in the portrayal of the African women, in the variety of female characters, old and young, that Sembène shows his greatest skill and versatility. [. . .] The lives of the women form, in fact, the central core of the drama"; Blair, *African Literature*, 237. In her overview of Senegalese literature, she reiterates: "The only novelist to depict women as heroines and victims, to champion their cause before any woman writer spoke up for her sisters was Ousmane Sembène"; Blair, *Senegalese Literature*, 132.

68. See Pfaff, *Cinema of Ousmane Sembène*, 154.

69. Blair, *African Literature*, 237.

70. Socé, *Mirages de Paris*; Kane, *L'aventure ambiguë*.

71. Diome, *Le ventre*; Gomis, *L'Afrance*.

72. Chevrier, "Afrique(s)-sur-Seine." See also D. Thomas, *Black France*, 5.

73. Diome, *Le ventre*, 88 (emphasis in original).

74. Ka, *La voie du salut*.

75. Ka, *La voie du salut*, 100.

76. Lyamlahy, *Évocation*.

77. Lyamlahy, *Évocation*, [9] (n.p.).

78. Blair, *African Literature*, 188.

79. Sembène, "La Noire de . . . ," 167.

80. Sembène, "La Noire de . . . ," 154.

81. Sembène, "La Noire de . . . ," 165.

82. See Warner, "Enacting Postcolonial Translation," 118–19.

83. Malčić, "Ousmane Sembène's Vicious Circle," 176.

84. See Warner, "Enacting Postcolonial Translation," 115.

85. Miller, "Hallucinations," 44.

86. Miller, "Hallucinations," 39.

87. Sembène, "La Noire de . . . ," 165–66.

88. Sembène, *La Noire de . . .* ("Scénario"), 17–18 (BFCA).

89. Senghor, *Négritude et humanisme*, 77–78; Senghor is drawing on a study by Legoff, "Les Noirs se suicident-ils en A.O.F.?," 20.

90. Niang and Sembène, "Interview," 75.

91. The suicide of Socé's exiled Fara, who hallucinates his native Cayor in the waters of the Seine before leaping to his death, rehearses the suicide by drowning of the deposed *dammel* of Cayor Samba Yaya Fall, who leapt from the Pont Faidherbe only a few decades earlier. Socé's novel also reworks the plot of the French sentimental novel by Pierre Loti *Roman d'un Spahi* (Calmann-Lévy, 1881), in which a Senegalese woman falls in love with a French soldier and strangles their child before committing suicide after he dies in battle. See Blair, *Senegalese Literature*, 52–53. The central drama of Kane's novel rewrites the story of Sidya Diop, whose ambiguous adventure and "assimilation manquée" also ended in suicide.

92. Patil et al., "Atypical Case," 492. See also Fukube et al., "Retrospective Study on Suicidal Cases."

93. Patil et al., "Atypical Case," 492.

94. Patil et al., "Atypical Case," 492.

95. Johnson, *Wicked Flesh*, 147.

96. Johnson, *Wicked Flesh*, 12.

97. D. Thomas, *Black France*, 115.

98. Sembène, "La Noire de . . . ," 172.

99. Sembène, "La Noire de . . . ," 152.

100. Sembène, "La Noire de . . . ," 159–60.

101. D. Thomas, *Black France*, 127.

102. Parascandola notes that she is "taken from Africa as if she were some sort of parcel, transported like unimportant cargo rather than by plane like the family"; Parascandola, "'What Are We Blackmen Who Are Called French?,'" 368.

103. For a similar comparison, see Jonassaint, "Le cinéma de Sembène Ousmane."

104. Kanor, *La poétique de la cale,* 277–78.

105. Spivak, "Scattered Speculations," 478.

106. The discourse of hygiene and indigeneity is even more significant when brought to bear on the death of a Senegalese maid. The history of French colonial Dakar is deeply intertwined with a history of segregationist sanitation policies that impacted Sembène's own family and his childhood in Casamance. See Bigon, *French Colonial Dakar*. See also Newell, *Histories of Dirt*, which, though focused on Lagos, also examines the cultural politics of dirt and conceptions of dirtiness during and after colonization more broadly.

107. The relationship between "purification" and suicide is explored by André Morel in an unpublished study of suicide in the Caribbean; Morel, "Suicide et tentatives de suicide à la Martinique" (1979, ANOM, BIB AOM TH 508), 55.

108. Pamela McCallum points out the striking similarity between David's painting and Sembène's framing of Diouana's suicide, reading the scene as a parodic reproduction of David's masterpiece that evokes "a canonical representation of heroic death in the suicide of a Senegalese domestic worker." However, McCallum analyzes the intertext of David's painting exclusively under the rubric of Revolution and Enlightenment, arguing that "Sembène's figuration of Diouana's death precipitates a series of reflections on the 'dialectic of Enlightenment' in the historical differences and continuities between Senegal and France." McCallum, "Irony, Colonialism and Representation," 161–62.

109. Sembène, "La Noire de . . . ," 171.

110. Dodman, *What Nostalgia Was*.
111. Dodman, *What Nostalgia Was*, 11.
112. See the chapter titled "Les 'maladies des nègres,'" in Dorlin, *La matrice de la race*, 231–76.
113. Sembène, "La Noire de . . . ," 175.
114. Sembène, "La Noire de . . . ," 175–76.
115. Sembène, "La Noire de . . . ," 177.
116. Sembène, "La Noire de . . . ," 177.
117. Sembène, "La Noire de . . . ," 175.
118. Amadou T. Fofana calls the song a "migration folk story of the Sereer people" and suggests that it is about the suicide of another maid; Fofana, *Films of Ousmane Sembène*, 223.
119. Langford, "Black and White," 15.
120. Petty, "Mapping the African 'I,'" 309.
121. Rofheart, *Shifting Perceptions of Migration*, 28. As Tobias Warner notes, the palimpsestic voice of Sembène's title character, in addition to nodding to "the way in which Diouana's voice is often subject to being captured and ventriloquized" also draws Diop/Bissainthe's performance of Diouana into a "diasporic," "transnational" diegetic space, by superimposing the voice of a Haitian actress onto Diop's actions and gestures; Warner, "Enacting Postcolonial Translation," 115.
122. As in the Wolof proverb "Ku mën na féy du xaru ci ndox" (Someone who knows how to swim does not commit suicide in the water).
123. My remarks here take inspiration from Christina Sharpe's reading of this scene and the figure of Zabou/Haiti in Sissako's film; C. Sharpe, *In the Wake*, 127–30.
124. Hartman, "Venus," 11.
125. Best, *None like Us*, 15.
126. Hartman, "Venus," 12.
127. Hartman, "Venus," 14.
128. Hartman, "Venus," 14.

4. MULTIPLE EXPOSURES

Epigraphs: Barthes, *Camera Lucida*, 6; Hughes, "Suicide's Note," in *Collected Works*, 53.

1. On Greene's calotypes, see Jammes, "John B. Greene." For a retrospective of Greene's work, see the exhibition *Signs and Wonders: The Photographs of John Beasley Greene* (San Francisco Museum of Modern Art in collaboration with Art Institute of Chicago, Summer 2020).
2. Nineteenth-century travel narratives expressed fear and fascination at the landscapes captured by Greene. Anne Dutertre, a Frenchwoman who traveled from Normandy to Algeria with her daughter in 1860 and published a narrative of their voyage, gives a detailed account of her first impressions of the Rhummel and Constantine's infamous abyss. See Dutertre, *Voyage*, 138.
3. Beginning with the monumental battle scenes depicted by the Orientalist painter Horace Vernet (1789–1863), image-making became a powerful tool of French colonizing presence in Algeria. French daguerreotypists such as Félix Moulin (1802–75)—whose three-volume *Algérie photographiée* (1856–57) was an official document of Napoléon III's

military campaigns in North Africa—and the photographer brothers Étienne Neurdein (1832–1918) and Louis-Antonin Neurdein (1846–1914) inaugurated an overtly Orientalist and ethnographic photographic tradition. For an overview of early photography in North Africa, see Killingray and Roberts, "Outline History of Photography." See also Stewart Howe, "North Africa." On colonial domination and image production, including the birth of photography and erotica, see the volume Blanchard et al., *Sexe, race et colonies*. See also Alloula et al., *Colonial Harem*, which discusses the role played by images of Algerian women, especially postcards, in the history of colonial photography. On the Neurdein brothers and their relationship to Orientalism and colonialism, see Rosenthal, "Neurdein Frères."

4. Greene held no official commissions and financed his own expeditions; as far as we know, he never captured human subjects—only photographing ruins, relics, and landscapes. This is not to say that Greene's interest in archeology and documentary photography was not part and parcel of an imperialist project. On the relationship between archeology and imperialism, see Effros and Lai, *Unmasking Ideology*.

5. Sealy, *Decolonising the Camera*, 106–7, 4.

6. Campt, *Listening to Images*; see also Campt, *Image Matters*.

7. Barthes's notion of the blind field comes from his remarks in *Camera Lucida* (1981). In *Ghostly Matters*, Avery Gordon reads the blind field as an invitation to haunting. Gordon writes: "The blind field is what the ghost's arrival signals. The blind field is never named as such in the photograph. How could it be? [. . .] If you are looking for the blind field, you first have to make your way to it, open to its particular mode of address. If you are not looking for it, it can take you to it without your permission"; Gordon, *Ghostly Matters*, 107.

8. Azoulay, "Photography," 77.

9. In addition to the work of Gordon, Campt, and Sealy, I am building here on Ariella Azoulay's thinking, in *The Civil Contract of Photography* (2012) and *Potential History* (2019), of the photographic "shutter," a technology of capture that she also reads as a moment of excision.

10. On the concept of "knots" or "nodes" on memory as an alternative to Pierre Nora's "sites of memory," see Rothberg, "Between Memory and Memory."

11. Abderrezak, "Mediterranean *Seametery* and *Cementery*."

12. Durkheim, *Le suicide*, 118.

13. See Livy, *History of Rome*, b. 30.12–15.

14. This scenario proved popular in Orientalist fiction set in Algeria after French conquest. Texts like Eugénie Foa's short story "La Kalissa" (1833) and Théophile Gautier and Noël Parfait's play *La Juive de Constantine* (1846) feature condemned women being tossed from cliffs—in Algiers in the case of Foa, in Constantine in the case of Gautier and Parfait. According to another legend, the saint Sidi M'Hammed-el-Ghrab was precipitated in a sack from the cliffs by Salah Bey but transformed into a crow and survived the fall; this legend is described in Robert, *L'Arabe tel qu'il est*.

15. Bennabi, *Mémoires d'un témoin*; cited in Cole, *Lethal Provocation*, 17–18.

16. One eyewitness notes how many Constantinians "rushed across the rocks towards the plain, on the south side [. . .] 200 corpses lay at the foot of the rocks"; "L'expédition, l'assaut, et la prise de Constantine," 125–26. Sylvain-Charles Valée, who commanded

the French artillery at the siege, writes, "a great number [of Arabs], however, died while trying to leap from the rampart to the plain." See *Recueil de documents*, 43.

17. Baudens, "Journal d'un médecin."

18. In 1955, the sight of the cadavers of Algerians in the gorge inspired Henri Maillot, a *pied noir* of the Algerian Communist Party, to desert from the French forces and join the resistance; he later published an expository article that was swiftly censured. See Kastell, *Le maquis rouge*, 88, 94.

19. See Chachoua, "Le suicide en Algérie," 402–3; Chachoua, "Genre, suicide et sexualité(s)"; and Sider, *Traumatisme psychologique*.

20. See "Self-Immolation in Algeria." Two Algerian films engage directly with the history of self-immolation in Algeria: Bahïa Bencheikh-El-Fegoun's *Fragments de rêves* (Allers Retours Films, 2017) and Meriem Achour Bouakkaz's *Nar* (Argus Films, Afkar Films, 2019).

21. The name of the river suggests sedimentation, the ocean floor, or the Sahara since *Oued Rhummel* or *Rummel* is a French transcription of the Arabic *rmel* "sand": the River of Sand.

22. For an example of "listening to images" in the context of French Algerian history, see Jarvis, "Radiant Matter."

23. Photography contributed in important ways to the creation of *anarchives* and alternative conduits for memory with respect to the history of Algerians in France and the history of France in Algeria. On the notion of "anarchive" as it relates to French Algerian history, in particular the 17 October 1961 massacre in Paris, see Brozgal, "In the Absence of the Archive" and *Absent the Archive*.

24. M. Silverman, *Palimpsestic Memory*.

25. M. Silverman, *Palimpsestic Memory*, 3.

26. Trouillot, *Silencing the Past*, 148.

27. Feraoun, *Les chemins qui montent*.

28. Yacine, *Parce que c'est une femme*; Halimi, *La Kahina*; Saint Pierre, *La Kahina*.

29. Wattar [Waṭṭār], *al-Zilzāl* and *The Earthquake*.

30. Mosteghanemi, *Dhākirat al-jasad*.

31. Laredj [al-Aʻradj], *Sayyidatu al-maqam* and *Les ailes de la reine*; Kacimi, *Yawm rāʼiʻ lil-mawt* and *Un jour idéal pour mourir*.

32. Haneke, *Caché*; Adimi, *Des ballerines de Papicha*.

33. For studies of this extensive literature and filmography, see Talbayev, *Transcontinental Maghreb*; Talbayev and elhariry, *Critically Mediterranean*; Esposito, *Narrative Mediterranean*.

34. Binebine, *Cannibales*; Essomba, *Le paradis du nord*.

35. Saadi, "Retour." The text later was republished with minimal additions and changes in Saadi, *Il n'y a pas d'os dans la langue*, 54–63.

36. Saadi, "Retour," 58.

37. See "Nomenclature des rues de Constantine," in *Plan monumental de Constantine*, 7–8. This is the street address that the protagonist of *La nuit des origines* associates with her childhood home.

38. Saadi, "Retour," 58.

39. Saadi, "Retour," 59.

40. The Inconnue was an unidentified young woman whose body police pulled out of the Seine at the Quai du Louvre during the late nineteenth century and whose death mask was reproduced as photographs and three-dimensional molds sold widely during the first few decades of the twentieth century. See Tillier, *La belle noyée*; Phillips, "In Search of an Unknown Woman"; Pinet, "L'eau, la femme, la mort." In his canonical study of suicide and literature, Alfred Alvarez writes in a footnote, "The Inconnue became the erotic ideal of the period." Alvarez, *Savage God*, 128–29.

41. The Inconnue served as the model for the head of Resusci Anne, the first aid mannequin used in CPR courses, making her "the most kissed face" of all time. Her story was reinvented in literary works, circulating widely enough to attract the attention of writers such as Maurice Blanchot and Albert Camus, the French writer—a Français d'Algérie—perhaps most readily associated with suicide for his remarks in "The Myth of Sisyphus" (1942). Both owned copies of the mask. On the literary afterlives of the Inconnue in works by Aragon, Breton, Céline, Man Ray, Nabokov, and Rilke, see Tillier, *La belle noyée*, 11–15.

42. The massacre was given an iconic visual representation in a photo by Jean Texier. On the history of this photograph and its circulation, see Lemire and Potin, "'Ici on noie les Algériens.'"

43. The Jardin Fatima Bedar in Saint-Denis now commemorates Fatima and the many unnamed victims of the 1961 massacre. On 17 October 1961, see House and MacMaster, *Paris 1961*.

44. We are not far here from Giorgio Agamben's famous characterization, adapted from Primo Levi and marked by a curious oversight or "silence," of (the Algerian) "Muslim" as the impossible witness: the Muslims, the drowned (*i musulmani, i sommersi*). See Jarvis, "Remnants of Muslims."

45. Maheke's installation, consisting of four digitally printed diaphanous curtains, was exhibited at the Diaspora Pavilion at the Fifty-Eighth Venice Biennale the year Sabally drowned. Scattered across the curtain panels are words that riff on Hughes's poem: "When it asked / for a / kiss, he obeyed without / resisting and the cold / evermoving surface swallowed him. / While the undertow / tosses his limbs around / he recalls the way / his river / flowed."

46. Saadi, "Retour," 60.

47. Saadi, "Retour," 60.

48. These are practically the same words that will open *Boulevard de l'abîme* ("L'inspecteur, stupéfait, ébaubi devant une telle garde-robe"); Saadi, *Boulevard*, 17.

49. Saadi, "Retour," 40.

50. The Baudelairean undertones seem evident. Like the speaker of Charles Baudelaire's "Le Cygne" (1860), the speaker of Saadi's "Retour à Constantine" wanders a city only in his mind (as Baudelaire writes, "Je ne vois qu'en esprit . . ." [I see only in my mind's eye . . .] and thinks of a river: not the "Old Paris" before Haussmannization, but Constantine before an earthquake that rendered it unrecognizable, not the Seine but the Rhummel. The minds of both speakers flood suddenly with an unexpected and nonlinear sense of memory that connects diverse figures of suffering and loss.

51. Saadi, *La nuit*, [205] (n.p.).

52. Alain inherits the studio from "le vieux Balbo" or "Œil-de-Bœuf," a character much like the nineteenth-century photographer Félix Moulin, who moonlighted as an art photographer but gained a living through touristic and erotic photos: "Œil-de-Bœuf had invented a rather singular posing technique: when the magnesium exploded, he burst into a great contagious laugh which provoked the hilarity of his model, thus eternalized by the white smoke in the cylinders"; Saadi, *La nuit*, 45.

53. See Froment-Meurice, "In the Name of the Other." Saadi's allusion to Nerval and his recourse to him as a literary model throughout the novel are pointed: as a vector of French Romanticism perhaps best known for his *Voyage en orient*, Nerval's literary-colonial "imaginary" had a role in sustaining and justifying French expansion in North Africa; see "Romanticism and the Saharan Sublime," in Brower, *Desert Named Peace*, 199–221.

54. Saadi, *La nuit*, [205] (n.p.; emphasis in original). Hereafter, citations for the novel are given parenthetically in the text.

55. Alain's first encounter with Abla suggests such a reading: he glimpses her on a rainy day wearing a white dress that makes her stand out against a "shapeless greyish crowd"; Saadi, *La nuit*, 144.

56. *Alba*: "Algerian white" like *Alger la Blanche*, like Blanche, the granddaughter of a French general in Saadi's *La maison de lumière* (2000), and like Bayda ("White"), the protagonist of Saadi's first novel *Dieu-Le-Fit* (1996). Abla's own name suggests a specific literary genealogy: the Beloved in the chivalric romances of the pre-Islamic Arab poet Antarah ibn Shaddad al-Absi (525–608 CE).

57. Thiais is an important *lieu de mémoire* since it houses the French Resistance monument as well as a memorial to the Paris-Brazzaville crash of 1961. In the novel, we also learn an important detail about the circumstances of the interment of Alain's mother: she was buried twice, first at Père Lachaise, where she was buried next to an Iranian poet, Sadeq Hedayat, who died by suicide, before being interred a second time in the *extra-muros* cemetery of Thiais; Saadi, *La nuit*, 101.

58. The *lit d'or* recurs throughout Saadi's oeuvre. In *Boulevard*, the inspector investigating the protagonist's death takes note of her "enormous gold four-poster bed," and the caretaker of the apartment building describes how "cumbersome cranes [were required] for a few days [...] to move this huge golden bed which was the curiosity of the whole neighborhood"; Saadi, *Boulevard*, 21, 104. In *La maison de lumière*, Marabout, the narrator's father, alludes to a "four-poster bed, a cage of gold, of arabesques and vaults"; Saadi, *La maison de lumière*, 128–29.

59. See Dewerpe, *Charonne*.

60. "Charonne" also points to another river, one that leads to Oblivion rather than to memory since Charonne is a feminization of *Charon*, the name of the mythic boatman who ferries souls across the Acheron, one of the rivers of hell, to the lake Lethe.

61. See Brozgal, *Absent the Archive*; House and MacMaster, *Paris 1961*, 255.

62. Brozgal, *Absent the Archive*.

63. On the history of this photograph, see Hanrot, *La Madone de Bentalha*.

64. Rose, *Last Resistance*, 3.

65. See Stora, *La gangrène et l'oubli*.

66. I have in mind here the analysis of Walid Benkhaled and Natalya Vince, who examine the ways different social and political groups collectively define and perform different forms of "Algerianness," as well as the ways national and transnational discourses have constructed an Algerian "identity crisis"; see Benkhaled and Vince, "Afterword: Performing Algerianness."

67. Ford, *Writing the Black Decade*.

68. Flood, "Women Resisting Terror," 116.

69. Flood, "Women Resisting Terror," 116.

70. Another reference to Nerval seems likely here: the poet's portable "Généalogie fantastique" (ca. 1841); on this, see the chapter "Unfolding Nerval," in Bray, *Novel Map*.

71. Saadi, *Boulevard*, 17.

72. Saadi, *Boulevard*, 21.

73. Saadi, *Boulevard*, 213 (emphasis in original). On the Améziane farmhouse, see "Rapport sur la ferme Améziane" (February 1961) in Vidal-Naquet, *La raison d'état*, 284–85; Einaudi, *La ferme Améziane*; as well as the survivor testimony and personal history of an FLN activist who was detained and tortured at Améziane, a young Algerian woman, Hadjira, presented by Mauss-Copeaux, *Hadjira*. On torture during the war, see Branche, *La torture et l'armée*.

74. Saadi, *Boulevard*, 20.

75. House and MacMaster, *Paris 1961*, 58–59; Einaudi, *La ferme Améziane*, 10.

76. Einaudi, *La ferme Améziane*, 10.

77. House and MacMaster, *Paris 1961*, 58–59. In *Boulevard*, one of A.'s memories transcribed in the *carnet noir* includes an image of Papon and his wife attending one of the lavish parties hosted at the farm; Saadi, *Boulevard*, 41.

78. Saadi, *Boulevard*, 124.

79. Saadi, *Boulevard*, 13–14 (emphasis in original).

80. Saadi, *Boulevard*, 212.

81. Saadi, *Boulevard*, [98] (n.p.).

82. I am echoing Elaine Scarry's claim that torture and pain have language-destroying functions; see Scarry, *Body in Pain*.

83. The SAS was a specialized military unit, not unlike the Bureaux arabes of the nineteenth century, created by the governor-general of Algeria, Jacques Soustelles, and tasked with both administrative functions as well as a "psychological" and "pacifying" mission aimed at establishing contact with Algeria's poor rural population. See Frémeaux, "Les SAS."

84. Saadi, *Boulevard*, 138–43.

85. Saadi, *Boulevard*, 137.

86. Saadi, *Boulevard*, 143.

87. Saadi, "Retour," 59.

88. This is the event that initially pushed Saadi to write a short story in *Méditerranéennes*, "Supplique pour une panne d'électricité dans la cave des suppliciés"; Chaulet-Achour, "'Cette maudite guerre d'Algérie.'"

89. Saadi, *Boulevard*, 26–27.

90. D. Thomas, *Black France*, 125.

91. Saadi, *Boulevard*, 28.

92. Sembène, "La Noire de . . . ," 153.

93. Saadi, *Boulevard*, 20.

94. Saadi, *Boulevard*, 20.

95. Saadi, *Boulevard*, 141; Einaudi, *La ferme Améziane*, 10.

96. To the best of my knowledge, there is no evidence that Monique died by suicide.

97. Einaudi, *La ferme Améziane*, 104.

98. Saadi, *Boulevard*, 14.

99. "What is it you want?," Jacques Soustelle and General Gilles supposedly said to her, "the *bac* or your brother's freedom?" See Einaudi, *La ferme Améziane*, 106. See also Perego, "Veil or a Brother's Life."

100. On unveiling ceremonies in Algeria, see MacMaster, *Burning the Veil*, especially the third chapter, "Unveiling: The 'Revolutionary *Journées*' of 13 May 1958," 114–51, which contextualizes Monique's role in unveiling rituals organized by the French.

101. See the chapter "L'Algérie se dévoile," in Fanon, *Sociologie d'une révolution (L'an V de la révolution algérienne)*, 16–51.

102. The episode is described in Einaudi, *La ferme Améziane*, 100, 105–7. His account is based on interviews with Mouloud and Monique Améziane in 1987.

103. Einaudi, *La ferme Améziane*, 106.

104. *Dépêche de Constantine*, 27 May 1958, 10 (BNF, L 1.15–MFM MICR D-314 [1958/04–1958/06]). The article is cited in Einaudi, *La ferme Améziane*, 112–13.

105. Saadi, *Boulevard*, 173.

106. Saadi, *Boulevard*, 169–72.

107. *Dépêche de Constantine*, 27 May 1958, 3.

108. Saadi, *Boulevard*, 198–99.

109. The story of Esther is especially salient given the history of Jews in Constantine since Jews but not Muslims were granted French citizenship after the Crémieux decree (1870), though this citizenship was revoked between 1940 and 1943 under the Vichy government.

110. Saadi, *Boulevard*, 182–86. For a local history of the black melaya in Constantine, see Kelkel, "La discrète éclipse de la m'laya."

111. The wartime photographer Marc Garanger's portraits "Femmes algériennes (1960)" are a famous example; Garanger, *Femmes algériennes*. On Garanger's photos, see André, *Femmes dévoilées*; K. Silverman, chap. 4, "The Gaze," in *Threshold*.

112. K. Silverman, "The Gaze," in *Threshold*, 147.

113. Saadi, *Boulevard*, 116–17.

114. Saadi, *Boulevard*, 173.

115. Saadi, *Boulevard*, 52.

116. Saadi, *Boulevard*, 52.

117. Saadi, *Boulevard*, 157.

118. These are the words of Fatima's brother Djoudi, reported in Ferroudj, "Fatima Bedar."

119. Ferroudj, "Fatima Bedar."

120. See Braudel, "History and the Social Sciences."

121. Chachoua, "Genre, suicide et sexualité(s)," 305. See also Chachoua, "Le suicide en Algérie."

122. Chachoua, "Genre, suicide et sexualité(s)," 302.

123. Especially the flood of Bab El Oued in 2001 and a devasting earthquake in the Boumerdès region in 2003; see Sider, *Traumatisme psychologique*.

124. Chachoua, "Genre, suicide et sexualité(s)," 302, 308. See also Kacha, "Contribution à l'étude du suicide"; Ammar, "Le suicide"; Chang, Yip, and Chen, "Gender Inequality and Suicide Gender Ratios."

125. Besnard, "Durkheim et les femmes," in *Études Durkheimiennes*, 100.

126. As Chachoua notes, "[It] is paradoxically this femininity that causes suicide presumed rare by common sense, official discourses, statistics"; Chachoua, "Genre, suicide et sexualité(s)," 305.

127. Chachoua, "Genre, suicide et sexualité(s)," 305 (my emphasis).

128. Chachoua, "Le suicide en Algérie," 389.

5. STRANGE BEDFELLOWS

This chapter is significantly revised and expanded from a previous publication, "Dead Narrators, Queer Terrorists: On Suicide Bombing and Literature," *New Literary History* 53, no. 2 (Spring 2022): 285–304, https://doi.org/10.1353/nlh.2022.0013.

Epigraphs: Shakespeare, *Tempest*, 2.2.40–41; Abu-Assad, *Paradise Now*.

1. Rose, *Last Resistance*, 125.

2. Rose, *Last Resistance*, 125.

3. Rose, *Last Resistance*, 125.

4. Best, *None like Us*, 92; Bosman, *New and Accurate Description*, 12.

5. Fanon, "L'Algérie se dévoile," in *Sociologie d'une révolution (L'an V de la révolution algérienne)*, 39.

6. Suicide bombing has become a "regular tool in the toolkit of violent nonstate actors," its use accelerating from 2002/2003 onward, in terms of raw totals and as a percentage of all terrorist attacks; Horwitz, "Rise and Spread," 81.

7. Rose, *Last Resistance*, 126 (my emphasis).

8. Houen, *Terrorism and Modern Literature*, 2 (emphasis in original). On suicide bombing and horror, see Asad, *On Suicide Bombing*, 65; Rose, *Last Resistance*, 127. See also Cavarero, *Horrorism*, especially chapter 15, "Suicidal Horrorism." Horror, Stanley Cavell writes, is "the perception of the precariousness of human identity, [...] the perception that it may be lost or invaded, that we may be, or may become, something other than we are"; Cavell, *Claim of Reason*, 418–19. Talal Asad calls horror an intransitive state that "explodes the imaginary"; Asad, *On Suicide Bombing*, 68.

9. I am drawing on Spivak's phrasing, "Suicide bombing [...] a confrontation between oneself and one-self—the extreme end of autoeroticism, killing oneself as other, in the process killing others"; Spivak, "Terror," 95.

10. Rose gives additional examples from the British political landscape. For instance, Downing Street issued an official apology after Cherie Blair, a barrister and wife of then-prime minister Tony Blair, suggested, "As long as young people feel they have got no hope but to blow themselves up you are never going to make progress"; Rose, *Last Resistance*, 126.

11. Watt, "Lib Dem MP."

12. Cited in Rose, *Last Resistance*, 126 (my emphasis).

13. Spivak, "Terror."

14. Spivak, "Terror," 93 (my emphasis).

15. See Heisbourg, *Hyperterrorisme*.

16. Rose, *Last Resistance*, 129.

17. Cavarero, *Horrorism*, 2–3.

18. Spivak, "Terror," 91.

19. For Bokhari, the female suicide bomber "commit[s] a double atrocity: using violence, and in the process destroying our safe, innocent and traditional view of women"; Bokhari, "Women and Terrorism," 52. Bokhari also suggests that the increasing involvement of women in terrorist organizations offers a strategic tactical as well as communicative advantage: "Symbolically female participation in terrorism sends a powerful message, blurring the distinction between perpetrator and victim"; Bokhari, "Women and Terrorism," 56. On the "horrorism" of female suicide bombers, see Cavarero, *Horrorism*, especially chapter 6, "The Crime of Medea," and chapters 15 and 16, "Suicidal Horrorism" and "When the Bomb Is a Woman's Body." See also Narozhna and Knight, *Female Suicide Bombings*; Bloom, *Bombshell*; Bloom, *Dying to Kill*; Fullmer, Mizrahi, and Tomsich, "Lethality of Female Suicide Bombers"; Alakoc, "Femme fatale"; Warner and Matfass, *Exploding Stereotypes*; Skaine, *Female Suicide Bombers*; Pearson, "Wilayat Shahidat."

20. See Bloom, "Female Suicide Bombers." The Sri Lanka Tamil Tigers and Chechen Black Widows are the best-known examples of terrorist organizations recruiting women as active guerrilla fighters. In recent years, the jihadist organization Boko Haram active in Nigeria, Chad, and Cameroon—known as Jama'ât Ahl as-Sunnah lid-Da'wah wa'l-Jihâd—has made prolific use of female suicide bombers. See Pearson, "Wilayat Shahidat."

21. Behind claims about non-Western "cultures of death" that do not respond to reason, glorify suicidal ideation, and defy comprehension lurks an Orientalist "subtext of racist dehumanization." Rose, *Last Resistance*, 129. Shortly after 9/11, US senator John Warner declared that suicide bombers "are not rational and are not deterred by rational concepts"; Atran, "Genesis of Suicide Terrorism," 1535. See also Atran, "Psychology of Transnational Terrorism." On "hyperbole" and suicide bombing, see Houen, *Terrorism and Modern Literature*.

22. Puar, *Terrorist Assemblages*, 38.

23. Puar, *Terrorist Assemblages*, 38 (emphasis in original).

24. Puar, *Terrorist Assemblages*, 37 (my emphasis).

25. Puar, *Terrorist Assemblages*, 41.

26. After 9/11, homophobic caricatures of Osama bin Laden being anally penetrated by the Empire State Building spread across midtown Manhattan with the caption "The Empire Strikes Back . . . So you like skyscrapers, huh, bitch?" Puar, *Terrorist Assemblages*, 37, 43.

27. This follows from Spivak's remarks that "terror" and its imperceptible slide into "terrorism" as social movement are alibis for the "legitimate" violence of war. Spivak, "Terror," 91.

28. Asad, *On Suicide Bombing*, 30.

29. Asad, *On Suicide Bombing*, 30.

30. Asad, *On Suicide Bombing*, 30–31. The link between suicide terrorism and religion, specifically Islam, has itself been shown to be largely illusory. Pape writes that "there is little connection between suicide and Islamic fundamentalism, or any religion for that matter" and that "what nearly all suicide terrorists have in common is a specific secular and strategic goal: to compel modern democracies to withdraw military forces from territory that the terrorists consider to be their homeland"; Pape, *Dying to Win*, 16. Asad makes a similar point, writing that suicide attacks are a means "to signal to the citizens of liberal democracies that they face an intolerable cost" if their armies do not withdraw; Asad, *On Suicide Bombing*, 54.

31. Rose, *Last Resistance*, 129.

32. Rose, *Last Resistance*, 129 (my emphasis).

33. Rose, *Last Resistance*, 135.

34. Rose, *Last Resistance*, 131. See also Reuter, *My Life Is a Weapon*; Victor, *Army of Roses*.

35. Best, *None like Us*, 92.

36. Asad, *On Suicide Bombing*, 3. Houen argues that "the figurative, if not the fictional" is always already at stake in terrorist attacks because figurative language is necessary to "express the inexpressible" and because the unity of "terrorism" itself is rhetorical, produced through a collusion and transference of figurative discursive practices and material events; Houen, *Terrorism and Modern Literature*, 4–5.

37. Pape, *Dying to Win*.

38. S. Thomas, "Outtakes and Outrage," 426.

39. Mustapha Hamil speaks of a "general 'terrorist genre'"; Hamil, "Plotting Terrorism," 550. Important examples of "terrorist fiction" from North Africa also exist in Arabic and in English. Examples in Arabic include Bashīr Muftī's novel concerning the Black Decade, *Ashbāḥ al-Madīnah al-Maqtūlah* (*The Ghosts of the Murdered City*, 2012), which sees its protagonist carry out a suicide mission, and, in English, Moroccan American writer Laila Lalami's *Secret Son* (2009), which takes place in the Casablanca slums.

40. Spivak, "Terror," 94.

41. Binebine, *Les étoiles*. Binebine's novel was originally published as a Moroccan imprint, at the Éditions Le Fennec in Casablanca. The novel is available in Arabic as *Nujum sidi Mumin* (Nashr al-Fanak, 2012), in English as *Horses of God* (Granta, 2013), and several other languages.

42. Weinmann, *"Je suis mort"*; Bennett, "Unquiet Spirits."

43. Alber, "Unnatural Narrative," 887.

44. Zaganiaris, "La question Queer," 147.

45. Binebine's novel is not mentioned in Gibson Ncube's *La sexualité queer au Maghreb à travers la littérature* (2018) or in William J. Spurlin's article "Contested Borders: Cultural Translation and Queer Politics in Contemporary Francophone Writing from the Maghreb." This is part of a broader disciplinary oversight, namely the persistent exclusion of Maghrebi literature from queer African studies, and African studies more broadly, in anthologies such as the *Queer African Reader* (2013), *Queer Africa 1* (2013), and *Queer Africa 2* (2017). See Ncube, "Renegotiating the Marginality of the Maghreb."

46. Lanser, "Queering Narrative Voice," 924.

47. Lanser, "Queering Narrative Voice," 926.

48. Nussbaum, *Not for Profit*, 95–96. For Nussbaum, the ability to imagine ourselves in the other's shoes "inspires distrust of conventional pieties and exacts a frequently painful confrontation with one's own thoughts and intentions"; Nussbaum, *Poetic Justice*, 6.

49. Boehmer and Morton, *Terror and the Postcolonial*.

50. Mahajan, *Association of Small Bombs*.

51. On the Algerian novel and *littérature de l'urgence*, see Leperlier, *Algérie, les écrivains de la décennie noire*; Leperlier, "Une littérature en état d'urgence?"; Khodja, "Écritures d'urgence de femmes algériennes." Examples include Rachid Boudjedra's *FIS de la haine* (1992), Yasmina Khadra's *Les agneaux du seigneur* (1998), Tahar Djaout's *Le dernier été de la raison* (1999), Boualem Sansal's *Le serment des barbares* (1999); Mohamed Sari's *Le labyrinthe* (2001), Salima Ghezali's *Les amants de Shahrazade* (2001), Arezki Mellal's *Maintenant ils peuvent venir* (2001), and Slimane Aït Sidhoum's *Les trois doigts de la main* (2002). Also noteworthy is Y. B.'s Algerian triptych *Comme il a dit lui* (1998), *L'Explication* (1999), *Zéro mort* (2001), as well as his later novels *Allah Superstar* (2003) and *Commissaire Krim* (2008). Saïd Oussad's *Les chemins inutiles* (2014) is a "belated" addition to terrorist literature related to the *décennie noire*, based on the author's role as a journalist during this period and in particular his interview of the head of a terrorist organization.

52. See Browning, "Frames of the Algerian War." See also M. Sharpe, *Late-Colonial French Cinema*.

53. Sansal, *Le village*; Khadra, *Les hirondelles*; Khadra, *Les sirènes*; Khadra, *L'attentat*. Khadra's *L'attentat* (Julliard, 2005), translated into English as *The Attack* (Doubleday, 2005), is perhaps the best-known example of terrorist fiction in French and remains a touchstone for critical reflection on the genre.

54. See Versluys, *Out of the Blue*. See also Keeble, *9/11 Novel*; Bāchī, *Moi, Khaled Kelkal*.

55. Julien, "Extroverted African Novel, Revisited," 374. See also Julien, "Extroverted African Novel." For rebuttals to and discussions of Julien, see Brouillette, *Postcolonial Writers*; Suhr-Sytsma, "Extroverted African Novel and Literary Publishing."

56. As one commentator notes, the 2003 attacks were "a brutal awakening." Senoussi, "La démocratie," 1.

57. Binebine, Galesne, and Scoppa, "Entretien."

58. The targets were all Western or Jewish-owned establishments: Café de Espana, the site of the deadliest bombing, where twenty people were killed; Hôtel Farah (also known as Hôtel Safir), where a security guard and porter were stabbed to death and one of the bombers arrested after he unsuccessfully tried to detonate his explosives; the Belgian consulate, where two police officers were killed, thought to be collateral damage of an attack at the Jewish-owned Italian restaurant the Positano; a Jewish cemetery, which was undamaged since one of the bombers mistook a different fountain for the one outside the cemetery and exploded, killing himself and three other people; the Cercle de l'Alliance Israélite, which was empty at the time of the blast but on the following day would have been filled with people. For a detailed report, see "Analysis: May 16, 2003."

59. Ezzakhraiy, "Horreur sur la place de Verdun" (BNF), 5.

60. In the days following the attacks, a number of newspapers announced special issues around the bombings: *Libération* published a special Sunday issue titled "Terrorisme: Les preuves de sang" (18 May 2003); *Al Bayane* likewise published a Sunday special with the

running head "Les terroristes frappent au cœur de Casablanca," and photos of the damage under the rubric "L'horreur terroriste par l'image"; *La Vie Éco* also published an eight-page special issue, "Tous contre le terrorisme." These are reviewed briefly in the section "Média-Express," 2.

61. See Weaver, "Short, Violent Life of Abu Musab al-Zarqawi."

62. For an analysis of the literary bidonville, including in Binebine's novel, see Pieprzak, "Zones of Perceptual Enclosure."

63. Binebine, Galesne, and Scoppa, "Entretien."

64. In a memo dated June 1939, the Contrôleur civil M. Girardière writes that "the constitution of the *bidonvilles* is a consequence of our establishment in Morocco. It has no specifically Moroccan characteristic but for the very nature of the *bidonvilles*, that is to say their mode of creation and structure" (ADM, E3195 44N).

65. See Huchzermeyer, *Cities with "Slums."*

66. Though the VSB program largely has been "successful"—in 2018, the ministry declared fifty-eight of Morocco's eighty-five cities "slum-free"—as Mona Atia documents, attempts at resettlement or rehousing have met with ongoing resistance from the inhabitants of these urban spaces, in the form of protest and "tactics of refusal." The efficacy of VSB as a counterterrorist initiative, too, has been called into question, since bombings have continued to plague Morocco: in April 2011, for instance, Abdel al-Othamni walked into a busy café in Marrakech disguised as a guitar-carrying "hippie" and planted two bombs that killed seventeen people. Atia, "Refusing a 'City without Slums.'"

67. New antiterrorist legislation introduced in the wake of the 2003 bombings has curbed publishing rights, extended incommunicado detention, and reduced the requirements for applying for the death penalty. Between 2003 and 2017, at least three thousand individuals were arrested and sentenced. In its 2010 annual report, the Human Rights Watch cited the detention of suspected terrorists as one of the reasons human rights conditions had deteriorated in Morocco in 2009. In 2005, King Mohammed VI announced the National Initiative for Human Development, which like the VSB program, focused on poverty and social inequality as factors contributing to radicalization. See Alami, "Morocco's Misguided War on Terror"; Maghraoui, "Morocco's Reforms after the Casablanca Bombings"; Masbah, "Limits of Morocco's Attempt"; Human Rights Watch, "Morocco/Western Sahara: Events of 2009."

68. See Houdzi, "Le roman contre la barbarie."

69. Literary examples include Mohamed Leftah's collection of short stories, *Un martyr de notre temps* (2007), and the novel *Le jour de Vénus* (2008); Mohamed Nedali's *La maison de Cicine* (2011); Youssouf Amine Elalamy's polyvocal novel *Oussama mon amour* (2011); Rachid Khaless's *Quand Adam a décidé de vivre* (2014); Mohammed Loakira's *La nuit des disgraciés* (2015); and Mounir Serhani's *Il n'y a pas de barbe lisse* (2016). Several films also grapple with religious fundamentalism and the figure of the suicide bomber, including Aziz Saâdallah's *Le temps du terrorisme* (2011), Mohcine Besri's *Les mécréants* (2011), and Nabil Ayouch's adaptation of Binebine's novel, *Les chevaux de dieu* (2012).

70. See Oktapoda, "Le 16 mai."

71. See the foundation's website: Fondation Ali Zaoua, http://fondationalizaoua.org/wp/acceuil/.

72. Binebine, Galesne, and Scoppa, "Entretien."

73. The original citation reads: "En fait, j'écrivais un livre qui me faisait peur, *car si je comprenais ces gamins, comment le dire* dans un récit moi qui combats le terrorisme de toutes mes forces?"; Binebine, Galesne, and Scoppa, "Entretien" (my emphasis).

74. Binebine, Galesne, and Scoppa, "Entretien."

75. De Man, "Autobiography as De-facement."

76. Binebine, *Les étoiles*, 10. Hereafter, citations for the novel are given parenthetically in the text.

77. Bennett, "Unquiet Spirits," 463.

78. On Bāchī's novel, see Terhmina, "Topographie de la terreur." On Muftī's novel and literature produced during and about the Black Decade, see Hamdi, "Writing Violence."

79. Barthes, *Œuvres complètes*, 4:435–36; Derrida, *La voix et le phénomène*, 108.

80. Bennett, "Unquiet Spirits," 476.

81. Blessington, "Politics," 117.

82. Bennett writes, "The voices of the dead de-sacralise closure and its revelations by adding supplementary time beyond the end and refusing to keep silent about what could fall outside any given plot"; Bennett, "Unquiet Spirits," 471.

83. On marginal sexualities in Morocco and the Maghreb, see Kendili, Berrada, and Kadiri, "Homosexuality in Morocco"; Hayes, *Queer Nations*. See also Zaganiaris, "La question Queer."

84. For instance, the opening image of the novel is that of the boys launching bowls of urine onto unsuspecting passerby through slits in the wall surrounding the bidonville.

85. Sedgwick, *Between Men*.

86. Tiger, "Rogue Males." See also R. Morgan, *Demon Lover*.

87. J. Ratier, "Étude sociologique des bidonvilles des carrières centrales de Casablanca" (ADM, E3195 1700N), 36.

88. René Girard's notion of the triangulation of (mimetic) desire is at the heart of Sedgwick's analysis. See Girard, *Mensonge romantique*, especially the first chapter, "Le désir 'triangulaire,'" 11–57.

89. Ratier, "Étude sociologique" (ADM), 6.

90. Hamil, "Plotting Terrorism," 558.

91. After 9/11, an American army missile (a GBU-31 JDAM), the so-called fag bomb aboard the USS *Enterprise*, was defaced with a graffitied message to its Afghan targets that read, "HIGH JACK [*sic*] THIS FAGS." A photograph of the missile was published by the Associated Press, then swiftly withdrawn. See Stuever, "The Bomb with a Loaded Message."

92. See Holden, "Learning to Empathize."

93. Binebine's "constellation" of six friends—a six-pointed star—is perhaps a nod to the fact that many of the targets and victims of the Casablanca bombings were Moroccan Jews, or otherwise a deeply ambivalent allusion to the boys' eventual status among radicals as luminaries, heroic martyrs whose explosive final acts would make Sidi Moumen synonymous with a terrorist threat.

94. Binebine, Galesne, and Scoppa, "Entretien."

95. Binebine, Galesne, and Scoppa, "Entretien."

96. Essomba, *Le paradis du nord*. Another noteworthy example of the literature on irregular migration is Youssouf Amine Elalamy's *Les clandestins* (2011).

97. Binebine, *Cannibales*, 87. Hereafter, citations for the novel are given parenthetically in the text.

98. Felwine Sarr, *Afrotopia*, 65n4.

99. Sharif, "Morocco's 'Culture of Death.'"

100. Al-Bakhsh, cited in Sharif, "Morocco's 'Culture of Death'" (my emphasis).

CONCLUSION

Epigraph: Vergès, "Museum without Objects," 32.

1. I am inspired by Michelle Caswell's discussion of the disconnect between archival studies (as a subfield of library and information studies) and humanistic inquiry into "the archive." Caswell, "'Archive.'"

2. Cvetkovich, *Archive of Feelings*, 268; cited in Caswell, "'Archive'" (my emphasis).

3. Gathara, "Path."

4. Gathara, "Path."

5. Sarr and Savoy, *Rapport*. See also Sarr and Savoy, *Restituer*.

6. Sarr and Savoy, *Rapport*, 36–37 (my emphasis).

7. Vergès, "Museum without Objects," 32.

BIBLIOGRAPHY

ABBREVIATIONS

ADAM	Archives départementales des Alpes-Maritimes, Nice, France
ADG	Archives départementales de la Guadeloupe, Gourbeyre, Guadeloupe
ADLA	Archives départementales de Loire-Atlantique, Nantes, France
ADM	Archives du Maroc, Rabat, Morocco
ADN	Archives de Nantes, Nantes, France
ADSSD	Archives départementales de la Seine-Saint-Denis, Bobigny, France
AFDF	Archives françaises du film du CNC, Bois d'Arcy, France
AMA	Archives municipales d'Antibes Juan-les-Pins, Antibes, France
ANOM	Archives nationales d'outre-mer, Aix-en-Provence, France
ANS	Archives nationales du Sénégal, Dakar, Senegal
ATM	Archives territoriales de Martinique, Fort-de-France, Martinique
ATNDS	Archives du Théâtre national Daniel-Sorano, Dakar, Senegal
AUCAD	Archives de l'Université Cheikh Anta Diop, Dakar, Senegal
BFCA	Black Film Center Archives, Indiana University, Bloomington, IN, USA
BNF	Bibliothèque nationale de France, Paris, France
BRBML	Beinecke Rare Book and Manuscript Library, Yale University, New Haven, CT, USA

WORKS CITED

Abderrezak, Hakim. "Harragas in Mediterranean *Illiterature* and Cinema." In *Reimagining North African Immigration: Identities in Flux in French Literature, Television and Film*, edited by Véronique Machelidon and Patrick Saveau, 232–53. Manchester: Manchester University Press, 2018.

Abderrezak, Hakim. "The Mediterranean *Seametery* and *Cementery* in Leïla Kilani's and Tariq Teguia's Filmic Works." In *Critically Mediterranean: Temporalities, Aesthetics, and Deployments of a Sea in Crisis*, edited by Edwige Tamalet Talbayev and yasser elhariry, 147–61. Cham, Switzerland: Palgrave Macmillan, 2018.

Abderrezak, Hakim. "The Mediterranean Spring, Sieve and Seametery." In *Refugee Imaginaries: Research across the Humanities*, edited by Emma Cox, Sam Durrant, David Farrier, Lyndsey Stonebridge, and Agnes Wooley, 372–91. Edinburgh: Edinburgh University Press, 2019.

Abouzeid, Rania. "Bouazizi: The Man Who Set Himself and Tunisia on Fire." *Time*, 21 January 2011.

Abu-Assad, Hany, dir. *Paradise Now*. Warner Independent Pictures, 2005.

Achour-Bouakkaz, Meriem, dir. *Nar*. Afkar Films, 2019.

Adélaïde-Merlande, Jacques. *Delgrès, ou, La Guadeloupe en 1802*. Paris: Éditions Karthala, 1986.

Adimi, Kaouther. *Des ballerines de Papicha: Roman*. Algiers: Éditions Barzakh, 2010.

Ahed, Mohamed. "La nuit de tous les maux." *Le Matin du Sahara*, 17 May 2003. https://lematin.ma/journal/2003/La-nuit-de-tous-les-maux/29182.html.

Aimard, Gustave. *Le chasseur de rats: Le commandant Delgrès*. Paris: E. Dentu, 1876.

Alakoc, Burcu Pinar. "Femme fatale: The Lethality of Female Suicide Bombers." *Studies in Conflict and Terrorism* 43, no. 9 (2020): 796–814.

Alami, Aida. "Morocco's Misguided War on Terror." *Foreign Policy*, 9 April 2010. https://foreignpolicy.com/2010/04/09/moroccos-misguided-war-on-terror-2/.

Alber, Jan. "Unnatural Narrative." In *Handbook of Narratology*, edited by Peter Hühn, Jan Christoph Meister, John Pier, and Wolf Schmid, 887–95. Berlin: De Gruyter, 2014.

Alloula, Malek. *The Colonial Harem*. Translated by Myrna Godzich and Wlad Godzich. Minneapolis: University of Minnesota Press, 1986.

Alvarez, Alfred. *The Savage God: A Study of Suicide*. New York: Random House, 1972.

Ammar, Sleïm. "Le suicide, problème de santé publique." *La Tunisie médicale*, no. 2 (March–April 1972): 3–24.

"'Ancerville' atteint 25 nœuds aux essais." *Le Monde*, 15 August 1962.

André, Marc. *Femmes dévoilées: Des Algériennes en France à l'heure de la décolonisation*. Lyon: ENS Éditions, 2016.

Annuaire général de l'Indo-Chine. Hanoi-Haiphong: Imprimerie d'extrême-orient, 1921.

"Anti-Racism Protesters in Martinique Tear Down Statue of Napoleon's Wife." RFI, 27 July 2020. https://www.rfi.fr/en/france/20200727-france-colonial-era-statues-torn-down-french-island-martinique-empress-josephine-beauharnais-racism-slavery.

Apap, Anabel. *Écrire par devoir de mémoire: La tragédie du Rwanda vue par le collectif "Écrire par devoir de mémoire."* Caen: Passage(s), 2019.

Aranke, Sampada. *Death's Futurity: The Visual Life of Black Power*. Durham, NC: Duke University Press, 2023.

Asad, Talal. *On Suicide Bombing*. New York: Columbia University Press, 2007.

Atia, Mona. "Refusing a 'City without Slums': Moroccan Slum Dwellers' Nonmovements and the Art of Presence." *Cities* 125 (June 2022). https://doi.org/10.1016/j.cities.2019.02.014.

Atran, Scott. "Genesis of Suicide Terrorism." *Science* 299 (2003): 1534–39.

Atran, Scott. "Psychology of Transnational Terrorism and Extreme Political Conflict." *Annual Review of Psychology* 72 (2021): 471–501.

Ayouch, Nabil, dir. *Les chevaux de Dieu / The Horses of God*. Les Films du Nouveau Monde, 2012.
Azan, H. "Notice sur le Oualo." *Revue maritime et coloniale* 9 (1863): 395–422, 607–55.
Azan, H. "Notice sur le Oualo." *Revue maritime et coloniale* 10 (1864): 327–60, 466–98.
Azim, Firdous. *The Colonial Rise of the Novel*. London: Routledge, 1993.
Azoulay, Ariella. *The Civil Contract of Photography*. New York: Zone Books, 2012.
Azoulay, Ariella. "Photography: The Ontological Question." *Mafte'akh* 2 (Summer 2011): 65–80.
Azoulay, Ariella. "Potential History: Thinking through Violence." *Critical Inquiry* 39, no. 3 (Spring 2013): 548–74.
Azoulay, Ariella Aïsha. *Potential History: Unlearning Imperialism*. London: Verso Books, 2019.
Bâ, Thierno. *Lat-Dior, le chemin de l'honneur: Drame historique en huit tableaux*. Dakar: Nouvelles Éditions Africaines, 1987.
Bāchī, Salīm. *Moi, Khaled Kelkal: Roman*. Paris: Grasset, 2012.
Bāchī, Salīm. *Tuez-les tous: Roman*. Paris: Gallimard, 2006.
Bakhtin, Mikhail M. *The Dialogic Imagination: Four Essays*. Edited by Michael Holquist, translated by Caryl Emerson and Michael Holquist. Austin: University of Texas Press, 1981.
Bancel, Nicolas, Pascal Blanchard, Gilles Boëtsch, Éric Deroo, and Sandrine Lemaire, eds. *Zoos humains: Au temps des exhibitions humaines*. Paris: La Découverte, 2004.
Bangou, Henri. *La Révolution et l'esclavage à la Guadeloupe, 1789–1802*. Paris: Messidor / Éditions Sociales, 1989.
Banier, Antoine. *Histoire des religions et des mœurs de tous les peuples du monde*. Vol. 1, *"Peuples idolâtres."* Paris: A. Belin, 1816.
Bargu, Banu. *Starve and Immolate: The Politics of Human Weapons*. New York: Columbia University Press, 2014.
Barillaud, Marie-Christine, Jacqueline Bièque, and Patrick Dahlet. "Le fait divers: Une didactique de l'incensé." *Français dans le monde*, no. 194 (July–August 1985): 76–88.
Barret, Paul. *L'Afrique occidentale: La nature et l'homme noir*. Vol. 1. Paris: Challamel, 1888.
Barry, Boubacar. *La Sénégambie du XVe au XIXe siècle: Traite négrière, Islam et conquête coloniale*. Paris: L'Harmattan, 1988.
Barry, Boubacar. *Le royaume du Waalo: Le Sénégal avant la conquête*. Paris: Maspero, 1972.
Barry, Boubacar. *Senegambia and the Atlantic Slave Trade*. Cambridge: Cambridge University Press, 1998.
Barry, Boubacar. *Sénégambie: Plaidoyer pour une histoire régionale*. Amsterdam: SEPHIS; Rio de Janeiro: CEAA, 2001.
Barthes, Roland. *Camera Lucida: Reflections on Photography*. Translated by Richard Howard. New York: Hill and Wang, 1981.
Barthes, Roland. *Œuvres complètes*. Vol. 4. Paris: Éditions du Seuil, 2002.
Barthes, Roland. "Structure du fait divers." In *Essais critiques*, 188–97. Paris: Éditions du Seuil, 1964.

Baucom, Ian. "Specters of the Atlantic." *South Atlantic Quarterly* 100, no. 1 (Winter 2001): 61–82.

Baucom, Ian. *Specters of the Atlantic: Finance Capital, Slavery, and the Philosophy of History*. Durham, NC: Duke University Press, 2005.

Baudelaire, Charles. *Œuvres complètes*. Edited by Claude Pichois. Paris: Gallimard, 1975–76.

Baudens, Lucien. "Journal d'un médecin de l'expédition de Constantine, dernière partie." *Revue de Paris (Bruxelles)* 4 (April 1838): 33–124.

Beenash, Jafri. "Reframing Suicide: Queer Diasporic and Indigenous Imaginaries." *GLQ* 27, no. 4 (2021): 577–601.

Bell, Richard. "Slave Suicide, Abolition and the Problem of Resistance." *Slavery and Abolition* 33, no. 4 (2012): 525–49.

Ben Jelloun, Tahar. *Par le feu*. Paris: Gallimard, 2011.

Ben Khelil, Mehdi, Amine Zgarni, Mounir Ben Mohamed, Mohamed Allouche, Anis Benzarti, Ahmed Banasr, and Moncef Hamdoun. "A Comparison of Suicidal Behavior by Burns Five Years before and Five Years after the 2011 Tunisian Revolution." *Burns* 43, no. 4 (2017): 858–65.

Bencheikh-El-Fegoun, Bahïa, dir. *Fragments de rêves*. Allers Retours Films, 2017.

Benkhaled, Walid, and Natalya Vince. "Afterword: Performing Algerianness: The National and Transnational Construction of Algeria's 'Culture Wars.'" In *Algeria: Nation, Culture and Transnationalism: 1988–2015*, edited by Patrick Crowley, 243–69. Liverpool: Liverpool University Press, 2017.

Benmiloud, Yassir. *Allah superstar: Roman*. Paris: Grasset, 2003.

Benmiloud, Yassir. *Comme il a dit lui*. Paris: J. C. Lattès, 1998.

Benmiloud, Yassir. *Commissaire Krim: Roman*. Paris: Grasset, 2008.

Benmiloud, Yassir. *L'explication*. Paris: J. C. Lattès, 1999.

Benmiloud, Yassir. *Zéro mort: Dernier volet du Triptyque algérois*. Paris: J. C. Lattès, 2001.

Bennabi, Malek. *Mémoires d'un témoin du siècle: L'enfant, l'étudiant, l'écrivain, les carnets*. Edited by Noureddine Boukrouh. Algiers: Samar, 2006.

Bennett, Alice. "Unquiet Spirits: Death Writing in Contemporary Fiction." *Textual Practice* 23, no. 3 (2009): 463–79.

Bénot, Yves, and Marcel Dorigny, eds. *Rétablissement de l'esclavage dans les colonies françaises 1802: Ruptures et continuités de la politique coloniale française (1800–1830)*. Paris: Maisonneuve et Larose, 2003.

Bertoncello, Brigitte, and Sylvie Brédeloup. "À la recherche du docker noir." In *Dockers de la méditerranée à la mer du nord: Des quais et des hommes dans l'histoire*, edited by Jean Domenichino, Jean-Marie Guillon, and Robert Mencherini, 139–51. Aix-en-Provence: Edisud, 1999.

Bertoncello, Brigitte, and Sylvie Brédeloup. "Le Marseille des marins africains." *Revue Européenne des Migrations Internationales* 15, no. 3 (1999): 177–97.

Besnard, Philippe. *Études Durkheimiennes*. Geneva: Droz, 2003.

Besri, Mohcine, dir. *Les mécréants*. Akka Films, 2011.

Best, Stephen. *None like Us: Blackness, Belonging, Aesthetic Life*. Durham, NC: Duke University Press, 2018.

Bèye, Alioune Badara. *Nder en flammes: Théâtre*. Dakar: Nouvelles Éditions Africaines, 1990.

Bèye, Alioune Badara. *Nder en flammes: Tragédie historique en 14 tableaux*. Paris: Radio-France Internationale, 1988.

Bhêly-Quénum, Olympe. *Un piège sans fin*. Paris: Librairie Stock, 1960.

Bigon, Liora. *French Colonial Dakar: The Morphogenesis of an African Regional Capital*. Manchester: Manchester University Press, 2016.

Binebine, Mahi. *Cannibales: Roman*. Paris: Fayard, 1999.

Binebine, Mahi. *Les étoiles de Sidi Moumen: Roman*. Paris: Flammarion, 2010.

Binebine, Mahi. *Horses of God: A Novel*. Translated by Lulu Norman. London: Granta, 2013.

Binebine, Mahi. *Nujūm sīdī Mūmin*. Translated by Muḥammad al-Mazdīwī. Al-Dār al-Bayḍā': Nashr al-Fanak, 2012.

Binebine, Mahi, Nathalie Galesne, and Cristiana Scoppa. "Entretien: Les étoiles de Sidi Moumen et les Chevaux de Dieu." *Mahi Binebine*, n.d. https://www.mahibinebine.com/single-post/2017/08/28/les-c3-a9toiles-de-sidi-moumen-et-les-chevaux-de-dieu-entretien.

Blair, Dorothy S. *African Literature in French: A History of Creative Writing in French from West and Equatorial Africa*. Cambridge: Cambridge University Press, 1976.

Blair, Dorothy S. *Senegalese Literature: A Critical History*. Boston: Twayne, 1984.

Blaise, Lilia. "Self-Immolation, Catalyst of the Arab Spring, Is Now a Grim Trend." *New York Times*, 9 July 2017.

Blanchard, Pascal, Nicolas Bancel, Gilles Boetsch, Dominic Thomas, and Christelle Taraud, eds. *Sexe, race et colonies: La domination des corps du XVe siècle à nos jours*. Paris: La Découverte, 2018.

Blessington, Francis. "Politics and the Terrorist Novel." *Sewanee Review* 116, no. 1 (Winter 2008): 116–24.

Bloom, Mia. *Bombshell: Women and Terrorism*. Philadelphia: University of Pennsylvania Press, 2011.

Bloom, Mia. *Dying to Kill: The Allure of Suicide Terror*. New York: Columbia University Press, 2007.

Bloom, Mia. "Female Suicide Bombers: A Global Trend." *Daedalus* 136, no. 1 (Winter 2007): 94–102.

Boehmer, Elleke, and Stephen Morton, eds. *Terror and the Postcolonial*. Malden, MA: Wiley-Blackwell, 2010.

Bokhari, Laila. "Women and Terrorism—Passive or Active Actors? Motivations and Strategic Use." In *Suicide as a Weapon, Proceedings of NATO Advanced Research Workshop on Motivation for Suicide Bombers (2007: Ankara, Turkey)*, edited by Centre of Excellence for Defence against Terrorism, 51–63. Washington, DC: IOS Press, 2007.

Bongie, Chris. *Islands and Exiles: The Creole Identities of Post/Colonial Literature*. Stanford, CA: Stanford University Press, 1998.

Bongie, Chris. "The (Un)Exploded Volcano: Creolization and Intertextuality in the Novels of Daniel Maximin." *Callaloo* 17, no. 2 (1994): 627–42.

Bordas, David Bravo. "Memorial to the Abolition of Slavery." *Public Space*, 5 February 2018. https://www.publicspace.org/works/-/project/g290-memorial-de-l-abolition-de-l-esclavage.
Borlandi, Massimo, and Mohamed Chakaoui, eds. *Le suicide: Un siècle après Durkheim*. Paris: PUF, 2000.
Bosman, Willem. *A New and Accurate Description of the Coast of Guinea*. London: J. Knapton, 1705.
Boudana, Sandrine. "The Unbearable Lightness of the *Fait Divers*: Investigating the Boundaries of a Journalistic Genre." *Critical Studies in Media Communication* 29, no. 3 (2012): 202–19.
Boudjedra, Rachid. *FIS de la haine*. Paris: Éditions Denoël, 1992.
Boudjedra, Rachid. *L'insolation*. Paris: Éditions Denoël, 1972.
Boudry, Robert. *Jean-Joseph Rabéarivelo et la mort*. Paris: Présence Africaine, 1958.
Boulègue, Jean. "À la naissance de l'histoire écrite sénégalaise: Yoro Dyao et ses modèles (deuxième moitié du XIXème siècle, début du XXème siécle)." *History in Africa* 15 (1988): 395–405.
Bourdieu, Pierre. *On Television*. New York: New Press, 1998.
Bourdieu, Pierre. *Sur la télévision, suivi de L'emprise du journalisme*. Paris: Liber—Raisons d'agir, 1996.
Branagan, Thomas. *The Penitential Tyrant; or, Slave Trader Reformed: A Pathetic Poem, in Four Cantos*. New York: Samuel Wood, 1807.
Branche, Raphaëlle. *La torture et l'armée pendant la guerre d'Algérie: 1954–1962*. Paris: Gallimard, 2001.
Brathwaite, Kamau. "Jou'vert." In *Islands*, 113. Oxford: Oxford University Press, 1969.
Braudel, Fernand. "History and the Social Sciences: The *Longue Durée*." Translated by Immanuel Wallerstein. *Review* 32, no. 2 (2009): 171–203.
Bray, Patrick M. *The Novel Map: Space and Subjectivity in Nineteenth-Century French Fiction*. Evanston, IL: Northwestern University Press, 2013.
Brigaud, Félix. "Le royaume du Waalo." In *Études sénégalaises*, f. 9, 61–82. Saint-Louis: CRDS, 1962.
Brisebarre, Anne-Marie. "L'évolution de la pratique du sacrifice de l'aïd el-kebir en contexte urbain français." *Ethnologie française* 168, no. 4 (2017): 607–22.
Brooks, George. "Peanuts and Colonialism: Consequences of the Commercialization of Peanuts in West Africa, 1830–1870." *Journal of African History* 16, no. 1 (January 1975): 29–54.
Brouillette, Sarah. *Postcolonial Writers in the Global Literary Marketplace*. London: Palgrave Macmillan, 2007.
Brower, Benjamin Claude. *A Desert Named Peace: The Violence of France's Empire in the Algerian Sahara, 1844–1902*. New York: Columbia University Press, 2009.
Brown, Ron. *The Art of Suicide*. London: Reaktion Books, 2001.
Browning, Cory. "Frames of the Algerian War: Pontecorvo's *La Bataille d'Alger* and the 'War on Terror.'" *Contemporary French and Francophone Studies* 23, no. 3 (2019): 316–23.
Brozgal, Lia. *Absent the Archive: Cultural Traces of a Massacre in Paris, 17 October 1961*. Liverpool: Liverpool University Press, 2020.

Brozgal, Lia. "In the Absence of the Archive (Paris, October 17, 1961)." *South Central Review* 31, no. 1 (Spring 2014): 34–54.

Burger, Hermann. *Tractatus Logico-Suicidalis: On Killing Oneself.* Translated by Adrian Nathan West. Cambridge, MA: Wakefield Press, 2022.

Busch, Annett, and Max Annas, eds. *Ousmane Sembène: Interviews.* Jackson: University of Mississippi Press, 2008.

Calhoun, Doyle. "Dead Narrators, Queer Terrorists: On Suicide Bombing and Literature." *New Literary History* 53, no. 2 (Spring 2022): 285–304.

Calhoun, Doyle. "A Fugue for the Middle Passage? Suicidal Resistance Takes Flight in Fabienne Kanor's *Humus* (2006)." *French Review* 95, no. 2 (December 2021): 111–28.

Calhoun, Doyle. "(Im)Possible Inscriptions: Silence, Servitude, and Suicide in Ousmane Sembène's *La Noire de . . .*" *Research in African Literatures* 51, no. 2 (Summer 2020): 96–116.

Calhoun, Doyle. "Looking for Diouana Gomis (1927–1958): The Story behind African Cinema's Most Iconic Suicide." *Research in African Literatures* 52, no. 2 (Summer 2021): 1–28.

Calhoun, Doyle. "Ousmane Sembène's *Black Girl* Is a Ghost Story." *Public Books*, 4 November 2021. https://www.publicbooks.org/sembenes-black-girl-is-a-ghost-story/.

Calhoun, Doyle. "Putting French Literary History on Trial." *Public Books*, 6 April 2022. https://www.publicbooks.org/mohamed-mbougar-sarr-yambo-ouologuem-prix-goncourt/.

Camille Sabatié, Alexandre. *Le Sénégal: Sa conquête et son organisation (1364–1925).* Saint-Louis: Impr. du gouvernement, 1925.

Campt, Tina M. *Image Matters: Archive, Photography, and the African Diaspora in Europe.* Durham, NC: Duke University Press, 2012.

Campt, Tina M. *Listening to Images.* Durham, NC: Duke University Press, 2017.

Canot, Théodore. *Les aventures d'un négrier: Trafiquant d'or, d'ivoire et d'esclaves.* 1854. Reprint, Paris: CLAEE, 2008.

Carré, Nathalie. "Between Mother Tongue and 'Ceremonial Tongue': Boubacar Boris Diop and the Self-Translation of *Doomi Golo.*" *International Journal of Francophone Studies* 18, no. 1 (2015): 101–14.

Caswell, Michelle. "'The Archive' Is Not an Archives: Acknowledging the Intellectual Contributions of Archival Studies." *Reconstruction* 16, no. 1 (2021). https://escholarship.org/uc/item/7bn4v1fk.

Cavafy, Constantine. "La Ville." In *Présentation critique de Constantin Cavafy, 1863–1933.* Translated by Marguerite Yourcenar and Constantin Dimarras, 93. Paris: Gallimard, 1998.

Cavarero, Adriana. *Horrorism: Naming Contemporary Violence.* Translated by William McCuaig. New York: Columbia University Press, 2008.

Cavell, Stanley. *The Claim of Reason: Wittgenstein, Skepticism, Morality, and Tragedy.* Oxford: Oxford University Press, 1999.

Center for Policing Terrorism. "Analysis: May 16, 2003, Suicide Bombings in Casablanca, Morocco." *Center for Policing Terrorism*, 2006.

Césaire, Aimé. "Mémorial de Louis Delgrès." *Présence Africaine*, no. 23 (1958): 69–72.

Chachoua, Kamal. "Genre, suicide et sexualité(s) en Algérie." *Revue internationale de sociologie* 20, no. 2 (2010): 301–19.

Chachoua, Kamal. "Le suicide en Algérie." In *Politique et religion en Méditerranée: Moyen âge et époque contemporaine*, edited by Henri Bresc, Georges Dagher, and Christiane Veauvy, 387–412. Paris: Éditions Bouchène, 2008.

Chamoiseau, Patrick. *L'esclave vieil homme et le molosse: Roman*. Paris: Gallimard, 1997.

Chang, Qingsong, Paul S. F. Yip, and Ying-Yeh Chen. "Gender Inequality and Suicide Gender Ratios in the World." *Journal of Affective Disorders* 243 (2019): 297–304.

Chapier, Henry. "La Noire de . . ." *Combat*, 10 April 1967.

Chaulet-Achour, Christiane. "'Cette maudite guerre d'Algérie': *Boulevard de l'abîme* de Nourredine Saadi." *Diacritik*, 15 December 2017.

Chaulet-Achour, Christiane. *La trilogie caribéenne de Daniel Maximin: Analyse et contrepoint*. Paris: Éditions Karthala, 2000.

Chevalier, Louis. *Splendeurs et misères du fait divers*. Paris: Perrin, 2003.

Chevrier, Jacques. "Afrique(s)-sur-Seine: Autour de la notion de 'migritude.'" *Revue des littératures du Sud*, nos. 155–56 (2004): 96–100.

Church, Christopher M. "The Last Resort of the Slave: Fire and Labour in the Late Nineteenth-Century French Caribbean." *French History* 32, no. 4 (December 2018): 511–31.

Clarkson, Thomas. *The History of the Rise, Progress, and Accomplishment of the Abolition of the African Slave-Trade by the British Parliament*. London, 1808.

Coats, Lauren, and Steffi Dippold. "Beyond Recovery: Introduction." *Early American Literature* 55, no. 2 (2020): 297–320.

Cole, Joshua. *Lethal Provocation: The Constantine Murders and the Politics of French Algeria*. Ithaca, NY: Cornell University Press, 2019.

Collomb, Henri, and René Collignon. "Les conduits suicidaires en Afrique." *Psychopathologie africaine* 10, no. 1 (1974): 55–113.

"Comité universitaire pour la célébration du cinquantenaire de la mort du poète, 1937–1987." In *Jean-Joseph Rabéarivelo, cet inconnu? Colloque international de l'Université de Madagascar*. Marseille: Sud, 1989.

Commander, Michelle D. *Afro-Atlantic Flight: Speculative Returns and the Black Fantastic*. Durham, NC: Duke University Press, 2017.

Conan, Eric, and Henry Rousso. *Vichy, un passé qui ne passe pas*. Paris: Fayard, 1994.

Condé, Maryse. *An tan révolisyon / In the time of revolution / Tiempos de revolución*. 1989. Reprint, Paris: Amandier, 2015.

Condé, Maryse. *Moi, Tituba, sorcière . . . Noire de Salem*. Paris: Mercure de France, 1986.

Confiant, Raphaël. *Le nègre et l'amiral*. Paris: Grasset, 1988.

Conklin, Alice L. *A Mission to Civilize: The Republican Idea of Empire in France and West Africa, 1895–1930*. Stanford, CA: Stanford University Press, 1997.

Corre, Armand. *Le crime en pays créoles, esquisses d'ethnographie criminelle*. Lyon: A. Storck, 1889.

Costello, Ray. *Black Salt: Seafarers of African Descent on British Ships*. Liverpool: Liverpool University Press, 2012.

Coulibaly, Bojana. "Senegalese Theater Unabashed: Wolof Drama and Cultural Liberation." *Alif: Journal of Comparative Poetics*, no. 39 (2019): 123–48.

Cultru, P. *Histoire du Sénégal du XVe siècle à 1870*. Paris: Emile Larose, 1910.

Cvetkovich, Ann. *An Archive of Feelings*. Durham, NC: Duke University Press, 2003.

D'Aguiar, Fred. *Feeding the Ghosts*. London: Vintage, 1998.

Daniel, Drew. *Joy of the Worm: Suicide and Pleasure in Early Modern English Literature*. Chicago: University of Chicago Press, 2022.

Danquin, Léon Rameau. "Contribution à une étude sur l'insurrection anti-esclavagiste de mai 1802." PhD diss., Basse-Terre, 1982.

Danquin, Léon Rameau. "Delgrès, figure du tragique." *Études guadeloupéennes*, no. 6 (1994): 67–130.

Danquin, Léon Rameau. "La postérité de 1802: Entre clameurs et discours." *Études guadeloupéennes*, no. 8 (2003): 36–60.

Day, Thomas, and John Bicknell. *The dying negro, a poem. By the late Thomas Day and John Bicknell, Esquires. To which is added, a fragment of a letter on the slavery of the negroes. By Thomas Day, Esq. Embellished with a frontispiece*. London: John Stockdale, 1793.

Day, Thomas, and John Bicknell. *The dying negro, a poetical epistle*. London: W. Flexney, 1773.

Day, Thomas, and John Bicknell. *The dying negro, a poetical epistle*. London: W. Flexney, 1775.

De Gouges, Olympe. *L'esclavage des Noirs ou l'heureux naufrage*. Paris: Chez la Veuve Duchesne, 1792.

De Gouges, Olympe. *Zamore et Mirza, ou l'heureux naufrage: Drame indien, en trois actes et en prose*. Paris: Chez l'Auteur et Chez Cailleau, 1788.

De Mackau, Ange. *Compte-rendu de l'exécution des lois des 18 et 19 juillet 1845 sur le régime des esclaves*. Paris: Impr. royale, 1847.

de Man, Paul. "Autobiography as De-facement." *MLN* 94, no. 5 (December 1979): 919–30.

Debbasch, Yvan. "Le marronage: Essai sur la désertion de l'esclave antillais." *L'année sociologique* 12 (1961): 1–112.

Debret, Jean Baptiste. *Voyage pittoresque et historique au Brésil, ou, Séjour d'un artiste français au Brésil, depuis 1816 jusqu'en 1831 inclusivement [. . .]*. Paris: Didot Frères, 1834–39.

Derrida, Jacques. *Archive Fever: A Freudian Impression*. Chicago: University of Chicago Press, 1998.

Derrida, Jacques. *Cinders*. Translated by Ned Lukacher. 1991. Reprint, Minneapolis: University of Minnesota Press, 2014.

Derrida, Jacques. *De l'esprit: Heidegger et la question*. Paris: Galilée, 1987.

Derrida, Jacques. *Feu la cendre*. Paris: Des femmes, 1987.

Derrida, Jacques. *Marges de la philosophie*. Paris: Éditions de Minuit, 1972.

Derrida, Jacques. *Sovereignties in Question: The Poetics of Paul Celan*. Edited by Thomas Dutoit and Outi Pasanen. New York: Fordham University Press, 2005.

Derrida, Jacques. *La voix et le phénomène: Introduction au problème du signe dans la phénoménologie de Husserl*. Paris: Presses universitaires de France, 1973.

Des Bruslons, Savary. *Dictionnaire universel de commerce*. Vol. 2. Paris: Chez la veuve Estienne et fils, 1723.

Dewerpe, Alain. *Charonne, 8 février 1962: Anthropologie historique d'un massacre d'État*. Paris: Gallimard, 2006.

Diakhate, Ousmane, Hansel Ndumbe Eyoh, and Don Rubin, eds. "Senegal." In *The World Encyclopedia of Contemporary Theatre: Africa*, 242. London: Routledge, 2013.

Diam Sy, Souleymane, and Ndiol Maka Seck. "'Thioural Goundiour': Le tombeau des combattants Peuls." *Le Soleil*, 22 September 2015.

Diawara, Manthia. *African Cinema: Politics and Culture*. Bloomington: Indiana University Press, 1992.

Diome, Fatou. *Le ventre de l'Atlantique*. Paris: Anne Carrière, 2003.

Diop, Aby. "Les suicides et tentatives de suicide à Dakar à partir des cas traités à l'hôpital principal et l'hôpital Aristide Le Dantec de 1998 à 2002." Master's thesis, Université Cheikh Anta Diop, 2003.

Diop, Alioune. "Sénégal, vidéo avant son immolation devant le palais: Cheikh Diop est mort." *Afrik.com*, 6 November 2018. https://www.afrik.com/video-avant-son-immolation-devant-le-palais-cheikh-diop-est-mort.

Diop, Boubacar Boris. *Bàmmeelu Kocc Barma*. Dakar: EJO Éditions, 2017.

Diop, Boubacar Boris. *Doomi Golo: Nettali*. Dakar: Éditions Papyrus Afrique, 2003.

Diop, Boubacar Boris. *Doomi Golo: The Hidden Notebooks*. Translated by Vera Wulfing-Leckie and El Hadji Moustapha Diop. East Lansing: Michigan State University Press, 2016.

Diop, Boubacar Boris. *Malaanum lëndëm*. Dakar: EJO Éditions, 2022.

Diop, Boubacar Boris. *Murambi, le livre des ossements: Roman*. Paris: Stock, 2000.

Diop, Boubacar Boris. *Murambi, the Book of Bones*. Translated by Fiona McLaughlin. Bloomington: Indiana University Press, 2006.

Diop, Boubacar Boris. *Les petits de la guenon*. Paris: Éditions Philippe Rey, 2009.

Diop, David. *La porte du voyage sans retour*. Paris: Éditions du Seuil, 2021.

Diop, Papa Samba. *The Oral History and Literature of the Wolof People of Waalo, Northern Senegal: The Master of the Word (Griot) in the Wolof Tradition*. Lewiston, ME: Edwin Mellen, 1995.

Diouf, Mamadou. *Le Kajoor au XIXe siècle: Pouvoir ceddo et conquête coloniale*. Paris: Éditions Karthala, 1990.

Djaout, Tahar. *Le dernier été de la raison: Roman*. Paris: Éditions du Seuil, 1999.

Djaout, Tahar. *Les vigiles*. Paris: Éditions du Seuil, 1991.

Djebar, Assia. *Le blanc d'Algérie*. Paris: Albin Michel, 1995.

"Djoudi n'oublie pas sa sœur Fatima Bedar." *Le journal de Saint-Denis*, 9 October 2014. https://lejsd.com/content/djoudi-n%E2%80%99oublie-pas-sa-s%C5%93ur-fatima-bedar.

Doane, Mary Ann. *The Emergence of Cinematic Time: Modernity, Contingency, the Archive*. Cambridge, MA: Harvard University Press, 2002.

Dodman, Thomas. *What Nostalgia Was: War, Empire, and the Time of a Deadly Emotion*. Chicago: University of Chicago Press, 2017.

Donadey, Anne. "Beyond Departmentalization: Feminist Black Atlantic Reformulations of *Outre-mer* in Daniel Maximin's *L'isolé soleil*." *International Journal of Francophone Studies* 11, nos. 1–2 (2008): 49–65.

Dorlin, Elsa. "Les espaces-temps des résistances esclaves: Des suicidés de Saint-Jean aux marrons de Nanny Town (XVIIe–XVIIIe siècles)." *Tumultes* 27, no. 2 (November 2006): 37–51.

Dorlin, Elsa. *La matrice de la race: Généalogie sexuelle et coloniale de la Nation française*. Paris: La Découverte, 2006.

Dorlin, Elsa. "Naissance de la race: Médecine esclavagiste, clinique négrière et étiologie raciale (XVIIe–XIXe siècles)." In *La Fabrique de la race dans la Caraïbe de l'époque moderne à nos jours*, edited by Marine Cellier, Amina Damerdji, and Sylvan Lloret, 27–45. Paris: Classiques Garnier, 2021.

Dorlin, Elsa. *Se défendre: Une philosophie de la violence*. Paris: Zones, 2017.

Dubied, Annik. *Les dits et les scènes du fait divers*. Geneva: Droz, 2004.

Dubois, Laurent. *A Colony of Citizens: Revolution and Slave Emancipation in the French Caribbean, 1787–1804*. Chapel Hill: University of North Carolina Press, 2004.

Dubois, Laurent. "Haunting Delgrès." *Radical History Review* 78 (2000): 166–77.

Dugoujon, Abbé Casimir. *Lettres sur l'esclavage dans les colonies françaises*. Paris: Pagnerre, 1845.

Duras, Claire de. *Œuvres romanesques*. Edited by Marie-Bénédicte Diethelm. Paris: Gallimard, 2023.

Duras, Claire de. *Ourika*. Paris: Ladvocat, 1826.

Duras, Claire de. *Ourika: The Original French Text*. Edited by Joan DeJean, with an introduction by Joan DeJean and Margaret Waller. New York: MLA, 1994.

Durkheim, Émile. *Le suicide: Étude de sociologie*. Paris: Félix Alcan, 1897.

Durpoix, Chantal. *Talaatay Nder*. Saint-Louis: Université Gaston Berger / Docmonde, 2016.

"Du suicide." *Mercure de France et Chronique de Paris*, no. 1 (August 1819): 269.

Dutertre, Anne. *Voyage de Vermont-Sur-Orne à Constantine-Sur-L'Oued-Rummel, Sétif, Bougie et Alger: Par une femme*. Caen: C. Hommais, 1866.

Dyâo, Yoro. "Légendes et coutumes sénégalaises: Publiées et commentées par Henri Gaden. Cahiers de Yoro Dyao." *La Revue d'Ethnographie et de Sociologie* 3–4 (March–April 1912): 119–37.

Dyâo, Yoro. "Légendes et coutumes sénégalaises: Publiées et commentées par Henri Gaden. Cahiers de Yoro Dyao." *La Revue d'Ethnographie et de Sociologie* 5–8 (May–August 1912): 191–202.

Edlmair, Barbara. *Rewriting History: Alternative Versions of the Caribbean Past in Michelle Cliff, Rosario Ferré, Jamaica Kincaid and Daniel Maximin*. Vienna: Braumüller, 1999.

Edwards, Brent Hayes. "The Taste of the Archive." *Callaloo* 35, no. 4 (Fall 2012): 944–72.

Effros, Bonnie, and Guolong Lai, eds. *Unmasking Ideology in Imperial and Colonial Archaeology: Vocabulary, Symbols, and Legacy*. Los Angeles: Cotsen Institute of Archaeology Press at UCLA, 2018.

Eileraas, Karina. "Reframing the Colonial Gaze: Photography, Ownership, and Feminist Resistance." *MLN* 118, no. 4 (2003): 807–40.

Einaudi, Jean-Luc. *La ferme Améziane: Enquête sur un centre de torture pendant la guerre d'Algérie.* Paris: L'Harmattan, 1991.

El Guabli, Brahim. *Moroccan Other-Archives: History and Citizenship after State Violence.* New York: Fordham University Press, 2023.

Elalamy, Youssouf Amine. *Les clandestins: Roman.* Casablanca: Éditions EDDIF, 2000.

Elalamy, Youssouf Amine. *Oussama, mon amour: Roman.* Casablanca: La Croisée des Chemins, 2011.

Ellerson, Beti. "M'Bissine Thérèse Diop: *La Noire de . . .* , a Black Woman from Senegal, Outside the Frame." *Black Camera* 15, no. 2 (2024): 244–52.

Émérigon, Balthazard-Marie. *Traité des assurances et des contrats à la grosse.* Marseille: J. Mossy, 1783.

Erickson, John D. "Maximin's *L'isolé soleil* and Caliban's Curse." *Callaloo* 15, no. 1 (1992): 119–30.

Esposito, Claudio. *The Narrative Mediterranean: Beyond France and the Maghreb.* Lanham, MD: Lexington Books, 2013.

Essomba, J. R. *Le paradis du nord: Roman.* Paris: Présence Africaine, 1996.

Etna, Max. "1802: La guerre de la Guadeloupe ou la géographie en marche avec la liberté." *Bulletin de la société d'histoire de la Guadeloupe*, no. 131 (January–April 2002): 47–60.

Evrard, Franck. *Fait divers et littérature.* Paris: Nathan, 1997.

Ezzakhraiy, Myriam. "Horreur sur la place de Verdun." *Le Matin du Sahara*, 18 May 2003.

Faidherbe, Louis. *Le Sénégal: La France dans l'Afrique occidentale.* Paris: Hachette, 1889.

Faithful-Velayoudom, Lucianne. "Réalité historique et fiction littéraire: Le passage de l'histoire au mythe: Louis Delgrès et Toussaint Louverture, deux figures emblématiques." PhD diss., Université des Antilles de la Guyane, 2006.

Fall, Babacar. "Orality and Life Histories: Rethinking the Social and Political History of Senegal." *Africa Today* 50, no. 2 (2003): 55–65.

Fall, Bilal. *Le serment: Pièce inspirée par le suicide de Xanju.* Dakar: Impricap, 1979.

Fanon, Frantz. *Les damnés de la terre.* Paris: Maspero, 1968.

Fanon, Frantz. *Sociologie d'une révolution (L'an V de la révolution algérienne).* Paris: Maspero, 1968.

Fanon, Frantz. *The Wretched of the Earth.* Translated by Constance Farrington. New York: Grove, 1963.

Farley, Anthony Paul. "The Apogee of the Commodity." *DePaul Law Review* 53, no. 3 (Spring 2004): 1229–46.

Fasolt, Constantin. *The Limits of History.* Chicago: University of Chicago Press, 2004.

Faye, Ayoba. "Fatou Sow Sarr en a marre de la célébration du 8 mars: Elle appelle les Sénégalais à plutôt fêter le 7 mars." *Pressafrik*, 8 March 2020.

Feindt, Gregor, Félix Krawatzek, Daniela Mehler, Friedemann Pestel, and Rieke Trimçev. "Entangled Memory: Toward a Third Wave in Memory Studies." *History and Theory* 53, no. 1 (2014): 24–44.

Feraoun, Mouloud. *Les chemins qui montent: Roman.* Paris: Éditions du Seuil, 1957.

Ferroudj, Hana. "Fatima Bedar, fille de tirailleur algérien, 'noyée' le 17 octobre 1961." *Le Bondy Blog*, 17 October 2013. https://www.bondyblog.fr/societe/fatima-bedar-fille-de-tirailleur-algerien-noyee-le-17-octobre-1961/.

Fierke, K. M. *Political Self-Sacrifice: Agency, Body and Emotion in International Relations.* Cambridge: Cambridge University Press, 2013.

Flood, Maria. "Women Resisting Terror: Imaginaries of Violence in Algeria (1966–2002)." *Journal of North African Studies* 22, no. 1 (2017): 109–31.

Foa, Eugénie. "La Kalissa (1833)." In *Les grands auteurs juifs de la littérature française au XIXe siècle: Nouvelles, une anthologie,* edited by Maurice Samuels, 25–42. Paris: Hermann, 2015.

Fofana, Amadou T. *The Films of Ousmane Sembène: Discourse, Politics, and Culture.* Amherst, NY: Cambria Press, 2012.

Ford, Joseph. *Writing the Black Decade: Conflict and Criticism in Francophone Algerian Literature.* Lanham, MD: Lexington Books, 2023.

Forsdick, Charles. "Interpreting 2004: Politics, Memory, Scholarship." *Small Axe* 27 (2008): 1–13.

Forsdick, Charles. "The Panthéon's Empty Plinth: Commemorating Slavery in Contemporary France." *Atlantic Studies* 9, no. 3 (2012): 279–97.

Forter, Greg. "Atlantic and Other Worlds: Critique and Utopia in Postcolonial Historical Fiction." *PMLA* 131, no. 5 (October 2016): 1328–43.

Foucault, Michel. *The History of Sexuality.* Translated by Robert Hurley. New York: Vintage Books, 1988–90.

Foucault, Michel. "Interview." In *The Final Foucault,* edited by James William Bernauer and David M. Rasmussen, 1–20. Cambridge, MA: MIT Press, 1988.

Foucault, Michel. "Lives of Infamous Men." In *Power: Essential Works of Foucault, 1954–1984,* vol. 3, edited by James D. Faubion and translated by Robert Hurley and others, 157–75. New York: New Press, 2000.

Frémeaux, Jacques. "Les SAS (Sections administratives spécialisées)." *Guerres mondiales et conflits contemporains* 4, no. 208 (2002): 55–68.

Freud, Sigmund. "Inhibitions, Symptoms and Anxiety (1926)." In *The Standard Edition of the Complete Psychological Works of Sigmund Freud,* vol. 10, edited and translated by James Strachey, 75–175. London: Hogarth, 1953–74.

Freud, Sigmund. "Mourning and Melancholia (1957)." In *The Standard Edition of the Complete Psychological Works of Sigmund Freud,* vol. 14, edited and translated by James Strachey, 243–58. London: Hogarth, 1953–74.

Freud, Sigmund. "Screen Memories (1899)." In *The Standard Edition of the Complete Psychological Works of Sigmund Freud,* vol. 3, edited and translated by James Strachey, 299–322. London: Hogarth, 1953–74.

Froment-Meurice, Marc. "In the Name of the Other: I . . . Gérard de Nerval." *Journal of European Studies* 33, nos. 3–4 (2003): 263–86.

Frossard, Benjamin S. *La cause des esclaves nègres et des habitants de la Guinée.* Lyon: Aimé de la Roche, 1789.

Fuentes, Marisa J. *Dispossessed Lives: Enslaved Women, Violence, and the Archive.* Philadelphia: University of Pennsylvania Press, 2016.

Fukube, S., T. Hayashi, Y. Ishida, H. Kamon, M. Kawaguchi, A. Kumura, et al. "Retrospective Study on Suicidal Cases by Sharp Force Injuries." *Journal of Forensic Legal Medicine* 15 (2008): 163–67.

Fullmer, Nyssa, Stephanie Lipson Mizrahi, and Elizabeth Tomsich. "The Lethality of Female Suicide Bombers." *Women and Criminal Justice* 29, nos. 4–5 (2019): 266–82.

Fyfe, Alexander, and Madhu Krishnan, eds. *African Literatures as World Literature*. New York: Bloomsbury Academic, 2023.

Gaden, Henri. "Légendes et coutumes sénégalaises: Cahiers de Yoro Dyao. Publiés et commentés par Henri Gaden." *La Revue d'ethnographie et de sociologie*, nos. 3–4 (1912): 119–37, 190–202.

Gadjigo, Samba. *Ousmane Sembène: The Making of a Militant Artist*. Translated by Moustapha Diop. Bloomington: Indiana University Press, 2010.

Garanger, Marc. *Femmes algériennes 1960*. Paris: Contrejour, 1982.

Gathara, Patric. "The Path to Colonial Reckoning Is through Archives, Not Museums." *Aljazeera*, 14 March 2019. https://www.aljazeera.com/opinions/2019/3/14/the-path-to-colonial-reckoning-is-through-archives-not-museums.

Gautier, Arlette. *Les sœurs de Solitude: Femmes et esclavage aux Antilles du XVIIe au XIXe siècle*. 1985. Reprint, Rennes: Presses universitaires de Rennes, 2010.

Gautier, Théophile, and Noël Parfait. *La Juive de Constantine, drame en cinq actes*. Paris: Marchant, 1846.

Gaye, Mamadou. "Sidiya Joop (1848–1878): L'itinéraire du brak virtuel du Walo." Master's thesis, Université Cheikh Anta Diop, 1990.

Ghezali, Salima. *Les amants de Shahrazade: Roman*. Algiers: Marsa, 2001.

Gilroy, Paul. *Postcolonial Melancholia*. New York: Columbia University Press, 2006.

Girard, René. *Mensonge romantique et vérité romanesque*. Paris: Grasset, 1961.

Glissant, Édouard. *Le discours antillais*. Paris: Éditions du Seuil, 1981.

Glissant, Édouard. *Une nouvelle région du monde*. Paris: Gallimard, 2006.

Glissant, Édouard. *Philosophie de la relation: Poésie en étendue*. Paris: Gallimard, 2009.

Glissant, Édouard. *Poetics of Relation*. Translated by Betsy Wing. Ann Arbor: University of Michigan Press, 1997.

Glissant, Édouard. *Poétique de la relation*. Paris: Gallimard, 1990.

Glissant, Édouard. *Le quatrième siècle*. Paris: Éditions du Seuil, 1964.

Glissant, Édouard. *Sartorius*. Paris: Gallimard, 1999.

Godineau, Dominique. *S'abréger les jours: Le suicide en France au XVIIIe siècle*. Paris: Armand Colin, 2012.

Goh, Irving. "Shared Unshareability, Suicidality, and the Melodrama of Living on after Failure in Yiyun Li." *Modern Fiction Studies* 69, no. 3 (2023): 539–62.

Goldblatt, Cullen. "Lëndëmtu: Réflexions sur *Doomi Golo* et *Les petits de la guenon*." In *Des mondes et des langues: L'écriture de Boubacar Boris Diop*, edited by Nsrin Qader and Souleymane Bachir Diagne, 61–83. Paris: Présence Africaine, 2014.

Gomez, Michael A. *Exchanging Our Country Marks: The Transformation of African Identities in the Colonial and Antebellum South*. Chapel Hill: University of North Carolina Press, 1998.

Gomis, Alain, dir. *L'Afrance*. Mille et Une Productions, 2001.

Gordon, Avery. *Ghostly Matters: Haunting and the Sociological Imagination*. Minneapolis: University of Minnesota Press, 1997.

Grégoire, Abbé Henri. *De la littérature des nègres*. 1808. Reprint, Paris: Perrin, 1991.

Gupta, Suman, Milena Katsarska, Theodoros A. Spyros, and Mike Hajimichael. *Usurping Suicide: The Political Resonances of Individual Deaths*. London: Zed Books, 2017.

Hacking, Ian. "Making Up People." In *Reconstructing Individualism: Autonomy, Individuality, and the Self in Western Thought*, edited by Thomas C. Heller, Morton Sosna, and David E. Wellbery, 222–36. Stanford, CA: Stanford University Press, 1986.

Halimi, Gisèle. *La Kahina*. Paris: Plon, 2006.

Hall, Gwendolyn. *Social Control in the Slave Plantation Societies: A Comparison of St. Domingue and Cuba*. Baltimore: Johns Hopkins University Press, 1971.

Hamdi, Houda. "Writing Violence in Bashīr Muftī's *Ashbāḥ al-Madīnah al-Maqtūlah (The Ghosts of the Murdered City)*." *Journal of North African Studies* 23, nos. 1–2 (2018): 140–53.

Hamil, Mustapha. "Plotting Terrorism: Mahi Binebine's *Les étoiles de Sidi Moumen* (2010)." *International Journal of Francophone Studies* 14, no. 4 (December 2011): 549–69.

Haneke, Michael, dir. *Caché*. France 3 Cinéma / Canal+ / Bavaria Film / Wega Film / Les films du losange, 2005.

Hanrot, Juliette. *La Madone de Bentalha: Histoire d'une photographie*. Paris: Armand Colin, 2012.

Hardy, Georges. *La mise en valeur du Sénégal de 1817 à 1854*. Paris: Émile Larose, 1921.

Harms, Robert. *The Diligent: A Voyage through the Worlds of the Slave Trade*. New York: Basic Books, 2002.

Hartman, Saidiya. *Lose Your Mother: A Journey along the Atlantic Slave Route*. New York: Farrar, Straus and Giroux, 2007.

Hartman, Saidiya. *Scenes of Subjection: Terror, Slavery, and Self-Making in Nineteenth-Century America*. New York: Oxford University Press, 1997.

Hartman, Saidiya. "Venus in Two Acts." *Small Axe* 12, no. 2 (2008): 1–14.

Hayes, Jarrod. *Queer Nations: Marginal Sexualities in the Maghreb*. Chicago: University of Chicago Press, 2000.

Hayet, Armand. *Chansons de bord*. Paris: Éditions Eos, 1927.

Heisbourg, François. *Hyperterrorisme: La nouvelle guerre*. Paris: Odile Jacob, 2001.

Helton, Laura, Justin Leroy, Max A. Mishler, Samantha Seeley, and Shauna Sweeney. "The Question of Recovery: An Introduction." *Social Text* 33, no. 4 (December 2015): 1–18.

Hennebelle, Guy. "'For Me, the Cinema Is an Instrument of Political Action, but...'" In *Ousmane Sembène: Interviews*, edited by Annett Busch and Max Annas, 7–17. Jackson: University of Mississippi Press, 2008.

Herbeck, Jason. "Entretien avec Fabienne Kanor." *French Review* 86, no. 5 (2013): 964–76.

Higonnet, Margaret. "Suicide: Representations of the Feminine in the Nineteenth Century." *Poetics Today* 6, nos. 1/2 (1985): 103–18.

Hinks, Peter. "Mémorial de l'abolition de l'esclavage (Memorial to the Abolition of Slavery), Nantes, France." *Journal of American History* 100, no. 1 (2013): 150–55.

"L'histoire méconnue du suicide collectif des femmes de Goundiour (Koumpentoum)." *Sunugox.info*, 5 May 2017. https://sunugox.info/histoire/histoire-meconnue-des-femmes/.

Hitchcott, Nicki. "A Global African Commemoration—*Rwanda: Écrire par devoir de mémoire*." *Forum for Modern Language Studies* 45, no. 2 (April 2009): 151–61.

Hitchcott, Nicki. "Writing on Bones: Commemorating Genocide in Boubacar Boris Diop's *Murambi*." *Research in African Literatures* 40, no. 3 (Fall 2009): 48–61.

Ho, Hai Quang. *Esclavagisme et engagisme: À la Réunion et à Maurice*. Saint-Clotilde: Poisson Rouge, 2016.

Hogarth, Rana A. *Medicalizing Blackness: Making Racial Difference in the Atlantic World, 1780–1840*. Chapel Hill: University of North Carolina Press, 2017.

Holden, Stephen. "Learning to Empathize with a Suicide Bomber." *New York Times*, 9 May 2007. https://www.nytimes.com/2007/05/09/movies/09day.html.

Horwitz, Michael. "The Rise and Spread of Suicide Bombing." *Annual Review of Political Science* 18, no. 1 (2015): 69–84.

Houdzi, Ahmed Aziz. "Le roman contre la barbarie: Récits d'un engagement pour le vivre ensemble dans la littérature marocaine d'expression française de la Nouvelle Génération." *Mouvances Francophones* 4, no. 1 (2019): 2–11.

Houen, Alex. *Terrorism and Modern Literature: From Joseph Conrad to Ciaran Carson*. Oxford: Oxford University Press, 2002.

Hourcade, Renaud. "Commemorating a Guilty Past: The Politics of Memory in the French Former Slave Trade Cities." In *Politics of Memory: Making Slavery Visible in the Public Space*, edited by Ana Lucia Araujo, 124–40. New York: Routledge, 2012.

House, Jim, and Neal MacMaster. *Paris 1961: Algerians, State Terror, and Memory*. Oxford: Oxford University Press, 2006.

Huchzermeyer, Marie. *Cities with "Slums": From Informal Settlement Eradication to a Right to the City in Africa*. Claremont, South Africa: University of Cape Town Press, 2011.

Hughes, Langston. *The Collected Works of Langston Hughes*, vol. 1: *The Poems: 1921–1940*. Edited by Arnold Rampersad. Columbia: University of Missouri Press, 2001.

Human Rights Watch. "Morocco/Western Sahara: Events of 2009." Accessed 28 January 2024. https://www.hrw.org/world-report/2010/country-chapters/morocco/western-sahara.

Huy, Minh Tran. *Les écrivains et le fait divers: Une autre histoire de la littérature*. Paris: Flammarion, 2017.

Irvine, Judith. "When Is Genealogy History? Wolof Genealogies in Comparative Perspective." *American Ethnologist* 5, no. 4 (November 1978): 651–74.

Jackson, Jeanne-Marie. *The African Novel of Ideas: Philosophy and Individualism in the Age of Global Writing*. Princeton, NJ: Princeton University Press, 2021.

Jammes, Bruno. "John B. Greene, an American Calotypist." *History of Photography* 5, no. 4 (1981): 305–24.

Jarvis, Jill. *Decolonizing Memory: Algeria and the Politics of Testimony*. Durham, NC: Duke University Press, 2021.

Jarvis, Jill. "Radiant Matter: Technologies of Light and the Long Shadow of French Nuclear Imperialism in the Algerian Sahara." *Representations* 160, no. 1 (Fall 2022): 54–89.

Jarvis, Jill. "Remnants of Muslims: Reading Agamben's Silence." *New Literary History* 45, no. 4 (Autumn 2014): 707–28.

Jensen, Deborah. *Beyond the Slave Narrative: Politics, Sex, and Manuscripts in the Haitian Revolution*. Liverpool: Liverpool University Press, 2012.

Johnson, Jessica Marie. *Wicked Flesh: Black Women, Intimacy, and Freedom in the Atlantic World*. Philadelphia: University of Pennsylvania Press, 2020.

Jonassaint, Jean. "Le cinéma de Sembène Ousmane, une (double) contre-ethnographie (Notes pour une recherche)." *Ethnologies* 31, no. 2 (2010): 241–86.

Jones, Nicholas R. "Debt Collecting, Disappearance, Necromancy: A Response to John Beusterien." In *Early Modern Black Diaspora Studies: A Critical Anthology*, edited by Cassander L. Smith, Nicholas R. Jones, and Miles P. Grier, 211–21. Cham, Switzerland: Macmillan, 2018.

Jordan-Zachery, Julia S. "Resistance and Redemption Narratives: Black Girl Magic and Other Forms of Black Girls and Women's Political Self-Articulations." *National Political Science Review* 19, no. 2 (2018): 2–10.

Jore, Léonce. "La vie diverse et volontaire du colonel Julien, Désiré Schmaltz." *Revue d'Histoire des Colonies* 41, no. 139 (1953): 265–312.

Jourdran, E., and M. Fontoynont. "Le suicide chez les malgaches." *Progrès Médical*, August 1909, 1–15.

Julien, Eileen. "The Extroverted African Novel." In *The Novel*, vol. 1: *History, Geography, and Culture*, edited by Franco Moretti, 667–700. Princeton, NJ: Princeton University Press, 2006.

Julien, Eileen. "The Extroverted African Novel, Revisited: African Novels at Home, in the World." *Journal of African Cultural Studies* 30, no. 3 (September 2018): 371–81.

Ka, Aminata Maïga. *La voie du salut, suivi de, Le miroir de la vie*. Paris: Présence Africaine, 1985.

Kacha, Farid. "Contribution à l'étude du suicide en milieu urbain." PhD diss., University of Algiers, 1971.

Kacimi, Samir. *Un jour idéal pour mourir*. Translated by Lofti Nia. Paris: Actes Sud, 2020.

Kacimi, Samir. *Yawm rā'i' lil-mawt: Riwāyah*. Algiers: El Elkhtilaf, 2009.

Kane, Cheikh Hamidou. *L'aventure ambiguë: Récit*. Paris: Julliard, 1961.

Kanor, Fabienne. *Humus*. Translated by Lynn E. Palermo. Charlottesville: University of Virginia Press, 2020.

Kanor, Fabienne. *Humus: Roman*. Continents noirs. Paris: Gallimard, 2006.

Kanor, Fabienne. *La poétique de la cale: Variations sur le bateau négrier*. Paris: Rivages, 2022.

Kanor, Fabienne, and Gladys Francis. "Entretien avec Fabienne Kanor, 'l'Ante-llaise par excellence': Sexualité, corporalité, diaspora et créolité." *French Forum* 41, no. 3 (Winter 2016): 273–88.

Kanouté, Dembo. *Tradition orale: Histoire de l'Afrique authentique*. Dakar: Impricap, 1972.

Kaplan, Alice. *Looking for "The Stranger": Albert Camus and the Life of a Literary Classic*. Chicago: University of Chicago Press, 2016.

Kasahara-Kiritani, Mami Kasahara-Kiritani, et al. "Reading and Watching Films as a Protective Factor against Suicidal Ideation." *International Journal of Environmental Research and Public Health* 12, no. 12 (2015): 15937–42.

Kastell, Serge. *Le maquis rouge: L'aspirant Maillot et la guerre d'Algérie, 1956*. Paris: L'Harmattan, 1997.

Keeble, Arin. *The 9/11 Novel: Trauma, Politics and Identity*. Jefferson, NC: McFarland, 2014.

Kelkel, Abdelkader. "La discrète éclipse de la m'laya, ou l'ultime adieu à Salah Bey: L'histoire du voile noir des femmes de l'Est." *Le Quotidien d'Oran*, 26–27 March 2006.

Kendili, I., S. Berrada, and N. Kadiri. "Homosexuality in Morocco: Between Cultural Influences and Life Experience." *Sexologies* 19, no. 3 (July–September 2010): 153–56.

Khadra, Yasmina. *Les agneaux du Seigneur: Roman*. Paris: Julliard, 1998.

Khadra, Yasmina. *L'attentat: Roman*. Paris: Julliard, 2005.

Khadra, Yasmina. *Les hirondelles de Kaboul: Roman*. Paris: Julliard, 2002.

Khadra, Yasmina. *Les sirènes de Baghdad: Roman*. Paris: Julliard, 2006.

Khaless, Rachid. *Quand Adam a décidé de vivre*. Casablanca: La Croisée des Chemins, 2015.

Khodja, Soumya Ammar. "Écritures d'urgence de femmes algériennes." *Clio* 9 (1999): n.p.

Killingray, David, and Andrew Roberts. "An Outline History of Photography in Africa to ca. 1940." *History in Africa* 16 (1989): 197–208.

Kirby, Jen. "The Political Crisis in Tunisia, Explained by an Expert." *Vox*, 27 July 2021. https://www.vox.com/22594759/tunisia-coup-president-arab-spring.

Klaa, Abla. "Le Pen Says 'Colonisation Gave a Lot' to Algeria." *Middle East Eye*, 26 April 2017. https://www.middleeasteye.net/news/video-le-pen-says-colonisation-gave-lot-algeria.

Klonsky, E. David, et al. "Ideation-to-Action Theories of Suicide: A Conceptional and Empirical Update." *Current Opinion in Psychology* 22 (2018): 38–43.

Konaté, Yacouba. "Le syndrome Amadou Hampâté Bâ ou comment naissent les proverbes." In *Amadou Hampâté Bâ, homme de science et de sagesse*, edited by Amadou Touré and N'Tji-Idriss, 23–45. Paris: Karthala, 2005.

Labat, Jean-Baptiste. *Nouveau voyage aux isles de l'Amérique*. Vol. 1. The Hague: P. Husson, T. Johnson et al., 1724.

"La classe politique unanime à condamner les actes criminels." *Le Matin du Sahara*, 18 May 2003. https://lematin.ma/journal/2003/La-classe-politique-unanime-a-condamner-les-actes-criminels/29191.html.

"La communauté internationale condamne ferment les attentats terroristes à Casablanca." *Le Matin du Sahara*, 18 May 2003.

Lacour, Auguste. *Histoire de la Guadeloupe: 1798–1803*. Vol. 3. Basse-Terre: Impr. du Gouvernement, 1858.

Lagercrantz, Annel B. S. *Geophagical Customs*. Uppsala: Almquist and Wiksell, 1958.

Lalami, Laila. *Secret Son: A Novel*. Chapel Hill, NC: Algonquin Books, 2009.

Landry, Timothy R. "Touring the Slave Route: Inaccurate Authenticities in Bénin, West Africa." In *Contested Cultural Heritage: Religion, Nationalism, Erasure, and Exclusion in a Global World*, edited by Helaine Silverman, 205–31. New York: Springer, 2011.

Langford, Rachael. "Black and White in Black and White: Identity and Cinematography in Ousmane Sembène's *La Noire de . . . / Black Girl* (1966)." *Studies in French Cinema* 1, no. 1 (2001): 13–21.

Lanser, Susan S. "Queering Narrative Voice." *Textual Practice* 32, no. 6 (2018): 923–37.

Lara, Christian, dir. *1802: L'épopée Guadeloupéenne*. Les Films du Paradoxe, 2004.

Laredj, Waciny [Waçiny al-Aʻradj]. *Les ailes de la reine*. Translated by Marcel Bois. Paris: Actes Sud, 2009.

Laredj, Waciny [Waçiny al-Aʻradj]. *Sayyidatu al-maqam: Marthiyat al-youm al-hazin*. Cologne/Beirut: Al-Gamal, 1993.

Larousse, Pierre, ed. *Grand dictionnaire universel du XIXe siècle*. Vol. 6. Paris: Administration du Grand dictionnaire universel, 1866–90.

Lee, Charles T. *Ingenious Citizenship: Recrafting Democracy for Social Change*. Durham, NC: Duke University Press, 2016.

Leftah, Mohamed. *Le jour de Vénus: Roman*. Paris: Éditions de la Différence, 2009.

Leftah, Mohamed. *Un martyr de notre temps: Nouvelles*. Paris: Éditions de la Différence, 2007.

Le Glaunec, Jean-Pierre. "Résister à l'esclavage dans l'Atlantique français: Aperçu historiographique et pistes de recherche." *Revue d'histoire de l'Amérique française* 71, nos. 1–2 (Summer–Fall 2017): 13–33.

Legoff, Germaine. "Le noirs se suicident-ils en A.O.F.?" *Bulletin du comité d'études historiques et scientifiques de l'Afrique occidentale française* 21, no. 1 (1938): 130–39.

Lemire, Vincent, and Yann Potin. "'Ici on noie les Algériens': Fabriques documentaires, avatars politiques et mémoires partagées d'une icône militante (1961–2001)." *Genèses* 49, no. 4 (2002): 140–62.

Leperlier, Tristan. *Algérie, les écrivains de la décennie noire*. Paris: CNRS, 2018.

Leperlier, Tristan. "Une littérature en état d'urgence? Controverses autour d'une notion stratégique dans la décennie noire." In *L'Algérie, traversées*, edited by Ghyslain Lévy, Catherine Mazauric, and Anne Roche, 99–110. Paris: Hermann, 2018.

Lester, David. "Suicidal Behavior in African-American Slaves." *OMEGA: Journal of Death and Dying* 37, no. 1 (1998): 1–13.

Leti, Geneviève. "L'empoisonnement aux Antilles françaises à l'époque de l'esclavage (1724–1848)." In *L'esclave et les plantations: De l'établissement de la servitude à son abolition*, edited by Philippe Hrodĕj, 209–27. Rennes: Presses Universitaires de Rennes, 2009.

Levacher, Michel-Gabriel. *Guide médical des Antilles et des régions intertropicales: À l'usage de tous les habitans de ces contrées*. Paris: Librairie médicale de Just Rouvier, 1840.

Levé, Édouard. *Suicide*. Paris: POL, 2008.

Leymarie, Isabelle. *Les griots wolof du Sénégal*. Paris: Servédit, 1999.

Liengme, Georges. "Le suicide parmi les noirs." *Bulletin de la société neuchâteloise de géographie* 8 (1894–95): 177–79.

Lim, Merlyna. "Framing Bouazizi: 'White Lies,' Hybrid Network, and Collective/Connective Action in the 2010–11 Tunisian Uprising." *Journalism* 14, no. 7 (2013): 921–41.

Little, Roger. "Pirouettes sur l'abîme: Réflexions sur l'absence en français de récits autobiographiques d'esclaves noirs." In *Littérature et esclavage, XVIIIe–XIXe*, edited by Sarga Moussa, 142–53. Paris: Desjonquères, 2010.

Livy. *History of Rome*. Translated by Canon Roberts. New York: E. P. Dutton, 1912.

Loakira, Mohammed. *La nuit des disgraciés: Roman*. Rabat: Marsam, 2015.

Loktev, Julia, dir. *Day Night Day Night*. IFC Films, 2006.

Londero, C. K. *Bonaparte et Delgrès*. Paris: Bookelis, 2020.

Loti, Pierre. *Roman d'un Spahi*. Paris: Calmann-Lévy, 1881.
Lowe, Lisa. "History Hesitant." *Social Text* 33, no. 4 (125) (2015): 85–107.
Ly, Boubakar. "L'honneur dans les sociétés Ouolof et Toucouleur du Sénégal (Contribution à l'étude sociologique des valeurs morales africaines)." *Présence Africaine*, no. 61 (1967): 32–67.
Lyamlahy, Khalid. *Évocation d'un mémorial à Venise: Roman*. Paris: Présence Africaine, 2023.
MacMaster, Neil. *Burning the Veil: The Algerian War and the "Emancipation" of Muslim Women, 1954–62*. Manchester: Manchester University Press, 2009.
Maghraoui, Abdeslam. "Morocco's Reforms after the Casablanca Bombings." *Sada*, 26 August 2008. https://carnegieendowment.org/sada/21592.
Mahajan, Karan. *The Association of Small Bombs*. New York: Penguin, 2016.
Mailhol, Gabriel. *Le philosophe nègre et les secrets des Grecs: Ouvrage trop nécessaire, en deux parties*. 1764. Reprint, Paris: L'Harmattan, 2008.
Malčić, Steven. "Ousmane Sembène's Vicious Circle: The Politics and Aesthetics of *La Noire de . . .*" *Journal of African Cinemas* 5, no. 2 (October 2013): 167–80.
Malkowski, Jennifer. *Dying in Full Detail: Mortality and Digital Documentary*. Durham, NC: Duke University Press, 2017.
"Man Dies after Setting Himself on Fire in Senegal." ABC 13, 18 February 2011. https://abc13.com/archive/7967344/.
Mannix, Daniel Pratt, and Malcolm Cowley. *Black Cargoes: A History of the Atlantic Slave Trade*. New York: Viking, 1962.
Margalit, Avishai. *The Ethics of Memory*. Cambridge, MA: Harvard University Press, 2002.
Martin, Gaston. *L'ère des négriers (1714–1774): Nantes au XVIIIe siècle*. 1931. Reprint, Paris: Éditions Karthala, 1993.
Martin, Gaston. *Négriers et bois d'ébène*. Grenoble: B. Arthaud, 1934.
Martin, Maurice. *Précis d'histoire de la Guadeloupe*. Basse-Terre: Imprimerie officielle, 1931.
Marty, Paul. *L'Émirat des Trarzas*. Paris: Ernest Leroux, 1919.
Marty, Paul. "Le suicide d'un gouverneur du Sénégal (1846)." *Revue de l'histoire des colonies, 8e année, 1er semestre* (1920): 129–44.
Masbah, Mohammed. "The Limits of Morocco's Attempt to Comprehensively Counter Violent Extremism." *Middle East Brief*, no. 118 (2018): 1–7.
Mauclair, Camille. *Servitude et grandeur littéraires*. Paris: Ollendorf, 1922.
Mauss-Copeaux, Claire. *Hadjira: La ferme Améziane et au-delà . . . .* Paris: Les Chemins du présent, 2017.
Maximin, Daniel. *L'isolé soleil*. Paris: Éditions du Seuil, 1981.
Mbembe, Achille. *Critique of Black Reason*. Translated by Laurent Dubois. Durham, NC: Duke University Press, 2017.
Mbembe, Achille. "Necropolitics." Translated by Libby Meintjes. *Public Culture* 15, no. 1 (Winter 2003): 11–40.
Mbembe, Achille. *Politiques de l'inimitié*. Paris: La Découverte, 2016.
Mbodji, Amadou. "*Nder en flammes* rejouée: Marie Auguste Diatta, victime du *Joola* 'ressucitée.'" *Le Quotidien*, 29 September 2014.
Mbougar Sarr, Mohamed. *La plus secrète mémoire des hommes*. Paris: Philippe Rey, 2021.

McCallum, Pamela. "Irony, Colonialism and Representation: The Case of Sembène Ousmane's *La Noire de*." *Mattoid* 52/53 (1998): 158–65.

McLaughlin, James T. "Resistance." In *Psychoanalysis: The Major Concepts*, edited by Burness E. Moore and Bernard D. Fine, 95–109. New Haven, CT: Yale University Press, 1995.

"Média-Express." *Le Matin du Sahara*, 19 May 2003.

Mellal, Arezki. *Maintenant ils peuvent venir: Roman*. Arles: Actes Sud, 2002.

Memmi, Albert. *The Colonizer and the Colonized*. Translated by Howard Greenfeld. London: Profile, 2021.

Mérimée, Prosper. *Tamango*. Paris: Charpentier, 1845.

Merleau-Ponty, Maurice. "Sur les faits divers." In *Signes*, 388–91. Paris: Gallimard, 1960.

Merrick, Jeffrey. "Patterns and Prosecution of Suicide in Eighteenth-Century Paris." *Historical Reflections / Réflexions Historiques* 16, no. 1 (1989): 1–53.

Métral, Antoine. *Histoire de l'expédition des Français, à Saint-Domingue, sous le consulat de Napoléon Bonaparte*. Paris: Fanjat Aîné, 1825.

Metref, Arezki. "Les obsessions romanesques de Nourredine Saâdi." *Le Soir d'Algérie*, 26 November 2017.

Mettas, Jean. *Répertoire des Expéditions négrières françaises au XVIIIe siècle*. Vol. 1, *Nantes*. Edited by Serge Daget. Paris: Société française d'histoire d'outre-mer, 1978.

Miano, Léonora. *La saison de l'ombre: Roman*. Paris: Grasset, 2013.

Michel, Johann. "A Study of the Collective Memory and Public Memory of Slavery in France." *African Studies* 75, no. 3 (2016): 395–416.

Michelsen, Nicholas. "The Political Subject of Self-Immolation." *Globalizations* 12, no. 1 (2015): 83–100.

Migerel, Hélène. *La migration des zombis: Survivances de la magie antillaise en France*. Paris: Éditions caribéennes, 1987.

Miller, Christopher L. *The French Atlantic Triangle: Literature and Culture of the Slave Trade*. Durham, NC: Duke University Press, 2007.

Miller, Christopher L. "Hallucinations of France and Africa in the Colonial Exhibition of 1931 and Ousmane Socé's *Mirages de Paris*." *Paragraph* 18, no. 1 (March 1995): 39–63.

Mills, Ivy. "Sutura: Gendered Honor, Social Death, and the Politics of Exposure in Senegalese Literature." PhD diss., University of California, Berkeley, 2011.

Moitt, Bernard. *Women and Slavery in the French Antilles, 1635–1848*. Bloomington: Indiana University Press, 2001.

Mondor, Henri. *Vie de Mallarmé*. Paris: Gallimard, 1941–42.

Monteil, Vincent. *Esquisses sénégalaises: Wâlo, Kayor, Dyolof, Mourides, un visionnaire*. Dakar: IFAN, 1966.

Monteil, Vincent. "Lat Dior, Damel du Kayor (1842–1886) et l'islamisation des Wolofs." *Archives de sociologie des religions* 8, no. 16 (1963): 77–104.

Montesquieu, Charles de Secondat, Baron de. "Lettre LXXVI: Usbek à son ami Ibben." In *Lettres persanes*, edited by André Lefèvre, 67–69. Paris: A. Lemerre, 1873.

Morel, André. "Suicides et tentatives de suicide à la Martinique." Master's thesis, Université de Rennes, 1979.

Morgan, Jennifer L. *Reckoning with Slavery: Gender, Kinship, and Capitalism in the Early Black Atlantic*. Durham, NC: Duke University Press, 2021.

Morgan, Robin. *The Demon Lover: On the Sexuality of Terrorism*. New York: Norton, 1989.

Moroccan Children's Trust. "A Different Path: Street and Working Children in Morocco." October 2010. https://www.moroccanchildrenstrust.org/wp-content/uploads/2015/09/2010-A-Different-Path-EN.pdf.

Mosteghanemi, Ahlam. *Dhākirat al-jasad*. 1993. Reprint, Beirut: Hachette Antoine, 2016.

Mosteghanemi, Ahlam. *Memory in the Flesh*. Translated by Baria Ahmar Sreih and Peter Clark. Cairo: American University in Cairo Press, 2003.

Moten, Fred. *In the Break: The Aesthetics of the Black Radical Tradition*. Minneapolis: University of Minnesota Press, 2003.

Muftī, Bashīr. *Ashbāḥ al-Madīnah al-Maqtūlah*. Algiers: El-Ikhtilef, 2012.

Munro, Pamela, and Dieynaba Gaye. *Ay Baati Wolof / A Wolof Dictionary*. Los Angeles: University of California Department of Linguistics, 1997.

Murdoch, H. Adlai. *Creole Identity in the French Caribbean Novel*. Gainesville: University Press of Florida, 2001.

Murdoch, H. Adlai. "Locating History within Fiction's Frame: Re-presenting the *Épopée Delgrès* in Maximin and Lara." *Journal of American Studies* 49, no. 2 (2015): 241–66.

Murphy, David. "Birth of a Nation? The Origins of Senegalese Literature in French." *Research in African Literatures* 39, no. 1 (2008): 48–69.

Murphy, Laura T. *Metaphor and the Slave Trade in West African Literature*. Athens: Ohio University Press, 2012.

N'Diaye, Tidiane. *Le génocide voilé: Enquête historique*. Paris: Gallimard, 2008.

Nahli Allison, Sophia. "Revisiting the Legend of Flying Africans." *New Yorker*, 7 March 2019.

Narozhna, Tanya, and W. Andy Knight. *Female Suicide Bombings: A Critical Gender Approach*. Toronto: University of Toronto Press, 2016.

Ncube, Gibson. "Renegotiating the Marginality of the Maghreb in Queer African Studies." *College Literature* 45, no. 4 (Fall 2018): 623–31.

Ncube, Gibson. *La sexualité queer au Maghreb à travers la littérature*. Paris: L'Harmattan, 2018.

Ndao, Cheik Aliou. "Abdou Anta Kâ et le théâtre africain." *Présence Africaine*, no. 159 (1999): 204–6.

Ndao, Cheik Aliou. *Bokk Afrig*. Dakar: OSAD, 2004.

Ndao, Cheik Aliou. *Guy Ndjulli*. Dakar: OSAD, 2002.

Nedali, Mohamed. *La maison de Cicine: Roman*. Casablanca: Éditions Le Fennec, 2010.

Nesbitt, Nick. "Aperçu de l'historiographie au sujet de Louis Delgrès." *Bulletin de la Société d'Histoire de la Guadeloupe* 110 (1996): 9–37.

Newell, Stephanie. "From Corpse to Corpus: The Printing of Death in Colonial West Africa." In *African Print Cultures: Newspapers and Their Publics in the Twentieth Century*, edited by Derek R. Peterson, Emma Hunter, and Stephanie Newell, 389–424. Ann Arbor: University of Michigan Press, 2016.

Newell, Stephanie. *Histories of Dirt: Media and Urban Life in Colonial and Postcolonial Lagos*. Durham, NC: Duke University Press, 2020.
Newton, Huey P. *Revolutionary Suicide*. New York: Harcourt Brace Jovanovich, 1973.
Ngom, Ousmane. "Militantisme linguistique et initiation littéraire dans *Doomi Golo*, roman wolof de Bubakar Bóris Jóob." *Repères DoRiF*, no. 2 (2012). https://www.dorif.it/reperes/ousmane-ngom-militantisme-linguistique-et-initiation-litteraire-dans-doomi-golo-roman-wolof-de-bubakar-boris-joob/.
Niang, Sada, and Ousmane Sembène. "An Interview with Ousmane Sembène by Sada Niang." *Contributions in Black Studies* 11 (1993): 75–94.
Niort, Jean-François, ed. *Du Code noir au Code civil: Jalons pour l'histoire du droit en Guadeloupe*. Paris: L'Harmattan, 2007.
Nussbaum, Martha. *Not for Profit: Why Democracy Needs the Humanities*. Princeton, NJ: Princeton University Press, 2010.
Nussbaum, Martha. *Poetic Justice: The Literary Imagination and Public Life*. Boston: Beacon, 1995.
O'Connell, David. "Victor Séjour: Écrivain américain de langue française." *Revue de Louisiane / Louisiana Review* 1, no. 2 (Winter 1972): 60–75.
O'Neill, Sean. "The Rebranding of Jonathan Walker." *Michigan Historical Review* 46, no. 1 (Spring 2020): 121–65.
Oktapoda, Efstratia. "Le 16 mai: Un roman pour la paix." In *Ahmed Beroho*, edited by Najib Redouane and Yvette Bénayoun-Szmidt, 147–64. Paris: L'Harmattan, 2010.
Oriol, T. *Les hommes célèbres de la Guadeloupe*. Basse-Terre: Imprimerie catholique, 1935.
Oumar Sall, Tamsir. "Yoro Dyao, un aristocrate waalo-waalo dans le système colonial." In *Contributions à l'histoire du Sénégal*, edited by Jean Boulègue, 161–76. Paris: Édition AFERA, 1987.
Oussad, Saïd. *Les chemins inutiles: Roman*. Paris: L'Harmattan, 2014.
Pacini, Alfred, and Dominique Pons. *Docker à Marseille*. Paris: Payot & Rivages, 1996.
Palmer, Tyrone S. "Otherwise than Blackness: Feeling, World, Sublimation." *Qui Parle* 29, no. 2 (December 2020): 247–83.
Pape, Robert. *Cutting the Fuse: The Explosion of Global Suicide Terrorism and How to Stop It*. Chicago: University of Chicago Press, 2010.
Pape, Robert. *Dying to Win: The Strategic Logic of Suicide Terrorism*. New York: Random House, 2005.
Parascandola, Louis J. "'What Are We Blackmen Who Are Called French?': The Dilemma of Identity in Oyono's *Un* [sic] *vie de boy* and Sembène's *La Noire de . . .*" *Comparative Literature Studies* 46, no. 2 (2009): 360–78.
Pariona, Amber. "What Languages Are Spoken in Senegal?" *WorldAtlas*, 27 September 2017. https://www.worldatlas.com/articles/what-languages-are-spoken-in senegal.html.
"Partie non officielle, état civil, ville de Haiphong: Relevé des actes de l'État Civil dressés du 16 au 29 Février 1928." *Bulletin Administratif du Tonkin*, no. 4 (1928).
Patil, Sachin Sudarshan, Ravindra Baliram Deokar, Sunil Gorakh Vidhate, and Shashank Tyagi. "An Atypical Case of Suicidal Cut Throat Injury." *Egyptian Journal of Forensic Sciences* 6, no. 4 (December 2016): 492–95.

Patterson, Orlando. *Slavery and Social Death: A Comparative Study*. Cambridge, MA: Harvard University Press, 1982.

Patton, Stacey. "Police Say Deaths of Black People by Hanging Are Suicides: Many Black People Aren't So Sure." *Washington Post*, 22 June 2020.

Pearson, Elizabeth. "Wilayat Shahidat: Boko Haram, the Islamic State, and the Question of the Female Suicide Bomber." In *Boko Haram beyond the Headlines: Analyses of Africa's Enduring Insurgency*, edited by Jacob Zenn, 33–52. West Point, NY: Combating Terrorism Center at West Point, 2018.

Perego, Elizabeth. "The Veil or a Brother's Life: French Manipulations of Muslim Women's Images during the Algerian War, 1954–62." *Journal of North African Studies* 20, no. 3 (2015): 349–73.

Petit, André. "Un suicide chez les noirs." *Revue d'ethnographie et des traditions populaires* 1 (1920): 113–14.

Pétré-Grenouilleau, Olivier. *Nantes et la traite négrière*. Nantes: Editions du château des ducs de Bretagne, 2007.

Petty, Sheila, ed. *A Call to Action: The Films of Ousmane Sembène*. Westport, CT: Greenwood, 1996.

Petty, Sheila. "Mapping the African 'I': Representations of Women in *La Noire de . . .* and *Histoire d'Orokia*." *Social Identities* 6, no. 3 (2000): 305–21.

Pfaff, Françoise. *The Cinema of Ousmane Sembène, a Pioneer of African Film*. Westport, CT: Greenwood, 1984.

Philip, Marlene NourbeSe. *She Tries Her Tongue, Her Silence Softly Breaks*. London: Women's Press, 1993.

Philip, Marlene NourbeSe. *Zong!* Middletown, CT: Wesleyan University Press, 2008.

Phillips, David. "In Search of an Unknown Woman: *L'Inconnue de la Seine*." *Neophilologus* 66, no. 3 (1982): 321–27.

Pieprzak, Katarzyna. "Zones of Perceptual Enclosure: The Aesthetics of Immobility in Casablanca's Literary *Bidonvilles*." *Research in African Literatures* 47, no. 3 (Fall 2016): 32–49.

Piersen, William D. "White Cannibals, Black Martyrs: Fear, Depression, and Religious Faith as Causes of Suicide among New Slaves." *Journal of Negro History* 62, no. 2 (April 1977): 147–59.

Pinet, Hélène. "L'eau, la femme, la mort: Le mythe de l'Inconnue de la Seine." In *Le dernier portrait: Exposition, Paris, Musée d'Orsay, 5 mars–26 mai 2002*, edited by Emmanuelle Héran and Joëlle Bolloch, 175–90. Paris: Réunion des musées nationaux, 2002.

Plan monumental de Constantine. Paris: Éditions Blondel la Rougery, 1951.

Powell, Timothy B. "Summoning the Ancestors: The Flying Africans' Story and Its Enduring Legacy." In *African American Life in the Georgia Lowcountry: The Atlantic World and the Gullah Geechee*, edited by Philip Morgan, 253–80. Athens: University of Georgia Press, 2010.

Prédal, René. "*La Noire de . . .* : Premier long métrage Africain." *Cinémaction* 34 (1985): 36–39.

Proust, Marcel. "Filial Feelings of a Parricide." Translated by Michael Wood. *Raritan* 25, no. 2 (Fall 2005): 107–31.

Puar, Jasbir K. *Terrorist Assemblages: Homonationalism in Queer Times*. Durham, NC: Duke University Press, 2007.

Puar, Jasbir K. "Towelheads, Diapers, and Faggots: Reviving the Turban." *CLAGSNews* 11, no. 3 (Fall 2001): n.p.

Puar, Jasbir K., and Amit S. Rai. "Monster, Terrorist, Fag: The War on Terrorism and the Production of Docile Patriots." *Social Text* 20, no. 3 (Fall 2002): 117–48.

Putney, Martha S. *Black Sailors: Afro-American Merchant Seamen and Whalemen Prior to the Civil War*. New York: Greenwood, 1987.

Radford, Daniel. *Zone dangereuse*. Paris: Seghers, 1978.

Recueil de documents sur l'expédition et la prise de Constantine, par les Français, en 1837. Paris: J. Corréard, 1838.

Rediker, Marcus. "History from Below the Water Line: Sharks and the Atlantic Slave Trade." *Atlantic Studies* 5, no. 2 (2008): 285–97.

Régent, Frédéric. "Figures d'esclaves à travers des procédures judiciaires en Guadeloupe de 1789 à 1848." In *Figures d'esclaves: Présences, paroles, représentations*, edited by Éric Saunier, 111–27. Mont-Saint-Aignan: Publications des universités de Rouen et du Havre, 2012.

Régent, Frédéric, Gilda Gonfier, and Bruno Maillard, eds. *Libres et sans fers: Paroles d'esclaves français*. Paris: Fayard, 2015.

Repinecz, Jonathon. "'The Tales of Tomorrow': Towards a Futurist Vision of Wolof Tradition." *Journal of African Cultural Studies* 27, no. 1 (2015): 56–70.

Repinecz, Jonathon. *Subversive Traditions: Reinventing the West African Epic*. East Lansing: Michigan State University Press, 2019.

Reuter, Christopher. *My Life Is a Weapon: A Modern History of Suicide Bombing*. Translated by Helena Ragg-Kirkby. Princeton, NJ: Princeton University Press, 2004.

Richard de Tussac, François. *Cri des colons contre un ouvrage de M. l'évêque et sénateur Grégoire [...]*. Paris: Chez Delaunay, 1810.

Robert, Achille. *L'Arabe tel qu'il est: Études algériennes et tunisiennes*. Algiers: Joseph Angelini, 1900.

Robinson, Cedric. *Black Marxism: The Making of the Black Radical Tradition*. Chapel Hill: University of North Carolina Press, 1983.

Rofheart, Mahriana. *Shifting Perceptions of Migration in Senegalese Literature, Film, and Social Media*. Lanham, MD: Lexington Books, 2013.

Rose, Jacqueline. *The Last Resistance*. New York: Verso, 2007.

Rosello, Mireille. *Littérature et identité créole aux Antilles*. Paris: Éditions Karthala, 1992.

Rosello, Mireille. *Postcolonial Hospitality: The Immigrant as Guest*. Stanford, CA: Stanford University Press, 2001.

Rosenthal, Donald. "Neurdein Frères." In *Encyclopedia of Nineteenth-Century Photography*, vol. 2, edited by John Hannavy. New York: Routledge, 2008.

Ross, Kristin. *Fast Cars, Clean Bodies: Decolonization and the Reordering of French Culture*. Cambridge, MA: MIT Press, 1996.

Ross, Kristin. *May '68 and Its Afterlives*. Chicago: University of Chicago Press, 2002.

Rothberg, Michael. "Introduction: Between Memory and Memory: From *Lieux de mémoire* to *Nœuds de mémoire*." *Yale French Studies*, nos. 118/119 (2010): 3–12.

Rothberg, Michael. *Multidirectional Memory: Remembering the Holocaust in the Age of Decolonization*. Stanford, CA: Stanford University Press, 2009.

Roumain, Jacques. *Bois-d'ébène*. Port-au-Prince: Imprimerie Henri Deschamps, 1945.

Rousseau, Raymond. "Le Sénégal d'autrefois: Étude sur le Oualo, cahiers de Yoro Dyâo." *Bulletin du comité d'études historiques et scientifiques de l'Afrique occidentale française* 12, nos. 1–2 (1929): 133–211.

Roy, Just-Jean-Étienne. *Histoire des colonies françaises et des établissements français [. . .]*. Tours: A. Mame, 1855.

R. S. "Why Boko Haram Uses Female Suicide-Bombers." *The Economist*, 23 October 2017.

Rupaire, Sonny (Soni Ripé). *Cette igname brisée qu'est ma terre natale: Recueil de poèmes en français / Gran parad ti kou baton: Krèy porèm an kréyol gwadloupéyen*. Paris: Éditions caribéennes, 1982.

S., Arslan. "Si la m'laya m'était contée." *El Watan*, 11 November 2004.

Saâdallah, Aziz, dir. *Le temps du terrorisme*. Ocean Film Productions, 2011.

Saadi, Nourredine. *Boulevard de l'abîme: Roman*. Algiers: Éditions Barzakh, 2017.

Saadi, Nourredine. *Dieu-Le-Fit: Roman*. Paris: Albin Michel, 1996.

Saadi, Nourredine. *Il n'y a pas d'os dans la langue: Rêves et autres histoires*. La Tour d'Aigues: Éditions de l'Aube, 2008.

Saadi, Nourredine. *La maison de lumière: Roman*. Paris: Albin Michel, 2000.

Saadi, Nourredine. *La nuit des origines: Roman*. La Tour d'Aigues: Éditions de l'Aube, 2005.

Saadi, Nourredine. "Retour à Constantine." In *Couleurs solides: Textes et paroles pour deux pays*, edited by Soumya Ammar Khodja, 58–60. Algiers: Marsa, 2003.

Sabatier, Peggy Roark. "Educating a Colonial Elite: The William Ponty School and Its Graduates." PhD diss., University of Chicago, 1977.

Sago, Kylie. "Beyond the Headless Empress: Gabriel Vital Dubray's Statues of Josephine, Edouard Glissant's *Tout-monde*, and Contested Monuments of French Empire." *Nineteenth-Century Contexts* 41, no. 5 (2019): 501–19.

Saint-Martin, Yves. "Léon Diop Sidia, une assimilation manquée." In *Perspectives nouvelles sur le passé de l'Afrique noire et de Madagascar: Mélanges offertes à Hubert Deschamps*. Paris: Publications de la Sorbonne, 1974.

Saint Pierre, Isaure de. *La Kahina, reine des Aurès: Roman*. Paris: Éditions Albin Michel, 2011.

Saint-Ruf, Germain. *L'épopée Delgrès: La Guadeloupe sous la révolution française*. Paris: Éditions L'Harmattan, 1977.

Saint-Ruf, Germain. *La leçon de Delgrès: Commémoration de l'anniversaire de sa mort: Discours prononcé le 28 mai 1955 à Paris*. Prague: Union internationale des étudiants, 1955.

Sala-Molins, Louis. *Le Code Noir, ou, Le calvaire de Canaan*. Paris: PUF, 1987.

Sall, Ibrahima. *Le choix de Madior: Suivi de Le prophète sans confession—Théâtre*. Dakar: Nouvelles Éditions Africaines, 1981.

Samb, Alaaji Momar. *Kujje*. Dakar: Éditions Papyrus Afrique, 2002.

Sankharé, Oumar. *Regard sur les œuvres de Alioune Badara Bèye: 1974–2009 (Essai, Poésie, Roman, Théâtre)*. Dakar: Éditions Maguilen, 2013.

Sansal, Boualem. *The German Mujahid*. Translated by Frank Wynne. New York: Europa Editions, 2009.

Sansal, Boualem. *Le serment des barbares: Roman*. Paris: Gallimard, 1999.

Sansal, Boualem. *Le village de l'Allemand ou le journal des frères Schiller: Roman*. Paris: Gallimard, 2008.

Sari, Mohamed. *Le labyrinthe: Roman*. Paris: Marsa, 2000.

Sarr, Fatou Sow. "Talaatay Nder et le message de Dialawali aux hommes politiques sénégalais." *leral.net*, 7 March 2018. https://www.leral.net/Talaatay-Nder-et-le-message-de-Dialawali-aux-hommes-politiques-senegalais-Fatou-Sow-SARR_a221942.html.

Sarr, Fatou [Sow]. *Talaatay Nder: La veritable histoire de Nder racontée aux enfants*. Dakar: Laboratoire Genre et Recherche Scientifique, Ifan—Université Cheikh Anta Diop de Dakar, 2010.

Sarr, Felwine. *Afrotopia*. Translated by Drew S. Burk and Sarah Jones-Boardman. Minneapolis: University of Minnesota Press, 2019.

Sarr, Felwine, and Bénédicte Savoy. *Rapport sur la restitution du patrimoine culturel africain: Vers une nouvelle éthique relationnelle*. Paris: Ministère de la culture, 2018.

Sarr, Felwine, and Bénédicte Savoy. *Restituer le patrimoine africain*. Paris: Phillipe Rey / Éditions du Seuil, 2018.

Savary, Jacques. *Le parfait négociant*. Paris: Chez Jean Guignard, fils, 1675.

Scarry, Elaine. *The Body in Pain: The Making and Unmaking of the World*. Oxford: Oxford University Press, 1985.

Schmaltz, Louis. *Carnet de voyage et destin d'une famille rescapée du naufrage de la frégate la Méduse, 1771–1827*. Colmar: Jérôme Do Bentzinger, 2017.

Schœlcher, Victor. *Histoire de l'esclavage pendant les deux dernières années*. Paris: Pagnerre, 1847.

Schwarz-Bart, André. *La mulâtresse solitude*. Paris: Éditions du Seuil, 1972.

Scott, A. O. "Ousmane Sembène's 'Black Girl' Turns 50." *New York Times*, 17 May 2016.

Scott, David. *Conscripts of Modernity: The Tragedy of Colonial Enlightenment*. Durham, NC: Duke University Press, 2004.

Scott, James C. *Domination and the Arts of Resistance: Hidden Transcripts*. New Haven, CT: Yale University Press, 1990.

Scott, James C. *Weapons of the Weak: Everyday Forms of Peasant Resistance*. New Haven, CT: Yale University Press, 1985.

Sealy, Mark. *Decolonising the Camera: Photography in Racial Time*. London: Lawrence and Wishart, 2019.

Sebold, Alice. *The Lovely Bones*. Boston: Little, Brown, 2002.

Sedgwick, Eve. *Between Men: English Literature and Male Homosocial Desire*. New York: Columbia University Press, 1985.

"Self-Immolation in Algeria, a New Chapter to Arab Spring?" *El Watan*, 5 May 2016.

Sembène, Ousmane, dir. *La Noire de = Black Girl*. . . . Filmi Doomi Reew, 1966. Criterion Collection, 2017.

Sembène, Ousmane. *Les bouts de bois de dieu*. Paris: Le livre contemporain, 1960.
Sembène, Ousmane, dir. *Ceddo*. Filmi Doomi Reew, 1977.
Sembène, Ousmane. *Le docker noir*. Paris: Nouvelles Éditions Debresse, 1956.
Sembène, Ousmane. "Liberté." *Action Poétique* ("Les peuples opprimés") 5 (1956): 29–32.
Sembène, Ousmane. "La Noire de . . . " In *Voltaïque: Nouvelles*, 149–77. Paris: Présence Africaine, 1962.
Sembène, Ousmane. *O pays, mon beau peuple!* Paris: Presses Pocket, 1957.
Sembène, Ousmane, dir. *Xala = The Curse*. Filmi Doomi Reew, 1974.
"Le Sénégalais Deba comparait aux Assises pour meurtre." *Paris-Dakar*, 24 December 1935.
"Senegal Man Dies in Dakar Fire Protest." BBC, 8 January 2013. https://www.bbc.com/news/world-africa-20947688.
Senghor, Léopold Sédar. *Négritude et humanisme: Liberté I*. Paris: Éditions du Seuil, 1964.
Senghor, Léopold Sédar. *Poèmes*. Paris: Éditions du Seuil, 1964.
Senoussi, Hicham. "La démocratie, ce bien si précieux à préserver." *Le Matin du Sahara*, 18 May 2003.
Serbin, Sylvia. *Reines d'Afrique et héroïnes de la diaspora noire*. Saint-Maur-des-Fossés: Sépia, 2004.
Serhani, Mounir. *Il n'y a pas de barbe lisse: Roman*. Rabat: Marsam, 2016.
Seye, El Hadji Amadou. *Walo Brack*. Dakar: Éditions Maguilen, 2003.
Shakespeare, William. *The Tempest*. Edited by Stephen Orgel. Oxford: Oxford University Press, 1987.
Sharif, Sa'eeda. "Morocco's 'Culture of Death.'" *raseef22*, 18 November 2022. https://raseef22.net/english/article/1090565-moroccos-culture-of-death-disturbing-numbers-reveal-the-spread-of-suicide.
Sharpe, Christina. *In the Wake: On Blackness and Being*. Durham, NC: Duke University Press, 2016.
Sharpe, Christina. *Ordinary Notes*. New York: Farrar, Straus and Giroux, 2023.
Sharpe, Mani. *Late-Colonial French Cinema: Filming the Algerian War of Independence*. Edinburgh: Edinburgh University Press, 2023.
Sider, Chérifa. *Traumatisme psychologique et suicide en Algérie*. Paris: L'Harmattan, 2018.
Sidhoum, Slimane Aït. *Les trois doigts de la main: Roman*. Algiers: Chihab, 2002.
"Sidya Léon Diop, fils de la Reine Ndatté Yalla Mbodj, un des plus grands héros de la résistance." *Ndarinfo.com*, 16 December 2017. https://www.ndarinfo.com/HISTOIRE-Sidya-Leon-DIOP-fils-de-la-Reine-Ndatte-Yalla-Mbodj-un-des-plus-grands-heros-de-la-resistance_a20548.html.
"Sidya Ndaté Yalla, une vie d'honneur et de courage pour le Brack du Walo." *Au-Sénégal.com*, 14 August 2017. https://www.au-senegal.com/sidya-ndate-yalla-une-vie-d-honneur-et-de-courage-pour-le-brack-du-walo,14658.html?lang=fr.
Silverman, Kaja. *The Threshold of the Visible World*. New York: Routledge, 1996.
Silverman, Max. *Palimpsestic Memory: The Holocaust and Colonialism in French and Francophone Fiction and Film*. New York: Berghahn, 2013.
Silverstein, Michael. "Texts, Entextualized and Artifactualized: The Shapes of Discourse." *College English* 82, no. 1 (2019): 55–76.

Skaine, Rosemarie. *Female Suicide Bombers*. Jefferson, NC: McFarland, 2006.
Snyder, Terri L. *The Power to Die: Slavery and Suicide in British North America*. Chicago: University of Chicago Press, 2015.
Snyder, Terri L. "Suicide, Slavery, and Memory in North America." *Journal of American History* 97, no. 1 (June 2010): 39–62.
Socé, Ousmane. *Mirages de Paris*. Paris: Nouvelles Éditions Latines, 1937.
Soumahoro, Maboula. *Le Triangle et l'Hexagone: Réflexions sur une identité noire*. Paris: La Découverte, 2020.
Spivak, Gayatri Chakravorty. "Can the Subaltern Speak?" In *Marxism and the Interpretation of Culture*, edited by Cary Nelson and Lawrence Grossberg, 271–313. Urbana: University of Illinois Press, 1988.
Spivak, Gayatri Chakravorty. "Rethinking Comparativism." *New Literary History* 40, no. 3 (2009): 609–26.
Spivak, Gayatri Chakravorty. "Scattered Speculations on the Subaltern and the Popular." *Postcolonial Studies* 8, no. 4 (2005): 475–86.
Spivak, Gayatri Chakravorty. "Terror: A Speech after 9/11." *boundary 2* 31, no. 2 (2004): 81–111.
Spurlin, William J. "Contested Borders: Cultural Translation and Queer Politics in Contemporary Francophone Writing from the Maghreb." *Research in African Literatures* 47, no. 2 (Summer 2016): 104–20.
Stevenson, Robert L. "Jumping Overboard: Examining Suicide, Resistance, and West African Cosmologies during the Middle Passage." PhD diss., Michigan State University, 2018.
Stewart Howe, Kathleen. "North Africa." In *Encyclopedia of Nineteenth-Century Photography*, vol. 1, edited by John Hannavy, 18–20. New York: Routledge, 2008.
Stora, Benjamin. *La gangrène et l'oubli: La mémoire de la guerre d'Algérie*. Paris: La Découverte, 1991.
Stratton, Florence. *Contemporary African Literature and the Politics of Gender*. New York: Routledge, 1994.
Stuever, Hank. "The Bomb with a Loaded Message." *Washington Post*, 27 October 2001.
Sturken, Marita. "Absent Images of Memory: Remembering and Reenacting the Japanese Internment." In *Perilous Memories: The Asia-Pacific War(s)*, edited by Takashi Fujitani, Geoffrey M. White, and Lisa Yoneyama, 33–49. Durham, NC: Duke University Press, 2001.
Sturken, Marita. "Absent Images of Memory: Remembering and Reenacting the Japanese Internment." *Positions* 5, no. 3 (1997): 687–707.
Suhr-Sytsma, Nathan. "The Extroverted African Novel and Literary Publishing in the Twenty-First Century." *Journal of African Cultural Studies* 30, no. 3 (2018): 339–55.
Sy, Alhamdou, dir. *Doomu Adama*. Dakar: Cauris Films Sarl, 2006.
Sylla, Aïda. "Les tentatives de suicide à Dakar: Étude descriptive de 439 cas colligés à l'hôpital principal." Master's thesis, Université Cheikh Anta Diop de Dakar, 1998.
Talbayev, Edwige Tamalet. *The Transcontinental Maghreb: Francophone Literature across the Mediterranean*. New York: Fordham University Press, 2017.

Talbayev, Edwige Tamalet, and yasser elhariry, eds. *Critically Mediterranean: Temporalities, Aesthetics, and Deployments of a Sea in Crisis*. Cham, Switzerland: Palgrave Macmillan, 2018.

Tansi, Sony Labou. *La vie et demie*. Paris: Éditions du Seuil, 1979.

Tasso, Torquato. *Jerusalem Delivered: An English Prose Version*. Edited and translated by Ralph Nash. Detroit: Wayne State University Press, 1987.

Terhmina, Imane. "Topographie de la terreur: Espaces (inter)textuels dans *Moi, Khalid Kelkal*." In *Salim Bachi*, edited by Agnès Schaffauser, 133–43. Paris: L'Harmattan, 2019.

Tervonen, Taina. *Au pays des disparus: PM390047, un mort en Méditerranée*. Paris: Fayard, 2019.

Thomas, Dominic. *Africa and France: Postcolonial Cultures, Migration, and Racism*. Bloomington: Indiana University Press, 2013.

Thomas, Dominic. *Black France: Colonialism, Immigration, and Transnationalism*. Bloomington: Indiana University Press, 2007.

Thomas, Leanna. "Daniel Maximin's *Lone Sun*: Disrupting the Tides of History and Memory." *Small Axe* 26, no. 1 (March 2022): 69–84.

Thomas, Samuel. "Outtakes and Outrage: The Means and Ends of Suicide Terror." *Modern Fiction Studies* 57, no. 3 (Fall 2011): 425–49.

"Three Students Set Fire to Themselves in Senegal." *News24*, 15 March 2013. https://www.news24.com/news24/3-students-set-fire-to-themselves-20130315.

Tiger, Lionel. "Rogue Males: What Makes Young Muslim Men Turn to Terrorism?" *Guardian*, 2 October 2001. https://www.theguardian.com/world/2001/oct/02/gender.uk.

Tillier, Bertrand. *La belle noyée: Enquête sur le masque de l'Inconnue de la Seine*. Paris: Les Éditions Arkhê, 2011.

Tirolien, Guy. *Balles d'or*. Paris: Présence Africaine, 1961.

Torrey, Jesse. *A Portraiture of Domestic Slavery, in the United States: With Reflections on the Practicability of Restoring the Moral Rights of the Slave, without Impairing the Legal Privileges of the Possessor; and a Project of a Colonial Asylum for Free Persons of Colour: Including Memoirs of Facts on the Interior Traffic in Slaves, and on Kidnapping*. Philadelphia: John Bioren, 1817.

Toudoire-Surlapierre, Frédérique. *Le fait divers et ses fictions*. Paris: Éditions de Minuit, 2019.

Toureille, Julien. "La dissidence dans les Antilles françaises: Une mémoire à préserver (1945–2011)." *Revue historique des armées* 270 (2013): 68–78.

Trouillot, Michel-Rolph. *Silencing the Past: Power and the Production of History*. Boston: Beacon, 1995.

Valente-Quinn, Brian. *Senegalese Stagecraft: Decolonizing Theater-Making in Francophone Africa*. Evanston, IL: Northwestern University Press, 2021.

Vergès, Françoise. "A Museum without Objects." In *The Postcolonial Museum: The Arts of Memory and the Pressures of History*, edited by Iain Chambers, Alessandra De Angelis, Celeste Ianniciello, Mariangela Orabona, and Michaela Quadraro, 25–38. London: Routledge, 2016.

Versluys, Kristiaan. *Out of the Blue: September 11 and the Novel*. New York: Columbia University Press, 2009.

Victor, Barbara. *Army of Roses: Inside the World of Palestinian Women Suicide Bombers*. London: Robinson, 2004.

Vidal-Naquet, Pierre. *La raison d'état: Textes publiés par le Comité Maurice Audin*. Paris: Éditions de Minuit, 1962.

Vieyra, Paulin Soumanou. *Ousmane Sembène, cinéaste: Première période, 1962–1971*. Paris: Présence Africaine, 1972.

Virtue, Nancy. "'Le film de . . .': Self-Adaptation in the Film Version of Ousmane Sembène's 'La Noire de . . .'" *Literature/Film Quarterly* 42, no. 3 (2014): 557–67.

Voltaire, François Marie Arouet de. *Œuvres complètes*. Paris: Garnier, 1876–83.

wa Thiong'o, Ngũgĩ. *Decolonising the Mind: The Politics of Language in African Literature*. Oxford: James Currey, 1986.

Wade, Amadou. "Chronique du Wâlo sénégalais, traduite du Wolof par Bassirou Cissé, publiée et commentée par Vincent Monteil." *Bulletin de l'Institut français d'Afrique noire, Série B: Sciences humaines* 26, nos. 3–4 (1964): 440–98.

Wade, Francis. "Gayatri Spivak: The Subaltern Speaks through Dying." *The Nation*, 6 July 2021.

Walcott, Derek. *Selected Poems*. Edited by Edward Baugh. New York: Farrar, Straus and Giroux, 2007.

Walker, Daniel. "Suicidal Tendencies: African Transmigration in the History and Folklore of the Americas." *The Griot* 18, no. 2 (October 1999): 10–18.

Walker, David H. *Outrage and Insight: Modern French Writers and the "Fait Divers."* Oxford: Berg, 1995.

Warner, Jason, and Hilary Matfess. *Exploding Stereotypes: The Unexpected Operational and Demographic Characteristics of Boko Haram's Suicide Bombers*. West Point, NY: Combating Terrorism Center at West Point, 2017.

Warner, Tobias. "Enacting Postcolonial Translation: Voice, Color and Free Indirect Discourse in the Restored Version of Ousmane Sembène's *La Noire de . . .*" In *Translating the Postcolonial in Multilingual Contexts*, edited by Judith Misrahi-Barak and Srilata Ravi, 113–26. Montpellier: Presses universitaires de la Méditerranée, 2017.

Warner, Tobias. *The Tongue-Tied Imagination: Decolonizing Literary Modernity in Senegal*. New York: Fordham University Press, 2019.

Waters, Sarah. *Suicide Voices: Labour Trauma in France*. Liverpool: Liverpool University Press, 2020.

Watt, Nicholas. "Lib Dem MP: Why I Would Consider Being a Suicide Bomber." *Guardian*, 23 January 2004. https://www.theguardian.com/politics/2004/jan/23/israel.liberaldemocrats.

Waṭṭār, Al-Ṭāhir. *Al-Zilzāl*. Algiers: Société nationale d'édition et de diffusion, 1974.

Waṭṭār, Al-Ṭāhir. *The Earthquake*. Translated by William Granara. London: Saqi Books, 2000.

Weaver, Mary Anne. "The Short, Violent Life of Abu Musab al-Zarqawi." *The Atlantic*, 15 August 2006. https://www.theatlantic.com/magazine/archive/2006/07/the-short-violent-life-of-abu-musab-al-zarqawi/304983/.

Weinmann, Frédéric. *"Je suis mort": Essai sur la narration autothanatographique*. Paris: Éditions du Seuil, 2018.

Werner, Michael, and Bénédicte Zimmermann. "Beyond Comparison: *Histoire Croisée* and the Challenge of Reflexivity." *History and Theory* 45, no. 1 (February 2006): 30–50.

White, Sophie. *Voices of the Enslaved: Love, Labor, and Longing in French Louisiana*. Williamsburg, VA: Omohundro Institute of Early American History and Culture; Chapel Hill: University of North Carolina Press, 2019.

Wilderson, Frank B., III. *Afropessimism*. New York: Liveright, 2020.

Wilson, Siona. "Severed Images: Women, the Algerian War of Independence and the Mobile Documentary Idea." *International Journal of Francophone Studies* 21, nos. 3–4 (2018): 233–54.

Wiredu, Kwasi. "Death and the Afterlife in African Culture." In *Person and Community: Ghanaian Philosophical Studies, I*, edited by Kwasi Wiredu and Kwame Gyekye, 137–52. Washington, DC: Council for Research in Values and Philosophy, 2010.

Woywodt, Alexander, and Akos Kiss. "Geophagia: The History of Earth-Eating." *Journal of the Royal Society of Medicine* 95, no. 3 (March 2002): 143–46.

Yacine, Kateb. *Parce que c'est une femme, suivi de La Kahina ou Dihya, Saout Ennissa, La voix des femmes, Louise Michel et la Nouvelle-Calédonie*. 1972. Reprint, Paris: Des Femmes, 2004.

Yaeger, Patricia. "Consuming Trauma; or, The Pleasures of Merely Circulating." *Journal X* 1, no. 2 (1996): 229–51.

Yale, Néba Fabrice. "La violence dans l'esclavage des colonies françaises au XVIIIe siècle." Master's thesis, Université Pierre Mendès-France, 2009.

Young, Jason R. "All God's Children Had Wings: The Flying African in History, Literature, and Lore." *Journal of Africana Religions* 5, no. 1 (2017): 50–70.

Zaganiaris, Jean. "La question Queer au Maroc: Identités sexuées et transgenre au sein de la littérature marocaine de langue française." *Confluences Méditerranée* 80, no. 1 (Winter 2011–12): 145–61.

INDEX

Page numbers in *italics* denote illustrations or photographs.

Abderrezak, Hakim, 34, 50, 66–67, 163–64, 168
abolition of French slavery, 6–7, 31, 58, 72
Absa, Moussa Sène, 85
Achebe, Chinua, 21
Adimi, Kaouther, 168
aesthetic works, 29, 34–35, 105, 115–16, 136, 207, 212, 235, 239; explanation of, x, 21–22; on "suicidal resistance," 23–25, 80. *See also* entextualization
African Novel of Ideas, The (Jackson), 21
Afropessimism, 14
Afrotopia (Sarr, Felwine), 79, 227
afterlife of slavery, 51
agricultural colonization, 82–83, 88–89
ailes de la reine, Les (al-A'radji), 167
Aimard, Gustave, 58
al-A'radji, Waçiny, 167
Algerian War of Independence, 3, 34, 109, 122, 164–65, 181, 184, 187
Allison, Sophie Nahli, 9–10
Al-Qaeda, 211
al-Zarqawi, Abu Musab, 211
al-Zilzāl (*The Earthquake*) (Waṭṭār), 167
anarchives, 29, 270n23
anti-Blackness, 115, 129
Arab Spring, 28
Aragon, Louis, 169
archive, explanation of, 26–29
Arékian, Roger, 58

ash/ashes, 25, 81, 91, 96, 98–104
Ashbāh al-Madīnah al-Maqtūlah (Muftī), 216
assimilation, 66, 139, 267n91
Association of Small Bombs (Mahajan), 210
Atlantics (Diop, Mati), 50, 168
attentat, L' (Khadra), 210
Aurélien (Aragon), 169
autothanatographic narration, 208–9, 216, 228
autothanatography, explanation of, 214
aventure ambiguë, L' (Kane), 90, 137–38
Ayouch, Nabil, 208, 213, 225–28
Azan, H., 84–85, 260n40
Azim, Firdous, 23
Azoulay, Ariella Aïsha, 31, 163

Bâ, Amadou Hampâté, 77, 103
Bâ, Thierno, 85
Bāchī, Salīm, 210
Bakhaw, Diawdine Amadou, 77, 257n3
ballerines de Papicha, Des (Adimi), 168
Bàmmeelu Kocc Barma (*The Grave of Kocc Barma*) (Diop), 95
bañ, 79
Barma, Kocc, 94–96, 102–3
Barse, Pierre, 6, 245n30
Barthes, Roland, 124, 159, 163, 195
barzakh, 214, 229
Bataille d'Alger, La (Pontecorvo), 210
Bedar, Fatima, 170, *172*, 195

bëkk-néég, 98, 103
Belain d'Esnambuc, Pierre, 42, 71
belly of the Atlantic, 49–50, 145
Beloved (Morrison), 45, 130
Benkhaled, Walid, 181, 273n66
Bennett, Alice, 208, 216
Beroho, Ahmed, 212
Best, Stephen, 20–21, 25, 27, 202, 207
Bèye, Alioune Badara, 33, 81, 83–94, 98–99, 101, 104–5, 261n58
Bhabha, Homi, 23
Bhaduri, Bhubaneswari, 29
Bicknell, John, 11, 37
bidonville, explanation of, 208
biens meubles, 3
Binebine, Mahi, 34–35, 65, 168, 208–9, 211–33
biopower, spectacles of, 5
Bissainthe, Toto, 152, 154, 268n121
Black Decade (*décennie noire*), 34–35, 168, 180, 182, 207, 210–11, 227, 229
Black Girl (Sembène). See *Noire de . . . , La* (Sembène)
Blair, Dorothy, 137, 266n67
Blessington, Francis, 217
Blessures secrètes: Port-Louis, 1943 (Saint-Eloy), 67
Boilat, Abbé David, 82
bois d'ébène, 67, 70
Bonaparte, Empress Joséphine, 42, 71
Bonaparte, Napoleon, 6–7, 56–57, 202
Bongie, Chris, 59, 256n64
bonnes, Les (Genet), 129
Borom Sarret (Sembène), 115, 122
boroom xam-xam, 77, 80, 98–99, 102–3
Bosman, Willem, 202
Bouazizi, Mohamed, 28, 81, 105, 106, 107, 263n105
Bouchikhi, Ahmed, 212
Boulevard de l'abîme (Saadi), 34, 166, 183–88
Bourdieu, Pierre, 124
bouts de bois de Dieu, Les (Sembène), 122
Bovary, Emma, 17, 29, 187
brak, 78, 82–84, 89, 96, 98
Brozgal, Lia, 29, 119, 180

Caché (Haneke), 168
cachexia Africana, 14
cale, la, 45, 51, 143

calotype, 161, 165. See also exposure, techniques of
Campt, Tina M., 163, 165
Camus, Albert, 116, 129, 271n41
Cannibales (Binebine), 35, 168, 208, 227–32
"Can the Subaltern Speak?" (Spivak), 28, 29
Cap 110 (Valère), 72
cathexis, 169–70
Cavarero, Adriana, 204
Ceddo (Sembène), 94, 137
ceintures de paradis, 223, 229
cendre-semence, 104
centre de renseignement et d'action (CRA), 164
Césaire, Aimé, 58, 65
Chamoiseau, Patrick, 44
champ aveugle. See photography: blind field in
chanson de bord, 53
chants marins, 52–53
Chapier, Henry, 116
Charonne massacre, 179–80
chasseur de rats, Le (Aimard), 58
chevaux de Dieu, Les (Ayouch), 208, 213, 225–26
Chirac, Jacques, 211
choix de Madior, Le (Sall, Ibrahima), 85
Christophe, Henri, 57
Church, Christopher M., 3–4, 17
claie d'infamie, 5, 6
Code Civil des Français (1804), 7, 30
Code de l'Indigénat (the Native Code), 30–31
Code Noir (1685), 3, 7, 18, 20, 30–31, 244n11
Code Pénal of 1791, 30
Code Pénal of 1810, 30
Colbert, Jean-Baptiste, 2
collective suicide, 9, 56, 79; of Louis Delgrès, 32, 41, 69, 72; of the women of Nder, 32, 45, 80–81, 84–92, 96, 101, 103–5, 108, 140, 146
Combat (newspaper), 116
Condé, Maryse, 44, 58, 72
Conscripts of Modernity (Scott), 23
Constantine, Siege of, 163–64
copycat effect, 105, 263n105
Coulibaly, Bojana, 87
CRA (*centre de renseignement et d'action*), 164
Criminal Ordonnance of 1670, 2
crypto genre, 115
Cugoano, Ottobah, 16–17
curateur, 2

Damas, Léon-Gontran, 65
Daniel, Drew, 19
David, Jacques-Louis, 146, *149*
Day, Thomas, 11, 37, 130
Day Night Day Night (Loktev), 226
Death and the King's Horseman (Soyinka), 21
death writing, 208–9
Debret, Jean, 15, *16*
décennie noire. *See* Black Decade (*décennie noire*)
Deckerinnerungen, 119. *See also* screen memory
Decolonising the Mind (wa Thiong'o), 95
De Gaulle, Charles, 122
Delgrès, Louis, 32, 41, 56–74, 202, 252n6, 254n46, 255n56
Demain la fin du monde (Bèye), 86
departmentalization, 58, 59
Derrida, Jacques, 25, 104–5, 208
Dessalines, Jacques, 57, 255n49
Dhākirat al-jasad (*Memory in the Flesh*) (Mosteghanemi), 167
Dialawali, terre de feu (Bèye), 86
Diatta, Marie Auguste, 85–86
Diaw, Yoro Booli, 82–85
Diome, Fatou, 33, 34, 49–50, 58, 66, 109, 137, 139, 168
Diop, Boubacar Boris, 33, 81, 83–84, 94–105
Diop, Cheikh, 105
Diop, David, 44
Diop, Fatima, 106–8, 120
Diop, Mati, 50, 168
Diop, Mbissine Thérèse, 113, 152, *153*
Diop, Ousmane Socé, 33, 66, 137, 139–40
Diop, Sidya "Léon," 79, 258n13
discours antillais, Le (Glissant), 57–58, 62
disillusionment, 139
displacement, 6, 32, 65–66; in *La Noire de . . .* , 137, 140, 142, 150; in Saadi's novels, 166, 171, 181
Dispossessed Lives (Fuentes), 27, 130
Doane, Mary Ann, 104
docker noir, Le (Sembène), 121–22
Doomi Golo: Nettali (Diop, Boubacar Boris), 33, 81, 87, 91, 94–104, 257n1, 262n78
dóomu taal yi, 101, 103
dóom yi, 96
double exposure. *See* multiple exposure
Drif, Zohra, 202

Dubois, Laurent, 57
Dugoujon, Abbé Casimir, 1, 3
Durbano, Magno, 128–29
Durkheim, Émile, 18, 164
Dying Negro, The (Day and Bicknell), 11, *13*, 37, 39, 130
dyom (*jom*), 10, 79, 106, 140
dysgraphia, 24–25, 29, 147, 156, 182, 188

Ebos Landing, 9–10
Edwards, Brent Hayes, 26
El Guabli, Brahim, 29
Elimane, T. C., 106, 108
Émérigon, Balthazard-Marie, 4
engagisme, 7
enquête, 34, 185
entangled history, 31
entextualization: definition of, 22; of Diouana Gomis's suicide, 124–25
epic, 23
Equiano, Olaudah, 17
esclave vieil homme et le molosse, L' (Chamoiseau), 44
Esquisses sénégalaises (Boilat), 82
Essomba, J. R., 229
Ethics of Memory, The (Margalit), 119
étoiles de Sidi Moumen, Les (Binebine), 34–35, 65, 208, 228–32
Évocation d'un mémorial à Venise (Lyamlahy), 33, 138, 171
exposure, techniques of, 161–62, 165, 170, 176, 189
extroversion, 227

fag bomb, 225, 280n91
Faidherbe, Louis, 79
fait divers: definition and discussion of the, 116, 124, 264n33; French literary tradition of, 129; in *La Noire de . . .* , *117*, 118, 120–22, *123*, 125–40, 147, 151; as a sign of necropower, 131
Fall, Samba Yaya, 79, 267n91
Fanon, Frantz, 5, 191, 202
Fasolt, Constantin, 21
Faye, Diégane Latyr, 106–8
Feindt, Gregor, 31
female suicide, 29, 32, 34, 94, 167, 170, 196, 205, 226, 276n19
Fillon, François, 71

INDEX · 317

flying African, 9–10, 44, 47
forgetting, 56–59, 115, 118–19, 136, 154. *See also* silencing
Forter, Greg, 23
Foster, Charles, 85
Foucault, Michel, 5, 24, 131
francophilie (Senghor), 87
francophonie, 87
French Atlantic Triangle, 30, 32, 44
French Atlantic Triangle, The (Miller), 16
French Protectorate, 212
Freud, Sigmund, 26, 118–19
Frossard, Benjamin, 9
Fuentes, Marisa, 27, 130
fugitivity, 9, 20
fugue, 44. *See also Humus* (Kanor)
Fuuta, 83, 86, 88, 90, 92, 259n29

gàcce, 79, 99
Garner, Margaret, 130
Gathara, Patrick, 238
Genet, Jean, 129
geology, genealogy of, 178
geophagia, 14, 15
géwél, 78, 80, 86, 103. *See also* griots
ghosts: in *La Noire de . . .*, 136, 156; in *Les étoiles de Sidi Moumen*, 214–18; in other works by Saadi, 195–96; in Retour à Constantine, 171–73
ghost story, 214, 216
Girardière, Millet de la, 6, 245n30
Glissant, Édouard, x, 39, 44, 49–50, 55–58, 62, 66, 72
Godineau, Dominique, 2
Gorée Island, Senegal, 43, 142
gouffre-matrice, 49
Greene, John Beasley, 161–65, 168, 269n4
griot de Marrakech, Le (Binebine), 213
griots, 78, 86. See also *géwél*
Guelwaar (Sembène), 85
Guide médical aux Antilles (Levacher), 15
Gupta, Suman, 28

Hacking, Ian, 18
haïk, 191–92, 202
Haitian Revolution, 57–58, 254n46
Halimi, Gisèle, 167
Haneke, Michael, 168

Hardy, Georges, 87–88
harraga, 32, 35, 208, 228–33
Hartman, Saidiya, 27, 51, 111, 131, 155–56
heteronormativity, 145, 209, 221–24
Higonnet, Margaret, 29
hirondelles de Kaboul, Les (Khadra), 210
histoire croisée, 31
historical tragedy, 84, 87
history hesitant, 31
homicidal suicide, 204, 228
homonationalism, 205
homophobia, 205, 219, 223, 226
homosexual panic, 221, 223
homosociality, 53, 209, 219–23, 226, 232, 254n41
horrorism, 205, 211
Houen, Alex, 203, 207, 277n36
Hughes, Langston, 161, 171, 271n45
Humus (Kanor), 41, 43–55, 61, 62, 63, 70–71, 254n41
hyperterrorism, 204

Ici on noie les Algériens, 173, 179
Ignace, Joseph, 6, 62
île et une nuit, L' (Maximin), 59
impossible message of suicide, 29, 207
impossible speech, 45, 156, 239
Inconnue de la Seine, 169–70
individual suicide, 30, 108, 232, 247n49
infanticide, 20, 65
"Inhibitions, Symptoms, and Anxiety" (Freud), 26
inscription of female suicide, 167
insurance policies, colonial, 3–4, 9, 16
Interesting Narrative (Equiano), 17
Interpretation of Dreams (Freud), 118
isolé soleil, L' (Maximin), 41, 55, 59, 72, 137, 170, 186, 256n66
istishhad, 229. *See also* martyrdom

jaam, 98
Jackson, Jeanne-Marie, 21, 23, 107
Jasmine Revolution in Tunisia, 28
jihadist, meaning of, 227
John Paul II (pope), 211
jom (*dyom*), 10, 79, 106, 140
Jones, Nicholas R., 131
Joola (vessel), 86
Jordan, Neil, 216

jour idéal pour mourir, Un (Kacimi), 168
journal de bord, 42
Joy of the Worm (Daniel), 19
Julien, Eileen, 23, 210–11
jumeaux de Sidi Moumen, Les (Bouchikhi), 212

Ka, Aminata Maïga, 138
Kacimi, Samir, 167–68
Kahina, La (Halimi), 167
Kahina, reine des Aurès, La (Saint Pierre), 167
Kahina ou Dihya, La (Yacine), 167
Kane, Cheikh Hamidou, 90, 137–38
Kanor, Fabienne, 32, 34, 41–56, 66, 70–71, 83–84, 109, 143–44
Karmen Geï (Ramaka), 85
Kef Chekara, 164
Khadra, Yasmina, 210
knotted memory, 31

Labat, Père, 14–15
larmes de la patrie, Les (Bèye), 86
Last Resistance, The (Rose), 26, 201
Lat-Dior, le chemin de l'honneur (Bâ, Thierno), 85
léep, 78, 85
Légitime défense, 59
Le Gray, Gustave, 161–63
Lemoine, Georges, 11
Le Pen, Marine, 71
Levacher, Michel-Gabriel, 15
Liengme, Georges, 8
lieu(x) de mémoire, 70–71, 163, 272n57
lingeer (*linguère*), 78, 84, 90, 91, 93, 96, 120, 257n6
lingeer-awo, 78
Loi Taubira, 58, 71–72
Loktev, Julie, 226
Louverture, Toussaint, 57–58, 72, *73*, 254n46
Lovely Bones, The (Sebold), 216, 226
Lowe, Lisa, 31
Lu Defu Waxu, 95
Lyamlahy, Khalid, 33, 138, 171

Mackau, baron de (Ange René Armand), 4
"Madonna of Bentalha" (Zaourar), 180, *181*
Mahajan, Karan, 210
Maheke, Paul, 171, *174*, 271n45
Mailhol, Gabriel, 17

Malaanum lëndëm (*The Cloak of Darkness*) (Diop), 95
maladies des nègres, 5
Marat, Jean-Paul, 146–47, *149*
Marat assassiné (David), 146–47, *149*
Margalit, Avishai, 119
marronage, 4, 20
martyrdom, 15, 20, 29, 65, 94, 220, 229; understanding suicide as heroic, 67
Maximin, Daniel, 32, 41–42, 44, 51, 55–62, 65, 67, 70–72, 137, 170, 186, 188, 190
mbandkat, 88
Mbaye, Coly, 85
Mbembe, Achille, xi, 5–6, 15
Mborso, Amar Fatim, 83
mélancolie, 5; Diouana Gomis and, 124, 126, 131, 137, 140–41, 150–51; *la mélancolie noire*, 14–15
melaya, 191–93
Memmi, Albert, 5
mémoire. See memory
Mémorial du sacrifice de Louis Delgrès (Arékian), 58
memorialization, 71
memory: Azor's trial of, 1–3; explanation of term, 1–2. See also *histoire croisée*
mens rea, 3
métissage, 66
Métral, Antoine, 14
Miano, Léonora, 44
migration, 32–35, 50; in *Cannibales*, 227–32; clandestine, 228–30; irregular, xii, 35, 227–28, 232; in *La Noire de...*, 109, 129, 142
migritude, 137, 168
military suicides, 18
Miller, Christopher L., 16, 44, 139
Mirages de Paris (Diop, Ousmane Socé), 33, 66, 137
miroir de la vie, Le (Ka), 138
mise en valeur du Sénégal, La (Hardy), 88
mission civilisatrice, 67, 86–88, 90
mnemic image, 118–19
Moi, Khaled Kelkal (Bāchī), 210
Moi, Tituba, sorcière... Noire de Salem (Condé), 44
monuments, 70–71
Morgan, Jennifer, 27
Morrison, Toni, 45, 130

mort de Marat, La (David), 146–47, *149*
Mosnier, Louis, 39–46, 54, 252nn2–3
Mosteghanemi, Ahlam, 167
mouth-locks, 15
Muftī, Bashīr, 216
mujāhid, 210
Mulâtre, Le (Séjour), 17–18
multidirectional memory, 31
multiple exposure, 34, 195; as anarchival technology of making visible, 165; in *Boulevard de l'abîme*, 167, 185, 187–95; explanation of, 165–66; in *La nuit des origines*, 176, 178–80, 183; metaphor and materiality of, 168; in Retour à Constantine, 170–71, 173, 175; using bodies of water, 171
Murphy, David, 82
music as a suicide deterrent, 53

Napoleonic Code Civil of 1804, 30
Napoléon III, 7
narrative imagination, 209, 225
nawetaan performances, 88
Ndao, Cheik Aliou, 86
Nder, Talaatay (Tuesday of), 32–33, 77–109, 120–21, 140–41, 146, 196, 236, 258n18, 258n22, 260n34
Nder en flammes (Bèye), 33, 81, 85–91, *90*, 101
Ndiaw, Treaty of, 83, 87
necromancy, 131
necropolitics, 6, 15
necroresistance, 15, 23
nègre/négresse, definition of, 3–4, 131
Nesbitt, Nick, 56
nettali, 78, 99–102, 104
New and Accurate Description of the Coast of Guinea (Bosman), 202
Newell, Stephanie, 22
Newton, Huey, 10, 248n59
Ngom, Ousmane, 95
Niaye (Sembène), 115, 122
nœud de mémoire, 163
Noire de . . . , La (Sembène), 33, 95, 108, 113–57, 166–69, 180, 188, 264n7
None like Us (Best), 20, 156, 202
nosopolitics, 8–9, 247n46
nostalgia, definition of, 148, 151
Notice sur le Oualo, 84

nuit des origines, La (Saadi), 34, 166–68, 175–83, 188, 189, 195–96
Nussbaum, Martha, 209, 219, 226

Octobre à Paris (Panijel), 180
Ô pays, mon beau peuple (Sembène), 122
oral history, 22, 32, 42, 78, 91
Ordinary Notes (Sharpe), 27
other-archives, 29

palimpsestic memory, 165, 268n121
Palmer, Tyrone, 20
Panijel, Jacques, 180
Pape, Robert, 207, 277n30
paradis au nord, Le (Essomba), 229
paradise, 32, 229
paraliterature, 82
parasuicide, 10–11, 14–15, 20, 80
parfait négociant, Le (Savary), 7
partus sequitur ventrum, 50–51, 145
Patterson, Orlando, 15
Paul et Virginie (1788), 17
Pellegrin, 88–89
Penda, Fara, 82, 84
petit nègre, 135
philosophe nègre, Le (Mailhol), 17
philosophical suicide, 21, 107
photography: blind field in, 163, 165, 269n7; colonial, 163, 193, 268n3; haptic objects in, 163, 165
pica, 14, 15
plus secrète mémoire des hommes, La (Sarr, M. M.), 33, 81, 105, 120, 138
Poétique de la relation (Glissant), 49, 55
points of resistance (Foucault), 24
police investigation, 34, 185
police violence, 67, 106, 170, 179, 188, 236–37
political suicide, x, 106, 120, 243n4
politicized looking, xii, 25
Pontecorvo, Gillo, 210
porte du voyage sans retour, La (Diop, David), 44
Portraiture of Domestic Slavery, A (Torrey), 11, *12*, 130
(post-)9/11 novel, 210
positivism, 156
postmortem narration, 208–9, 214, 216–17
potential history, 31

Pouye, Baye, 105
Power to Die, The (Snyder), 17
Prévost, Abbé, 2
proverbs, 59, 62, 94
psychiatry, 167
psychoanalysis: resistance in, 26, 118, 175; *séance* of, 188–89
Puar, Jasbir, 205, 225, 227
public suicide, 105–6, 120, 128
purple, 49–50

quatrième siècle, Le (Glissant), 44
queering, 65, 208, 219, 225, 232–33; definition of, 209
queerness, 205, 209, 226, 232–33
queer practice of the archive, 26
queer voice, 209

Rabéarivelo, Jean-Joseph, 66–67
rachat préalable (1856), 7
racism, 32, 129; in *La Noire de . . .*, 115–16; in *Le docker noir*, 121; in *L'isolé-soleil*, 65, 137
Radford, Daniel, 58
Ramaka, Joseph Gai, 85
Rapport sur la restitution du patrimoine culturel africain (Sarr and Savoy), 238
Raynaud, Jean, 4
reading suicide, x, 21, 24–25, 28, 30, 65, 70, 81, 104
Reckoning with Slavery (Morgan), 27
recovery in archival studies, 26–27, 33, 115, 118
Reines d'Afrique et héroïnes de la diaspora noire (Serbin), 80
Repinecz, Jonathon, 94–95, 102, 257n4
resistance fighter, 56, 203
revenant, 171, 175
revolutionary suicide, 10, 19–20, 248n59
rhetorical force of suicide, xi, 22, 24–26, 30, 207–8, 239
Rhummel River Gorge, 34, 161–75, *162*, 178–85, 189–90, 195–96, 270n21
Richepanse, Antoine, 6–7, 56, 58
River Asked for a Kiss, The (Maheke), 171, *174*
rocher des femmes adultères (rocher du sac), 164. See also *Kef Chekara*
roman, origin of word, 23
romance, 23
Rosalie l'infâme (Trouillot, Évelyne), 44

Rose, Jacqueline, 26, 181, 201, 203, 206–7, 219, 233
Rosello, Reij M., 63, 114
Ross, Kristen, 119
Rothberg, Michael, 31, 119–20
Rousseau, Raymond, 82–83
rumor, 25–26, 42
Rupaire, Sonny, 58

Saadi, Nourredine, 34, 166–79, 183–93
sacre du Ceddo, Le (Bèye), 86
sacrificial violence, xi, 19, 31, 57, 201–33, 275n6, 276n21, 277n30; in *Les étoiles de Sidi Moumon*, 34–35, 65, 208–13, 228–33; Louis Delgès and, 6–7; role of women in, 29–30
Said, Edward, 23
Saint-Domingue, Revolution of, 14, 83
Saint-Eloy, Luc, 67
Saint Pierre, Isaure de, 167
Saint-Ruf, Germain, 58, 255n56
saison de l'ombre, La (Miano), 44
Salafia Jihadia, 211
Sala-Molins, Louis, 16
Sall, Ibrahima, 85
Sall, Macky, 105–6, 236
Samb, El Hadji Momar, 86
Sansal, Boualem, 210
Sarr, Fatou Sow, 80, 87
Sarr, Felwine, 79, 227, 238
Sarr, Mohamed Mbougar, vi, 33, 81, 85, 105–8, 138, 210
sati, 8
Savary, Jacques, 7
Savoy, Bénédicte, 238
Sayyidatu al-maquam (al-A'radji), 167
Schmaltz, Julien Désiré, 83–85, 88, 258n22
Schœlcher, Victor, 8, 42, 71
Scott, David, 23
Scott, James C., 24
screen memory, 33, 118–20, 140, 165; silver, 165
"Sea Is History, The" (Walcott), 70
seametary, 34, 50, 66–67, 163–64
sea shanties, 52–53
Sebold, Alice, 216, 226
Seck, Samba, 86
secret, 3, 32, 59, 65–67, 80, 99–100
Sedgwick, Eve, 219

INDEX · 321

Séjour, Victor, 17–18
self-disappearance, 28, 106, 235
self-immolation, 20–21, 105, 107, 207; of Sidi Bouzid, 28, 33, 81, 105, 107, 165, 263n105; of the women of Nder, 32–33, 87, 89, 92, 98, 140
self-killing, 2, 15; 9/11 terrorist attacks and, 104; entextualization and, 22–24; explanation of, 19; as *les suicides obsidionaux*, 164. *See also* sacrificial violence
Sembène, Ousmane, 33, 34, 85, 94, 95, 98, 108–9, 113–57, 166–69, 183–84, 188–89, 195, 229, 267n106
Senegalese Independence, 30, 108–9
Senegalese Stagecraft (Valente-Quinn), 86
Senghor, Léopold Sédar, 10, 122, 140
seppuku, 8
Serbin, Sylvia, 80
sexual violence, 215, 223
Shade (Jordan), 216
shared memory, 119–20
Sharpe, Christina, 25, 27, 51
siggi, 79
silencing, 16–20, 40–41
Silverman, Maxim, 165
single-image icon, 118
sirènes de Baghdad, Les (Khadra), 210
Sissako, 154, 210
16 Mai, Le (Beroho), 212
slavery: psychological effects of, 5; silencing of, 16–20
slow suicide (*lent suicide*), 15
Snyder, Terri, 17
Socé Diop, Ousmane, 33, 66, 137, 139–40
Soleil, Le (ship and story), 39–55, 72, 73, 79, 80, 121, 196, 254n41
Solitude, La Mulâtresse, 41, 59, 68, 252n6
Sonko, Ousmane, 236
Soufrières (Maximin), 59, 62, 188
Soyinka, Wole, 21
speculum oris, 9, 10
Spivak, Gayatri, 20, 25, 28, 145, 204, 208, 219, 226, 233
state violence, 30, 32, 67, 179, 188, 195, 203, 206, 228
statistics on slave suicide, 9
statuefication, 41–42, 71
Sturken, Marita, 118
subaltern speech, 21, 23, 28–29, 94

Subversive Traditions (Repinecz), 95, 257n4
suicidal resistance, 23–26, 29, 31, 41–43, 83, 85, 94, 239; in *Doomi Golo*, 101; explanation of term, 24–25; genealogy of, 34, 107–8, 173; geologies (sites) of, 164; in *Humus*, 44, 63; in *La Noire de . . .* , 136, 140, 156; in *L'isolé soleil*, 55–56, 65; Louis Delgrès and, 32, 41, 57; rhetorical force of, 207–8; in Saadi's novels, 166, 173; screening of, 114, 116; systemic violence and, 30; and the women of Nder, 33, 79–81, 236
suicide: as amplifying semantic instability, 25; "causes" of, 5; criminalization of, 2–3, 6, 30–31; difficulty and challenges of writing about, ix, 19–20, 25, 27, 213; etymology of word, 2; as failure, 57, 156, 182; interpretation problems of, 21, 24, 29, 196; in metropolitan literature, 17; as pathology, 4, 18, 19, 148; as performance, 14, 28; as political protest, 30; in the press, 11, 106, 116, 123–24, 129–30, 180; prevention of, 9, 53, 247n53; as refusal of enclosure, 20; as sonic production, 25; as speech act, 24–25; usage of word, 19, 29–30; vestimentary markers of, 11; as a Western phenomenon, 8. *See also* parasuicide
suicide, Le (Durkheim), 18
suicide bombing: as beyond the pale of understanding, 206; early example of, 6, 57, 69, 202; as a paradox, 204, 206; as unthinkable, 203. *See also* sacrificial violence
suicide contagion, 9
suicide epidemics: in 2000s metropolitan France, 18; in Algeria, 164–65; explanation of, 9, 247n49
Suicide of Xanju, The, 80
"suicide parmi les noirs, Le" (Liengme), 8
suicide terrorism, 31, 34–35, 204–15, 227–32
suicide zones, 164
suicidology, 18–20, 196
sutura, 79–80, 91, 140

Talaatay Nder. *See* Nder, Talaatay (Tuesday of)
Taubira Laws (Loi Taubira), 58, 71–72
Teranga Blues (Absa), 85
Terre ceinte (Sarr), 210
terrorism: semantics, 204; and sexual othering, 205. *See also* suicide bombing
terrorist fiction. *See* terrorist genre

terrorist genre, 207; in African literature, 210, 212, 216; in *Les étoiles de Sidi Moumen*, 208, 222, 225
testimony, 103–4
theater of exposition, 86
Things Fall Apart (Achebe), 21
Thioural Goundiour, 79
Thomas, Dominic, 50, 114, 252n156
Thomas, Leanna, 59–60
Thomas, Samuel, 207
Timbuktu (Sissako), 154, 210
tirailleurs, 89
Tirolien, Guy, 58
Tongue-Tied Imagination, The (Warner), 95
Torrey, Jessey, 11
torture, 5–6; *séances de*, 189
trade (*troc*), 46, 48
tragedy, 23
transference, 26, 177
Traoré, Seyba, 88
Trarzas, 78, 82–84, 88–97, 260n34, 260n39
Tribal Scars (Sembène), 115
troc, 46, 48
Tropiques, 59
Trouillot, Évelyne, 44
Trouillot, Michel-Rolph, 17
Tuesday of Nder. *See* Nder, Talaatay (Tuesday of)
Tuez-les tous (Bāchī), 210

unnatural narrative, 209
unveiling, 97, 191–94, 202
Usurping Suicide (Gupta), 28

Valente-Quinn, Brian, 86–87
Valère, Laurent, 72
veil, 140, 191–93, 215. *See also* unveiling
ventre de l'Atlantique, Le (Diome), 33, 49–51, 137, 168

"Venus in Two Acts" (Hartman), 27, 111, 155
Vergès, Françoise, 235, 239
village de l'Allemand ou le journal des frères Schiller, Le (Sansal), 210
Vince, Natalya, 181, 273n66
violence, contemporary, 182–83, 203–7
voicing, 152; in *Étoiles*, 215, 218, 233
voie du salut, La (Ka), 138
voix-off, 51, 152
Voltaïque (Sembène), 114, 122, 147
Voyage pittoresque et historique au Brésil (Debret), 15, *16*

Waalo, 46, 77–94, 97–98, 141, 259n29, 260n34
Wade, Abdoulaye, 105, 260n34
wake, the (Sharpe), 51, 64, 154
Walcott, Derek, 45, 70, 230
Warner, Tobias, 95, 268n121
wa Thiong'o, Ngũgĩ, 95
Waṭṭār, al-Ṭāhir, 167
Weinmann, Frédéric, 208
Werner, Michael, 31
Wheatley, Phillis, 16
Wiredu, Kwasi, 9
Wolof theater, 86–87, 260n50

Xala (Sembène), 137
xaru, 79–80, 154
Xaru Xanju, 80

Yacine, Kateb, 167
Yaum Rai'a lil-Mawt (Kacimi), 168

Zaganiaris, Jean, 209
Zaourar, Hocine, 180, *181*
Zimmermann, Bénédicte, 31
zomaï, 40, 253n12
zoos humains (human zoos), 6, 67

Printed and bound by CPI Group (UK) Ltd, Croydon, CR0 4YY
25/03/2025